CONTRACEPTIVE RISK

BIOPOLITICS: MEDICINE, TECHNOSCIENCE, AND HEALTH IN THE 21ST CENTURY

General Editors: Monica J. Casper and Lisa Jean Moore

Contraceptive Risk

The FDA, Depo-Provera, and the
Politics of Experimental Medicine

William Green

NEW YORK UNIVERSITY PRESS
New York

NEW YORK UNIVERSITY PRESS
New York
www.nyupress.org

References to Internet websites (URLs) were accurate at the time of writing. Neither the author nor New York University Press is responsible for URLs that may have expired or changed since the manuscript was prepared.

ISBN: 978-1-4798-7699-0 (hardback)
ISBN: 978-1-4798-3698-7 (paperback)

For Library of Congress Cataloging-in-Publication data, please contact the Library of Congress.

New York University Press books are printed on acid-free paper, and their binding materials are chosen for strength and durability. We strive to use environmentally responsible suppliers and materials to the greatest extent possible in publishing our books.

Manufactured in the United States of America

10 9 8 7 6 5 4 3 2 1

Also available as an ebook

For Rowena

CONTENTS

PREFACE AND ACKNOWLEDGMENTS

My initial reason for writing about the FDA and Depo-Provera was the need to fulfill a law school course requirement. As a student in a Seminar in Criminal Law offered by Professor John Batt at the University of Kentucky College of Law, I was searching for, but unable to find a suitable paper topic. I asked him for a suggestion. "Depo-Provera" was his telegraphic reply. "What's that?" I asked. "That's your problem" was his equally terse reply. I took his suggestion and wrote a seminar paper later published as "Depo-Provera, Castration, and the Probation of Rape Offenders."[1] Since law school, I have presented papers on Depo-Provera's twenty-five-year approval controversy, its unapproved contraceptive use, its direct-to-consumer advertising, and its risk of osteoporosis at state, regional, and national professional conferences and published them as a book chapter, four law review articles, and two encyclopedia essays.

When I decided to use my publications to write this book, I made three decisions that define its structure and purpose. First, I would use a risk management framework to understand Depo-Provera's domestic odyssey as a struggle between scientific risk assessment and the risk acceptability of the drug's marketing and use. Second, I would study the FDA as a federal agency with limited risk management authority and as one participant in a fragmented system of drug risk management. Third, I would put a human face on Depo-Provera's odyssey and tell it, not as one narrative, but as three overlapping stories of people who, as participants in the drug's odyssey, serve symbolically as ethical standards for the evaluation of the drug's approval and its contraceptive and criminal justice uses. Together they would tell a collective story that provides a common set of lessons for managing the drug's risk.

Along the way, I have accumulated a large body of documents and debts. My understanding of the national controversy over Depo-Provera benefited immensely from the official documents provided by U.S. Food and Drug Administration and Richard Marshall, a Columbus, Indiana, attorney. These documents included the FDA advisory committee and Depo-Provera Public Board of Inquiry transcripts, the FDA Grady Clinic Data Audit, and the FDA's Depo-Provera marketing approval documents.

I am deeply grateful to public health and women's health organizations, including the Boston Women's Health Book Collective, the National Women's Health Network, and the Public Citizen Health Research Group for allowing me to copy memoranda, correspondence, testimony, and articles critical to my understanding of the scientific and political controversy over the drug's contraceptive and criminal justice uses.

I am also indebted to Michael Ericksen and Richard Kupfer, Anne MacMurdo's attorneys, and to William Fette, Roger Gauntlett's attorney, for supplying me with the trial and appellate court documents that allowed me to write about *Upjohn v. MacMurdo* and *People v. Gauntlett*. I also appreciate the articles supplied by Sherry Fletcher of Kalamazoo, Michigan, and Anne MacMurdo of St. Augustine, Florida.

My research has benefited from interviews of Dr. Judith Weisz, Professor of Obstetrics and Gynecology at the University of Pennsylvania Hershey Medical Center; Judy Norsigian, Executive Director of the Boston Women's Health Book Collective; Dr. Sidney Wolfe, Senior Advisor and former Director of the Public Citizen Health Research Group; Cynthia Pearson, Executive Director of the National Women's Health Network; Dr. Fred Berlin, Director of the National Institute for the Study, Prevention, and Treatment of Sexual Trauma; Drs. Ridgely Bennett, Robert Temple, and Solomon Sobel of the U.S. Food and Drug Administration; and Anne MacMurdo.

My interviews, acquisition of documents, and presentation of papers at professional conferences were made possible with the financial support provided by Morehead State University Faculty Research Grants. Without the late John Batt's terse seminar paper suggestion, I would not have begun my personal and professional odyssey that has finally produced this study of the FDA and Depo-Provera. I thank Richard C. Ausness, Associate Dean for Faculty Research and the Everett H. Metcalf, Jr., Professor of Law at the University of Kentucky College of Law, for his helpful comments on my law review articles and his critique of this book. I deeply appreciate the many helpful comments of Caelyn Cobb, my New York University Press editor, which did so much to improve the book.

My two previous attempts at writing this book were cut short when life interfered. This, the third time around, my government colleagues provided an environment in which research is encouraged and rewarded. Still, the most consistently helpful and supportive person has been my wife, Rowena. She has read, corrected, and critiqued all my conference papers, articles, and this book, all of which have profited from our discussions of health policy issues and female contraceptive methods. I would have found it very difficult, if not impossible, to write this book without her assistance. I dedicate this book to her. At her request, I also dedicate this book to Anne MacMurdo and to all women who have suffered from their use of Depo-Provera.

William Green
Lexington, KY

NOTE TO THE READER

This study of the FDA and Depo-Provera contains medical and legal terms. When they first appear in the text, they are explained there or in endnotes and defined in the Glossary of Legal and Medical Terms at the end of the book. One medical regulatory term that is not used is "off label." Instead, the popular term "unapproved use" identifies Depo-Provera's FDA-unapproved contraceptive use prior to 1992 and its continuing unapproved criminal justice use.

Introduction

The Odyssey of Depo-Provera

The Pill, the IUD, and Norplant have dominated public awareness and debate over contraceptive technologies. Depo-Provera, a three-month injectable drug, held out the promise that it could also play a leading role in the contraceptive revolution, but it has not received much more than episodic public attention.[1] Still, the drug has raised difficult questions about its experimental, contraceptive, and criminal justice uses. After the FDA approved The Upjohn Company's application to test Depo-Provera as a female contraceptive in 1963, the drug was administered to 11,400 women at the Grady Memorial Hospital's Family Planning Clinic in Atlanta, the drug's major domestic clinical trial. The drug was also administered to convicted male sex offenders at the Johns Hopkins Hospital in Baltimore, but without the FDA's experimental authorization. Neither at Grady nor at Johns Hopkins did the men and women involved in these studies give their informed consent. Depo-Provera's approval for other medical purposes as early as 1960 meant that for thirty-two years prior to its FDA contraceptive approval in 1992, physicians were able to prescribe the drug as a contraceptive and state trial court judges were able to impose it as a probation condition for sex offenders. Depo-Provera's FDA contraceptive approval has made little difference in the drug's contraceptive and criminal justice uses. Physician prescribing practices and judicial use of the drug continue to raise serious ethical and legal issues. Female patients and male defendants are still injected with the drug without being informed of Depo-Provera's short- and long-term side effects.

The odyssey of Depo-Provera is a study of the politics of contraceptive drug risk management.[2] According to the conventional two-stage model of risk management, risk assessment, the first stage, "is the use of the factual base to define the health effects of exposure of individuals or populations to hazardous materials or situations."[3] Risk acceptability, the second stage, "is the process of . . . integrating the results of risk assessment . . . with social, economic, and political concerns to reach a decision."[4] This model allows us to identify the risk assessment and risk acceptability elements of a regulatory decision, but it cannot explain the controversy over the assessment of the drug's risk and the determination of its acceptability, because the model assumes a separation of fact and value. This study adopts an alternative view: the strict separation of facts and values cannot be maintained in practice, because the scientific basis of risk assessment is often incomplete and policies based on that information become enmeshed in larger debates.[5] In the case of Depo-Provera, those debates concern issues such as pharmaceutical innovation, human experimentation, and the FDA's marketing authority; population control, reproductive health, and state medical malpractice and products liability law; and deviant sexual behavior, alternative criminal punishments, and defendants' constitutional rights.

Depo-Provera has received only occasional attention as a twenty-five year national struggle over Upjohn's FDA application to license it as a contraceptive drug. Rarely has its story been linked to state medical malpractice and products liability issues raised by its contraceptive use or to the criminal justice issues raised by its use as a sentencing alternative. To tell the story of contraceptive drug risk, this study turns to Judith Weisz, a reproductive biologist who evaluated Upjohn's Depo-Provera research, to Anne MacMurdo, a college student who received the drug for contraception, and to Roger Gauntlett, an Upjohn heir, who was ordered to take the drug as a probation condition. Together they tell a collective story of Depo-Provera's fifty-year odyssey, which connects the national controversy over its FDA approval to the state civil and criminal legal issues raised by the use of the drug.[6]

Depo-Provera and Contraceptive Risk

This introduction presents the principal participants; identifies the leading ethical, scientific, and political issues; defines the administrative, civil, and criminal legal risk management arenas; and establishes the criteria to evaluate contraceptive risk in terms of the stories told by Judith Weisz, Anne MacMurdo, and Roger Gauntlett. Their stories portray contraceptive drug risk management as a fragmented activity structured by the Federal Food, Drug, and Cosmetic Act, state negligence and products liability law, state probation and parole law, and the federal Constitution. Their stories have been framed by the FDA's marketing decisions, state medical malpractice and products liability law, and state criminal sentencing law and practice, and have been driven by the competing values of pharmaceutical innovation and profits, professional medical autonomy, population control and women's reproductive health, and civil and criminal justice. In sum, the odyssey of Depo-Provera is a study in the politics of contraceptive risk.

Three Stories of Contraceptive Risk

JUDITH WEISZ'S STORY

Judith Weisz's story views the odyssey of Depo-Provera as a study in the politics of risk management. Why choose Dr. Judith Weisz, a reproductive biologist at the University of Pennsylvania's Hershey Medical Center, from among all the people involved in the drug's administrative controversy? As chair of the FDA's Depo-Provera Public Board of Inquiry, a scientific court established by the agency to analyze the drug's medical research, she studied the scientific evidence, heard testimony from all interested parties, and wrote a report recommending that the FDA not grant Upjohn a license to market Depo-Provera. Her scientific impartiality, objectivity, and expertise provide a vantage point for examining the FDA's risk assessments of the drug's research, the agency's policy judgments about the drug's health risk acceptability, and the scientific and political scrutiny of its drug marketing decisions by Upjohn, by health, women's, and population control organizations, and by members of Congress. She provides the same vantage point for understanding the state medical malpractice and products liability lawsuits brought by women to recover for their injuries from the drug's use and the state criminal justice use of the drug as a probation and parole condition for sex offenders.

ANNE MACMURDO'S STORY

Anne MacMurdo's story examines Depo-Provera's contraceptive use. She and thousands of American women received "the Shot." Some of these women sued their physicians and Upjohn for the adverse effects they suffered: depression, high blood pressure, depressed libido, excessive weight gain, irregular and heavy menstrual bleeding, infertility, breast cancer, and osteoporosis. Why choose Anne MacMurdo of all these women? The medical malpractice and products liability cases brought by other women were dismissed or settled for undisclosed amounts. Only Anne MacMurdo's was tried successfully in 1986 and appealed to the Florida Supreme Court. As the leading pre-approval Depo-Provera contraceptive use case, hers is a story of Upjohn's marketing practices, physician use of an unapproved drug, often without a woman's informed consent, and the state medical malpractice and products liability consequences. Anne MacMurdo's story continues to provide the paradigm for women who claim to be injured by Depo-Provera's contraceptive use, the legal remedies they can use to be compensated for their injuries, and the challenges they will face in suing their physician or Pfizer, Upjohn's multinational corporate heir.

ROGER GAUNTLETT'S STORY

Roger Gauntlett's story explores Depo-Provera's unapproved criminal justice use. He and other convicted sex offenders were ordered by state court judges to use Depo-Provera as a probation condition. Why choose Roger Gauntlett of all these men? In other cases, the defendants "voluntarily" accepted the drug as an alternative to incarceration. At his 1984 trial for sexual assault, the judge ordered him to take the drug as "castration by chemical means."[7] He refused, appealed, and had the judge's probation condition overturned. As the leading case involving Depo-Provera's use as a criminal sanction, Roger Gauntlett's is the story of the drug's FDA-unapproved use by Johns Hopkins Clinic researchers and criminal court judges, which still provides the precedent for sex offenders to challenge state statutes that grant judges the discretion or mandate them to use Depo-Provera as a parole condition, frequently without the offender's informed consent. They can use, as he did, state statutory and federal constitutional arguments to personally manage the drug's risk to their health.

A COMMON THREAD OF CONTRACEPTIVE DRUG RISK

Judith Weisz's, Anne MacMurdo's, and Roger Gauntlett's stories all have a common thread: they involve personal encounters with a risky drug and the failure to control its use. Depo-Provera has not always been tested in accordance with FDA experimental procedures; not approved for contraceptive use until 1992, and still is not FDA-approved as a criminal sentencing alternative. Nevertheless, physicians have administered the drug to women for contraception, and judges have ordered sex offenders to use it as a probation and parole condition. Together, these three stories raise scientific, ethical, political, and legal questions about the existing approach to contraceptive drug risk. Together, they reveal that the failure to manage drug risk is rooted in the flawed character of risk assessment, in the political calculations of risk acceptability, and in the competing values and interests of the individuals and institutions that have a stake in making risk management decisions about Depo-Provera's approval and use. All of these threads are woven into the three stories which are structured by three legal systems: federal drug law, state civil law, and state criminal law.

Federal Drug Law

The Federal Food, Drug, and Cosmetic Act (FFDCA) of 1938 and its 1962 amendments established the basic structure for federal drug regulation by enlarging the Food and Drug Administration's (FDA) authority to manage pharmaceutical risk.[8] The FFDCA authorizes pharmaceutical companies to apply to the FDA for authorization to conduct human clinical trials and to provide the agency with accurate scientific evidence of a drug's safety and effectiveness. Once the FDA reviews this company-supplied evidence, approves the drug for marketing for a specific medical purpose, and defines its labeling and advertising, the statute authorizes the agency to require drug companies to report adverse drug reactions, conduct post-marketing studies, and withdraw its products from the market.

Otherwise, the act passes drug risk responsibility to the pharmaceutical companies, physicians, and patients. Companies have the responsibility to manage risk by complying with FDA experimental testing protocols, by promoting only FDA-approved drug uses, by following FDA procedures in conducting post-marketing studies, and by reporting adverse drug experiences to FDA. Physicians have a professional responsibility to manage risk by providing their patients with accurate information about a drug's uses, side effects, and adverse reactions. Patients have a personal responsibility to manage drug risk by using their physician's information to make an informed decision. Finally, the FFDCA recognizes that the FDA's drug marketing approval decisions constitute minimum standards for safety and effectiveness. These standards do not limit a physician to prescribing a drug only for uses in the FDA-approved labeling, nor do they preempt the right of patients to bring state civil actions against pharmaceutical companies and physicians.

State Civil Law

State civil law authorizes courts to participate in the management of drug risk by means of private litigation.[9] When a pharmaceutical company's manufacturing and marketing practices or a physician's prescribing practices fail to manage a drug's risk, the legal doctrine of negligence based on state case law, along with state products liability and medical malpractice statutes, provide the legal means for patients and research subjects to claim that their personal injuries are due to the failure of a pharmaceutical company or a physician to exercise reasonable care and to seek financial compensation for their injuries.

Judicial risk management is, however, limited by the ability of the adversarial process to assess drug risk and its acceptability. The legal system imposes substantial financial and personal barriers to a woman who claims, as Anne MacMurdo did, to have been harmed by her use of Depo-Provera. As a plaintiff, she will confront a variety of civil discovery methods, directed verdict motions, and the temptation to settle her case.[10] At trial, she will have the burden of proving that the pharmaceutical company's and physician's negligent behavior is the legal cause of her injuries. Her task will be made more difficult by the rules of evidence, which limit her use of scientific evidence and expert testimony, and by the need to confront defense counterclaims that she either assumed the risk in using the drug or contributed to her injuries.[11] If she receives a judgment in her favor, the pharmaceutical company may subject her to the demands and uncertainties of the appellate court review.

State Criminal Law

State criminal law also authorizes courts to participate in contraceptive drug risk management. Once a defendant is found guilty of a sexual assault in violation of a state criminal law, as Roger Gauntlett was, a judge has the discretion to imprison him or grant him probation. If the defendant is imprisoned, six states specifically authorize a trial court judge to grant him parole. In making this decision, state statutes grant a judge the authority to assess the risks of imprisonment and conditional freedom and to make a judgment about their acceptability: whether probation or parole is a more humane and effective means of rehabilitation and reintegration into the community than imprisonment.

Since Depo-Provera has never been approved by the FDA for use as a probation or parole condition, the critical issue is whether a judge has the authority, even if specifically granted by statute, to order the drug's use as an alternative to or as a condition of release from imprisonment and whether the defendant can make an informed decision to accept the condition. Judicial risk management is, once again, limited by the ability of the adversarial process to assess drug risk and determine its acceptability. A convicted defendant, such as Roger Gauntlett, has the legal right to object to a judge's risk assessment and risk acceptability decisions about a Depo-Provera condition, because they are an unreasonable or impractical exercise of a state's probation and parole authority to which he cannot give his informed consent, and because they violate his federal constitutional rights to freedom of thought, to freedom from cruel and unusual punishment, and to due process privacy, and equal protection.

Contraceptive Drug Policy Environment

Judith Weisz's, Anne MacMurdo's and Roger Gauntlett's stories provide a common thread for understanding the management of Depo-Provera's risk, which is situated in the wider world of contraceptive drug policy. In this world, the principal policy-makers are the FDA, drug companies, research scientists, physicians, population control organizations, state legislatures, and courts. They control drug approval and use on the basis of their authority, rooted in state and federal law and in their political, economic, and professional influence. Their control over contraceptive drug policy and their assessment and acceptability of drug risk are contested by health activists and organizations that speak for vulnerable women by critiquing and challenging FDA, drug company, physician, and population control program practices and by having a voice in FDA drug-approval decision-making.

Depo-Provera's domestic odyssey began in 1963, the year after Congress enacted the 1962 Kefauver-Harris Amendments to the Federal Food, Drug, and Cosmetic Act.[12] These amendments created a more powerful FDA and a more demanding drug approval process for companies. Previously, the act had required that drugs be tested only for their safety before they were marketed, "but there were no particular scientific or medical guidelines from the FDA about what evidence was required."[13] The 1962 Amendments, enacted partially in response to the Thalidomide tragedy,[14] create a detailed and lengthy drug approval process, outlined below, which places the burden on companies of providing the agency with scientific proof that a drug is both safe and effective for its proposed medical use.

The drug development and approval process begins with an initial screening and animal studies of the drug's safety, toxicity, and biological activity. Next, the company is required to file with the FDA a Notice of Claimed Investigational Exemption for a New Drug (IND).[15] The IND describes the drug, provides the results of the initial screening and animal studies indicating that human testing would be reasonably safe, and details the company's plan for human testing. Clinical testing then takes place in three phases that together evaluate the drug's safety and effectiveness, define its dosage requirements, and identify its side effects on the basis of randomized, double-blind placebo-controlled studies.[16]

Once the company completes the three clinical trial phases, it may submit a New Drug Approval (NDA) application supported by evidence from the drug's animal and human studies.[17] The FDA then reviews the evidence to determine whether the drug is safe and effective for its proposed use. If the agency decides to approve the drug, it will, as the final step, determine in consultation with the drug company the content of the package insert, which is the official description of the drug received by physicians. As a condition of approval, the FDA may require a company to conduct Phase IV post-marketing studies to address any safety and effectiveness concerns.

With these changes, the 1962 Amendments created a new drug regulatory regime that shifted power from the pharmaceutical companies to the FDA. Upjohn was required to comply with the new drug development and approval standards and to demonstrate that Depo-Provera was a safe and effective contraceptive. At the same time, the 1962 Amendments left untouched Upjohn's responsibility to conduct Depo-Provera's research, the discretion of physicians to prescribe Depo-Provera, and the authority of state legislatures and courts to impose the drug as a criminal sentence.

Depo-Provera's odyssey was also defined by two events that bracketed the enactment of the 1962 Amendments and that together altered drug risk management: the FDA's approval of the oral birth control pill in 1960[18] and the publication in 1963 of Betty Friedan's *The Feminine Mystique*,[19] acknowledged as having begun the second wave of feminism.[20] The FDA's approval of the Pill was based on the pre-1962 Amendments' drug company deferential standards, but the poor quality of the field trials in Haiti and Puerto Rico and the side effects suffered by women and documented in Barbara Seaman's *The Doctor's Case Against the Pill* (1969) focused feminist attention on women's health issues[21] and led to Senate hearings in 1970, which provoked even more criticism of the FDA, physicians, and pharmaceutical companies. Later the same year, the pathbreaking book about women's health and sexuality, *Our Bodies Ourselves*, was published by the Boston Women's Health Book Collective.[22]

Still, the women's health movement needed a political voice. Barbara Seaman, along with Belita Cowan, publisher of *Herself* newspaper, aware of the successful consumer activism of Ralph Nader's Public Citizen and its Health Research Group, headed by Dr. Sidney Wolfe, decided to "form a woman's health lobby, descend on Washington, be a key player and influence national health policy."[23] In 1976, together with other feminists, they created the National Women's Health Network as the policy wing of the women's health movement and the first national lobbying group for women's health advocacy, in order to monitor the FDA and "ensure that the voice of a national women's health movement would be heard on Capitol Hill."[24] Since then, the Network has become a clearinghouse for information on women's health, a forum to improve women's health, and a voice for women's health issues, including the safety of contraceptive drugs and devices.[25]

The Network and women's health advocates addressed the risk management faults in the worldwide testing by pharmaceutical companies and use by population control organizations of long-acting birth-control techniques: intrauterine devices, injectables, and implants. The International Planned Parenthood Foundation, the United Nations Fund for Population Activities, and the World Health Organization favored these contraceptives, because they were easy to administer and effective in preventing pregnancy and lowering fertility rates in developing countries.[26] There were, however, substantial risk assessment and acceptability issues in the research and use of these drugs.

When Upjohn applied for FDA approval, stating that Depo-Provera's research confirmed that the drug was a safe and effective contraceptive, the company met with withering criticism from the Network, the Health Research Group, and women's health advocates. They found serious design flaws in the research, a failure to provide women who participated in the trials with informed consent, and evidence suggesting that the drug was a potential carcinogen with significant side effects. They also took issue with the claim that Depo-Provera was an acceptable risk for a domestic female population,[27] because the research was conducted in developing countries where the quality of health care was poor, life expectancy was low, and the benefit of lowering fertility rates outweighed the risk of breast, uterine, and endometrial cancer in women, who were "more likely to die of malaria, cholera, dysentery, or in childbirth before they get cancer."[28] FDA approval of Depo-Provera would open up a large overseas market for the drug by permitting the U.S. Agency for International Development to use it in population control programs, bestowing legitimacy on its use in developing countries, and substantially increasing Upjohn's profits.

In sum, Depo-Provera's odyssey has been shaped by the principal participants in contraceptive drug policy-making, the drug's international research and fertility control use, and three events that altered the drug policy making environment: the controversy over the contraceptive Pill, the 1962 Kefauver-Harris Amendment's creation of a more demanding drug approval process, and the participation of health activists and the woman's health organizations in drug policy-making. In this setting, Upjohn found the FDA's approval process more demanding, and the agency found its decisions challenged by the National Women's Health Network and the Health Research Group, which involved the media and members of Congress in questioning the FDA's assessment and acceptability of Depo-Provera's risk to women's health.

A Collective Story

The odyssey of Depo-Provera has been primarily a story of the national struggle over the FDA's authority to license the drug's contraceptive use. Seldom has this story been connected to the state civil and criminal legal issues raised by the drug's use. Never has the story been told as three concurrent stories, nor as three partially overlapping stories that together tell a collective story about the politics of contraceptive drug risk management. Together the stories provide the opportunity to explore the relationship between Depo-Provera's national experience and the drug's state contraceptive and criminal justice uses, to evaluate civil litigation as a means of managing contraceptive risk, and to appraise the authority of judges to impose the drug as an alternative criminal sentence and of state legislatures to grant trial court judges the discretion or mandate that a convicted sex offender will use the drug. An overview of each chapter will suggest the ways these three stories are interwoven to tell Depo-Provera's collective risk management story.

In Chapter 1, Judith Weisz's story of the politics of drug risk management begins with the FDA's limited control of Depo-Provera's contraceptive research and its focus on the Grady Memorial Hospital Family Planning Clinic, which conducted the drug's major domestic clinical trial by administering the drug to 11,400 principally poor African-American women from 1967 to 1978. When the FDA audited the Grady Clinic's study, the agency found serious deficiencies in the design and conduct of the clinic's testing protocol, including inaccurate screening, defective informed consent procedures, and no follow-up of the women. The FDA concluded that the clinic had sacrificed scientific standards for its assessment of the drug's health risks to its value in promoting family planning goals. The agency terminated the clinic's program, but its risk management flaws were not publically exposed and its research was not discredited until a Public Board of Inquiry, chaired by Judith Weisz, held hearings in 1983. Yet, the women whose health had been harmed by their participation in the Grady Clinic's study were unable to obtain a legal remedy.

In Chapter 2, Judith Weisz's story of the politics of drug risk management shifts its focus to Depo-Provera's lengthy FDA marketing approval process and analyzes the scientific and political controversy over the FDA's assessments of the drug's health risk and its policy judgments about the risk acceptability of its marketing approval, which was dominated by the fear that the drug could cause breast, endometrial, and cervical cancer. The controversy began when the FDA relied on its Obstetrics and Gynecology Advisory Committee to grant the drug limited marketing approval in 1974, which the agency withdrew after congressional criticism, and then, following a lengthy intra-agency review, disapproved the drug for general contraceptive marketing in 1978. An FDA Public Board of Inquiry, convened at Upjohn's request and chaired by Judith Weisz, conducted an intensive scientific assessment of the drug's animal and human studies at its 1983 hearings and then made a recommendation, accepted by the FDA in 1986, to disapprove the drug for general contraceptive marketing.

Chapter 3 turns from the national controversy over Depo-Provera to Anne MacMurdo's story of the drug's unapproved contraceptive use and the personal risks faced by women, because of the FDA's limited authority over Upjohn's marketing practices and over physicians, mental health facilities, and family planning clinics nationwide, which used Depo-Provera without the informed consent of women. Unlike the focus of Judith Weisz's story of Depo-Provera's long-term risk of cancer, Anne MacMurdo's concerns the drug's short-term side effects, such as excessive menstrual bleeding, depression, and weight gain. Her legal odyssey began in 1974, after her use of the drug was followed by a hysterectomy to stop her continuous bleeding. She brought a products liability suit against Upjohn, which was not tried until 1986, when a Florida jury awarded her $186,000, a verdict reversed on appeal by the state supreme court. Her story exposes the failure of Upjohn and physicians to manage the drug's risk, the limited access of women, often poor white women and women of color, to a legal remedy, the risk management role of courts, and the limited ability of state civil law to address the drug's short-term side effects.

Chapter 4 returns to Judith Weisz's story of the national politics of drug risk management and finds an altered risk assessment environment for Depo-Provera, because of the FDA's decision to eliminate animal experiments and to rely solely on improved World Health Organization human clinical trial data, a decision that paved the way for the agency to approve the drug in 1992. Approval came with the condition that Upjohn conduct a post-approval study of bone mineral density loss, and its results led the FDA to revise the drug's package insert in 2004 to include a "black box" warning of the risk of osteoporosis and a two-year limitation on the drug's use.[29] In Depo-Provera's post-approval world, Anne MacMurdo's story is told by the women who claimed that the drug caused their osteoporosis. Their stories, like hers, raise state medical malpractice and products liability issues, and they, too, faced formidable legal obstacles. None of their cases, unlike hers, went to trial. Pfizer, Upjohn's corporate heir, had the cases dismissed on the basis of its motions for summary judgment.[30] Her story explains how Pfizer was able to use Depo-Provera's package labeling, state products liability law, the learned intermediary doctrine,[31] and expert evidence to avoid liability.

Chapter 5 brings Judith's Weisz's story of the politics of drug risk management full circle by returning to the FDA's limited control of Depo-Provera's experimental use first discussed in Chapter 1. Now her story focuses on the drug's criminal justice use by Dr. Fred Berlin at the Johns Hopkins Clinic and explains why the clinic failed to acquire an IND to test the drug on convicted sex offenders, why it failed to receive their informed consent, and why its published research failed to provide credible scientific evidence of the drug's safety and effectiveness. Roger Gauntlett's story joins Judith Weisz's when he was arrested, convicted of criminal sexual conduct, and sentenced by a Michigan trial court judge to five years probation conditioned on his use of Depo-Provera based on the Johns Hopkins program, a sentence that was reversed by the state supreme court. His story provides the opportunity to analyze the risk management roles of state trial court judges, who use their discretion to impose the drug as probation condition and of state legislatures, which enact statutes granting trial court judges authority to use the drug as a parole condition for sex offenders. At the same time, his story advises convicted sex offenders to protect themselves from the drug's serious side effects by relying on their federal constitutional rights.

The conclusion draws together Judith Weisz's, Anne MacMurdo's, and Roger Gauntlett's separate, but interwoven stories of the politics of contraceptive risk. Of the three stories, Judith Weisz's is the one that provides the risk management framework for the conduct of Depo-Provera's research, its FDA approval, and state civil and criminal litigation over its use. Her story and the other two provide a collective story that identifies the individuals and institutions that failed to manage Depo-Provera's contraceptive and criminal justice uses, their joint responsibility for the harm they have caused, and the actions they should take to change their management of the drug's risk and to acknowledge their lack of respect for human dignity of the women who have taken Depo-Provera for contraception and the men who were ordered to take the drug as a condition of probation or parole.

1

The Grady Hospital Study

The Corruption of Contraceptive Research

Judith Weisz's story of the politics of drug risk management begins with
the Food and Drug Administration's authority to permit a pharmaceutical company to conduct human clinical studies of a drug.[1] For her, a
critical period in the drug's approval process occurs after the FDA grants
an IND, the agency's official authorization for the conduct of human
clinical testing,[2] and before the company submits a New Drug Approval
application.[3] During this time, drug testing is out of the FDA's hands and
in those of the company and its researchers, who are required to follow
the IND protocol and make periodic reports to the agency. The research
protocol, the defining feature of the IND process, is designed to provide
evidence of the drug's safety and effectiveness, which is necessary for the
FDA to make a marketing approval decision.[4]

The IND research protocol is supposed to create a boundary between
evidence of risk assessment and risk acceptability. Inside this boundary,
the IND study can be assessed on scientific criteria: Is it sufficient in
scale, design, and execution to establish the drug's safety and effectiveness? Yet the temptation is to cross the boundary at the research site and
allow decisions to be influenced by practice-of-medicine standards and
by social, economic, and political interests.

When the FDA allowed human clinical trials to continue in spite of
animal study evidence suggesting that Depo-Provera was a suspected
carcinogen and when the Grady Memorial Hospital Family Planning Clinic conducted its IND studies of the drug's contraceptive use,
they crossed the risk assessment boundary and failed to assess Depo-
Provera's risk to the research subjects. This chapter will examine why
this boundary was crossed by the FDA and the Grady Clinic; why two
FDA medical officers, Drs. J. W. Armistead and Michael Popkin, found
fault with Upjohn animal studies and why Dr. Alan Lisook, head of the

FDA team investigating the Grady Clinic study, and Dr. Judith Weisz, chair of the FDA's Public Board of Inquiry, found the Grady Clinic's IND plagued with failures; and why the women in the clinic's study failed to find a legal remedy for the harms they had suffered.[5]

Depo-Provera Contraceptive Research

The Food and Drug Administration first approved Depo-Provera, a synthetic progestogen, in 1960 to treat endometriosis and miscarriage.[6] When Upjohn found that the drug could also prevent conception by suppressing the hormones that induce ovulation, it conducted an initial screening and animal tests. In 1963, the company received an IND to conduct human clinical trials of the drug's contraceptive safety and effectiveness.[7] Two years later, it initiated clinical trials in seventy-six foreign countries. In 1967, the Grady Memorial Hospital Family Planning Clinic in Atlanta, Georgia, received its own IND to conduct the drug's major domestic clinical trial for use as a female contraceptive.[8]

Upjohn's and Grady Memorial Hospital's INDs for Depo-Provera's contraceptive use became the focus of scientific and political controversy. When the FDA granted and then withdrew Upjohn's New Drug Approval (NDA) for Depo-Provera's limited marketing approval in 1974,[9] refused to grant the drug a general marketing license in 1978,[10] and created a public board of inquiry to resolve scientific issues about the drug's safety,[11] the agency was concerned that the animal studies revealed a risk of breast and endometrial cancer, and the human clinical studies also suggested an increased risk of breast, endometrial, and cervical cancer.[12] The Upjohn-sponsored clinical studies and the medical reports and journal articles they generated were also criticized for their research designs and conclusions about the drug's safety. These studies, reports, and articles, which will be examined in Chapter 2, became the subject of substantial public debate, but they make only passing references to their subjects' informed consent and provide no window on the realities of these clinical trials.

The Grady Clinic's study does, however, allow us to go beyond the face of Upjohn's and the clinic's scientific reports and journal articles to explore how its protocol, informed consent procedures, record-keeping, and research findings crossed the boundary between the conduct of scientific research and the practice of medicine and to grasp the impact of the Grady Clinic study on the lives of women who were its subjects. The Grady Clinic study also allows us to examine the FDA's supervision and investigation of the clinic's IND process and the agency's role and that of its Obstetrics and Gynecology (OB/GYN) Advisory Committee and its Depo-Provera Public Board of Inquiry in reviewing the scientific evidence and making risk assessments and risk acceptability judgments related to all Depo-Provera clinical trials, including the Grady Clinic's.

The Grady Memorial Hospital Study

Grady Memorial is a large inner-city public hospital in Atlanta, Georgia, which serves an almost exclusively low-income and indigent African American population. Dr. W. Newton Long, the Director of Research and Training in Grady's Maternal Health and Family Planning Clinic and the Deputy Chief of Obstetrics at the Grady Hospital, was the chief sponsor of the clinic's IND study of Depo-Provera.[13] The clinic drew its subject population for the study from its inner-city clientele and enrolled women throughout their childbearing years. "The 'average' Depo-Provera user at Grady, [was] 28.8 years old, black and unmarried. She [was] most likely to have attended school through between 10th and 12th grade, have two children and be acting as the head of her family. She [was] earning 100 dollars per month per family member, and [was] subsidized by [M]edicaid or Title XX."[14]

The Grady Clinic IND Protocol

The Grady Clinic's IND protocol provided for the drug to be given to women "for whom pregnancy was contraindicated (cardiac patients), women with medical problems associated with menses (sickle cell disease, menorraghia), [and] women who had experienced contraceptive failure with two other methods."[15] Use of Depo-Provera was halted on November 3, 1972, because of a concern about the drug's teratogenic effects and then reinstated a month later with a revised protocol containing two additional stipulations that the drug be given to women "receiving the rubella vaccine immediately postpartum and to those unable to use another contraceptive method," including those who were mentally challenged.[16]

Women became participants in the Grady study once they complied with the procedures set forth in the clinic's IND protocol. At their first visit, they completed a questionnaire about their age, marital status, education, reproductive experience, and medical history. Then they were given a physical examination that included a pregnancy test, a pelvic examination, and a Pap smear to test for cervical cancer.[17] Once they read and signed the consent form, they were given an injection of the drug. At the three-month follow-up visits, they were given a pregnancy test and counseled about any complications they were experiencing. At their fourth injection, they received an annual examination, which repeated the elements of the initial examination.[18]

The Grady Clinic IND provided a large data base for Depo-Provera's contraceptive research, which was used to study the drug's discontinuation rates; estrogen use to manage bleeding; breast, uterine, and ovarian cancer; and mortality among black contraceptive users.[19] Journal articles based on the Grady Clinic data were published in *Public Health Reports*, *Contraception*, and the *Journal of the American Medical Association*; and unpublished reports appeared in *Medroxyprogesterone Acetate*, a Grady Clinic research collection.[20] In spite of this large volume of research and the clinical procedures that appear to have been unexceptional, the Grady Clinic study was deeply flawed.

The Grady Clinic and Informed Consent

A research subject's participation in an experimental drug program requires that she give her voluntary and knowing consent to the health risk involved. Assuming that her decision is voluntary, a key element in making a knowing decision is the information in the consent form. When the Grady Clinic's study began in 1967, women read and signed a consent form that stated *in toto*: "I hereby acknowledge that I am Voluntarily [sic] receiving an injection of Depo-Provera. I am also aware that as a result of the injection I may experience the following side effects: 1. Amenorrhea (loss of periods), 2. Irregular bleeding, 3. Possible absence of return to fertility."[21]

The Grady Clinic's form raises a basic informed consent issue: What is the duty of researchers to disclose a drug's risk to their subjects? Assuming, once again, that the subjects gave their voluntary consent, the Grady consent form they signed was seriously deficient in providing them with the information necessary for them to give their knowing consent to the use of Depo-Provera. The form failed to disclose that the drug was not an FDA-approved contraceptive, nor did it disclose that the drug's only approved uses were treatment for amenorrhea, irregular uterine bleeding, miscarriage, endometriosis, and kidney and endometrial cancer. The form also failed to identify, nor was it ever modified to include, the evolving body of clinical research that documented that the short-term side effects from the drug's use included loss of libido, depression, and weight gain, and suggested that it was a suspected human carcinogen. The form failed to list any contraindications for the drug's use, including thrombophlebitis, thromboembolic disorders, cerebral vascular disease, liver dysfunction or disease, undiagnosed vaginal bleeding, known or suspected pregnancy, and miscarriage.[22] Finally, the consent form did not inform the women that they were subjects in an experimental drug study, but implicitly represented the drug as an approved contraceptive and the clinical experiment as the practice of medicine.

When the National Women's Health Network created a registry of Depo-Provera users in 1979 and encouraged women nationwide to request questionnaires, thirty-two women who had received the drug at the Grady Clinic prior to 1973 requested and returned the registry questionnaire.[23] Their answers provide anecdotal data on the Grady Clinic's informed consent practices. One woman cast doubt on whether the clinic's consent practices were voluntary when she wrote: "My welfare worker ordered me to take this drug. She said if I didn't my check would be cut off."[24] The thirty-two Grady women overwhelmingly agreed that they did not give their knowing consent. Thirty informed the Network that they were not given any information about the drug's unapproved status, and twenty-eight indicated that they received no information about the drug's potential risks or hazards. One woman took the time to write: "I do not remember signing any papers. I did not know until over three months later that it was experimental. They told me nothing at the hospital just that it would protect me from getting pregnant. I would not have taken the shot knowing it was experimental."[25] Even Dr. Robert Hatcher, the Director of the Grady Clinic, admitted in his testimony before the Public Board of Inquiry that Depo-Provera was "being administered as [if] it were a fully approved drug with established risks."[26] Still, even if the drug had been an approved contraceptive, the Grady Clinic's consent form did not provide its patients with sufficient information about the drug's risks for them to make an informed choice.

The FDA Review of Upjohn's Research

The Grady Clinic had been using its consent form for three years when the future of its clinical trial was jeopardized by Upjohn's report to the Food and Drug Administration in September 1970 that its seven-year dog study had found tumors in three of the beagles.[27] FDA policy required the agency to terminate all clinical trials if animal studies revealed significant negative findings, but risk acceptability considerations came into play, because of the drug's uniqueness as the only injectable contraceptive currently in development.[28] Since "the occurrence of malignant and nonmalignant tumors had caused the rejection of . . . two NDA's," the question, according to the FDA's Dr. Victor Berliner, was "Should the same thing apply to Depo-Provera or should the uniqueness of use overrule the malignancy of the Beagles [sic]?"[29] If, however, the FDA overruled the animal test results, because of Depo-Provera's uniqueness, then it would not only permit the IND experimental studies to continue, but also authorize Depo-Provera's unapproved contraceptive use by two specific groups of women: those who were mentally challenged and those, like Anne MacMurdo, who were unable or unwilling to use other contraceptive methods.[30]

Conflicting IND Recommendations

The FDA's Bureau of Drugs informed its medical officer, Dr. J. W. Armstead, and its Obstetrics and Gynecology (OB/GYN) Advisory Committee about the beagle findings, and the following year, the agency temporarily suspended all human clinical trials of Depo-Provera, including the Grady Clinic's, while it discussed the relevance of the beagle test results.[31] A central feature of the agency's deliberations over the next two years was the conflicting advice it received from its medical officers and its OB/GYN Advisory Committee. The medical officers were committed to making a decision solely on the basis of risk assessment criteria while the advisory committee was willing to cross the boundary and bring risk acceptability considerations into play.

Dr. Armstead favored termination of the drug's clinical tests. On January 21, 1971, he recommended that "further testing of Depo-Provera as a contraceptive should not be done until . . . the relevance of the dog study lesions to human breast disease has been determined."[32] When the OB/GYN Advisory Committee met on July 2, 1971, and learned that three dogs had developed malignant tumors, it recommended that the testing continue, that the IND consent form be amended to indicate that tumors had been found in the beagles, and that "any physician [be permitted] to utilize Depo-Provera as an injectable contraceptive in patients who could not tolerate or for whom other forms of contraception are unacceptable and who agreed to take the risk of the side effects . . . demonstrated by the beagle tumors."[33] Subsequently, the FDA adopted the advisory committee recommendation and authorized limited clinical trials to obtain metabolic data,[34] and, pending its receipt of this data and the results of the dog studies, the agency permitted IND studies to continue and physicians to prescribe the drug for women unable to use other contraceptives.

When the OB/GYN Advisory Committee met eleven months later on June 2, 1972, Dr. Berliner informed them that the three dogs treated with twenty-five times the human dose had developed malignant and invasive mammary nodules that had become cancerous.[35] In light of these findings, Dr. Elizabeth Connell, the panel chair, believed the committee was confronted with three options for Depo-Provera's contraceptive use: "you kill it, you pass it, or you let it dangle for a while."[36] She did not think the committee was "about to approve it or encourage . . . [the FDA] to approve it."[37] So the question was "whether to let it go since we don't know what is involved totally or whether to say this has now become a dangerous drug and we should recommend its total discontinuance for any indication."[38]

With her guidance, the committee initially discussed delay and disapproval in risk assessment terms. Unwilling to accept Dr. Armstead's report and disapprove the drug, the committee wanted to know how rapidly a reasonable amount of data would be available from the new seven-year beagle studies. Dr. Berliner estimated that the FDA would not know for two years, because a new beagle study had just begun in January 1972 and the first malignancies had not occurred until fourteen or fifteen months after the earlier beagle study had begun.[39] At the same time, he pointed out that the monkey studies' negative results revealed no necessary indication that Depo-Provera caused breast cancer in women.[40]

Since the committee appeared to be willing to wait for the results of the new beagle study, it turned to a consideration of risk acceptability issues, or as Dr. Philip Corfman, an FDA consultant to the committee, phrased it: "How important [is] this particular method?"[41] Aside from the Pill and the IUD, Dr. Raymond Vande Wiele told his fellow committee members that there were no other contraceptives, including injectable ones, currently in development and there was a need, albeit a small one, for Depo-Provera's use by a "specialized population such as retarded people."[42] Given the drug's unique features, the committee turned to the informed consent issue.

Once again, Dr. Corfman provided them with guidance when he distinguished between IND investigators who were required to provide their subjects with the FDA's revised informed consent form and private physicians who were not required to provide their patients with any information about the drug, including its unapproved status.[43] Would it be important, he asked, to inform these physicians about the drug's limited use?[44] Given the choice of recommending that Depo-Provera be removed from the market or tolerating its unapproved contraceptive use, the committee was persuaded by Dr. Connell to warn physicians about the drug's adverse side effects.[45]

After further discussion on these risk acceptability matters, the committee reached enough of a consensus to recommend that Depo-Provera's IND status be continued on a highly restricted basis, including a consent form informing research subjects about the animal test results and the medical community about the danger of its unapproved contraceptive use.[46] In sum, the OB/GYN Committee was not willing to disapprove Depo-Provera, because it did not believe enough animal data were yet available, but there was also "great reluctance about recommending approval of an NDA for unrestricted use."[47] In Dr. Connell's phrase, the committee let Depo-Provera's fate "dangle" while it awaited the accumulation of more pertinent animal data.

Seven weeks later, the FDA received a contrary recommendation from its medical officer, Dr. Michael Popkin. In his July 28 statement, he reviewed Upjohn's clinical studies, which revealed four cases of breast cancer and, most significantly, that "sixteen subjects have developed Grade IV pap smears . . . [all] showed carcinoma in situ[,] . . . and all subsequently underwent [a] hysterectomy."[48] His review included a pivotal Upjohn study that had not been discussed by the OB/GYN Advisory Committee: Drs. Paul C. Schwallie and J. Robert Assenzo's multi-center study involving 3,857 women, which contained data on the drug's adverse short-term side effects, including menstrual bleeding.[49] "The only problem has been bleeding and/or spotting which occurs in 30–100% of [the] subjects, depending on the dosage regimen employed. This bleeding (predominately spotting) is unpredictable and tends to be somewhat prolonged in those subjects receiving Depo-Provera alone."[50] The dropouts from the studies also troubled him: 65 percent for all reasons and 25 percent for medical reasons and side effects. "Of these bleeding had the highest rate of 7.8%."[51] In sum, Dr. Popkin's review of the clinical data, along with the malignant tumors found in the beagles, led him to recommend that, despite Depo-Provera's uniqueness, "this IND should be discontinued and no further studies be permitted by the FDA."[52]

The FDA's Depo-Provera IND Decision

The FDA announced its decision three weeks later in a terse August 9, 1972, postscript to Dr. Popkin's recommendation: to leave open Depo-Provera's IND "with fully informed consent" so the drug could be used by women "who cannot use any other means of contraception."[53] The agency's announcement avoided any reference to the Schwallie and Assenzo study's findings on breast and cervical cancer and to the prolonged and unpredictable bleeding, which Dr. Popkin had reported as increasing from "28.1 [percent in] month 3 . . . to 92.9 [percent in] month 69," as being a major reason for women dropping out of the Upjohn studies.[54] Instead of taking the opportunity to place the Schwallie and Assenzo study on the agenda of the OB/GYN Advisory Committee's next meeting, the FDA approved Depo-Provera's continued IND use, aware that its action permitted any physician not governed by an IND to prescribe the drug as a contraceptive without formal FDA approval and without the patient's informed consent.

The FDA's decision failed to attract the attention of the Senator Edward Kennedy's Labor and Public Welfare Committee, which called hearings the following year to explore the drug's nationwide unapproved contraceptive use by private physicians and family planning clinics.[55] The agency's decision did, however, gain some congressional interest when the House Committee on Government Operations held hearings in 1974 on the FDA's use of its OB/GYN Advisory Committee to grant Depo-Provera limited marketing approval the year before.[56] Representative L. H. Fountain, the committee chair, found the agency's postscript to Dr. Popkin's recommendation puzzling, because it "suggest[ed] approval on the part of the FDA of the unapproved use of Depo-Provera. . . . Why," he asked Dr. J. Richard Crout, the Director of the Bureau of Drugs, "didn't the FDA come out and approve its use? Why throw the ball to an advisory committee, who . . . arrived at the same decision?"[57] Dr. Crout delivered a lengthy narrative on the agency's deliberations and the advisory committee's role in providing support from the scientific community, but he avoided the issue of the drug's unapproved use.[58] Mr. Fountain did not pursue the matter, nor did he inquire about the agency's willingness to dismiss its medical officer's assessments of the drug's risk and to continue clinical trials for risk acceptability reasons.

The Grady Clinic Revised Consent Form

On December 5, 1972, the Grady Clinic adopted the FDA's redesigned Depo-Provera consent form, which required all IND subjects to be informed about the beagle test results and the side effects they could experience in using the drug.[59] The form explicitly stated that Depo-Provera was an experimental drug and informed women of the existence of other non-experimental methods of preventing conception.[60] Then it addressed the two major risk issues.

The redesigned form told women that they might encounter problems, similar to those with the Pill, including "blood clots, tender breasts, nausea, vomiting, weight gain, weight loss, spotty darkening of skin of the face, mental depression, elevated levels of sugar and fatty substances in the blood, dizziness, loss of hair, increase in body hair and increased or decreased sex drive."[61] Women taking the drug were also told that they could experience menstrual irregularities, including "unexpected vaginal bleeding, completely irregular menstrual cycles or no menstrual bleeding at all," as well as fertility problems, including "unpredictable and prolonged delay" in becoming pregnant and permanent sterility.[62]

The redesigned form also told women about the beagle test results and their possible consequences for them. "I have been told that tests in dogs injected with this drug showed that some of them developed tumors in their breasts. Some of these tumors were cancer[ous] and spread to other organs. It is not known whether or not similar tumors or cancers will grow in my breasts after receiving the drug."[63] Then the consent form concluded by limiting Depo-Provera's use to women who had tried and either could not use or refused to use other birth control methods and who volunteered of their "own free will to receive an experimental drug" with "full knowledge and understanding" of the animal test results and the lack of scientific knowledge about the consequences of these test results for breast cancer in women.[64]

The FDA supplemented the redesigned consent form with a mandatory physician's certification form, which reflected an interest in continuing Depo-Provera's IND use on a highly restricted basis and incorporating practice of medicine standards into an IND study. Physicians were required to certify that they had "explained to the patient the facts, risks and alternatives" contained in the revised consent form and that she had consented to receive Depo-Provera for any one or more of five reasons largely related to other contraceptives: the failure of other methods, her inability to use other methods, unacceptable side effects with other methods, her refusal to accept the "responsibility demanded by other methods," and her need for a method not using estrogen.[65]

When the Grady Clinic implemented the revised consent form, it had a devastating effect on the size of the subject/patient participation. Dr. Robert Hatcher, Director of the Grady Clinic, informed the members of the House Select Committee on Population in 1978 that over 1,300 women were using Depo-Provera, but after "the staff explained the complicated and rather frightening new consent form in detail to the patients . . . the number of Depo-Provera users dropped within six months to its current level of 800 women."[66] As a 1980 Grady Clinic document reported: "It was the impression of the clinic staff that a 30–40% decrease in the number of active patients" occurred following implementation of the new consent form.[67]

The FDA Investigation of the Grady Clinic

The 1978 House Select Committee on Population hearings provided a favorable forum for Dr. Hatcher. Representatives of the World Health Organization, the International Planned Parenthood Federation, and the Population Council used the hearings to critique the FDA's decision two months earlier to deny Depo-Provera marketing approval, not for the scientific basis of the agency's decision, but for its risk acceptability implications for family planning and international population control. Four months later, however, Dr. Hatcher received a less friendly reception when the FDA visited the Grady Clinic to determine whether it had complied with IND requirements and employed the scientific criteria necessary to provide reliable evidence of the drug's safety and effectiveness. A five-person team, headed by Dr. Alan Lisook, conducted a week-long inspection, technically an IND Data Audit, and found "severe deficiencies" not only in the clinic's use of the FDA's 1972 consent form, but also in its protocol, its patient records and follow up, and its data, which had been used in journal articles and research reports.[68]

The FDA Grady Audit Report

The FDA's January 1979 report found that the Grady protocol failed to include the essential criteria for the selection of a participant in the study: the "age parameters, physical condition of subject (e.g. history of cancer), or the estimated duration of the clinical trial."[69] The FDA audit report did acknowledge that Dr. Hatcher had parameters for selecting subjects, but these had not been submitted to the agency with the original protocols.[70] He had, however, provided the House Select Committee on Population with these parameters when he identified the clinical settings in which the drug was "most likely" and "least likely" to be considered as an appropriate contraceptive.[71]

The FDA report did not, however, explain that Dr. Hatcher's congressional testimony had identified the standards for using a contraceptive in a family planning clinic, not for the conduct of an IND study. If he had been conducting an IND study, he would not have used Depo-Provera in many of the ten "clinical settings" where it was "most likely to be considered as an appropriate contraceptive."[72] A clinical study would not have admitted women who

> want a safe, effective method for a short period of time prior to a sterilization operation, are over thirty years, are mentally retarded, are receiving a rubella vaccine and must be protected against pregnancy for three months, have sickle cell disease, experience unplanned pregnancies or refuse other methods of birth control, are at particularly high risk of developing cardiovascular complications from estrogen-containing birth control pills or estrogen-related complications while taking combined oral contraceptives, are postpartum, or are being evaluated for suspicious Pap smears.[73]

These are practice of medicine standards, not criteria for a clinical study of a drug's safety and effectiveness. In fact, the drug should not have been used in two non-IND settings, because its use would have been contrary to the medical evidence about Depo-Provera, available in 1978, that women who had used the drug had subsequently undergone hysterectomies after developing Grade IV Pap smears[74] and that women who had used the drug postpartum experienced an unusually significant amount of menstrual bleeding.[75]

The FDA audit report did not explain that the clinical settings in which Dr. Hatcher stated that Depo-Provera was "least likely to be considered as an appropriate contraceptive" confirm that he was not conducting an IND clinical study.[76] If he had been conducting an IND study, he would not have used two of the eight criteria. An IND clinical study would not have included "women unwilling to take a drug that is not FDA approved . . . [or] to sign the consent form," because these are not medical criteria for excluding a woman in an IND clinical study,[77] nor are they "relative contraindications as he told the Public Board of Inquiry, elements of informed consent."[78] Women would, however, have been rejected for the other five reasons that Dr. Hatcher listed—"a history of breast cancer, benign breast mass, cancer of the cervix, abnormal glucose tolerance during pregnancy, and diabetes"—as they would have been rejected if they had had problems taking injections, desired more children, were never pregnant, or were teenagers, because the medical evidence, available in 1978, would clearly have justified excluding these women.[79]

The FDA report did, however, reveal substantial discrepancies in the number of women who participated in the Grady study. The clinic's protocol initially identified 1,100 women who participated in the study, but Dr. Hatcher reported in 1980 that 11,400 women had received Depo-Provera from April 1967 to May 1979.[80] This figure is still widely disputed. In his appearance before the House Select Committee on Population, he testified that there had been "4,600 and some odd [women] from 1967 to 1973, and then about 2,500 since then. So we've had a total of 7,500 women using Depo-Provera."[81] Then in his prepared statement, he said that the contraceptive had been provided "to over 5,000 women at Grady."[82] They were not, however, the same 5,000 women, nor even the 800 who were receiving the drug in 1978, because the dropout rate in the Grady program was about 40 percent.[83] As the FDA audit report disclosed, there was a loss and gain of approximately fifty subjects a month, which created "a patient turnover of approximately 75%" and exceeded the number of subjects identified in the protocol.[84] Dr. Hatcher had told the Select Committee on Population that the patients had discontinued their use of the drug, because of irregular menstrual periods, an absence of menstrual periods, depression, a loss of libido, weight gain, and "concern about issues raised by the Depo-Provera consent form."[85] But the clinic did not know what happened to these women, because, as the audit team found, that clinic personnel had not established a "tickler" system or any other method to follow their subjects who had dropped out of the study and determine the reasons they dropped out, including pregnancy and cancer.[86] As a consequence, the high dropout rate biased the study's conclusions and undermined the validity of its published research.

Even though the FDA had conditioned Depo-Provera's experimental use after 1972 on a substantially revised consent form, the agency's audit team found that Grady Clinic's use of the form was a mere formality, often observed in the breach. Patients were admitted to the program and received Depo-Provera prior to signing the consent forms.[87] One patient did not sign the consent form until almost four months later, another not until a year later.[88] Some consent forms were not routinely completed by all parties.[89] Some forms failed to have the patient's, the witness's, or the physician's signature certifying the subject's participation.[90] Still other forms were pre-witnessed, undated, or not included in the patients' charts.[91]

The National Women's Health Network Registry questionnaires returned by Grady patients supported the FDA data audit findings. Twelve of the twenty-two women who said they had received Depo-Provera after the clinic was required to use FDA's revised consent form reported that they were given no information on the drug's potential risks.[92] Fifteen out of twenty-four women reported receiving no information that the drug was not FDA-approved for contraception.[93] One woman wrote: "I feel like my life, my health, and the health of future children I might have had was [sic] put in jeopardy by not being told about this drug. As a result, I almost hemorrhage[d] to death. And . . . I had to have a complete hysterectomy. Since then a lot of the symptoms still remain and I feel that they will until death and that's very depressing."[94]

The FDA audit team examined the clinic's case histories of fifty-nine subjects and found that twenty-seven did not have recorded the reasons for their participation in the study.[95] "At least five subjects were admitted with no prior contraceptive history."[96] One subject was allowed to participate even though she had "a biopsy of proven carcinoma-in-situ of the cervix [and] . . . had a documented depression with a suicide attempt."[97] Two other subjects were admitted even though one was a diabetic and the other had a history of depression.[98] "Subjects were . . . admitted with undesirable characteristics: . . . a woman desiring more children, a never pregnant woman, or teenagers."[99] In spite of Dr. Hatcher's 1978 House testimony that the clinic was not able to provide Depo-Provera to teenagers and did not generally provide the drug to women who wanted to have children, because of the drug's experimental status and unresolved questions about return to fertility following its use,[100] the FDA investigators found that "teenagers are routinely admitted to the Depo-Provera study."[101]

Patient records disclosed that Grady personnel did not follow the protocol in giving the injections every three months.[102] Informed consent was not always included on the patients' charts or was undated, and not all the dates of injections were recorded.[103] One patient was given

Depo-Provera at a postpartum exam, without any reason stated in her chart, and another following a rubella vaccine, but "without any documented reason for her continuation in the study."[104] One patient had "dizziness and leg pains, another fainting spells, headaches with blurred vision, cramps in legs, and hypertension [and still] another had hypertension and possible seizures, but none had any clinical evaluation of their reactions to the drug."[105] The FDA audit team suggested that some of these failures could be explained by the fact that about "20% of the subjects . . . [were] seen without chart review."[106]

The Grady Clinic had a contract with the Georgia Department of Human Resources (GDHR) for its computers to evaluate the clinical data, but the clinic had not obtained any data for evaluation. "Drs. Long and Hatcher explained to the FDA audit team that on numerous occasions they had requested the data . . . [but] they have not gotten any cooperation."[107] Upon further investigation, the FDA team found that even if the GDHR had been cooperative, its computer could not have provided the clinical data, because the data were not "clinical in nature. . . . The data shows tests, but does not show any results of tests."[108] No data were available, because the Grady Clinic form used to supply the data showed the type of test to be provided—for example, blood pressure, breast exam, Pap smear—but "this form does not allow for the results of the test."[109] Not all patient visits were coded for computer usage. "Outpatient visits and diagnoses are not coded. . . . Only inpatient discharge diagnoses are coded. If this data is to be used for review and evaluation of this drug study," the audit report concluded, "not only inpatients', but outpatients' clinical information should be coded for [the] computer."[110]

Finally, the FDA audit team discovered that the Grady personnel failed to submit any reports to the Emory University Institutional Review Board,[111] nor did they, as Dr. Hatcher later told the Public Board of Inquiry, submit to the FDA any required annual reports.[112] Even though the 1972 consent form emphasized the beagle test results and informed women and physicians about the lack of scientific knowledge of developing breast cancer, the FDA audit team found that the clinic had not reported to the agency "any findings or summaries to [the] FDA . . . of subjects developing breast cancer while on Depo-Provera. . . . [or of the] 2 subjects that died from breast cancer while using Depo-Provera."[113] When Dr. Solomon Sobel of the FDA's Center for Drugs and Biologics (formerly the Bureau of Drugs),[114] was asked at the Public Board of Inquiry about the clinic's conduct, he stated that its failure to report such serious adverse effects in an annual report implied "a great degree of culpability."[115]

Dr. Lisook and his FDA audit team met with Drs. Long and Hatcher on the last day of their investigation and informed them of their findings.[116] They agreed with all the FDA findings, and Dr. Long expressed an interest in discontinuing the study, but he was also interested in using the data and resubmitting a new IND.[117] In that event, the FDA team suggested that the clinic should consider writing a more detailed protocol, exercising more control during the study, and providing a better follow-up of their patients.[118] The FDA team also met with Dr. Arthur Richardson, Dean of the Emory University School of Medicine, who agreed that the study should be discontinued unless there were any data that could be used in the resubmission of a new IND.[119] In sum, the FDA's investigation of the Grady Clinic's IND had been a narrowly focused scientific review of research procedures, but it led to no regulatory action except the termination of the clinic's IND for Depo-Provera.[120] The FDA team did not analyze the clinic's research reports and publications in professional journals, nor did it address the short-term health-related consequences for the women who had received the drug without their informed consent. These matters would be addressed at the FDA's Public Board of Inquiry hearings in 1983 and by the National Women's Health Network litigation in 1984.

The Discontinuation of the Grady IND Study

The Grady Family Planning Clinic discontinued its IND study of Depo-Provera and stopped offering the drug by June 1, 1979.[121] Dr. George Tucker, a Grady resident, was less than forthright when he informed his colleagues that the clinic's decision was due to "the high cost of providing any experimental drug due to the stringent FDA research requirements . . . [and] the tremendous amount of controversy and publicity surrounding the issue."[122] Missing from his report was any meaningful reply to the FDA audit or any acknowledgement that the "controversy and publicity" were rooted in the clinic's failure to follow the "stringent FDA research requirements" that bind all IND researchers.[123]

When the Grady Clinic informed its patients in a pamphlet entitled "Why Are You Stopping the Birth Control Shot at Grady Hospital?," it also avoided any reference to the FDA's data audit findings and sought to merely allay their fears that the clinic had not been "doing the right thing" in providing the injectable contraceptive. Depo-Provera, the pamphlet asserted, was "the best approach for some individuals" and it was "*safer and more effective than the pills.*"[124] Why was the shot discontinued? The clinic was not aware of something "new or suspicious" about the drug, or that it would cause cancer.[125] "We do *not* expect that you will get cancer, because of the shot. *It has not been proven that the birth control shot causes cancer . . .* [nor has] the shot been proven not to cause cancer."[126]

The pamphlet's simplistic reassurances sacrificed scientific honesty by blaming the FDA. The deeply flawed research on Depo-Provera, as this chapter and the following one will explain, made a comparative assessment of the drug safety impossible and allowed the clinic to say that there was no proof of cancer. No proof was possible. If the patients had read the clinic's informed consent form, they would have known that the research, in spite of its faults, identified the drug as a suspected carcinogen. After telling their patients that the drug was no longer available, because the FDA had "never approved the shot" for contraception,[127] the pamphlet avoided taking the next step and informing them that for the past twelve years they had been given the drug as subjects in a faulted IND clinical study, not as patients at a family planning clinic.

The pamphlet went on to express the clinic's disappointment in not being able to provide "this excellent contraceptive" and then offered to send its patients' personal views of their need for the drug to the FDA and members of Congress.[128] Even though the FDA had disapproved Depo-Provera the previous year (1978) for all women, the pamphlet expressed the clinic's hope that the FDA "will soon approve this drug for *some* women."[129] At the same time, the pamphlet encouraged Depo-Provera's continued unapproved use when it informed patients that they would not be able to obtain the contraceptive from private physicians, but it encouraged them to try.[130] If they decided to discontinue the shot, the clinic's cautious prognosis was that "the average woman could become pregnant in 6–12 months but there is no way to be exactly sure."[131] If they did not want to become pregnant, the pamphlet provided them with information on other birth control methods available at the clinic, including the Pill and tubal ligation.[132]

What contraceptive choices did the Grady women make? According to Dr. Tucker, of 509 women remaining in the clinic's patient registry, "forms were found for 492 or 97%. Of these 334 or 68% had returned for another visit after discontinuation . . . [and] 92% selected a method of contraception at that visit."[133] Why did they return? As Dr. Hatcher testified at the Public Board of Inquiry, they returned, as did oral contraceptive users, "to get the subsequent supplies,"[134] but the clinic did not have a protocol to follow up on the 40 percent who did not return.[135]

The Depo-Provera Public Board of Inquiry

When the FDA disapproved Depo-Provera for general marketing on June 22, 1978, Upjohn had the right to challenge the agency's action in a formal public hearing before an administrative law judge, but waived the right and requested an informal hearing before a public board of inquiry.[136] The FDA Commissioner, Arthur Hull Hayes, subsequently appointed Dr. Judith Weisz as chairperson and Drs. Griff T. Ross and Paul Stolley as members.[137] The Public Board of Inquiry on Depo-Provera heard five days of medical and scientific testimony from January 10 to 14, 1983, from all major participants: the pharmaceutical industry; medical organizations; population control, health, and women's groups; and government agencies, including the FDA.[138] Since Upjohn's New Drug Application (NDA) for Depo-Provera had included clinical studies based on Grady Clinic data and since the clinic was the major domestic clinical study of the drug, the Public Board of Inquiry was particularly interested in its protocol and research findings.

The Grady Clinic Protocol

The Public Board of Inquiry was aware that the FDA had inspected the Grady Clinic's IND in 1978, but was concerned that the FDA had not exercised any meaningful supervision over the Grady Clinic's program during the prior eleven years. When Dr. Robert Temple, the FDA's Acting Director of the Office of New Drug Evaluation, appeared before the board, Dr. Griff Ross asked him about the FDA's surveillance of the

Grady program.[139] Dr. Temple preferred to answer in general terms, because his office was responsible for new drug evaluations, not IND investigations. "After supplying an IND and protocol," he explained, "the only requirement is that a sponsor has is to report certain kinds of adverse events, and to provide an annual report."[140] The FDA does not, he said, oversee the approximately five thousand active INDs, but leaves the daily management of the trials "to the responsibility of the sponsor [carrying out the study] and his Institutional Review Board, which is supposed to be watching this with him."[141] Typically, Dr. Temple explained, the FDA reviews the results of studies supplied by the sponsor and does not inspect a study site unless there is a specific need, but he was unsure about what prompted the 1978 data audit of the Grady Clinic.[142]

The board shifted its scrutiny to Grady's IND when Dr. Robert Hatcher appeared to testify. Dr. Hatcher described himself as a clinician who ran a "hospital-based family planning program; [taught] medical students, nurse practitioners, and nurse midwives"; and was involved in several writing projects, including *Contraceptive Technology*, "a practical manual for providers of contraceptives," but he said, "I do minimal research and I am not a sophisticated epidemiologist."[143] Thereafter, he discussed the clinic's consent forms, the "close attention" the clinic's personnel paid to patient complaints, the most likely and least likely reasons they provided Depo-Provera, and the Grady-based research.[144]

Once he had concluded his formal remarks, Dr. Judith Weisz, the board chair, conducted a critical inquiry of the clinic's protocol and its published research. She began with the Grady IND protocols and elicited from Dr. Hatcher for the first time the public admission that the clinic had never operated under either its 1967 or 1973 protocol.

> DOCTOR HATCHER: We never operated under the '73 one, we never operated under a protocol from 1968 on. We provided the contraceptives from 1968 on as a contraceptive in our program. We followed up our patients, but there was no formal protocol.
>
> CHAIRPERSON WEISZ: There was no formal protocol under which— under what group was this administered?

DOCTOR HATCHER: We had an IND number and we provided it with known consent forms and known contraindications for providing the drug.

CHAIRPERSON WEISZ: But without any specific protocol being defined and there being no connection between the way this was used, administered, data collected, etc., and the protocol that I have before me which is 1973. . . .

DOCTOR HATCHER: That's correct. . . . The protocol was not operant.[145]

Dr. Weisz pressed on. Dr. Hatcher agreed with her statement that the Emory University's Institutional Review Board was "not in any way involved" in the clinic's IND administration, nor had the clinic provided the FDA with IND-required annual reports.[146] When he told her that the clinic had submitted a report to the FDA audit team, she turned to the FDA's data audit report:

CHAIRPERSON WEISZ: If one reads the report of the audit by the FDA in 1978, it . . . appears that there was [sic] flaws in the translation of intent into actual action.

DOCTOR HATCHER: I agree.

CHAIRPERSON WEISZ: What is the magnitude of this failure of translation of intent into action?

DOCTOR HATCHER: I think it was a serious failure. But, however, I do not believe that it was detrimental to our patients.

CHAIRPERSON WEISZ: . . . If no system was instituted to follow the patients adequately, what is the basis for the statement that no harm was done for obtaining the data of evaluating what particular risks the patients were actually exposed to?[147]

Dr. Hatcher referred to "one fairly intensive study initially," periodic audits, and an "extensive analysis of the risk of developing three types of cancer."[148] When he tried to explain that Depo-Provera was one of a number of contraceptive options that the clinic provided in an urban service setting undergoing a decrease in funding,[149] Dr. Weisz acknowledged that family planning clinics worked under difficult conditions, but since there was no protocol, the clinic appeared to be providing an unapproved contraceptive drug under the guise of an IND.

> CHAIRPERSON WEISZ: I understand that this drug was being ad-
> ministered, as if it were a fully approved drug with established risks
> rather than adhering to a protocol which would be necessary during
> the data collection period under an IND. Is that correct?
> DR. HATCHER: That's correct.
> CHAIRPERSON WEISZ: And, therefore, it was not possible to collect
> the kind of data that one would be able to use subsequently for estab-
> lishing a better risk/benefit ratio.[150]

Since the Grady Clinic had an IND, but was not using its own proto-col, Dr. Griff Ross asked Dr. Hatcher about his self-imposed protocol: "Would you tell me for any patient receiving contraceptive advice and prescriptions in your clinic, was it customary to see these persons on some anniversary date quarterly, six monthly, annually, and . . . how vigorously were these persons pursued when they failed to maintain a follow-up? . . . [What was the] customary practice as related to the way you followed these patients?"[151] Dr. Hatcher explained that the clinic ex-amined Depo-Provera patients annually. "They were asked about danger signals, the pregnancy test was done and we had another small protocol every three months. We made sure that they knew how to do a breast examination and that they were doing it. So that was basically our pro-tocol for Depo-Provera patients. If they failed to come back, . . . we did not have a protocol, period, for our contacting them."[152]

Dr. Ross returned to the Grady Clinic IND when Dr. Solomon Sobel of the FDA's Center for Drugs and Biologics appeared the following day. He drew Dr. Sobel's attention to the Grady Clinic's abandonment of its protocol after the first year and its failure to file any annual reports. "I find no evidence of even an annual report, during the course of this eleven year period. And that's dereliction . . . [which] should have trig-gered somebody's interest in the fact that not everything was proceed-ing according . . . to the minimal rules and regulations with respect to the proper rules of conduct."[153] Dr. Sobel agreed with him and Dr. Weisz that the investigators were culpable for failing to submit annual reports or even reports of "any significant departure from the original protocol" immediately and not waiting to include a protocol departure in the annual report.[154] Still, neither Dr. Ross nor later Dr. Weisz was able to obtain from Dr. Sobel any explanation for the FDA's failure to discover this egregious departure from standard IND oversight procedures. All they received from him was an assurance that "systematic follow-up through computer technology [would now] . . . avoid as much as possible this type departure from good investigative practice."[155]

The Grady Clinic's Published Research

The Public Board of Inquiry had been convened to examine the Upjohn reports and the published research that the company had used to support Depo-Provera's NDA application for contraceptive marketing approval. At its hearing, the board listened to a devastating critique of the research based on Grady data: the unpublished reports assembled by Dr. Hatcher in *Depo-Medroxyprogesterone Acetate: Experience at the Grady Memorial Family Planning Clinic in Atlanta Georgia: 1967–1978*,[156] the articles published in the *Journal of the American Medical Association*, *Public Health Reports*, and *Contraception*,[157] and the research reports and publications submitted by Upjohn in support of Depo-Provera's NDA.

Dr. Robert Hoover, the acting chief of the National Cancer Institute's Environmental Epidemiology Branch, began his critique of studies using the Grady data. He found that their sample sizes did not provide the studies with "substantial statistical power to detect meaningful differences in risk"; that their populations "received minimal exposure to Depo-Provera, the average being less than a year"; that their "relatively short follow-up period after exposure wasn't evaluated"; and that their designs "failed to introduce any substantial control for a variety of potential confounding factors."[158]

Then Dr. Hoover turned his attention to the design problems of three Grady studies. The Greenspan study (1980) of breast cancer was limited to those cases diagnosed at Grady, but no similar restriction applied to the control group, which resulted in the potential for bias.[159] The Liang study (1983) of breast, uterine, and ovarian cancer estimated that the "potential losses to follow-up was approximately 45% of the study population," but its attempt to adjust for these cases was "dubious at best," because the losses were so great.[160] The Ory study (1982) of mortality among young black contraceptive users "avoided many of these major design defects, . . . [but] the sample size concerns . . . were profound. . . . [and the] study has virtually no power to address meaningful differences in risk from death from cancers at the individual sites."[161] In sum, the Grady studies, along with many of the other Upjohn-sponsored studies, contained major design flaws that made the research scientifically and medically useless.

Dr. Charles Annello of the FDA's Bureau of Drugs echoed Dr. Hoover's assessment of the Grady studies for the inappropriateness of their study designs, their lack of follow-up, and their limited statistical power.[162] These scientific problems also concerned representatives of health and women's organizations. Dr. Gary Richwald of UCLA's School of Public Health, testifying on behalf of the National Women's Health Network, found that the Grady Clinic studies suffered from a lack of appropriate control groups, small sample sizes, inadequate length of exposure, and loss of users to follow-up.[163] Dr. Richwald was particularly disturbed by the Ory study's 45 percent loss to follow-up and the extent to which this loss biased the study's conclusions.[164] Dr. Sidney Wolfe, Director of the Public Citizens Health Research Group, also focused on the Grady Clinic's high loss of its subjects to follow-up. When people are "lost to follow-up at a rate of 30 to 40%," he said, "one should be more concerned about such questions as carcinogenicity, as return to fertility, [and] continued bleeding."[165] Loss of such a magnitude, he argued, not only undermines "the validity of a carcinogenicity study, but it also seriously diminishes the usefulness of the study in terms of looking at some of these other problems."[166]

The Public Board of Inquiry Report

The Public Board of Inquiry's Report, published in October 1984, upheld the FDA's decision to deny general marketing approval for Depo-Provera, because the "facts related to long term consequences of the use of the drug are inadequate and insufficient to provide a basis for risk assessment."[167] The board found "particularly unfortunate" the failure to collect reliable data at the Grady Clinic, as confirmed by the FDA audit, because the clinic could not provide an assessment of the drug's safety and effectiveness drawn from a domestic population.[168]

The unpublished study by Greenspan on endometrial cancer, which appeared in Dr. Hatcher's *Depo-Medroxyprogesterone Acetate* (1980), demonstrated the problems of relying on information from inadequate patient questionnaires and "trying to obtain data when no appropriate record system was set up in the beginning."[169] The Greenspan study of breast cancer in *Contraception* (1980) and the Liang study of breast, uterine, and ovarian cancer in the *Journal of the American Medical Association* (1983) had limited value, because of the short exposure of their subjects to Depo-Provera [170] and because they were retrospective studies based on information retrieved from patient files and records, the accuracy and completeness of which the 1978 FDA audit had questioned.[171]

In all, the Grady studies, along with other equally poor Upjohn human studies, could not dispel the animal study results that suggested the risk of breast, endometrial, and cervical cancer.[172] Upjohn appealed the board's report, but then withdrew its appeal, announcing that it would resubmit a supplemental NDA "supported by the most current scientific data."[173] Shortly thereafter, the FDA accepted the board's recommendation as a final agency decision to disapprove Depo-Provera's marketing license application.[174]

The National Women's Health Network Class Action Lawsuit

The Public Board of Inquiry's hearings answered the question about whether the scientific evidence was sufficient to assess Depo-Provera's carcinogenic risk, but the hearings left unaddressed the drug's adverse short-term side effects, though it acknowledged that they were "not trivial."[175] The board did not address issues related to pharmaceutical risk management and human experimentation, because its mandate did not extend to making any recommendations about the FDA's supervision and the Grady Clinic's conduct of its IND clinical studies.[176] Nor was it likely that the FDA would take any further action against the Grady Clinic for its IND violations. When Representative Ted Weiss, now chair of the House subcommittee that had scrutinized the agency's limited marketing approval of Depo-Provera in 1974, wrote to FDA Commissioner Arthur Hull Hayes in June 1983 about two articles in the *Journal of the American Medical Association* that had used Grady data, he also asked the commissioner about the agency's response to the 1978 data audit.[177] FDA Assistant Commissioner Robert Wetherell tersely replied: "The FDA has not taken any other significant regulatory action regarding the IND other than to permit its discontinuance."[178]

The Grady women were, however, given the opportunity to join the National Women's Health Network's nationwide class action suit against Upjohn. The Network, founded in 1976 as a national woman's consumer organization devoted to women's health, took the initiative three years later to create the National Stop Depo-Provera Coalition. Composed of 463 individuals, health professionals, and women's health advocates, the coalition coordinated "a direct media and publicity effort around the Board of Inquiry hearing."[179] Shortly thereafter, the Network also created a National Depo-Provera Registry[180] and then placed stories in women's magazines, including *MS.*, *McCall's*, *Mademoiselle*, *Mother Earth News*, *Women and Health*, and *Working Mother*, informing women about the drug and requesting them to register. Over one thousand women returned questionnaires detailing their experiences using the drug.[181] The Network provided them with free information on Depo-Provera and used the registry information to prepare for the Public Board of Inquiry hearings and to identify potential plaintiffs for a national class action lawsuit.[182]

The Network was aware that it would have to focus on the presentation of scientific testimony at the hearings and would not be permitted to make presentations addressing the social, political, or economic dimensions of Depo-Provera's use and introducing the testimony of its victims.[183] So the Network held a news conference on January 10, 1983, the opening day of the hearings. Sybil Shainwald, the Network's board chair, announced it would bring a lawsuit against Upjohn and then presented three women—Sandra Martin, Barbara Askinoise, and Adele Butterfield—who spoke about how they had been harmed by Depo-Provera.[184] Then the Network, along with women's and health advocates, including Helen Holmes, Stephen Minkin, Judy Norsigian, and Dr. Sidney Wolfe, testified at the five-day hearing.[185]

After the Public Board of Inquiry hearing, the Network encouraged the women involved in the Grady Clinic studies to join its lawsuit. Byllye Avery, coordinator of the newly formed and Atlanta-based Black Women's Health Project, issued a press release on February 2, 1983, announcing: "Atlanta women who participated in Grady Hospital's experimental use of the unapproved birth control drug called 'depo-provera,' can join a nationwide class-action suit against its manufacturer, the Upjohn Company."[186] Then the Public Citizen Health Research Group, the Network, and the Project engaged in a joint effort "to gather information about women who were given Depo-Provera at Grady."[187]

Of the fifty-six Depo-Provera Registry questionnaires the Network received from Grady subjects, fifty-one respondents said they had not been informed about the drug's unapproved status, and forty said they had not been informed about its risks: thirty out of thirty-two prior to 1973 and nine out of fourteen thereafter.[188] On their Registry forms, forty-six Grady women also reported bleeding, ten identified it as hemorrhaging, and four of those had had a hysterectomy.[189] All but one said they would like "to be considered for the class action suit against Upjohn."[190] Drawing upon these Registry questionnaires, the Health Research Group, working in cooperation with the Network, sent confidential questionnaires "designed to determine the sequence of events, the woman's health status before and after Depo-Provera use, and other possible causes of health problems such as heavy bleeding and infertility.[191] At the Network, Susan Seidler reported the disappointing results:

> Cary LaCheen [of the Health Research Group] sent out questionnaires to 35 women and received 12 responses. At least 6 were returned with no forwarding address, so those women are lost to us. . . . A lot of the women had other health problems that might account for the difficulties they have experienced since taking Depo. Cary is trying to isolate problems that could only be related to Depo. She wrote back to 3 women asking for more information because they might have serious problems as a result of using Depo. She wants to look at the medical records of all of them and has requested this in the letters.[192]

On March 12, 1984, Sybil Shainwald announced that the Network had formally filed suit, but it was not a nationwide suit, nor one involving women who had received Depo-Provera at the Grady Clinic, but one on behalf of nine California women.[193] In *National Women's Health Network v. The Upjohn Company* (1984), the Network asked the San Francisco Superior Court to hold Upjohn liable for distributing Depo-Provera to physicians and clinicians who the company would know were using the drug as a contraceptive not approved by the FDA.[194]

Sybil Shainwald promised a nationwide suit in several months as well as another state-wide class action suit in Texas, but they were never filed.[195] In September 1985, James Kreindler, a New York City attorney, advised her that "a class action against Upjohn is not viable."[196] Since "the vast majority of women received the drug from private physicians and not health clinics," he concluded, "I do not see any evidence that Upjohn was shipping Depo-Provera to entities that had no business ad-ministering the drug to any patients. . . . Upjohn could justifiably claim that it was shipping the drug to physicians who presumably were using the drug for approved purposes."[197] Mr. Kreindler's legal opinion also suggested that the Network's California case was in jeopardy. Later that year, the Network's California attorneys withdrew from the suit.[198] Un-able to find another California attorney to take the case on a *pro bono* basis, the Network left the case pending until 1988, when the California trial court dismissed the case at Upjohn's request.[199] As a consequence, the California plaintiffs had no recourse, except to consult an attorney about bringing a medical malpractice action.

Summary

Dr. Judith Weisz's story of the politics of drug risk management, as told by her and by Drs. J. W. Armstead, Michael Popkin, and Alan Lisock, is defined by their commitment to the FDA's drug IND research, based on animal studies and human clinical trials and conducted in accordance with the agency's IND standards. Her story documents how the FDA and the Grady Clinic crossed the risk assessment boundary and allowed risk acceptability and practice of medicine interests to permit the Grady Clinic to conduct the major domestic Depo-Provera clinical trial for twelve years (1967–1979). Her story also documents how the clinic crossed the boundary between risk assessment and the practice of medicine in a family-planning setting and in the process behaved unethically toward its subjects and the scientific community. The clinic failed to provide its sub-jects the information about Depo-Provera that would have enabled them to give their informed consent; it failed to use a well-designed protocol that would have provided criteria for selecting subjects and for collecting, analyzing, and reporting data; and it failed to provide periodic reports to the FDA and the Emory Institutional Review Board.

The Food and Drug Administration engaged in an exercise of risk management science when it disregarded the precedent of negative animal study results, which would have permitted it to terminate Upjohn's and the Grady Clinic's Depo-Provera INDs. Instead, the agency allowed the drug's INDs to continue, albeit on a restricted basis with enhanced informed consent, because the drug's supposed unique advantages overrode the unsettled state of the animal studies. At the same time, the FDA crossed the boundary between the approved and unapproved drugs when it authorized Depo-Provera's continued IND use for restricted groups of women knowing that it would be used in non-IND settings by private physicians and family-planning clinics. The FDA was even derelict in its duty for not investigating the Grady Clinic's failure to submit annual reports for eleven years, because, once it did investigate, it found how seriously the clinic had crossed the boundary between the conduct of a human clinical trial and the practice of medicine.

The Grady Clinic's failure to observe the standards for the conduct of a human clinical study deeply affected the quality of its research. The Grady research reports and professional journal articles became part of the general public debate over the scientific evidence in support of Depo-Provera's marketing approval, but they did not receive any thoroughgoing analysis until the Public Board of Inquiry hearing, when they were dissected by scientists at the FDA, the Centers for Disease Control, and medical researchers testifying on behalf of women' health organizations for their failure to follow the canons of scientific research—a failure that made them, along with many other Upjohn-sponsored studies, medically and scientifically useless.

The Grady Clinic's failure to conduct a clinical study in accordance with the standards of informed consent had personal consequences for women, which remain unremedied. The FDA audit exposed the extent of the clinic's research failures, but the audit led only to the termination of the clinic's IND. The FDA's Public Board of Inquiry was deeply troubled by the Grady Clinic's failure to use its protocol and the agency's lack of IND oversight, but did not hear the anecdotal testimony from women adversely affected by the drug, because it had a mandate to examine only the scientific evidence and make a marketing recommendation.

Congressional committees spoke with a divided voice in response to the FDA's recommendation for limited marketing approval in 1974 and general marketing approval in 1978—they were critical of the agency's failure to sufficiently assess the scientific evidence in the first instance and critical of its failure to give sufficient emphasis to risk acceptability considerations in the second, but in neither instance did these committees give any attention to the personal experiences of the research subjects. The National Women's Health Network seriously considered a nationwide class action lawsuit that would include Grady women, but they were difficult to find and the harm to their health was difficult to attribute to their unknowing use of Depo-Provera.

2

The Twenty-Five-Year FDA Approval Controversy

Cancer and the Politics of Acceptable Risk

Judith Weisz's story of the politics of drug risk management shifts its focus to the Food and Drug Administration's new drug approval authority.[1] Up to this point, her story has been confined to the FDA's focus on the Grady Clinic's IND. Now a critical period for her is the drug approval process, which occurs after the FDA receives a company's New Drug Approval (NDA) application. During this time, drug evaluation is usually in the FDA's hands. Yet Upjohn's submission of its Depo-Provera NDA application in 1967 expanded the scope of the risk management conflict over the drug to include members of Congress and representatives of women's, public health, and population control organizations, who, together with the FDA, engaged in a twenty-five-year risk management controversy over Depo-Provera's approval for contraceptive use.

In this public arena, Judith Weisz's story addresses the risk management issues raised by Upjohn's animal and human clinical studies.[2] Her story explains why the FDA and Upjohn crossed the risk assessment boundary and allowed risk acceptability policy arguments—the drug's uniqueness as a long-acting injectable contraceptive,[3] its approval by other countries, and its use in international population control programs—to influence its marketing approval decisions and why this boundary crossing became the subject of scientific scrutiny by Dr. Weisz, the FDA's Drs. Michael Popkin and Bertram Litt, the National Cancer Institute's Dr. Robert Hoover, Representative L. H. Fountain, and the Health Research Group's Dr. Sidney Wolfe, among others.

This twenty-five-year scientific and political controversy was, however, limited in its scope. It did not consider the drug's short-term risks, such as excessive menstrual bleeding, weight gain, depression, and delayed return to fertility. Cancer, the long-term risk, drove the engine of national risk management. Fear that Depo-Provera could cause breast,

cervical, and endometrial cancer defined the FDA's marketing decisions: its limited marketing approval in 1974, later withdrawn, and its
1978 decision to deny the drug general marketing approval. Thereafter,
the agency turned to a public board of inquiry, chaired by Dr. Weisz,
to make a risk management decision based principally on a scientific
assessment of the drug's risk, which justified the agency's 1986 decision
to, once again, deny Upjohn approval to market Depo-Provera as a contraceptive drug.

1974 Limited Marketing Disapproval

Upjohn had just submitted its NDA in 1967 when breast tumors were discovered in the animal testing of another progestogen.[4] Subsequently, the
FDA ordered the company to conduct a seven-year study of beagle dogs
and a ten-year study of rhesus monkeys.[5] In September 1970, Upjohn
reported to the agency that it had found malignant breast tumors in
three of the dogs. As discussed in Chapter 1, the Bureau of Drugs turned
to its medical officers and Obstetrics and Gynecology (OB/GYN) Advisory Committee, but it received conflicting advice about whether to
terminate the drug's IND. The bureau's medical officers recommended
an end to clinical testing, but the FDA decided to follow the July 1971
recommendation of its OB/GYN Advisory Committee and allow limited
clinical trials to obtain metabolic data on menstrual bleeding and weight
gain[6] and to await the outcome of the animal studies, because Upjohn's
clinical trials were almost complete. When the bureau consulted the
advisory committee at its June 2, 1972 meeting, it became aware that the
committee had sufficient reservations about the drug's safety and would
not encourage the agency to grant general marketing approval,[7] but the
committee's discussion suggested that it might endorse limited approval
of the drug for institutionalized women who were mentally challenged
and women who could not tolerate the Pill or an IUD.[8]

By late 1972, the FDA had become increasingly aware of two risk
acceptability issues that had been explored by its OB/GYN Advisory
Committee. At its July 1971 meeting, a Department of State official had
informed the committee about Depo-Provera's "considerable importance to the policy interests of the United States in assisting developing
countries . . . [to] bring down their exceedingly high birth rates."[9] At its

June 1972 meeting, the committee had discussed Depo-Provera's widespread unapproved contraceptive use by private physicians and family planning clinics nationwide.[10] The drug's unapproved use had also attracted the interest of Senator Edward Kennedy, who planned to hold hearings in early 1973 on human experimentation and the widespread use of Depo-Provera and DES, a synthetic hormone, for medical treatments not approved by the FDA. In these circumstances, the agency concluded that approval of Depo-Provera for limited marketing would be a solution to the drug's unapproved domestic use and to the demand for its use in controlling population growth overseas.

The OB/GYN Advisory Committee Recommendation

When the OB/GYN Advisory Committee met on February 22, 1973, it was aware that Senator Kennedy's hearings had begun the day before[11] and that it would be asked to address Depo-Provera's unapproved use and to recommend that the drug be granted a limited marketing license.[12] Dr. J. Richard Crout, Acting Director of the FDA's Office of Scientific Evaluation, began the meeting by telling the committee that it was "being asked to pull together the evidence and help us with a decision . . . [involving the] open use of drugs when that use is not part of approved indications. We believe when this is occurring, the Food and Drug Administration has an obligation to address the issue and either approve the indication, with appropriate labeling, or tell doctors why it cannot be approved."[13]

The advisory committee first heard from Upjohn researchers. Dr. Paul Schwallie, who was principally responsible for the drug's clinical trials, presented the results of the company's human studies, including the pivotal efficacy and safety study that he had conducted with Dr. J. Robert Assenzo.[14] Then Dr. Robert Carlson, an Upjohn toxicologist-pathologist, explained the animal studies and the company's misgivings about the relevance of the beagle test results.[15] The advisory committee also heard from representatives of the United States Agency for International Development and population control organizations that favored Depo-Provera's approval, but the committee heard no presentations critical of the Upjohn research.[16] The FDA did not make a presentation, nor did the agency provide the committee with the July 20, 1972, report by Dr. Michael Popkin, a Bureau of Drug's medical officer who had critiqued the Upjohn clinical studies, including the Schwallie and Assenzo study, and found four cases of breast cancer, sixteen cases of cervical cancer, and a 65 percent dropout rate, all of which led him to recommend that "this IND be discontinued and no further studies be permitted by the FDA."[17]

In sum, the advisory committee's questions indicate that it had heard a one-sided presentation, which did not provide a sufficient amount of evidence to make a proper assessment of the drug's risk. Nor did the committee hear any meaningful testimony about the need for an injectable contraceptive. As Dr. Sheldon Segal, a consultant to the committee, observed: "There has been no survey or study concerning the question of how useful an injectable contraceptive would be."[18] All he had heard were "anecdotal comments that tend to be difficult to evaluate."[19]

When the advisory committee met that afternoon in executive session, Dr. Marion Finkel, Acting Deputy Director of the Bureau of Drugs, turned to Senator Kennedy's hearings on Depo-Provera's unapproved use and to the evidence his committee had heard about family-planning clinic patients who had not been adequately informed about the drug's experimental status and its possible risks and about the guardians of girls in an institution for the mentally challenged who were asked to sign a grossly inadequate informed consent form.[20] For Dr. Finkel, these unapproved uses of Depo-Provera provided rather convincing evidence that the agency's 1971 IND decision, discussed in chapter 1, was not serving its purpose of allowing Upjohn to complete its metabolic studies and permitting the drug to be used by women who could not use other contraceptives.[21] Still, she argued, that "there exists a certain segment of the population for whom an injectable contraceptive remains a viable contraceptive."[22] She then concluded that the FDA was interested in a committee recommendation for the drug's limited use based on informed consent by means of patient and physician package inserts.[23]

Dr. Finkel's remarks suggested that the FDA was not seriously interested in the advisory committee's critique of the Upjohn research. Dr. Segal, one of the few concerned about the agency's ability to make an assessment of the drug's risk, was not pleased by its apparent willingness to "disregard the beagle data as having implications for the human."[24] Upjohn's clinical studies also prompted him to inquire about the ability of the company to reach meaningful conclusions about the drug's long-term carcinogenic potential, because of the high discontinuation of research subjects: "50 percent in the first year . . . [and] 40 to 50 percent in the second year."[25] He was troubled by Upjohn's failure to include in its presentation an infertility study by Dr. F. Douglas Scutchfield, based on Grady Clinic data, which concluded that only 52.9 percent of the women who used the drug resumed normal menses.[26] Since Dr. Segel was aware that the committee's discussion was defined by the agency's interest in limited approval accompanied by informed consent safeguards, he expressed the hope that the risk of infertility would not be "buried in the package insert" because of the "psychological problems" and "potential for tragedy" from the drug's use by young women.[27]

Dr. Finkel's remarks also suggested that the FDA had been pleased to hear the favorable risk acceptability testimony presented at the advisory committee's open session, which emphasized Depo-Provera's uniqueness as the only available long-acting injectable contraceptive and the need for it to be used by a restricted population described by Dr. Schwallie as composed of women who were unable to accept the responsibility demanded by other methods, including the mentally challenged; those who found conventional birth control means unsuitable, ineffective, or unacceptable; and those who lacked the motivation to use oral contraceptives.[28] At the executive session, committee members speculated that these women, perhaps 3 percent of contraceptive drug users, had a need for an injectable contraceptive. Dr. Philip Corfman, the other committee consultant, was, however, willing to reject even these speculations, because "we all have a gut feeling that injectables could be very important in a certain population and that could be justification for using a compound that happens to cause beagle tumors."[29]

In sum, the advisory committee did not have the scientific data to assess the drug's risk or any clear standards to make a risk management recommendation. Instead, the committee members had little more to rely upon than their anecdotal and impressionistic views and their professional speculations in discussing the package insert's value in assuring that the restricted population of women would be able to give their informed consent. Would these women really understand the patient insert's explanation,[30] would they would be filled with anxiety once they read it,[31] and would it be necessary for them to read it at all? As Dr. Elizabeth Connell remarked, "I think if a patient wants a shot, she is going to get it, and the doctor is going to down-play it if he feels it is in her best interest."[32] In the end, the committee approved, 6 to 1, Depo-Provera's limited use with a patient insert and, thereby, provided the FDA with the means to legitimize the drug's unapproved contraceptive use.[33] Only Dr. Ernest Lowe voted "no," because he "preferred to see the development of another drug in as much as this drug has demonstrated all the limitations we have discussed."[34]

The FDA's Limited Marketing Proposal

The FDA announced its proposed order to approve Depo-Provera for limited contraceptive use on October 10, 1973. The *Federal Register*[35] notice largely reflected the OB/GYN Advisory Committee recommendation seven months earlier.[36] The FDA notice first cited Depo-Provera's uncontested benefit: the drug was 99.4 percent effective in preventing conception for at least three months.[37] Then the notice identified the drug's health risks: the "potential" for breast cancer, the "possibility" of permanent infertility, and "unexpected" bleeding.[38] The risk of breast cancer, suggested by the results in the beagle dog studies, had led to the removal of Provest, the oral form of Depo-Provera used daily, but the agency proposed to approve the injectable drug, because of its "unique advantage" of being used at the "infrequent interval of every three months. . . . [by] a limited patient population."[39] For this restricted population with no other suitable means of contraception, the FDA "concur[red] with the opinion of the Advisory Committee that the benefits of . . . [the drug] outweigh its risks."[40]

The FDA's proposed order was not, however, based on a meaningful risk-benefit analysis. In fact, the agency had misapplied risk-benefit analysis, because Depo-Provera's "unique advantage" is not a benefit, but a risk acceptability factor. The FDA notice identified two risk acceptability grounds for approving Depo-Provera. First, it largely adopted Upjohn's definition of the "very limited and carefully defined patient population" for whom the drug would be an acceptable risk: women who could not use other methods of contraception or whose use of other methods had "repeatedly failed," women who refused or were unable "to accept the responsibility demanded by other contraceptive methods, women who were unable to tolerate the side effects of conventional oral contraceptives . . . or other effective methods of contraception," and women who understood and accepted the risks of using Depo-Provera.[41] Second, the FDA notice claimed that the drug would be "properly used" by this patient population, because the proposed order contained two "cautionary measures": a leaflet and a detailed brochure that would accompany each dose to assure informed consent[42] and a distribution restriction that would require physicians, clinics, and hospitals to order the drug from Upjohn and participate in "a registry of physicians who have utilized the drug for contraception."[43]

The FDA's proposed order also raised serious doubts as to whether the agency's action satisfied all the regulatory criteria in the Code of Federal Regulations for the approval of a new drug.[44] CFR 314.105 (a) states: "the FDA will approve an application if none of the [16] reasons in 314.125 for refusing to approve the application apply."[45] The tests that Upjohn used and the evidence it supplied to the agency and the advisory committee were, however, of dubious value in overcoming the three reasons for disapproval in CFR 314.125: first, the studies were not adequate to show the drug was safe, even for a limited population; second, the test results did not show the drug was not safe; and third, "sufficient information" did not exist to determine that the drug was safe for use under the conditions stipulated in its proposed labeling.[46] Clearly Upjohn had not met its burden of proving that Depo-Provera was "safe for its intended use," but the FDA accepted the company's risk management arguments. The agency's proposed order approved the drug for limited marketing subject to two "cautionary measures" to ensure informed consent: the leaflet and brochure that would accompany each dose.

Congressional Scrutiny

The FDA's proposed order received a number of written comments. In the spring of 1974, the rule also attracted intense congressional scrutiny. When the House Subcommittee on Intergovernmental Relations, chaired by L. H. Fountain, held hearings to explore the agency's greatly increased use of advisory committees in making new drug approval decisions,[47] the subcommittee inquired about the agency's reliance on the OB/GYN Advisory Committee in approving Depo-Provera's limited use. Mr. Fountain directed his questions to Dr. J. Richard Crout, the Director of the Bureau of Drugs, and to his opening comments at the February 22, 1973, OB/GYN Advisory Committee meeting in which one of the choices he gave the committee was to "revise the labeling to legitimate its non-approved use."[48] Mr. Fountain suspected that Depo-Provera's proposed limited approval was one more example of the FDA "throw[ing] the ball to advisory committees . . . to legitimize the unapproved use of drugs by restrictive labeling changes."[49] Dr. Crout sought to assure the congressman that the advisory committee members "had a very good idea of what scientific evidence is" and would not have recommended a change in the labeling unless there was evidence to support the change.[50]

Mr. Fountain had his doubts and turned to the FDA medical officers' review of the Upjohn data in 1971 and 1972 and to their recommendation that Depo-Provera's IND be terminated, because the preliminary results from the beagle dog studies suggested the potential for breast cancer in women and clinical studies revealed cervical cancer rates in excess of national incidence.[51] He was particularly interested in the issue of cervical cancer and drew Dr. Crout's attention to Dr. Popkin's July 1972 report on the Upjohn research, including Drs. Schwallie and Assenzo's pivotal study of 3,856 women which had found sixteen cases of cervical cancer[52] as compared to the nine cases identified by Upjohn in the written material that Dr. Schwallie had supplied to the advisory committee.[53] Mr. Fountain was disturbed that these cervical cancer "figures were not discussed at any time during the committee's consideration of the safety of Depo-Provera" and that the FDA officials had not taken the initiative to have the committee address the variations among Dr. Popkin's cervical cancer findings, Upjohn's, and those reported in the Third National Cancer Survey.[54]

Mr. Fountain informed Dr. Crout that his subcommittee staff had computed the incidence of cervical cancer using Dr. Popkin's and Upjohn's figures and found that "the Upjohn figures add[ed] up to an incidence of 235 per 100,000 and for Dr. Popkin's figures, an incidence of 410 per 100,000. In either case, the figures greatly exceeded the recorded incidence of 36 per 100,000" in the National Cancer Survey.[55] Then he asked Dr. Crout a rhetorical question: "Is this possible discrepancy of sufficient importance to have warranted bringing this matter to the attention of the OB/GYN Advisory Committee for consideration and discussion?"[56] Dr. Crout agreed: "If the data you are presenting are correct, we have missed the point and there is absolutely no question that the benefit risk of this drug changes."[57] In fact, the doubts that the data raised meant that "the Federal Register statement we are proposing to publish will not get published in this form."[58]

Still, Mr. Fountain was not satisfied, but asked Dr. Crout a final lengthy question that summarized the absence of any meaningful scientific evidence to support the agency's decision:

> If the evidence or data presented to the committee by Upjohn was not complete, as the participants at the committee meeting indicated during the closed session; if the significance for humans of cancer and tumor results in beagles is not known, as is revealed in the verbatim transcripts and in the FDA's October 10, 1973, *Federal Register* notice; if the facts, nature, and significance of the cases of [cervical] cancer-in-situ were not presented to the committee or in any way discussed, as is apparent from the verbatim transcript; [and] if there is not enough experience, because of the high discontinuation rate and other factors, to determine the extent of infertility caused by the drug, as indicated by the consultants; . . . was the committee ready to make a benefits, risk determination?[59]

Dr. Crout attempted to deflect the question, replying: "I think you are discovering that the approval process involves a lot of ifs."[60] Mr. Fountain, not amused, persisted. "I just summarized the findings. . . . What is the answer to my question?"[61] To his utter amazement, Dr. Crout answered, "Yes."[62] Dr. Crout's further replies and his attempts to defend the FDA's actions were unconvincing, because his earlier testimony had revealed that the advisory committee did not have before it the scientific evidence on cancer, infertility, and bleeding necessary to make an assessment of the drug's risk, nor did it have any meaningful evidence of the need for an injectable drug to make a risk acceptability judgment.

The FDA's Revised Limited Marketing Proposal

In the months following Mr. Fountain's devastating critique, the FDA focused its attention on consumer comments and congressional questions about its 1973 proposal to grant Depo-Provera limited marketing approval. Then on September 17, 1974, the agency issued a final patient labeling rule in anticipation of the drug's limited approval.[63] The *Federal Register* notice reflected the agency's willingness to alter its proposed approval order in response to fourteen comments, including those sent by physicians, family planning organizations, and consumer groups.[64] The revised patient leaflet and brochure were reworded "to more simply express the nature and hazards of the drug" and to include information on oral contraceptives that would allow women to make a comparative risk decision.[65] The final patient label rule was, however, a bold step for the agency, because Mr. Fountain's criticism clearly indicated that the scientific evidence did not support even limited approval.

The FDA's reanalysis of the cervical cancer data threw down the risk assessment gauntlet, because it accepted the argument that the incidence of cervical cancer was higher than that reported by the National Cancer Institute (NCI) for the general population, but it then dismissed the NCI findings as unimportant. According to the *Federal Register* notice, the increase in the incidence of cervical cancer in women who received Depo-Provera was "not compatible with known behavior of chemical carcinogens, because most of the cases were detected within 2 years of the start of the trials. . . . Documented examples of chemical carcinogenesis in man has [*sic*] occurred after a lag time of 3 years or longer, and in most instances this lag time has been a decade or more."[66] Studies of rodents, rabbits, and monkeys had not demonstrated any carcinogenic potential. Only the beagle dog had raised a concern about breast cancer, not cervical cancer.[67] Nor was Upjohn's clinical trial comparable to the group the NCI used, because the company's clinical trial involved women who had previously taken oral contraceptives, who were under more intensive surveillance, and who were members of a socioeconomic population normally at higher risk for cervical cancer.[68] In sum, the notice concluded that the agency's reanalysis of the cervical cancer data, subjects, and clinical trials did not provide any new evidence that would alter its decision to grant the drug marketing approval.

Congressional Intervention and FDA Retreat

The *Federal Register* notice provoked Mr. Fountain to write a letter of protest to Health, Education, and Welfare (HEW) Secretary Casper Weinberger, which "strongly urged" him to revoke Depo-Provera's approval and require additional studies to ensure a "sound safety determination."[69] In his eleven-page single spaced critique, the congressman detailed for the secretary the conclusions he had drawn from his oversight hearings about the agency's misuse of its advisory committee and the detailed analysis his staff had conducted of the risk analysis in the agency's *Federal Register* notice and the information in its patient leaflet and brochure.

Mr. Fountain began by dismissing the FDA's claim that its approval was based on its advisory committee's evaluation of the drug's benefits and risks. FDA documents suggested both "a prior intent to approve Depo-Provera regardless of the insufficiency of the available information"[70] and a committee "motivated to recommend approval because the drug was administered by injection."[71] The FDA's reanalysis of the cervical cancer data was also deeply flawed. Using information he had acquired from the FDA and NCI officials and experts, he argued that the agency's reanalysis was "a casual dismissal of the high incidence of cervical cancer when so little was known on the subject."[72] The FDA's statement that Depo-Provera had not demonstrated carcinogenic potential in rodents, rabbits, and monkeys was "grossly misleading."[73] None of the FDA pharmacologist reviews supported the conclusion that the drug was non-carcinogenic.[74]

The FDA's conclusions about the lack of comparability of Upjohn's clinical trial and the NCI group of women were based on conjecture, because "most of the NCI patients had taken oral contraceptives prior to entering the trials."[75] Dr. Bertram D. Litt, an FDA statistician, could not evaluate "the prior use of oral contraceptives . . . from the available information."[76] The NCI had reported that prescreening and more intensive surveillance of women in the Depo-Provera clinical trials would result in a lower detection rate of cervical cancer, not a higher one as the FDA argued.[77] Then using Dr. Schwallie's FDA Advisory Committee testimony and the NCI survey, Dr. Litt found that the higher rate of cervical cancer could not be explained either by race or socioeconomic status.[78]

Finally, Mr. Fountain disputed the conclusion that the agency's re-analysis did not provide any new evidence since Dr. Litt's June 17, 1974, memo had reported thirty-five known cervical cancer cases.[79] This "two fold increase in known cancer cases is new information,"[80] he declared, and then asked if these cases were the "minimal figures . . . because over 40 percent of the women in the Depo-Provera study had dropped out for various reasons in the first twelve months."[81] As a consequence, he concluded that the patient leaflet would not provide a woman with the information she needed for an informed judgment, because it made no mention of the higher incidence of cervical cancer.[82]

Mr. Fountain closed his letter to Secretary Weinberger by drawing his attention to the FDA's failure to comply with Section 505(d) of the Federal Food, Drug, and Cosmetic Act. Section 505(d) requires that all new drug approvals be based on test results that provide sufficient information to determine whether the drug is safe for its labeled use.[83] Mr. Fountain's inquiries had satisfied him that there were enough serious and unresolved questions about the drug's safety to conclude that there was insufficient evidence under Section 505(d) to find that the drug was safe.[84] So he "strongly urged" the HEW secretary "to take prompt action" and revoke the FDA's approval of Depo-Provera and require additional studies of the drug.[85]

Mr. Fountain received the prompt action he requested. Secretary Weinberger wrote to him the next week, saying that he shared his "significant and justifiable concerns" about the drug's carcinogenicity, and informed him that "FDA Commissioner Dr. Alexander Schmidt is writing to you today, outlining a course of action that will include staying the order and holding a public hearing."[86] Dr. Schmidt, citing the need for public confidence in drug safety, informed Mr. Fountain that he would stay the order and delay a decision until the issues raised by the congressman were examined in an open hearing before the agency and its Obstetrics and Gynecology Advisory Committee.[87]

1978 General Marketing Disapproval

The FDA's review of its limited marketing order began the following spring, lasted three years, and led to its decision to disapprove the drug for general marketing. The Bureau of Drugs began the review process by admitting that the Obstetrics and Gynecology Advisory Committee had never considered the relationship of cervical cancer to Depo-Provera use.[88] In order to provide the OB/GYN Advisory Committee with the benefit of statistical expertise on this issue and on the general issue of the relationship of steroidal contraceptives to cervical cancer, the bureau decided to convene a joint open hearing of the OB/GYN Advisory Committee and the Biometrics and Epidemiological Methodology (BEM) Advisory Committee.[89]

OB/GYN and BEM Advisory Committee Hearing

On April 7, 1975, the advisory committees listened to representatives of the FDA, Upjohn, and the Centers for Disease Control testify that scientific studies were unable to provide reliable evidence about the relationship of Depo-Provera to cervical cancer. Dr. L. C. Powell, whose research had called attention to the increased risk of cervical cancer,[90] acknowledged: "We have not designed a study to look for a carcinogenesis in Depo-Provera."[91] Upjohn spokesmen, Dr. Noel Mohberg, agreed. The company, he said, had studied "the drug as a contraceptive and not as a possible carcinogen," and it had not used any controls for cancer.[92] As a consequence, it could not determine the drug's long-term carcinogenic risk, nor engage in any meaningful comparison of its cervical cancer findings with those of the National Cancer Institute's survey and the published research literature. Upjohn's pivotal multi-center study, which was composed of fifty-four trials and coordinated by Drs. Schwallie and Assenzo, was troublesome, because it had a significant loss of its subjects to follow up. According to Dr. Bertram Litt, an FDA statistician, the study had 1,513 dropouts out of a total of 3,856 women—722 for unexplained reasons, 491 for personal ones, and 30 for irregular bleeding—and these losses limited the ability to statistically evaluate whether women would be at higher risk of cervical cancer.[93]

The advisory committees also heard assessments of Depo-Provera's carcinogenic risk from representatives of women's, consumer, welfare rights, and public health organizations. Anita Johnson, representing the Health Research Group and the National Organization of Women, and Dr. Sidney Wolfe, Director of the Health Research Group, reminded the committees that the human data would not support a limited marketing order based on the September 1974 *Federal Register* notice.[94] Dr. Wolfe emphasized that the "extraordinarily high" dropout rate of 45 percent in the Upjohn studies made it difficult to assess Depo-Provera's health risk. The use of estrogen to control "severe bleeding" also undercut the drug's uniqueness as a three-month injectable, and the uncertainty of return to fertility following its discontinuance raised questions about involuntary sterilization.[95]

Marcia Greenberger, who spoke on behalf of the Consumer's Union, National Welfare Rights Organization, and Women's Equity Action League, discussed the risk acceptability problems identified by Anita Johnson.[96] Approval for "limited and well-defined patient populations," she argued, would target mentally challenged and indigent women who would be given the drug in circumstances, identified in the 1973 Senate DES and Depo-Provera hearings, and would raise substantial doubts about their ability to give their informed consent.[97] The FDA's patient leaflet raised even more doubts, because it provided no information about the possible harm to infants from breast-feeding mothers given Depo-Provera postpartum or about the risks of using other contraceptive methods.[98] Nor was there any requirement that physicians explain the drug's benefits and risks prior to giving an injection.[99]

At the conclusion of the open hearing, Gilbert Goldhammer, a consultant to Mr. Fountain's subcommittee, drew the advisory committees' attention to Anita Johnson's argument that Upjohn had the burden of proving that the drug is safe.[100] The Food, Drug, and Cosmetic Act, he reminded the committees, permits the HEW secretary to approve a drug only if all appropriate tests establish that the drug is safe or, in the alternative, the drug is not unsafe.[101] Therefore, he requested the addition of one question to be answered by the advisory committees before they decided whether to recommend approval of Depo-Provera on the basis of the September 1974 order: Did the test results establish that the drug is not unsafe?[102] Dr. Crout agreed to add the question.

After the hearing, the FDA created a joint OB/GYN–BEM subcommittee, which was composed of three members of each advisory committee, met on April 30, 1975, and prepared a report that concluded that the human and animal data were ambiguous and recommended that marketing approval be delayed pending a study of cervical cancer incidence and an informal survey of available databases.[103] Five months later, the subcommittee met again and concluded that there were no databases available for a retrospective study to determine the relationship of Depo-Provera and the incidence of cervical cancer; and that no prospective study could reveal the drug's carcinogenicity prior to marketing, because of the time lag in the development of cervical cancer.[104] Nevertheless, the subcommittee recommended limited marketing approval on the basis of the 1974 *Federal Register* order.[105] On December 15, 1975, the OB/GYN Advisory Committee unanimously approved the subcommittee report on the condition that studies exploring the drug's effect on fertility, birth defects, nursing mothers and infants, and breast and cervical cancer be continued.

The Bureau of Drugs agreed with the advisory committee recommendations, but conditioned its approval on post-marketing studies of Depo-Provera's effect on bone density, because of its concern about osteoporosis, and on the incidence of breast and cervical cancer, because there were no adequate data available.[106] At the same time, the bureau rejected the need for a study of infertility, because the labeling could be written to restrict the drug's use to women who accepted the risk of permanent infertility. In sum, the FDA had satisfied the terms of Secretary Weinberger's letter by staying the order and holding a public hearing before the OB/GYN and BEM Advisory Committees, but these agency actions left unaddressed whether its post-marketing research conditions would satisfy Mr. Fountain and whether Upjohn could conduct the research.

The FDA's Disapproval Decision

Over the next two years, the FDA discussed the design of epidemiological studies with Upjohn, but the Bureau of Drug's staff had serious reservations about the company's ability to conduct studies that would provide meaningful data.[107] The FDA staff thought that Upjohn's relatively low projections of loss to follow-up over a ten-year period were unrealistic, given the large loss of clinical subjects to follow-up in its pivotal study by Drs. Schwallie and Assenzo, and that a much larger study was needed to compensate for these losses. The FDA staff was also concerned about the contamination of control and Depo-Provera study groups by patients switching to oral contraceptives and, thereby, decreasing the uncontaminated subject population available for long-term follow-up.

Since the Bureau of Drugs concluded that these safety issues could not be resolved, it rejected the OB/GYN Advisory Committee's 1974 limited marketing approval recommendation. On August 30, 1977, the bureau requested Upjohn to withdraw its New Drug Approval application for marketing Depo-Provera as a contraceptive. Otherwise, it informed the company, it would publish a notice of rejection. A week later Upjohn notified the agency that it would not withdraw the NDA. After further review, the FDA sent Upjohn a non-approval letter on March 7, 1978, and in a *Federal Register* notice on June 22, 1978, the agency explained the grounds for its disapproval and gave Upjohn the opportunity for a hearing.[108]

Risk Assessment Criteria

The Food, Drug, and Cosmetic Act requires that drugs be tested for their safety, but the act does not specify a risk assessment criterion. Instead, the Code of Federal Regulations provides that the FDA will make a marketing approval decision on the basis of "adequate tests," meaning "well-controlled clinical investigations," and then proceeds to define their major characteristics.[109] The CFR also grants the agency broad discretion in assessing the drug's risk by recognizing the agency's need "to exercise its scientific judgment to determine the kind and quality of data and information . . . required to meet" these standards.[110]

The FDA's disapproval of the limited and general marketing of Depo-Provera was formally based on two statutory grounds: insufficient information to determine whether the drug was a safe contraceptive and test results that did not show it was safe.[111] The disapproval decision was not, however, based on a published regulation that sets forth the agency's risk criteria, nor is it clear which risk criteria the FDA applied to disapprove the drug's NDA. There are three possibilities, but the first two—no-risk analysis and risk-risk analysis—give no attention to the drug's benefits, nor to weighing its benefits and risks, while the third, a risk-benefits analysis, does.[112]

A single risk factor, assessing the animal test results, provided one explanation for the FDA's disapproval. In 1978, Dr. Victor Berliner, an FDA Bureau of Drugs medical officer, informed the House Select Committee on Population about "an old toxicological principal, [which] is to spread the risk over species, at least two, preferably more, and to go by the least favorable results in any one of the species, as the leading deciding factor for evaluating toxicity or risk from a drug to the human."[113] Since Depo-Provera had been tested on three animal species, mice, rats, and dogs, the FDA could have used the single risk factor to disapprove the drug for contraceptive use, because the beagle dogs had developed breast cancer. As the *Federal Register* notice stated: "No other contraceptives that have such safety data are approved for marketing."[114] In fact, FDA Commissioner Donald Kennedy had used the single risk factor in his testimony before the House Select Committee in 1978. "No other contraceptive approved for marketing," he said, "has shown a similar carcinogenic potential in the beagle assay."[115]

A multiple risk analysis provided another explanation for the agency's disapproval. The FDA notice cited three potential risks: breast cancer suggested by the beagle dog study, increased congenital malformations from the drug's failure, and the risk from estrogen therapy to control irregular bleeding.[116] The notice also cited risk-risk analysis data. Risk-risk analysis involves weighing the health risks of non-approval against the health risk of approval in order to determine whether disapproval would deprive the public of any countervailing health benefits.[117] Using this criteria, the notice stated that Depo-Provera was disapproved, because there were available "many safe and effective alternative methods of contraception and sterilization which have decreased the need for a long-term, potentially high risk injectable contraceptive."[118]

A risk-benefit analysis provided a final explanation for the agency's notice. If the notice is read in conjunction with its 1973 and 1974 proposed patient labeling regulation, then it is clear that in 1978 the agency gave attention to the drug's risks and benefits. The FDA was satisfied when it proposed its 1973 regulation that the research findings had proven Depo-Provera's high contraceptive effectiveness.[119] At the same time, the FDA acknowledged that the beagle dog studies had revealed the drug's potential for malignant breast tumors, and the human clinical trials had demonstrated the drug's potential for "prolonged and possibly even permanent infertility . . . [along with] less significant adverse reactions."[120] Nevertheless, the agency concluded that Depo-Provera's benefits outweighed its risks for the institutionalized mentally challenged, as long as the drug was provided subject to two conditions: the women would receive a patient leaflet and brochure explaining the risks associated with its use, and their parents or guardians would give their informed consent prior to the administration of the drug. When the FDA issued its patient label regulation in 1974, it reaffirmed its belief that the drug's benefits outweighed its risks for the same limited groups of women subject to the same informed consent requirements set out in the proposed rule.[121] In 1978 the FDA disapproved Depo-Provera, in part, because it found there was "no significant patient population meeting the criteria proposed in 1974 for use of the drug and for whom the benefits of the drug outweighed the risks."[122]

This risk-benefit analysis does not explain the agency's refusal to give the drug limited approval in 1978, because its disapproval did not depend, any more than its limited approval in 1974, on risk assessment considerations, but on a risk acceptability ground—the absence of a significant patient population—which will be discussed below. Nor does this risk-benefit analysis apply to the agency's disapproval of the drug's general marketing. The *Federal Register* notice provides no evidence that Depo-Provera had the same benefit for general marketing that it had for limited marketing or that those benefits had been outweighed by the risk(s) identified under the no-risk or risk-risk analyses.

The FDA might have given less weight to Depo-Provera's risks under any of the three risk analyses if it had been impressed with a related risk-assessment factor: Upjohn's proposed post-marketing study. The agency had required the drug company to submit a proposed post-marketing study as part of its NDA, because its pre-marketing research had limited value in assessing the drug's long-term carcinogenic risk. When the FDA denied Upjohn approval to market Depo-Provera, its decision relied, in part, on "serious reservations about the ability of Upjohn's proposed post-marketing study for breast and cervical carcinoma to yield meaningful data."[123] Upjohn's proposed study, the FDA concluded, "would require a much larger patient population than proposed [and] Upjohn would have difficulty finding enough patients to complete it within a reasonable time."[124]

Risk Management Judgment

After the FDA reached a negative risk assessment, relying upon one or more of the three possible risk analyses, the agency had to confront the question: Are the risks of Depo-Provera's use identified by the animal and human studies acceptable in light of the drug's demonstrated benefits? Risk management requires an agency to integrate "the results of risk assessment . . . with social, economic, and political concerns to reach its decision."[125] The FDA's disapproval notice states that the agency had three non-scientific concerns about Depo-Provera, which made the drug an unacceptable risk.

The need for the drug, the FDA decided, had been decreased by the "availability . . . of many safe and effective alternative methods of contraception and sterilization which have become increasingly popular in recent years."[126] The agency also decided that the labeling requirements would have limited value in controlling physician prescription practices and in assuring patient consent. In 1974, the FDA had proposed to approve Depo-Provera's limited contraceptive use subject to leaflet and brochure requirements. By 1978, it doubted the value of such "cautionary measures," because there was "strong evidence Depo-Provera is being used for non-labeled indications."[127] Approval would only increase the likelihood that "Depo-Provera will be put to non-approved uses for which the benefits do not exceed the risks."[128] Finally, the FDA decided that approval would increase a woman's risk of cancer, because "physicians would be likely simultaneously to prescribe estrogens to patients in attempt to control irregular uterine bleeding" caused by Depo-Provera's use.[129] In sum, the FDA's *Federal Register* notice prohibited the drug's domestic marketing and its export "based upon the agency's analysis of risk-benefit considerations in the United States."[130]

On these terms, the agency's order was a limited risk management decision. It did not alter Depo-Provera's IND status; nor prohibit physicians on their own authority from prescribing the drug as a contraceptive, because it was FDA-approved for at least one other medical use. The order did not affect Depo-Provera's manufacture and sale by Upjohn's foreign subsidiaries to the seventy foreign nations that had approved the drug's contraceptive use and to international population organizations, including the World Health Organization (WHO) and the International Planned Parenthood Federation (IPPF), for use in their Third World population control programs.[131] Nor did the order seriously limit the drug's use in U.S. foreign aid programs. The U.S. Agency for International Development (USAID) policy prohibited the export of non-approved drugs or direct financing for their overseas purchase, but USAID policy did not prohibit the indirect financing of the United Nations Fund for Population Activities, the International Fertility Research Program, and the Family Planning International Assistance, which supplied contraceptives, including Depo-Provera, to developing nations.

At the same time, FDA disapproval did have an impact on Depo-Provera's contraceptive use overseas. Disapproval raised doubts in Third World nations that rely on the FDA's risk management decisions, and led five countries to reverse their approvals to avoid charges of distributing an unsafe drug.[132] The agency's decision also deeply troubled the international population control organizations that relied on the FDA's drug risk management decisions. They voiced their displeasure at House Select Committee hearings on development assistance, which had been convened coincidentally on the same day that the FDA had notified Upjohn that Depo-Provera was not approvable for contraceptive use.

Congressional Scrutiny

The House Select Committee on Population decided to hold hearings to examine the scientific bases for the FDA's risk assessment and the international consequences of the agency's risk management decision. On August 8, 9, and 10, 1978, the committee listened to and questioned William Hubbard, Upjohn's president, and Donald Kennedy, the FDA commissioner, along with FDA Bureau of Drugs staff members, professors of obstetrics and gynecology involved in contraceptive drug research, leaders of international family planning and population control organizations, and representatives of health, consumer, and women's groups.

James Scheuer, the House Committee chair, began the inquiry by asking FDA Bureau of Drugs staff members about the agency's use of animal test results to assess Depo-Provera risk. "If there can't be a consensus among experts as to the basic suitability of the beagle, how can we use beagle testing as the basis of making very important national policy with extraordinary international implications?"[133] Dr. Victor Berliner explained that all drugs have to be tested on animals for their human safety. The scientific disagreement over the beagle was whether the breast and cervical cancer results from the dog tests could be extrapolated to humans. The FDA, he said, was aware of this scientific disagreement and had disapproved Depo-Provera, just as it had removed Provest, a contraceptive pill containing medroxyprogesterone acetate, from the market because it had also produced breast cancer in beagles. At the same time, he added, the FDA had approved the marketing of other contraceptives containing progestins that had not produced that carcinogenic response.[134]

Mr. Scheuer then turned to Upjohn's human tests results, including its pivotal study by Drs. Schwallie and Assenzo. When he asked Dr. Ridgely Bennett of the FDA Bureau of Drugs whether he had done an analysis of the Upjohn study, Dr. Bennett dismissed the study as "just an observational report that out of 3,800 some odd patients, there were 7 women who had breast tumors, 2 of which were cancerous."[135] In his testimony, Dr. Ronald Gray of the World Health Organization also criticized the Schwallie and Assenzo study for its absence of internal controls. He told Congressman Paul McCloskey that the FDA's OB/GYN Advisory Committee had found that the Upjohn studies on "cervical abnormalities were methodologically unsatisfactory . . . [and] bore absolutely no valid scientific information."[136]

Mr. Scheuer and his committee also learned that the Fountain subcommittee had used the National Cancer Institute's Third National Cancer Survey (NCS3) as an external control group, but when the NCS3 revealed dramatic increases in the cervical cancer rates of women given Depo-Provera, it was criticized as not providing a valid comparison.[137] Since the NCS3 rates were considered too low, the Health Research Group (HRG) turned to the research literature, chose studies with similar groups to use as external controls, and found excessive cervical cancer rates among Depo-Provera users.[138] Mr. Scheuer asked Anita Johnson, the author of the HRG study, about her study: "But you would concede that those tests have no scientific validity for comparison. They offer a suggestion, but they are not proof."[139] Ms. Johnson agreed, but then she continued: "They are important because they confirm the beagle studies. They show that the manufacturer has not proven the safety of the product. The law says that the manufacturer must bear the burden of proving safety."[140]

While the House Committee was satisfied with this testimony and deferred to the FDA's evaluation of animal and human studies and the agency's doubts about Upjohn's proposed post-market research, the committee was quite critical of the agency's disapproval of limited marketing. Mr. McCloskey claimed the FDA had gone "beyond [its] scientific and pharmacological expertise and beyond FDA safety questions."[141] When Dr. Bennett and Dr. Bernard St. Raymond told him that the agency's decision had been based not on scientific studies, but on letters, phone conversations, and the "clamor for approval," Mr. McCloskey replied: "Public clamor—I would hope that an agency like the FDA, in order to preserve its scientific integrity, would not be reacting to public clamor. The minute scientists start reacting to public clamor, I think you'd concede that we've abandoned science, would you not?"[142] Dr. St. Raymond replied: "Yes, sir."[143] Mr. McCloskey's harsh inquiry was reminiscent of Mr. Fountain's four years earlier when he had asked Dr. J. Richard Crout about the agency's limited approval of the drug.

In the end, the House Select Committee hearing did provide the WHO and the IPPF representatives, along with those from the International Fertility Research Program and the Population Council, with the opportunity to testify that the FDA's decision had made a needed contraceptive less available to women in Third World nations and that pending legislation, the Drug Regulation Reform Act of 1978, would improve the situation by permitting the export of non-approved drugs. Still the House Select Committee did not disturb the FDA's 1978 decision.[144] As a consequence, Upjohn's only immediate recourse was to request an internal agency review.

Depo-Provera Public Board of Inquiry

Upjohn had the right to challenge the FDA's disapproval action in a full evidentiary public hearing before an administrative law judge.[145] The company had made the request on July 24, 1978, but waived that right two weeks after the House Select Committee hearings and requested instead a review procedure that had been invoked only once before in the FDA's history: a hearing before a public board of inquiry.[146] FDA regulations permit the agency to create this "administrative law tribunal"[147] to "review medical, scientific, and technical issues."[148] When a board of inquiry is convened, agency regulations provide that its proceedings will be conducted as an informal hearing[149] and its findings and conclusions will have the legal status of an initial agency decision.[150]

FDA Commissioner Donald Kennedy accepted Upjohn's request for a public board of inquiry on October 24, 1978, and approved the company's request to delay the hearing until it could analyze the data from the recently completed ten-year rhesus monkey study. Upjohn notified the FDA the following April that its review was complete. Three months later, Commissioner Kennedy ordered a public board of inquiry hearing,[151] but more than two years intervened before his successor, Arthur Hull Hayes, appointed its members: Dr. Judith Weisz as chairperson and Drs. Griff T. Ross and Paul Stolley as members.[152]

The Interim Years

As the FDA was proceeding at a stately pace to create and convene the public board of inquiry, the debate over Depo-Provera outside the agency became increasingly defined by two communities with opposing interests in international population control and women's health. "Upjohn, [the] World Health Organization (WHO), the International Planned Parenthood Federation (IPPF), and the U.S. Agency for International Development (USAID) sought to demonstrate Depo-Provera's safety by reviews of the medical evidence based on what is known and certain about the drug," while the National Women's Health Network and the Health Research Group "tried to give wide publicity to the risks associated with what is still unknown and uncertain."[153]

In 1979 and 1980, the IPPF, WHO, and USAID convened scientific panels that issued reports supporting Depo-Provera's use in family planning programs worldwide.[154] USAID's Ad Hoc Consultative Panel found that the drug had substantial benefits for women in Third World countries, including its long-lasting effectiveness, its advantage for women who breastfeed, and its ease and infrequency of administration, and that these benefits outweighed the risks of cancer, congenital malformations, and infertility.[155] The report dismissed the risk of breast cancer, because the beagles metabolize progestins differently from humans, were given high doses, and are prone to mammary tumors.[156] The monkey study findings were unclear because the high doses of the drug and a lack of data on endometrial cancer in monkeys were coupled with evidence that progestins do not proliferate in the endometrium and promote cancer, but shrink the endometrium and protect against cancer in women.[157] The clinical trials provided no strong evidence of cervical cancer.[158] Infants were at no higher risk of congenital defects from Depo-Provera than they were from other methods of hormonal contraception.[159] Women who discontinued Depo-Provera showed a delay in the return to fertility, but there was no significant difference from women who discontinued IUD use.[160] Even the metabolic effects, such as bleeding and weight gain, were generally milder than those of women who used the Pill.[161] In sum, the USAID panel, like the WHO and IPPF committees, concluded that Depo-Provera's benefits outweighed its risks.[162]

The National Women's Health Network, one of the most prominent critics of the drug's current unapproved use and its potential future approval, initiated a National Stop Depo-Provera Campaign to document the drug's risks and make women aware of them.[163] The Network, along with other women's, consumer, and health organizations, critiqued the WHO, IPPF, and USAID scientific assessments, rejecting their claims of methodological difficulties in extrapolating from the animal studies that suggested a risk of human cancer and finding that the human studies refuting the risk of cancer were methodologically flawed.[164] At the same time, they argued that the human studies tied the drug's use to birth defects and promoted the use of estrogen therapy to control severe menstrual bleeding, but that these studies did not adequately address the drug's effect on infants of mothers who breastfeed.[165] They further argued that these scientific assessments were influenced by a symbiotic relationship between Upjohn and international population control organizations, which linked a corporate interest in finding a market for a contraceptive drug to the population control organizations' use in the Third World of an extremely effective method of birth control.[166] They did, however, agree with the international population control and health organizations about the need for further research on Depo-Provera's long-term effects, but argued that the uncertainties of the drug's risks made post-marketing research unacceptable in light of the post-approval problems encountered with the Pill, DES, and estrogen.[167]

Pre-Hearing Activities

After their appointments, Dr. Judith Weisz and her fellow board members, Drs. Griff Ross and Paul Stolley, took over a year to review the vast amount of material that had accumulated over the past fifteen years. Then on September 23, 1982, they held a pre-hearing conference to establish the procedures for a five-day hearing.[168] The first two days, they decided, would be devoted to presentations by the two parties, Upjohn and the FDA's Center for Drugs and Biologics (formerly the Bureau of Drugs);[169] the third and fourth days to testimony by the non-party participants, representatives of population control, and women's and public health organizations; and the fifth to summary remarks by all participants and their comments on other presentations.

Dr. Weisz announced that the hearing would not involve a mirror image review of the grounds for the FDA's 1978 disapproval decision, but would be governed by the July 27, 1979, *Federal Register* notice creating the Public Board of Inquiry and defining the seven questions for it to consider.[170] Four questions addressed risk assessment issues, which had served as the basis for FDA disapproval. Did the animal studies data, that now included a second beagle dog study and the ten-year rhesus monkey study, suggest a potential risk of breast and endometrial cancer in humans?[171] Did the human data successfully refute the risk of cancer suggested by the animal data?[172] Was there an increased risk of teratogenic effects in the event of a contraceptive failure?[173] Would estrogen be likely to be prescribed for a significant number of patients to control the adverse side effects of bleeding?[174] One risk assessment issue that served as the basis for the FDA's 1978 disapproval decision was not included: whether Upjohn's proposed post-marketing study of breast and cervical cancer could yield meaningful data.[175]

The *Federal Register* notice also identified three risk acceptability issues defined by the drug's domestic use. Two questions raised general marketing issues. Would the benefits of Depo-Provera in comparison with other FDA-approved contraceptives outweigh its risks? Would general marketing be likely to increase the drug's use "as a contraceptive under conditions not stipulated in approved labeling or . . . increase its use for unrelated indications for which safety and effectiveness have not been established (for example, for hygienic purposes in mental retardees)?"[176] A third issue addressed the FDA's 1973 limited marketing proposal, withdrawn in 1974 and then rejected in 1978. Were there labeling or distribution controls that would permit marketing on a limited basis?[177] The July 27, 1979, *Federal Register* notice required the board to hear scientific testimony assessing Depo-Provera's risk and policy arguments supporting the drug's acceptability in making a domestic risk management recommendation for the drug's limited or general contraceptive use.

The Board of Inquiry Hearing

Dr. Judith Weisz opened the Public Board of Inquiry on Depo-Provera on January 10, 1983, by informing the participants that the board had been selected to conduct an impartial scientific investigation concerning "a complex and emotional issue on which people have taken certain viewpoints and taken them strongly."[178] In this setting, she emphasized, the board could achieve its purpose and serve the public interest only if it used the rules of scientific evidence. "The rules of scientific evidence are what we wish to apply and what we have applied over the last year and a half to our reading of the data that has accumulated around this subject."[179] This meant that the board would give primary, if not exclusive attention to the risk assessment issues in the FDA's July 27, 1979, *Federal Register* notice.

Dr. Weisz and her fellow board members listened to and questioned fifty-three participants who were specialists in obstetrics, gynecology, epidemiology, toxicology, and pathology, who were deeply involved in the research on and the use and criticism of Depo-Provera, and who together defined two distinct scientific arguments supportive of either Upjohn or the FDA. Dr. Gordon Duncan, Upjohn's Manager of Research, was joined by J. Robert Assenzo, who with Paul Schwallie had conducted Depo-Provera's pivotal clinical study; Robert Hatcher, Director of the Grady Clinic; Elizabeth Connell, a former member of the FDA's OB/GYN Advisory Committee and now Professor of Obstetrics and Gynecology at Emory University; Charles Hammond of the American College of Obstetricians and Gynecologists; and representatives of the leading international population control organizations, including the U.S. Agency for International Development, the World Health Organization, the International Planned Parenthood Federation, Family Health International, and the Population Council. The FDA Center for Drugs and Biologics officials Drs. Robert Temple and Solomon Sobel were supported by medical and research specialists from the National Institutes of Health, the National Cancer Institute, and the Environmental Protection Agency; by representatives of women's and public health organizations, including Diane Silberstein of the National Women's Health Network and Dr. Sidney Wolfe, Director of the Health Research Group; by women's health activists and authors, Judy Norsigian, Gena Corea, and Stephen Minkin; and by specialists in biology, gynecology, family health, pharmacology, and toxicology.

Dr. Weisz had identified the assessment of Depo-Provera's risk as the board's primary task. On the first day of the hearing, Dr. Gordon Duncan outlined Upjohn's case for the drug's approval arguing that the animal test results should be discounted and the clinical trial results should be relied upon to demonstrate the drug's safety. First, Dr. Duncan addressed the animal studies and argued that the beagle dog was an inappropriate test model, because it metabolized progestogens differently from humans and was prone to mammary tumors.[180] The monkey studies should also be discounted, because endometrial cancer developed spontaneously from a cell type that had no human counterpart.[181] Then he turned to the human studies and emphasized that the drug's extensive clinical trial experience, its positive evaluation in the scientific literature, and its favorable recommendations from USAID, WHO, and the IPPF provided strong arguments in favor of the drug's safety. The human test data from over forty studies disclosed no major risks, only some low magnitude ones that were currently under investigation, including WHO's nine-nation study of the drug's potential for cancer and congenital abnormalities.[182] Estrogen therapy to correct any bleeding abnormalities was "a non-issue" for the company.[183] Other Upjohn witnesses dismissed the drug's adverse side effects. Dr. Daniel Mishell, a University of Southern California Professor of Obstetrics and Gynecology and clinical researcher, found that "the amount of bleeding is not excessive and is frequently characterized as spotting."[184] Dr. Elizabeth Connell viewed weight gain and diminished libido as "non-serious adverse side effects" and found "no permanent evidence of infertility."[185] In sum, Upjohn found that the human research reassuring and provided no meaningful scientific basis for concern that the drug was a carcinogen or teratogen.

Any advantage Upjohn may have acquired from appearing first and presenting its case uninterrupted by any questions until the end was undercut the following day by the FDA presentations and those on the fourth day by women's and health organizations. Dr. Robert Temple set the terms for the critique when he informed the board that Upjohn could have shown that "the animal data were not pertinent by discrediting the dog and monkey studies" or it could have shown "through persuasive human studies that the feared carcinogenic risk was not present."[186] Upjohn had done neither. The company had not provided a persuasive argument on behalf of its animal studies; but it had made only assertions that "the beagle is too sensitive and that the monkey tumors may have arisen from a special endometrial structure."[187]

Upjohn's human studies could not refute these animal studies. Dr. Robert Hoover of the National Cancer Institute found that the clinical research suffered from serious flaws, including inappropriate control groups, small sample size, inadequate length of exposure, and loss of subjects to follow-up.[188] Yet even these unreliable studies, according to FDA and consumer and women's health organization witnesses, suggested that Depo-Provera was a potential carcinogen and teratogen with other significant adverse side effects that could not be ignored in analyzing the drug's risk.[189] Dr. Sidney Wolfe found that Upjohn's pivotal study by Drs. Schwallie and Assenzo reported heavier prolonged bleeding, and another study reported bleeding so erratic that it amounted to "menstrual chaos."[190] In fact, Dr. Wolfe found that the delay in return to fertility was so severe, often amounting to permanent infertility and that Upjohn had acknowledged that the drug "should not be used in women who wish to have additional children."[191] In sum, Depo-Provera's poorly designed human studies could not dispel the risk of cancer suggested by the animal studies.

Dr. Weisz had identified the scientific assessment of the drug's risk as the board's principal task, but risk acceptability issues were its subtext.

The 1979 *Federal Register* notice identified three issues for the Public Board of Inquiry to address in making a risk management recommendation. Upjohn argued that Depo-Provera's clinical studies and its lengthy worldwide experience indicated that it was as safe as oral contraceptives for general marketing.[192] Dr. Jacob Stucki, Upjohn Vice President for Pharmaceutical Research, testified that it was unnecessary for the board to address the other two risk acceptability questions, because they were "beyond the scope of a scientific inquiry."[193] Nevertheless, he argued that general marketing would not increase unapproved use, because the drug had already been used for twenty years.[194] Limited distribution of the drug with labeling and distribution controls, which had been the focus of the company's approval efforts for a decade, could benefit a specific population of women.[195] But Upjohn was no longer interested in limited approval, because of the drug's safety under general marketing conditions worldwide supported its domestic approval.[196]

The FDA's Dr. Robert Temple disagreed, but he was pleased that Upjohn had decided to focus on general marketing approval and had not argued that "there is a tiny population that needs this drug approach. Arguments like that," he explained, "are very difficult for us, as we try to calculate who will really get the drug."[197] Fletcher Campbell, an FDA attorney, agreed that limited marketing was "a non-issue. Upjohn doesn't want it. They want the whole ball of wax."[198]

The FDA's 1979 *Federal Register* notice had mandated a risk-benefit recommendation for domestic marketing. In making its recommendation, the board would be bound by the FDA's legal standards for judging the drug's safety. Dr. Robert Temple[199] and Diane Silberstein, counsel for the National Women's Health Network,[200] identified and discussed those standards and then on the last day of the hearing, Fletcher Campbell summarized and applied them to the evidence the board had heard. Upjohn, he observed, bore the burden of proving that Depo-Provera was safe for its intended use on the basis of all reasonably applicable tests.[201] The FDA interpreted "reasonably applicable tests" to include "the adequacy of those studies as well as what those studies say"[202] and "safe for its intended use" to mean that the risks were outweighed by the benefits of treatment.[203] Judged by this standard, he concluded, the animal data did not establish the drug's safety. The monkey study's finding of endometrial or endocervical tumors did not prove the drug's safety, nor did the dog study's mammary tumors.[204] The human studies did not dispel these findings. "No adequate test shows the safety of Depo-Provera, not one."[205] In sum, Mr. Campbell found that these reasonably applicable tests did not lead to the conclusion that Depo-Provera was safe for its intended use, because the benefit of convenience "paled into obscurity" when weighed against the risks of cancer.[206]

The Public Board of Inquiry hearing ended, as it had begun, with attention to the assessment of Depo-Provera's risk. Participants informed the board that its inquiry had fulfilled Dr. Weisz's promise. Perhaps Paul Brenner, Professor of Obstetrics and Gynecology at the University of Southern California, expressed it best. He was "very impressed with [Griff Ross's] . . . ability to extract the maximum amount of information," Paul Stolley's "ability to probe and persist until you got every piece of information from every witness"; and Judith Weisz's: "ability to ask precise questions and delve to the heart of the matter. Whatever your decision, I cannot picture a more impartial hearing."[207]

The Board of Inquiry Report

The Public Board of Inquiry members took over a year to examine the research data and analyses and to write the report, a 207 page document, issued on October 17, 1984.[208] The board considered its "primary task to be to evaluate the scientific validity of the information available."[209] Since the report had the legal status of an initial agency decision,[210] the board "attempted to determine how much of this information qualified as facts [as distinguished from assumptions and hypotheses] on which definitive conclusions could be based."[211] Then it reordered the seven questions that it had been required to address in accordance with the distinction between scientific assessment of risk and policy judgments about risk acceptability. "We have reordered the sequence," the report stated, "so that the scientific evidence available for assessing the risks . . . required to arrive at a regulatory decision, is presented first and evaluated before considering the regulatory decision itself."[212] As a consequence, the board first gave detailed consideration to Questions 2, 3, 5, and 6, which concerned Depo-Provera's carcinogenic and teratogenic potential and the need for estrogen therapy and then briefly discussed Questions 1, 4, and 7, which involved judgments about the drug's marketing.

Risk Assessment Analysis

The Board of Inquiry's review of the scientific evidence began with the issue raised by Question 2: Do the beagle dog and rhesus monkey study data indicate a potential risk of breast or endometrial cancer in humans from Depo-Provera?[213] The examination of this research focused on three sub-issues: Were the malignancies drug-related, was there a dose-response relationship, and was the animals' progestogen response applicable to humans?[214]

The board found that the first beagle dog study, conducted by the International Research and Development Corporation (IRDC) from 1968 to 1975, was unable to address these issues because it was poorly designed and executed.[215] However, the second study, conducted by the Dawson Corporation from 1972 to 1979, was well-designed and executed and provided "evidence that the mammary carcinomas in the dogs were drug-related. . . . There was also [a] good indication of dose-response relationship: malignancies developed both more frequently and earlier with increasing doses of DMPA."[216] The monkey data were more problematic because the development of malignancies in the rhesus monkey, unlike the beagle dog, were unanticipated.[217]

Dr. Weisz established an expert committee of six pathologists to review the monkey research.[218] At a second hearing on August 12, 1983,[219] the pathologists unanimously concluded that "progestogens can elicit a malignant transformation in the uterus of monkeys."[220] The board was, however, unable to determine whether there was a dose-response relationship, because "the study was poorly designed and executed: the number of controls and animals receiving lower doses of DMPA was much too small and the pathological examinations too inadequate."[221]

The board then dismissed Upjohn's argument that the beagle dog and rhesus monkey were appropriate models for testing the long-term effects of progestogens on human females. Since Depo-Provera had "exhibited the characteristics of a potential carcinogen [in the animal studies] according to generally accepted criteria," the board was unwilling "to dismiss the findings as irrelevant to the human . . . [because there was no] conclusive evidence of fundamental differences among the species in the basic mechanisms of action of the hormone or in the response of target cells."[222] Little research supported Upjohn's argument that the beagle responds differently to progestogens than a woman.[223] No research supported Upjohn's argument that monkeys possessed a special cell type that made them more prone to endometrial cancer.[224]

Question 3 asked whether the human data submitted by Upjohn could successfully refute the risk of human cancer from Depo-Provera suggested by the animal data.[225] In general, the board found that the human data were inadequate, because they were not based on studies that addressed the issue of cancer, they were not derived from epidemiological studies, and if they were, they suffered from major research design and execution limitations.[226] The board's critique of the human studies was organized in terms of the research findings on breast, cervical, and endometrial cancer.

The breast cancer data came from IND studies of 11,631 women, but the board found the data of limited value, because the studies were "pooled" from over eighty different research centers.[227] As a consequence, it was "not possible to assess the significance of five cases of breast cancer in a mixed population of subjects."[228] They were descriptive clinical reports that were not designed to provide epidemiological data.[229] Whether retrospective or prospective studies, they included too few long-term users, too short a period of follow-up, a lack of information about the subject's medical history, inadequate or inappropriate controls, and a lack of documentation.[230] Thus, the board concluded that "if the same standards are applied equally to all studies, we are left essentially without information on the effect that the use of DMPA as a contraceptive may have on the incidence of breast cancer."[231]

Cervical cancer findings from an IND research study had provoked a confrontation between the FDA and Representative Fountain and led to a stay of Depo-Provera's proposed limited approval in 1974. The Public Board of Inquiry was critical of the IND study not only because "the cervical abnormalities were diagnosed only a short time after the initiation of drug use," but also because the study was poorly designed and executed.[232] "The data were collected from subjects at various centers, both in and outside the United States and representing different populations with unknown background incidence of cervical cancer."[233] The board also found that no other appropriately designed epidemiological study addressed the issue of cervical cancer until after the FDA's disapproval action in 1978. The World Health Organization had initiated a study in

1979, but that had not been completed by the time the board issued its report. So the board was able to dismiss "the early suggestions that the drug may increase the incidence of cervical neoplasia."[234]

Endometrial cancer evidence was based primarily on endometrial biopsies.[235] The early biopsies, the board found, were not designed to study endometrial cancer.[236] The studies conducted after the discovery of endometrial cancer in the rhesus monkey were flawed because the number of subjects in the three biopsy studies was too small and the two retrospective epidemiological studies had a serious lack of information on the subjects.[237] In the Thai study, the subjects were identified from hospital records, and in the Mexican study, diagnoses were obtained from death certificates.[238] Thus, the board concluded: "There are no data available that could serve as a basis for deciding whether the use of DMPA as a contraceptive has an effect on the incidence of [human] endometrial cancer."[239]

After an exhaustive survey of this scientific data on breast, cervical, and endometrial cancer, the Board of Inquiry rejected Upjohn's argument that the quantity of this data could substitute for its quality and that voluntary reporting could substitute for specific studies.[240] What was needed, but what had only begun after the FDA's 1978 disapproval action, were appropriately designed studies that would "collect data in a systematic manner from humans on the consequences of long-term use of Depo-Provera."[241] Then in one page, the board brought its risk assessment examination to a close by dismissing the estrogen therapy issue, Question 6, with the finding that estrogen use was unlikely because "there appears to be a consensus . . . that estrogen is ineffective in either treating or arresting uterine bleeding caused by DMPA."[242]

Risk Acceptability Judgments

When the Board considered the three risk acceptability issues on marketing, Questions 1, 4, and 7, its treatment was brief, a mere ten pages, and its analysis of all three issues together was almost exclusively scientific. Depo-Provera's general marketing approval depended upon its benefits outweighing its risks in comparison with other FDA-approved contraceptive drugs, but the board was unable to weigh them and was, therefore, unable to conduct a risk-benefit analysis.[243] The drug's benefits, it said, were clear and its short-term side effects had been well-documented and not trivial.[244] "Neither the short-term side effects of the drug, nor its teratogenic potential should constitute a reason for not proposing to use DMPA."[245] The board was, however, troubled by its inability to assess the drug's long-term carcinogenic effects. "The available evidence presented fails to provide an adequate, scientifically justifiable basis for concluding whether the use of DMPA as a contraceptive does or does not pose any long-term risks."[246]

In the absence of this evidence, the board was unable to recommend general marketing approval, because there was "no valid basis for comparing the risks of DMPA with those of other contraceptives."[247] This conclusion allowed the board to avoid as "largely irrelevant" the issue of the drug's potentially increased unapproved use under general marketing conditions.[248] The board did, however, reject the view that a drug's possible non-approved uses should influence an NDA decision, because "it . . . is FDA policy not to regulate the physician's practice of medicine in prescribing approved drugs for unapproved indications."[249]

Depo-Provera's limited marketing approval, per Question 7, depended upon the control of its distribution to patients with special needs. The board acknowledged that this patient population existed, but disagreed over limited approval. Dr. Ross recommended approval, if feasible, for the mentally challenged and drug addicts,[250] but Drs. Weisz and Stolley were unwilling to recommend limited approval. They did not "think it desirable that the FDA set up broad categories of indications . . . since . . . the drug is likely to be appropriate only for selected patients within each category."[251] They preferred instead to have the decision about Depo-Provera's use be made on "an individual basis and with informed consent" because it would avoid the need for limited marketing approval.[252] "DMPA is currently approved . . . for use for other indications."[253] They did not think that the FDA had any effective mechanisms to limit the drug's distribution to patients with special needs or to collect information from them about its use in a systematic manner.[254] These two risk acceptability judgments, unlike those the board made about general marketing, needed to be better argued and documented. The first expressed a preference for Depo-Provera's unapproved use as a lesser evil while the second was briefly stated in conclusory language without any supporting evidence.

Risk Management Recommendation

The Public Board of Inquiry recommended that Depo-Provera should not be approved for general marketing. The action was based on the following finding of scientific fact: the "data available on the long-term risks of DMPA are insufficient and inadequate to provide a basis for a decision whether the benefits of the drug as a contraceptive outweigh its disadvantages under conditions of general marketing in the USA."[255] This factual finding led the board to reach a conclusion of law identical to the FDA's 1978 disapproval action: Upjohn's NDA for Depo-Provera for contraceptive use "does not contain reports of investigations adequate to show that the drug is safe for use under the conditions prescribed, recommended, or suggested in the labeling . . . [which when] combined with other information about the drug, does not provide [a] sufficient basis from which FDA can determine that DMPA is safe for general marketing."[256] This finding of fact and conclusion of law had the status of an initial agency decision.[257] The Board of Inquiry did not, however, reach any factual findings or legal conclusions about limited marketing, but its risk management recommendation did provide substantial scientific support for the FDA's decision to deny Depo-Provera general marketing approval.

1986 General Marketing Disapproval

Upjohn challenged the Public Board of Inquiry report on January 24, 1985, by taking exception to the board's findings on each of the seven questions identified in the FDA's 1979 *Federal Register* notice and to the board's conclusion that the NDA had not shown Depo-Provera to be safe for general contraceptive use.[258] The company also claimed that it had been denied a fair hearing for two reasons. The board failed to conduct a systematic inquiry and make findings on the central issue before it—whether Depo-Provera's benefits outweighed its risk in comparison to other drugs approved for contraception—because it had separated the four risk assessment questions from the three risk acceptability questions, reformulated the three questions, and discussed them jointly. The board had also acknowledged that there were women for whom Depo-Provera would be an appropriate contraceptive, but had failed to offer persuasive reasons for refusing to recommend limited approval.[259] To remedy this prejudice, Upjohn requested the commissioner to set aside the board's decision and grant Depo-Provera general marketing approval. If the commissioner determined that general marketing approval was "inappropriate" until the World Health Organization's interim studies, then underway, were completed, the company argued that the board's report supported limited marketing approval.[260] If, however, the commissioner decided not to approve the NDA, Upjohn argued that he should grant the company a new hearing, or if it were refused, at least the opportunity to make an oral presentation.[261]

The FDA's Center for Drugs and Biologics rejected Upjohn's arguments. The board had properly found that Upjohn had not met its burden of providing adequate long-term animal studies to demonstrate that the drug is safe and that the human data are adequate to refute the animal data.[262] "A group of poor quality studies . . . cannot, when combined, be transformed into reliable scientific evidence to be used to evaluate the safety of a drug."[263] The board's decision to combine and reformulate Questions 1, 4, and 7 did not avoid a comparative risk-benefit analysis, but "tackled the risk/benefit issue head on and found that no such comparison was possible, because Upjohn had failed to satisfy its burden of presenting adequate evidence to delineate the risks."[264] The Center for Drugs and Biologics also objected to Upjohn's advocacy of limited approval, now that general marketing was in jeopardy, because the board did not find that the risk-benefit ratio would be favorable to all women in these specific patient groups, but only to a few for whom a decision would be made on an individual basis with informed consent.[265]

The World Health Organization requested that the board's administrative record be reopened to admit three recently completed WHO studies concerning the carcinogenicity of Depo-Provera. FDA Commissioner Dr. Frank Young reopened the record on February 8, 1985,[266] but the following September, he refused an Upjohn request to reopen the record to permit additional material and to hold an oral argument on the WHO data.[267] The commissioner did not want to "forestall indefinitely final agency action" in an already lengthy proceeding by allowing Upjohn to periodically introduce new information, nor was he willing to grant Upjohn an oral argument.[268] The commissioner's decision was supported by the board members who informed him that nothing in the

WHO interim studies would affect their conclusions in the report.[269] Thereafter, the commissioner informed Upjohn that he would proceed to make his decision, but would allow the company to voluntarily withdraw its NDA and "resubmit the reports and studies that are the subject of its request to reopen the record."[270] On September 29, 1986, Upjohn withdrew Depo-Provera's NDA for contraception with the promise that it would reapply.[271] Shortly thereafter, the commissioner accepted the company's withdrawal and the termination of its appeal of the Public Board of Inquiry's report, aware that the company's nineteen-year effort to gain approval for Depo-Provera would continue.[272]

Summary

Judith Weisz's story of the politics of drug risk management, as told by her, by Drs. Michael Popkin and Bertram Litt at the FDA, Dr. Robert Hoover at the National Cancer Institute, Representative L. H. Fountain, and Dr. Sidney Wolfe at the Health Research Group, among others, was defined by their commitment to scientific standards in making drug approval decisions. As such, her story continues to provide the risk assessment framework for understanding the Food and Drug Administration's market approval decisions as the interplay of science and politics. Upjohn's pre-market testing assured that the FDA would have to rely on uncertain scientific research, because the human clinical studies were designed to assess the drug's effectiveness and short-term risks, not its long-term risk of cancer. At the same time, the IND tests suggested a risk of breast, endometrial, and cervical cancer that doomed the approval of the drug for general marketing. Still, Depo-Provera's extensive unapproved contraceptive use nationwide and the interest in using the drug to combat population growth in developing countries tempted the FDA to minimize the drug's health risk and justify its use for a limited population of women.

Even though the FDA's decision relied on two cautionary measures, informed consent and a physician registry, and on the OB/GYN Advisory Committee's approval recommendation, the agency disregarded its risk assessment mandate and twice brought political intervention to bear by Congressman L. H. Fountain. His subcommittee hearings provided a devastating critique of the FDA's proposed order to approve Depo-

Provera for limited use. When the agency disregarded the critique and published its proposed rule, his letter to HEW Secretary Caspar Weinberger quickly led the FDA to stay its approval order. Chastened, the agency conducted a two-year internal review, disregarded the limited approval recommendations of its OB/GYN Advisory Committee, and issued an order, firmly grounded in its statutory mandate, disapproving the drug for general marketing approval. Still, the FDA's decision met with congressional criticism, not for its assessment of the drug's risk, but for its decision to make a risk management judgment based on the drug's domestic and international acceptability.

The FDA's Public Board of Inquiry was mandated to consider both risk assessment and acceptability issues in reviewing the agency's 1978 decision, but it confined its analysis to a scientific assessment of the animal and human research, briefly discussed the marketing issues, and then reminded the agency that a risk management recommendation, based on a concern for physician prescribing practices, was beyond its mandate. In sum, the Public Board of Inquiry's report, as an initial agency decision, provided the scientific basis for the FDA's refusal to grant Depo-Provera general marketing approval, but not its refusal of limited approval for a well-defined patient population.

When the FDA disapproved Depo-Provera for general marketing, based on the Public Board of Inquiry's recommendation, the agency expressed a willingness to certify the drug's safety and approve an amended NDA for general marketing if Upjohn demonstrated that the animal test results were not relevant and that better designed human studies showed the drug was not carcinogenic. The FDA also appeared willing to grant Depo-Provera limited approval if a well-defined patient population existed for which the carcinogenic risks suggested by the animal and human studies were overcome by unusually great benefits. When Upjohn decided to voluntarily withdraw its NDA in 1986, the agency informed the company that it would take a look at new evidence. Six years later, the research landscape changed significantly when the FDA examined a new NDA for Depo-Provera. In the meantime, though the drug's contraceptive use was not FDA-approved, it was widely prescribed, and, as the next chapter explains, women who suffered its short-term side effects sued their physicians for medical malpractice and Upjohn for products liability in state courts.

3

Contraceptive Chaos

Unapproved Use and Upjohn v. MacMurdo

Anne MacMurdo's story leaves behind Depo-Provera's national marketing approval controversy to explore risk management beyond the
Food and Drug Administration's authority to permit a pharmaceutical
company to sell and physicians to prescribe a drug for specific medical
purposes. Once the FDA approves a drug, the agency may regulate how
manufacturers promote the drug, but it does not have the authority to
regulate the practice of medicine. As a consequence, the use of drugs is
largely out of the FDA's hands and in those of physicians, who are free
to prescribe a drug for a use or in a manner not approved by the FDA.[1]

Anne MacMurdo's story provides a window on Depo-Provera's use
during the thirty years before the FDA's 1992 approval of the drug for
contraceptive use. During this time, the drug was widely prescribed by
private physicians, family planning clinics, and state mental health facilities throughout the country, because the drug had been FDA-approved
for at least one other medical purpose since 1960. Senate hearings in
1973 first documented the drug's contraceptive use, the National Wom-
en's Health Network's Registry Depo-Provera provided further evidence
of its nationwide use in the early 1980s, and House hearings in 1987 confirmed that the drug had been routinely used by the federal government's Indian Health Service.[2]

Congress did not examine the availability and adequacy of the legal
remedies for women who claimed to have been harmed by Depo-
Provera and their reliance on state malpractice and products liability
law and on state courts to sue their physicians and Upjohn. These cases
were usually settled or dismissed, but not Anne MacMurdo's. Her story
began in 1974 with her first injection of Depo-Provera, and then made
its slow and lengthy journey through the Florida court system, ending in
1990 with the Florida Supreme Court's decision in *Upjohn v. MacMurdo,*

which raised critical questions about the usefulness of state products liability law and the role of state courts in contraceptive risk management.

Depo-Provera's Unapproved Contraceptive Use

The FDA's authority to regulate the drugs it approves extends to how pharmaceutical companies promote their products to physicians and patients, but not to physician prescription practices. The agency's authority to manage drug risk is limited by the freedom of physicians to practice medicine as it is defined by the profession's ethical standards and its peer review procedures. The practice of medicine exception, as explained in Chapter 1, traces its origins to the Federal Food, Drug, and Cosmetic Act of 1938 and its legislative history, which clearly indicate that in granting the FDA the authority to regulate the safety of drugs, Congress did not intend for the agency to exercise its authority to interfere with a physician's use of drugs for treatment purposes not listed in the FDA's approved labeling.[3]

The FDA has respected this congressional limitation on its authority to manage drug risk. In 1972 the agency proposed a rule, never adopted, that extended its authority to regulate the promotion by pharmaceutical manufacturers of approved drugs for unapproved (off-label) uses, but did not interfere with practice of medicine. In fact, the FDA later provided physicians with explicit encouragement to prescribe for unapproved uses. A 1982 *FDA Drug Bulletin* described approved drug labeling as "informational only" and recognized an unapproved use as accepted medical practice.[4]

Depo-Provera's unapproved contraceptive use, as discussed in Chapter 2, was known to the FDA and its Obstetrics and Gynecology Advisory Committee in 1972, but first came to public attention during the February 1973 hearings on the "Quality of Health Care—Human Experimentation" before the Senate Public Welfare Subcommittee on Health chaired by Edward M. Kennedy.[5] The hearings revealed that private physicians, university hospitals, mental health physicians, and family planning clinics throughout Tennessee had used Depo-Provera as a contraceptive beginning as early as 1963.[6] The National Women's Health Network's Depo-Provera Registry provided additional anecdotal evidence that women across the socioeconomic spectrum and in virtually every state had received Depo-Provera for contraception.[7] Together, they provide a national setting for Anne MacMurdo's story by revealing how Upjohn, physicians, and patients failed to manage the drug's risk.

The Upjohn Company

Pharmaceutical companies manage risk in physician use of their drugs by means of package inserts. The insert describes the drug, identifies its FDA-approved uses (indications), disapproved uses (contraindications), warnings and precautions in its use, and adverse reactions associated with its use. From 1974 until Depo-Provera was approved in 1992, its package insert stated that it was approved only as chemotherapy. The 1974 insert's warning section stated: "The use of Depo-Provera (medroxyprogesterone acetate) for contraception is investigational since there are unresolved questions relating to its safety for this indication. Therefore, it is not an approved indication for this purpose."[8] Then the insert listed the following adverse reactions: "breakthrough bleeding, spotting, and change in menstrual flow."[9]

What responsibility does a pharmaceutical company have when one of its drugs is being used in an FDA unapproved manner? At the 1973 Senate hearings, Dr. William N. Hubbard, Jr., Executive Vice President of Upjohn, testified that Depo-Provera's promotional materials made no reference to the drug's contraceptive use and its sales force was not permitted to initiate discussions regarding the drug's contraceptive use. If physicians wrote requesting information on the drug's use, he said, Upjohn "will give reference citations to the published literature . . . but will not comment upon that literature."[10] Beyond these measures, he testified, Upjohn had been careful in monitoring its marketing of Depo-Provera, because "it would be inappropriate for the company to supply the drug directly to physicians who had declared their intention to use it for an unapproved use."[11] Dr. Hubbard also recognized that there were medical professional limits to its monitoring of unapproved drug use, which "if pursued too energetically runs the risk of having the company intrude on the legal rights of the physician to utilize medicinals as he judges to be in the best interests of his patient."[12]

At the same time, the 1973 Senate hearings revealed that Upjohn was unable or unwilling to limit the marketing of Depo-Provera to its approved uses. In 1978, the FDA disapproved the drug for general marketing, in part because the agency concluded that the labeling requirements would have limited value in controlling physician prescription practices and assuring patient consent.[13] In 1984, the FDA Public Board of Inquiry recommended against general approval on other grounds, but based its disapproval of limited marketing, in part, on the absence of any effective mechanisms to limit the drug's distribution to patients with special needs.[14] Even after Upjohn withdrew Depo-Provera's New Drug Approval (NDA) application in 1986, the company continued to make the drug available to private physicians, mental health professionals, and family planning clinics nationwide for contraceptive use.[15]

Physicians

Physicians manage risk by making an informed and individualized decision about patient use of prescription drugs. In making these decisions, they do not restrict their choice of drugs to their FDA approved uses. Depo-Provera was approved for four medical uses prior to 1992: as a treatment for endometriosis (1960–1972) and miscarriage (1960–1974) and as a palliative treatment and adjunctive therapy for endometrial cancer (after 1972) and kidney cancer (after 1978).[16] The National Women's Health Network's Registry revealed that physicians continued to use Depo-Provera to treat endometriosis after the FDA concluded that the drug was ineffective and withdrew its approval.[17] Physicians also used the drug to treat threatened and habitual abortions after the FDA withdrew its approval in 1974, because of the drug's suspected teratogenic potential.[18] After 1974, Depo-Provera's FDA-approved use as chemotherapy permitted physicians to use the drug for other medical purposes including chronic cystic ovaries, fibroid tumors, heavy menstrual flow, premature labor, premenstrual syndrome, and rheumatoid arthritis—purposes for which Upjohn had never received IND authorization to test or FDA approval to market.[19] Still, it was Depo-Provera's contraceptive use that attracted widespread public attention and debate.

The Network's Registry suggests that physicians widely prescribed the drug irrespective of their patient's physical or mental condition or their socioeconomic status, but the witnesses who testified at the 1973 Senate hearings and appeared before the FDA's Public Board of Inquiry claimed that physicians largely restricted the drug's use to women in special circumstances. At the Senate hearings, Dr. Robert Hutchinson, Assistant Commissioner of the Tennessee Department of Health, identified circumstances similar to those relied upon by Upjohn in its argument in support of Depo-Provera's limited contraceptive approval in 1974 and by Dr. Robert Hatcher for the drug's use at the Grady Family Planning Clinic.

Some of the circumstances Dr. Hutchinson cited were arguably risk assessment based: women who had not tolerated the IUD, who could not take an oral contraceptive (OC), or who were nursing their infants and could not use OCs.[20] Others were risk acceptability grounded: women who were mentally challenged, who lacked privacy, who were poor, young Appalachian women living in remote rural settings, who had completed child bearing and wanted contraceptive protection until they could arrange for a tubal ligation, and women "who had demonstrated by several accidental pregnancies their inability to properly use the pill."[21] The women who lacked privacy and were not sufficiently disciplined to control their own fertility were identified as young Latino and African American women in large urban centers and institutionalized mentally challenged women. These women lived at the margins of society and, women's health advocates argued, were subject to contraceptive abuse by physicians, even those with the best of motives.

Why did physicians use Depo-Provera even in these special circumstances when the FDA had identified it as an experimental contraceptive drug and had refused to approve its marketing on either a limited or general basis, because of concerns about its carcinogenic potential? Dr. Hutchinson testified that Depo-Provera's unapproved contraceptive status created a dilemma for physicians who claimed that they had to decide whether to use an unapproved drug to prevent unwanted pregnancies by women in special circumstances or allow them to take their chances with another pregnancy.[22]

Physicians resolved this dilemma by using Depo-Provera and justified their actions by reaching their own risk assessments or by claiming the agency's decisions were politically motivated. Some dismissed the FDA's reliance on animal studies in making a contraceptive marketing decision. One Depo-Provera user reported to the Network Registry that her doctor told her "not to worry unless I was a beagle dog."[23] Dr. Raymond Jannett, a Phoenix gynecologist, was less forthcoming to his patients: "I don't tell them that rhesus monkeys did strange things. . . . Most parents don't have rhesus monkey children."[24]

Other physicians made risk assessment judgments on the basis of their own independent review of the medical literature. In commenting upon the Tennessee Department of Health's decision, Dr. Hutchinson observed: "We came to realize that many of the initial reasons for our reluctance to use the drug were being removed by medical studies."[25] What those reasons were, aside from return to fertility, he did not disclose, but it is likely that they were drawn from studies that were scientifically flawed. According to the Public Board of Inquiry, the clinical studies conducted prior to 1983, which addressed the drug's carcinogenic risks and its effect on a woman's return to fertility, were "inadequate and insufficient to provide a basis for risk assessment."[26] When physicians rejected the FDA's risk assessment standards and its marketing decision and made their own risk assessment judgments, they denied women the information necessary for them to make an informed contraceptive choice.

Patients

Patients manage risk by taking the information that their physicians provide them about a drug's risks and benefits and then making a knowing and voluntary decision. A major focus of the 1973 Senate hearings was whether women who received Depo-Provera at Tennessee family planning clinics gave their informed consent. Anna Burgess, a welfare mother from rural Tennessee, was the first patient to publicly address the lack of informed consent and the social welfare control rationale for Depo-Provera's use. She testified that she was pressured into taking the drug "because they [the welfare office] said they would rather pay for one child as two."[27] When she went to the health department for her injection, she also testified that the clinic doctors did not tell her Depo-Provera was unapproved for contraceptive use, nor did they inform her about its side effects.

Anna Burgess's personal experience was supported by Dr. Norman Kase, Chair of the Department of Obstetrics and Gynecology at the Yale

University Medical School, who testified at the Senate hearings that he had interviewed women in Cumberland County, Tennessee. "Informed consent," he said, "was not obtained, nor was an attempt made to achieve patient awareness or acceptance of this issue. In particular, the potential short and long term hazards of the drug were not discussed" even though the consent form specifically mentioned two major known side effects: "(a) an irregular menstrual pattern following the shot which sometimes leads to periodic heavy bleeding during the first few months, or no monthly periods while on the shot; [and] (b) a possibility of a delay in the ability to have children following discontinuation of this shot."[28]

Dr. Hutchinson agreed that the women who signed the consent form did not know that Depo-Provera was not approved by the FDA for contraception, nor did they know the value of the drug as opposed to its side effects. "They will not know of it if the clinic physician has not explained it to them, but," he added, "we have advised them to explain it."[29] The FDA's October 1972 revision of Depo-Provera's package insert, based on the evidence that the drug had induced breast cancer in beagle dogs did, however, have an impact on its use in Tennessee as it had at Grady Memorial Hospital in Atlanta. Dr. Hutchinson acknowledged that the "patient load had dropped from 1,400 to 942," but he did not elaborate on who was responsible: state health officials, family planning physicians, or patients.[30]

Depo-Provera's unapproved use was not limited to poor rural and urban women and those with special needs.[31] The National Women's Health Network received letters from women across the socioeconomic spectrum who told their stories about receiving an injection on the basis of scanty information about the drug's risks.[32] A statistical analysis of the Network's Registry provides anecdotal data suggesting that over 80 percent of the women who returned their registry forms were not informed about Depo-Provera's risks, over 60 percent were not told about its unapproved status, and over 70 percent said that more information would have changed their minds about using the drug.[33] Even when physicians informed their patients that Depo-Provera had not been FDA-approved for contraception, they represented the drug as being safe and attributed the agency's decision to political motives: to "internal politicking and bureaucratic red tape" and "the financial gains for big companies."[34] If consent forms were used, they were incomplete or contained editorial comments.[35] Physician control of medical information and the unwillingness to share it with their patients made informed consent the most troublesome ethical issue in Depo-Provera's lengthy unapproved use.

In sum, the 1973 Senate and 1987 House hearings exposed the fragmented system of risk management. The congressional hearings and the Network's Registry documented that the FDA was a licensing agency with limited direct control over drug marketing and physician prescription practices, that Upjohn had made Depo-Provera available for unapproved contraceptive use, and that physicians failed to provide women with information about the drug's FDA status and the risks its use posed to their personal health. As a consequence, women who were injected with Depo-Provera were not able to make informed contraceptive choices.

Upjohn v. MacMurdo

The 1973 Senate and 1987 House hearings left unanswered two questions about Upjohn's and physicians' legal duties, which added another dimension to the fragmented system of drug risk management: the division between federal and state legal authority. In selling Depo-Provera, what were Upjohn's legal duties to discourage its unapproved contraceptive use and to disclose in its package insert the risks of its contraceptive use? In prescribing Depo-Provera for contraception, what were a physician's legal duties to disclose the drug's risks in order to enable patients to make informed decisions? The FDA has no authority to address these questions, because they are governed exclusively by state law and decided principally by state courts.

If a woman believes she has been harmed by the use of a drug, because of the manufacturer's failure to warn her physician, her legal remedy is a state products liability suit. If she believes that her physician has failed to provide her with the information necessary to make a personal judgment, her legal remedy is a state medical malpractice suit. In initiating these two state negligence actions, she has the burden of proving all four elements of a negligence claim: that she was owed a legal duty by the physician or pharmaceutical company to avoid an unreasonable risk to her; that they breached their duty by failing to conform their conduct to a standard of reasonable care; that their breach was the proximate or legal cause of her injuries; and that she suffered actual compensable injuries. In risk management terms, state negligence law is the means a women can use to target the failure of two critical linkages in the contraceptive risk management system: the pharmaceutical company and the physician.

Any woman who decides to use state negligence law to provide herself with a personal remedy will most likely use state courts, which as judicial risk managers, will apply the state's rules of civil procedure and negligence law in assessing the evidence of the drug's risk and determining whether it was an acceptable risk for her to bear. Prior to trial, she and her attorney will have to build her case through the use of rules governing discovery (depositions, interrogatories, and documents) and protect her case from summary judgments.[36] If she and Upjohn do not settle her case, her attorney will have to win her case at trial by using the rules governing the choice of jurors, the presentation of evidence by means of direct and cross examination of her and other witnesses, and the jury's evaluation of that evidence. On appeal, her attorney will have to protect or attack the trial court's verdict by using the rules governing the filing of briefs and making of oral arguments before an intermediate court of appeal and a state supreme court. Her ability to navigate the pathways of the law will depend upon her initiative, her choice of a skillful and determined legal advocate, and her willingness to engage in a frequently costly and time-consuming struggle with a physician or a pharmaceutical company.

Anna Burgess was the first woman to publicly report the side effects she experienced from Depo-Provera (nervousness and excessive bleeding for three to four weeks) when she testified before Senator Kennedy's subcommittee. She took no legal action, but Secundina Perez and Gloria Popham, among many others, sued their physicians and Upjohn for medical malpractice and products liability.[37] None of them endured Anne MacMurdo's lengthy and tortuous thirteen-year journey through the Florida state court system, which raises serious questions about the roles and responsibilities of state courts in the pharmaceutical risk management system.

Anne MacMurdo

Anne MacMurdo was neither an urban African American woman at the Grady Hospital, nor a poor white Appalachian woman at a family planning clinic, nor a Native American woman in an Indian Health Service school for the mentally challenged. She was a twenty-three-year-old middle-class white woman who had graduated from business school and was a Loyola University psychology major with an A average when her story began. On May 27, 1974, she visited Dr. Donald Levy, a gynecologist at the Ochsner Clinic in New Orleans. At the time, she had had been bleeding from an intrauterine device (IUD), which had been removed, and was considering an alternative means of contraception. Having read the package insert, Dr. Levy knew that Depo-Provera was being investigated for contraceptive use, but he did not advise her that Depo-Provera was not FDA-approved for contraception; nor did he inform her of the risks of its use. Nevertheless, he prescribed the drug for contraception, because she had previously experienced adverse reactions to oral contraceptives and two IUDs. The first injection acted as expected and caused amenorrhea (absence of bleeding).

When she moved to Miami, Florida, she visited Dr. Arthur Shapiro, a gynecologist at the University of Miami's Family Services Clinic, on August 6, 1974, to request an abortion only to discover that she was not pregnant. Nine days later, she returned, and Dr. Shapiro, knowing that Depo-Provera was not FDA-approved for contraception, that it was routinely used by family planning clinics, and that she had used the drug, gave her a second injection, but without informing her of its risks or that its contraceptive use was not FDA-approved. This time, she experienced a totally different reaction: continuous and heavy menstrual bleeding. At first, she attempted to control her bleeding though nutrition, but the treatment did not stop her bleeding. When she returned to New Orleans, she visited Dr. Levy on January 7, 1975, complaining about her bleeding. The next day, he performed a hysterectomy on her.[38] Why she experienced the menstrual bleeding and why the operation was performed became the central features of her lawsuit.

Origins of Upjohn v. MacMurdo

Anne MacMurdo did not take legal action immediately, but researched Depo-Provera and learned about Edward Kennedy's 1973 Senate hearings on the drug's unapproved use and L. H. Fountain's 1974 House hearings on FDA advisory committees.[39] In December 1975, she wrote to them about the injections of Depo-Provera that led to her hyster-ectomy and requested information about the drug.[40] In her letter she informed them that she had "never been told that this method did not have FDA approval, nor was I shown a consent form, . . . [but was told] that it was a safe method with none of the possible side effects of the pill."[41] As a result, she had suffered physically, psychologically, and financially from her use of the drug. She asked that her case "serve as an example by establishing better safeguards in human experimenta-tion" and suggested a legislative remedy for women like her to avoid "lengthy litigation to recover . . . medical expenses."[42] Still, she was resolved to pursue existing legal remedies in spite of the time it would take and the personal costs involved. "If I can find proper representa-tion, I am taking my case to court which will probably result in my being subjected to a couple of years of embarrassing litigation con-cerning a personal matter."[43]

Anne MacMurdo did not initiate any legal action until May 19, 1978. Instead of suing Dr. Levy in New Orleans, she filed a complaint in Broward Circuit Court in Ft. Lauderdale, Florida, against Dr. Shap-iro, the University of Miami, and Upjohn claiming negligence, breach of warranty, and strict liability; unspecified compensatory damages for her dysmenorrhea (painful and dysfunctional bleeding) and hys-terectomy; and $1 million in punitive damages.[44] The defendants denied virtually all her allegations. Dr. Shapiro and the University of Miami specifically denied they were sellers of Depo-Provera and claimed that she was contributorily negligent.[45] Upjohn asserted that any harm she suffered was due to either her assumption of the risk and/or her negligence.[46]

One might expect, as Anne MacMurdo did, that after discovery and a variety of pretrial motions and orders, her case would be settled or tried within several years, but *MacMurdo v. Upjohn* did not go to trial until December 1, 1986. What happened to delay the trial? The defendants brought two pretrial challenges to her complaint. The trial court deci-sions in both were appealed to the Florida Court of Appeals. *MacMurdo I* indirectly addressed her medical malpractice claim, and *MacMurdo II*, her products liability claim. When the Florida courts decided her case and its appeal, they made risk management judgments about who shall bear the risk: the pharmaceutical company, the physicians, or the patient.

MacMurdo I: Medical Malpractice

Anne MacMurdo's complaint did not state a claim for medical malpractice against Dr. Shapiro and the University of Miami, because it was barred by Florida's two-year statute of limitations.[47] Instead, she claimed that in prescribing and administering an injection of Depo-Provera, they were liable for breach of warranty, because they had sold her a defective drug that they had warranted to be safe for her use. She also claimed that they were strictly liable, because they did not warn her that Depo-Provera was an experimental and dangerous drug and that she might risk serious and deleterious side effects from its use.

Dr. Shapiro and the University of Miami moved immediately for summary judgment. In Broward Circuit Court, Judge Raymond Hare treated Anne MacMurdo's complaint as a medical malpractice claim and, on the defendants' motion, dismissed her complaint without leave to amend "without first proceeding through medical mediation."[48] Anne MacMurdo appealed. In October 1980, Judge George Hersey, speaking for a unanimous court of appeals, acknowledged that her complaint did not state a claim for medical malpractice, but that even if it had, the Florida Supreme Court in *Aldana v. Holub* (1980) had recently declared the state's medical malpractice statute unconstitutional.[49] Then he turned to her implied warranty and strict liability claims. "We are not prepared at this stage of the pleadings," he declared, "to accept as an inevitable conclusion that appellant will not be able to state a cause of action against the appellees on any theory."[50] Remand was appropriate, he concluded, "to give appellant her day in court . . . to seek redress for her injuries."[51]

Anne MacMurdo survived a second summary judgment motion in October 1981,[52] but she was not so fortunate in September 1985, when she faced a motion to dismiss her case.[53] Dr. Shapiro and the University of Miami claimed that her suit was based on a medical malpractice claim barred by the statute of limitations. They persuasively argued that she had "styled her claim as one of strict liability and breach of warranty, rather than medical malpractice in order to avoid the Statute of Limitations for such a cause of action. . . . However, the law is not so easily circumvented."[54]

A breach of warranty claim, the defendants argued, did not apply to the administration of drugs supplied as part of medical services provided by a hospital and physician. Florida courts had recognized the distinction between a sale and a service and also recognized the distinction between the sale of goods and "the incidental transfer of property as a necessary part of . . . [individual contracts for professional] services."[55] Her case, they concluded, did not involve a sale within the contemplation of the Uniform Commercial Code and, therefore, did not give rise to a breach of warranty claim.[56] On the issue of strict liability, citing *Carmichael v. Reitz* (1971),[57] they argued that it would be inappropriate to impose strict liability on a hospital or physician when a drug is administered as a part of a course of treatment.[58]

Anne MacMurdo, recognizing that the law could not be "so easily circumvented" and aware that her implied warranty and strict liability theories were weak, took a voluntary dismissal in December 1985.[59] In sum, the Florida statute of limitations had proven to be a formidable barrier to her medical malpractice claim against Dr. Shapiro and the University of Miami. No court would decide whether Dr. Shapiro had been negligent in failing to inform her about Depo-Provera's risks. No court would decide whether they had harmed her by failing to manage Depo-Provera's risk. Now the only defendant was the drug's manufacturer, The Upjohn Company, which would use the issue of medical malpractice and a lack of informed consent in its defense to her products liability suit.

MacMurdo II: Products Liability

Anne MacMurdo's complaint against Upjohn stated a products liability claim. Upjohn, she argued, was negligent in marketing Depo-Provera, and its package insert warnings were inadequate to inform Dr. Levy that the drug could cause her dysmenorrhea (painful and dysfunctional bleeding) and her heavy and prolonged bleeding. As a result, he had misdiagnosed her problem and performed a hysterectomy. Her complaint also held Upjohn strictly liable for her injuries, because, she claimed, Upjohn knew Depo-Provera was an experimental drug with serious and deleterious side effects, but the company had failed to inform her that she was an experimental subject.

Upjohn moved for summary judgment in Broward Circuit Court.[60] At the October 1983 hearing, Judge Mark Polen found the package insert warnings adequate as a matter of law, because there was no conflicting evidence, but his comments on his lack of faith in the jury system revealed the subjective basis for his decision. "The reason I love to give summary judgments is when you put six people in the [jury] box, God knows what they'll come out of the [jury] room with."[61] Anne Mac-Murdo once again appealed.

In December 1983, Judge James Walden, speaking for a divided court of appeals, reversed and remanded her case for jury trial. "It is not for judges, but for the jury to determine if a particular warning is adequate under the circumstances."[62] He relied principally on the Florida Supreme Court decision in *Tampa Drug Co. v. Wait* (1958),[63] which held that the adequacy of the warning on a prescription drug label was a jury question, but he also found support in *Lake v. Konstantinu* (1966).[64] There the Florida Court of Appeals had held that "the question of the sufficiency of the warnings of the drug's extremely dangerous potentiality and the inherent danger in its use. . . . must certainly be submitted to the jury."[65] Judge Walden also disposed of Upjohn's argument that summary judgment was proper, because there was no conflicting testimony. In *Lake*, he said, the appellate court had stated: "Florida is committed to the 'slightest doubt' rule and even though there is no conflict in evidence, a motion for summary judgment should be denied where inferences are reasonably deducible therefrom."[66]

In his concurrence, Judge Garvin Letts sympathized with the trial court judge's view that in reaching a finding about the adequacy of the warning, a jury might be swayed by the plaintiff's injuries. Citing the federal district court decision in *Dunkin v. Syntex Laboratories* (1977),[67] he would have preferred the view that the package insert warnings were adequate as a matter of law. Yet he concurred, because he agreed that "Judge Walden's remarks . . . fairly reflected the state of law in Florida."[68]

Judge Hersey was not persuaded and argued in his dissent that the record disclosed that "reasonable men could not disagree as to the adequacy of the warnings, let alone reasonable physicians."[69] And even if they could disagree, the federal district court decisions in *Chambers v. G.D. Searle* (1975) and *Dunkin v. Syntex Laboratories* (1977)[70] supported the position that the adequacy of the warnings could be a question of law.

In sum, the court of appeals' decision, reversing the trial court's grant of Upjohn's summary judgment motion, eliminated the barrier to Anne

MacMurdo's products liability case against Upjohn. Depo-Provera's labeling was a question of fact, and a jury would decide on the basis of the evidence at trial whether the labeling was adequate to warn a physician about the risk of the drug's contraceptive use. Whether the Florida Supreme Court would agree when Upjohn appealed the trial court's decision was another matter.

Broward Circuit Court Trial

After the Court of Appeals December 1983 decision, Anne MacMurdo's attorney, Dominic Brandy, did not take the initiative and prepare her case for trial. When he failed to respond to Upjohn's interrogatories and produce a physician expert who would testify that the drug caused her bleeding problems, Upjohn moved for summary judgment on July 25, 1986, because it had retained a physician expert who, along with Drs. Levy and Schapiro, did not attribute her medical problems to her Depo-Provera injections.[71]

In reply, Anne MacMurdo's co-counsel, Eric Golden, requested Broward Circuit Court Judge Miette Burnstein, who would preside at the trial, to grant a thirty-day extension for him to respond to Upjohn's interrogatories, because he had not been active in the case for two years, and Dominic Brandy had been "advised by a physician to suspend his trial preparations . . . for six months."[72] Judge Burnstein allowed him ten days and set the case for trial in early September,[73] but by August 22, he had not fully complied with Upjohn's requests.[74]

Anne MacMurdo, aware of her upcoming trial date, but without any expert to testify that Depo-Provera caused her bleeding and with her attorneys unprepared to try her case, submitted an affidavit on August 27 stating she had contacted eight law firms specializing in products liability litigation and that "all of these law firms have indicated to me that they would be willing to handle my case, but not without a sixty (60) to ninety (90) day continuance of the trial."[75]

She retained the West Palm Beach firm of Cone, Wagner, Nugent, Johnson, Roth, and Romano. One of the firm's attorneys, Michael Ericksen, who had tried Dalkon Shield cases, became her new co-counsel. On September 11, Judge Burnstein granted Anne MacMurdo a continuance and set her trial date for December 1. Preparations for trial moved swiftly. With less than ninety days, Michael Ericksen planned "a bare bones trial."[76] He amended the answers to Upjohn's expert witness interrogatories, requested Upjohn to provide documents, deposed three witnesses,[77] and acquired from Dr. Sidney Wolfe's Health Research Group the minutes of FDA Obstetrics and Gynecology Advisory Committee's 1972 through 1974 meetings on Depo-Provera, but he was unable to settle her case. Eric Golden had previously made a settlement demand of $400,000, but Upjohn had refused to negotiate.[78] A hysterectomy case, according to Michael Ericksen, was worth $300,000 to $500,000, assuming a liability verdict, but even when he reduced his settlement demand to $75,000, Upjohn would offer nothing in return.[79]

Theories of the Case

Anne MacMurdo's products liability case finally went to trial in Broward Circuit Court on December 1 before Judge Burnstein. For six days, the trial would be defined by two theories of her case: one presented by her attorney, Michael Ericksen, and the other by Upjohn's attorney, David Covey. The theory of each case would tell the jury a story that "explains not only the legal theory and factual background, but ties as much of the evidence as possible into a coherent and credible whole."[80] The negligence theories in Anne MacMurdo's case were defined in her complaint and Upjohn's answer. The factual background was detailed in the documents the attorneys had acquired, the depositions they had taken, and the interrogatories they had served on each other. The two contradictory theories would define the conduct of the trial, the strategies of the attorneys, and the evidence the jury would hear.

Michael Ericksen situated Anne MacMurdo's story within the wider world of Upjohn's pursuit of FDA approval of Depo-Provera for contraception.[81] He was interested in the company's animal and human clinical testing programs, scholarly journal articles' reports of the research, the FDA's Obstetrics and Gynecology (OB/GYN) Advisory Committee's recommendations, and the FDA's marketing decisions. He wanted to include Senator Kennedy's hearings on the drug's unapproved contraceptive use and Representative Fountain's hearings on the FDA's and the OB/GYN Advisory Committee's role in approving Depo-Provera for limited marketing. Upjohn's Depo-Provera marketing program and package insert, along with the depositions of Upjohn officials and researchers and expert witnesses, would provide the evidence to support his two legal theories: that Upjohn was negligent in marketing Depo-Provera by failing to control the drug's unapproved contraceptive use at the University of Miami Hospital; and that Upjohn was negligent by failing to provide an adequate warning to physicians in the Depo-Provera package insert stating that the drug's unapproved contraceptive use could cause the menstrual bleeding suffered by Anne MacMurdo and lead her to have a hysterectomy.

David Covey took a narrower view of Anne MacMurdo's story. He focused on Upjohn's program to limit Depo-Provera's marketing to its approved use and on the drug's package insert. He wanted to examine her life: her failed marriage, the stillbirth of her only child, her suicide attempts, her use of prescription and illegal drugs, her menstrual history of irregular periods and heavy bleeding, her use of the contraceptive Pill, two IUDs, and Depo-Provera, and her decision to have a hysterectomy. The depositions of Anne MacMurdo, her physicians, and expert witnesses, along with her medical history, would provide the evidence to support his three legal theories: that Upjohn had acted responsibly by creating and implementing a marketing program to limit Depo-Provera to its approved uses; that the drug's package insert adequately warned physicians about its unapproved contraceptive use and abnormal bleeding; and that if anyone acted negligently, it was not Upjohn, but Drs. Levy and Shapiro, who gave Anne MacMurdo injections without her informed consent and Dr. Levy who provided her with no medical alternatives to a hysterectomy to which she consented, because she wanted to be sterilized.

In sum, Anne MacMurdo's products liability trial became a story subject to two contradictory tellings that can be viewed in risk management terms. As Michael Ericksen told her story, she expected Upjohn to manage Depo-Provera's risk by creating and implementing a program to limit the drug to its FDA-approved use, to assess the drug's contraceptive risk, and to express its risk of heavy and prolonged bleeding in its FDA-approved package insert. She expected her physicians, as learned medical intermediaries, to have read the package insert and, knowing the drug's risks and her medical history, to have made an informed medical judgment that the drug posed an unacceptable risk for her. Her physicians were, however, unable to make that risk acceptability judgment, because Upjohn had failed to disclose in the drug's package insert an assessment of the extent of the bleeding risk reported by its research.

As David Covey would tell her story, Upjohn had assessed Depo-Provera's risk by conducting research on Depo-Provera's short-term side effects, including menstrual bleeding, and had provided adequate FDA-approved warnings in the package insert about the risk of bleeding and stated that its contraceptive use was experimental and unapproved for birth control. Upjohn had also taken action to manage the drug's risk by creating and implementing a program to monitor its unapproved use. Anne MacMurdo and her physicians had, however, failed to manage Depo-Provera's risk. Her physicians knew Upjohn's assessment of the drug's risk for contraception, because they had read the package insert before they gave her injections of the drug and Dr. Levy had terminated her bleeding with a hysterectomy at her request.

Pretrial Conference

Michael Ericksen's and David Covey's opportunity to present their two contradictory tellings of Anne MacMurdo's story to the jury depended on their pretrial conference with Judge Burnstein. The conference addressed the legal theories that would underpin the trial and the evidence the jury would hear to support each theory.

Anne MacMurdo's negligent marketing claim was based on the argument that Upjohn knew of Depo-Provera's nationwide unapproved contraceptive use, but that the company's monitoring program failed to police the drug's use. David Covey was, however, able to convince Judge Burnstein that Upjohn's monitoring program had not targeted Planned Parenthood clinics and, as she told Michael Ericksen, he would have to show that Upjohn knew or should have known that the quantities of Depo-Provera it shipped to the University of Miami Hospital "could not possibly be used for other than family planning."[82] Michael Ericksen believed that the evidence to support this claim depended upon the admissibility of the 1973 Senate testimony of Dr. William Hubbard, Upjohn's Executive Vice President. After listening to both attorneys, Judge Burnstein decided that there was "no purpose for its admission, not only hearsay, but also for relevance."[83] Michael

Ericksen protested: "It's really important to our case to show that Upjohn was on notice there was widespread unapproved use" and that the
program Dr. Hubbard described was not carried out.[84] Still she failed
to see its relevance, but if an Upjohn employee testified that he did
not know about Depo-Provera's unapproved contraceptive use, then
she would allow Michael Ericksen to use Dr. Hubbard's testimony to
impeach the witness.[85]

Anne MacMurdo's claim that Upjohn failed to warn about Depo-
Provera's side effect of heavy and prolonged menstrual bleeding raised a
legal causation issue. David Covey argued that she could not claim that
Depo-Provera caused her bleeding that "necessitated the performance of
her hysterectomy."[86] Michael Ericksen replied that he would argue not
that the drug caused the medical operation, but that it "cause[d] a condition that had to be operated on."[87] Judge Burnstein was satisfied that
he had an expert who would testify to the causal connection between
the drug and the operation. When David Covey wanted to introduce
"medical testimony that [Anne MacMurdo's] drug use, psychiatric problems, and stress are all contributing factors to the injury of bleeding,"[88]
Judge Burnstein would allow the testimony on drug use only if expert
witnesses could establish its relevance to her bleeding. When he wanted
to probe even further into Anne MacMurdo's personal life in 1974 and
let the jury know "she was living as a mistress, a kept woman to a mar-
ried man and . . . she didn't want children,"[89] Judge Burnstein would
allow the testimony only if it were relevant to show that "she wanted a
hysterectomy and her lifestyle precluded her having children."[90] At the
same time, she agreed with Michael Ericksen that using words such as
"mistress" and "kept woman" would be irrelevant and prejudicial.[91] As
she told David Covey: "Those are very moralistic and judgmental ac-
cusations that I don't think are appropriate for a court."[92]

In sum, Judge Burnstein's rulings focused the trial on the evidence
that was directly relevant to the two legal theories— negligent marketing and failure to warn—and would avoid the dual perils of politicizing
and personalizing the trial. In spite of Michael Ericksen's concern that
the jury not look at the case in a vacuum, it was unavoidable.[93] Otherwise, as both Michael Ericksen and David Covey agreed, introducing
evidence from "extraneous areas" could prejudice their clients in the
eyes of the jury.[94]

Opening Statements

A jury of four women and two men would hear and decide Anne Mac-
Murdo's case. Unlike the FDA's Public Board of Inquiry, the jury had no
specialized knowledge of the FDA's prescription drug approval process,
the package inserts accompanying prescription drugs, the marketing of
drugs by pharmaceutical companies, and the use of drugs by physicians
for purposes not approved by the FDA. Nor did the jury know about
Depo-Provera's research and regulatory history or the effect of Depo-
Provera on the menstrual cycle, and the two men were unlikely to know
about a woman's reproductive system and the functioning of her menstrual cycle. The jury's knowledge of these matters would begin with
Michael Ericksen's and David Covey's opening statements: their outlines
of the facts and issues in the case and the evidence they would present to
support a jury verdict on behalf of their clients.

Michael Ericksen told the jury Anne MacMurdo's story. As a
twenty-three-years-old woman, she had received two injections of
Depo-Provera, a cancer drug not approved by the FDA for contraception. After the second injection for contraception, she had a hysterectomy to relieve her continuous menstrual bleeding. He would
call three expert witnesses whose evidence would show that Upjohn
was responsible for Anne MacMurdo's bleeding and hysterectomy. Dr.
David Benjamin, a pharmacologist and expert in drug package inserts,
would explain that Upjohn knew Depo-Provera was being used for
contraception and that, although the company created a program to
control its unapproved use, it did not implement the program.[95] Dr.
Benjamin would also explain that one of the drug's effects is heavy
and prolonged bleeding for eleven to thirty days and that this was
experienced by 25 to 35 percent of the women who used it, but the
drug's package insert did not explain this side effect to physicians,
and the physician who performed her hysterectomy "did not recognize that her bleeding was coming from this particular drug."[96] Dr.
Paul Schwallie, an Upjohn researcher who had published the pivotal
study on Depo-Provera side effects, would testify that Depo-Provera
could cause heavy and prolonged bleeding. Dr. Soroh Roshan, a gynecologist, would confirm that the drug "was causing Anne MacMurdo's
bleeding,"[97] even though Upjohn witnesses would "suggest that every-

thing else but Depo-Provera in Anne MacMurdo's life was the cause of her bleeding."[98] Finally, Anne MacMurdo would tell the jury about her use of the Pill, IUDs, and Depo-Provera and her hysterectomy for which Upjohn was responsible.[99]

David Covey outlined for the jury a quite different story. The evidence would show that Upjohn did not sell the drug to her physicians or to their family planning clinics.[100] Anne MacMurdo's physicians had obtained Depo-Provera from their hospital pharmacies. "That's not The Upjohn Company's fault."[101] The drug's package insert informed her physicians that it had not been FDA-approved for contraception, because "there were unresolved questions relating to its safety for this use," but the FDA did not have the authority to forbid doctors from using Depo-Provera for contraception.[102] The evidence would show that Anne MacMurdo's physicians knew the drug was unapproved for contraception, but injected her with it anyway. After her second injection, her bleeding was terminated with a hysterectomy even though other medical and surgical procedures could have been used. Why then did she consent to a hysterectomy? The evidence would show that after the stillbirth of her acephalic child, "she was not going to subject herself to that risk again."[103] When she thought she was pregnant after her first injection, she requested an abortion, and after her second injection, she knowingly and voluntarily signed a consent form to be sterilized by having a hysterectomy.[104] "Her choice, her body, her right," David Covey told the jury.[105] "Upjohn is not responsible. That's the evidence."[106]

Presentation of the Case

With the opening statements completed, Michael Ericksen began the presentation of his case that Upjohn had been negligent in marketing Depo-Provera and in failing to warn Anne MacMurdo's physicians, Drs. Donald Levy and Arthur Shapiro, that the drug could cause heavy and prolonged menstrual bleeding and that its failure had led Dr. Levy to terminate Anne MacMurdo's bleeding with a hysterectomy. Thereafter, David Covey would present his case denying Upjohn's liability and asserting that Anne MacMurdo and her physicians were responsible for her injuries. Throughout the trial, each attorney would use objections for relevance and hearsay to control the introduction of evidence supporting his theory of the case and use cross examination to question the evidence introduced to support the other's theory and to elicit evidence favorable to his theory. Judge Burnstein would rule on their objections to avoid the twin perils of politicizing and personalizing the trial. In risk management terms, the trial would become the venue for answering the question of who should bear the legal responsibility for the assessment and acceptability of Depo-Provera contraceptive risk: Upjohn or Anne MacMurdo and her physicians.

NEGLIGENT MARKETING CLAIM

To prove Anne MacMurdo's claim of negligent marketing, Michael Ericksen first called Dr. David Benjamin, a PhD pharmacologist and the plaintiff's chief expert witness on patient package inserts. Dr. Benjamin testified that between 1972 and 1974, "there was sufficient evidence available to the company . . . [to] have concluded there was a widespread unapproved use of Depo-Provera for contraceptive . . . purposes."[107] When Dr. Elizabeth Connell, a defense witness and a chair and member of the FDA's Obstetrics and Gynecology (OB/GYN) Advisory Committee from 1970 to 1974, testified on direct examination that Depo-Provera's unapproved contraceptive use "was occurring in many areas of the United States,"[108] her answer led Michael Ericksen on cross examination to ask if she "were aware of extensive use of that drug for contraceptive purposes," to which she replied: "I wouldn't say extensive."[109] He then read from the transcript of the OB/GYN Advisory Committee's July 2, 1972, meeting at which she had observed: "I think all of us who are involved clinically recognize that the drug is being used for more than endometriosis, and . . . we recognize there's an extensive use of this drug not covered by an IND."[110] She reluctantly agreed: "If it's in the record, I assume I did" make the statement.[111] After she denied that the drug's use was a "national scandal," they had the following colloquy:

Q. Is it not a fact that it was so notorious and was the subject of a congressional inquiry into the scope of unapproved use . . . in [February] 1973?

A. There was a hearing with Senator Fountain [sic Kennedy] [on] the issue of Depo-Provera, that's true.

Q. Didn't most of the hearing consist of an inquiry into the scope and extent of the use of this drug for purposes other than indicated on the label?

A. That was part of it.[112]

Michael Ericksen wanted the jury to know about the actions Upjohn had failed to take, as a reasonable pharmaceutical company, to address this "national scandal." He turned to his deposition of Frank Fletcher, an Upjohn regional sales manager from 1972 to 1974, and read a redacted excerpt of Dr. William Hubbard's 1973 Senate testimony, which did not identify its venue, nor Senator Kennedy by name.

Dr. Hubbard stated: "The company policy is quite clear and that is that the drug should not be distributed for unapproved use." Question to Dr. Hubbard: "Do you inquire as to what use they put the drugs?" and Dr. Hubbard: "We now do precisely that." Question: "Since when?" Dr. Hubbard: "Last summer." Question: "What do you ask?" Dr. Hubbard: "What they intend to use the drug for in places like family planning clinics where there is reason to infer what they intend to do with it. We simply ask them.[113]

Frank Fletcher, now Upjohn's Vice President for Domestic Pharmaceutical Sales, confirmed that Upjohn had a "Depo-Provera Monitoring System" described by Dr. Hubbard. The system required all Depo-Provera orders to be referred to regional service managers who were not to release an order if there were any reason to question its proposed use and then to contact the customer.[114]

While Michael Ericksen was able to establish Depo-Provera's national contraceptive use and Upjohn's national program to monitor the drug's unapproved use, he had difficulty in providing convincing evidence that Upjohn had been negligent in marketing Depo-Provera at the University of Miami Hospital by failing to exercise reasonable care in controlling its sale. His difficulty lay in the fact that the company's policy, as described by Dr. Hubbard and Mr. Fletcher, contained both a passive order monitoring component and an active inquiry component: asking family planning clinics and physicians about their use of Depo-Provera for contraception.

Glen Wright, Upjohn's Miami Services Manager in 1973 and 1974, testified that the company's order monitoring program required him to review all University of Miami Hospital orders. Upjohn could not, however, really monitor Depo-Provera's contraceptive use at the hospital's Family Services Clinic and by Dr. Shapiro, because neither maintained an account with the company. All hospital orders, he told the jury, were placed by its pharmacy, and its orders were for small quantities of the drug.[115] Since the hospital had an oncology program, which could use the drug for chemotherapy, Mr. Wright was not aware of any noticeable change in Depo-Provera orders and had "no reason to suspect quantities of Depo-Provera were being ordered . . . for contraception."[116]

Joseph Paternetti, the Upjohn hospital sales representative (detail person), testified that his duties at the University of Miami Hospital did not involve taking orders from physicians and that he was not allowed to enter the Family Services Clinic to promote the drug.[117] At the University of Miami Hospital, he visited only its pharmacy and then forwarded the purchase orders to his local service manager.[118] Dr. Shapiro confirmed that when he gave Anne MacMurdo her second injection of Depo-Provera on August 15, 1974, the Family Services Clinic did not order the drug from Upjohn, did not keep it in stock, and did not use it for contraception, because it was an abortion clinic.[119] When he gave Anne MacMurdo her injection at the Family Services Clinic, he had ordered it from the hospital pharmacy.[120]

Michael Ericksen also found it difficult to prove Upjohn's negligent marketing by arguing that Dr. Hubbard had misled the Senate subcommittee when he informed Senator Kennedy that Upjohn asked about the intended use of Depo-Provera. Frank Fletcher confirmed that company policy required sales managers to ask customers if there were "any large or frequent orders" for the drug.[121] Glen Wright had delegated this task to Joseph Paternetti, and therein lay the problem of proving negligent marketing. Mr. Fletcher told Michael Ericksen that asking physicians how they were using Depo-Provera would be contrary to company policy and federal law.[122] Then he added: "Most physicians would tell them it wasn't any of their damn business."[123] Glen Wright echoed Mr. Fletcher's comment on a physician's response to an inquiry about the use of Depo-Provera for contraception.[124] Joseph Paternetti added that he was guided by Upjohn's company policy, which did not permit him to discuss a drug's unapproved uses with physicians, because "the indication [for contraception] did not exist."[125] Nor did he discuss with the pharmacists, who ordered Depo-Provera for the University of Miami Hospital, the drug's unapproved contraceptive use by physicians, including those at the Family Planning Clinic.[126]

Overall, the evidence established Depo-Provera's nationwide contraceptive use, but did not fit well with Michael Ericksen's theory that Upjohn was negligent in marketing Depo-Provera when it filled orders for the drug placed by the University of Miami Hospital. Federal law, company policy, and physician prescription autonomy did not allow Upjohn to engage in active inquiry of physicians about their use of Depo-Provera for contraception, but limited the company to passively monitoring orders placed by the hospital pharmacy.

NEGLIGENT FAILURE TO WARN CLAIM

To prove Anne MacMurdo's claim of Upjohn's failure to warn her physicians that Depo-Provera could cause prolonged menstrual bleeding, Michael Ericksen had her tell the jury her story from the stillbirth of her acephalic child in 1970 to her hysterectomy in 1975. She provided its broad outlines, but he would rely on her physicians, expert witnesses, and legal and medical documents to tell the jury about her menstrual history, her use of Depo-Provera, and her hysterectomy. Three themes would define her negligence claim: first, she had had no history of heavy and prolonged menstrual bleeding until she received her second injection of Depo-Provera; second, Upjohn had failed to warn her physicians that the drug could have this effect; and third, as a result of Upjohn's failure, she had suffered five months of prolonged bleeding, which Dr. Levy terminated with a hysterectomy.

To prove that Anne MacMurdo did not have a history of abnormal menstrual bleeding before her second injection of Depo-Provera, Michael Ericksen turned to Dr. Sorosh Roshan, the plaintiff's gynecological expert, and played her taped deposition in court. Dr. Roshan testified that Anne MacMurdo had seen Dr. Hutchinson, her pediatrician from age six to nineteen, and that his records did not disclose "any abnormal bleeding patterns."[127] On cross examination, Dr. Elizabeth Connell, a former chair of the FDA's OB/GYN Advisory Committee, agreed that Dr. Hutchinson's records documented that Anne MacMurdo did not have an abnormal menstrual history, except for one episode of pelvic inflammatory disease (PID) in 1968.[128]

Dr. Connell further testified that when Dr. Victor Brown, a gynecologist at the Touro Infirmary in New Orleans, saw her on January 9, 1973, his records confirmed that she had no menstrual irregularities, except for the one PID episode.[129] Three months later, he removed her intrauterine device (IUD) and performed a dilation and curettage (D&C), which addressed her complaint of "heavy bleeding with clots and cramps."[130] When she visited Dr. Jack Jacob at the Ochsner Clinic on April 26, 1974, having discontinued the Pill and having had a second IUD implanted, she once again complained about "heavy periods and clotting for six months."[131] He removed the IUD and diagnosed it as having caused her bleeding.[132]

Finally, Dr. Connell testified that when Dr. Levy gave Anne Mac-Murdo the first injection of Depo-Provera a month later, his medical records stated that her pelvic exam was normal and her medical history made no reference to any kind of history of abnormal or irregular bleeding, except in connection with her PID and two IUDs.[133] In sum, Dr. Roshan's and Dr. Connell's evidence confirmed that Anne MacMurdo's medical history, up until she received her second injection of Depo-Provera, did not provide an explanation for her abnormal menstrual bleeding.

Drs. Levy's and Shapiro's use of Depo-Provera contributed another critical piece of evidence to her story: the drug's package insert. Dr. David Benjamin testified that Upjohn, like other pharmaceutical companies, drafted the Depo-Provera package insert and then submitted it for FDA approval. Upjohn was also responsible for amending the drug's package inserts to include important information on a drug's side effects.[134]

Michael Ericksen then asked him about the article written by Drs. Paul Schwallie and J. Robert Assenzo, Upjohn researchers, which had been published in the journal *Fertility and Sterility* in 1973.[135] Dr. Benjamin testified that the article revealed that Depo-Provera usually produces amenorrhea (absence of menstruation), but after three months, 40 percent of women had no bleeding, 25 percent had 1 to 7 days of bleeding, 5 to 7 percent had 8 to 10 days of bleeding, and "those who had bleeding from between 11 and 30 days in that period would be about 27 percent."[136] After six months, "50 percent had no bleeding, 30 percent had from 1 to 7 days, 10 percent had from 8 to 10 days of bleeding, and 15 percent had from 11 to 30 days of bleeding."[137]

Michael Ericksen and Dr. Benjamin then had the following colloquy about the implications of the Schwallie and Assenzo article's findings for the Depo-Provera package insert.

> Q. Assuming that we have a study . . . that demonstrates there is an incidence of bleeding from 11 to 30 days . . . that information . . . normally should be in a package insert?
>
> A. I think it would be appropriate to include. . . .
>
> Q. Is there anything in the [1974] package insert that says anything about women bleeding from 11 to 30 days using this drug? . . .
>
> A. It doesn't specifically say bleeding of 11 to 30 days can occur.[138]

Dr. Benjamin then explained that it would be a violation of an industry standard[139] not to include the Schwallie and Assenzo bleeding data in the package insert's Adverse Warning section,[140] because, as he told David Covey on cross examination, the evidence of bleeding differed substantially from the prior state of knowledge.[141]

Did Drs. Levy and Shapiro know about Depo-Provera's package insert? Dr. Levy testified that that he was aware that the drug's package insert stated that its use was contraindicated for women suffering from undiagnosed vaginal bleeding, but he had diagnosed Anne MacMurdo's bleeding as "secondary to her IUD" when he gave her an injection on May 27, 1974.[142] The first injection acted as expected and caused amenorrhea (absence of bleeding). Except for one episode of spotting in June 1974, she had no menstrual periods for three months.[143]

During the summer Anne MacMurdo moved from New Orleans to Miami and was seen by Dr. Arthur Shapiro at the University of Miami Family Services Clinic on August 6. As she testified, she told Dr. Shapiro that the injection of Depo-Provera "may not be working properly."[144] If she were pregnant, she wanted an abortion, but he examined her and found she was not. A week later he gave her an injection of Depo-Provera. Dr. Shapiro testified that he had read the package insert and knew that the drug's primary effect was to eliminate menstrual periods, but the package insert did not contain any information about heavy and prolonged bleeding for up to thirty days a month.[145]

Unlike her pre-Depo-Provera menstrual history and her experience with her first injection, her second injection produced nonstop bleeding for five months. She first addressed her bleeding by attending Essner Natural Hygiene in Lake Worth, Florida, for two weeks. There she had followed a regimen of a vegetarian diet of fruits and vegetables, vitamins, and rest.[146] Dr. Sorosh Roshan testified that "nine out ten women respond to rest and vitamins and iron."[147] Anne MacMurdo was the one in ten whose bleeding problem did not respond to this therapy.

When she returned to Dr. Levy's office on January 7, 1975, she was suffering not only from prolonged menstrual bleeding, but also from dysmenorrhea (painful and dysfunctional bleeding), which is not listed on the Depo-Provera package insert.[148] At her visit to Dr. Levy's office, she was desperate to have relief from her bleeding, and she would agree to anything Dr. Levy would recommend.[149] As she testified: "I had tried the organic way . . . and I was still bleeding my brains out."[150]

Dr. Levy had read the 1974 package insert and knew that Depo-Provera's adverse reactions included only "spotting, breakthrough bleeding, and change in menstrual flow."[151] The package insert did not, however, inform him that Depo-Provera might have caused her heavy and prolonged bleeding because, as he stated, it was supposed to have the opposite effect of amenorrhea.[152] Dr. Levy admitted that he did not offer Anne MacMurdo any alternatives to a hysterectomy,[153] but told her, as she recalled, "You need a hysterectomy and that will solve your bleeding."[154] She recounted her visit in the following colloquy with Michael Ericksen.

Q. Did you initiate the discussion relative to a hysterectomy?
A. No.
Q. At any time did you indicate in any way, shape or form to Dr. Levy that you desired to be sterilized for the purpose of not having children in the future?
A. No.
Q. What was your understanding about the necessity of a hysterectomy at the time?
A. That it would stop the bleeding and at that point if they hung me from a tree if that would stop it, fine.[155]

Did Depo-Provera cause Anne MacMurdo's bleeding? She did not have any doubts, nor did Dr. Roshan, who testified that her bleeding was "causally related" to Depo-Provera.[156] Did Depo-Provera cause the hysterectomy? That was an issue of fact, but Anne MacMurdo had no doubt. When David Covey asked her on cross examination, "You blame the Upjohn Company for having this hysterectomy, don't you?" she replied, "It's your drug."[157]

In sum, Michael Ericksen provided the jury with evidence documenting that Upjohn had caused Anne MacMurdo's injuries, because it had breached its duty to warn Drs. Levy and Shapiro that the use of Depo-Provera could cause dysmenorrhea and the prolonged menstrual bleeding that necessitated her hysterectomy. In risk management terms, Upjohn had assessed the drug's risk, but failed to provide in Depo-Provera's package insert the finding from the Schwallie and Assenzo article, which documented that women who received an injection had a 27 percent risk of painful and prolonged menstrual bleeding. Without knowledge of this finding, Anne MacMurdo's physicians were unable to determine whether the drug's use was an acceptable risk for her. Without this knowledge, Dr. Levy did not use estrogen, perform a D&C, or allow the drug's effect to wear off, but gave Anne MacMurdo only one option, a hysterectomy, to which she agreed, desperate as she was to stop the bleeding.

David Covey provided an alternative reading of Anne MacMurdo's story. Three themes defined his defense of Upjohn. He would begin with Anne MacMurdo's personal life, including her menstrual history, stressful lifestyle, and drug use, which, in turn, could explain her bleeding, and the birth of her acephalic child, which, in turn, could explain her decision to request a hysterectomy. Then he would argue that the Depo-Provera package insert provided an adequate warning to her physicians about menstrual bleeding. He would end his defense of Upjohn with the argument that Dr. Shapiro and Dr. Levy failed to exercise reasonable care by disregarding clear warnings in Depo-Provera's package insert and prescribing the drug for contraception, and that Dr. Levy performed a hysterectomy disregarding alternative medical means to treat Anne MacMurdo's bleeding.

David Covey began by probing deeply into Anne MacMurdo's personal life. The medical history she gave Dr. Shapiro on August 6, 1974, documented her irregular menstrual cycles and painful menstrual periods with heavy menstrual bleeding.[158] After her second injection of Depo-Provera, as she admitted on cross examination, she waited five months before she saw a doctor even though, as she testified, "I was bleeding my brains out."[159] Then, in spite of having "serious protracted vaginal bleeding," she had elective surgery to correct a problem with her breast implants ten days before her hysterectomy.[160]

Dr. Elizabeth Connell, contrary to her testimony on cross-examination, told David Covey that her review of Anne MacMurdo's medical records confirmed that her "periods were always irregular, that birth control pills controlled the irregularity and after they were discontinued she would return to irregular bleeding often called dysfunctional bleeding."[161] Dr. Sorosh Roshan disagreed. Anne MacMurdo's August 6, 1974 University of Miami menstrual history did indicate heavy menstrual flow, but "no intermenstrual bleeding," and it was not clear that she "had very irregular cycles with heavy flow and heavy pain in the onset of her menstrual history."[162]

Was Depo-Provera the cause of Anne MacMurdo's menstrual condition at the time she had her hysterectomy? Drs. Connell and Roshan gave David Covey conflicting answers. When Dr. Connell reviewed the pathology report of Anne MacMurdo's uterus, she found that it did not reveal that Depo-Provera had caused her bleeding.[163] Dr. Roshan disagreed: for her the pathology report's findings were "consistent with the effect of Depo-Provera."[164] For her, Anne MacMurdo's dysfunctional bleeding at the time of her hysterectomy was caused by Depo-Provera[165] and "fit the pattern I observed in most of the patients I have followed who had heavy, irregular bleeding after Depo-Provera."[166]

Since there was doubt as to whether Depo-Provera could cause her bleeding, could her stressful life and drug use account for her bleeding problems that led to her hysterectomy? Anne MacMurdo's lifestyle, including her illegal recreational and prescription drug use, provided a second element in David Covey's story of her personal life. She had admitted to the use of mescaline and LSD in the late 1960s and to marijuana and hashish "very seldom" after 1970.[167] In 1972 when her marriage had broken up, she attempted suicide using Thorazine and Stelazine.[168] She also admitted to using Quaaludes, because of sleeping problems and on the night before her D&C in 1973[169] and of bringing Nembutal and

Seconal to the hospital for pain from the bleeding and as a sedative the night before her hysterectomy.[170]

Stress, anxiety, and emotional trauma, Dr. Roshan told the jury, were known to cause abnormal bleeding.[171] Dr. Connell agreed that stress could effect irregular bleeding and that Anne MacMurdo's life in the five years prior to her hysterectomy was defined by stressful activities, which could have contributed to her dysfunctional bleeding.[172] She and Dr. Roshan also agreed that Anne MacMurdo's prescription drug use at the time she was taking Depo-Provera and even the night before her hysterectomy would not have caused her bleeding.[173]

What about illegal drug use, such as marijuana? Dr. Roshan told the jury that the drug might have had an effect on menstrual bleeding.[174] Dr. Connell agreed and then added that human clinical data suggests that marijuana "actually interferes with reproduction."[175] On cross examination, her testimony led to the following colloquy with Michael Ericksen.

> Q. Does the data rise to the level to where it would allow the jury to conclude, if she's using marijuana during this period of time that was causing her bleeding?
> A. I do not believe that's an isolated factor. No. Maybe an additive factor.
> Q. Let's assume . . . that marijuana maybe does cause bleeding, wouldn't you have to know if the patient was using marijuana for sure in order to render a scientific opinion to the jury?
> A. We have no data in this case that would warrant anybody making any kind of judgment. . . . If you are asking me are there data to support the position that marijuana caused her [menstrual] abnormality, the answer is no.[176]

David Covey had engaged in a detailed examination of Anne MacMurdo's menstrual history, stressful life, and use of prescription and illegal drugs, but he had found it difficult to establish that they had caused her heavy and prolonged menstrual bleeding that had been terminated by hysterectomy. To explain why she had a hysterectomy, other than her use of Depo-Provera, he turned to a final element in his story of her personal life: the stillbirth of her acephalic child in 1970.

After the stillbirth, she went to a genetic clinic for counseling and was told that the stillbirth was caused by a genetic abnormality and that she had a one in twenty chance that it would happen again."[177] Ten days later, she attempted suicide.[178] As David Covey told her story, she decided not take that chance again. When she went to see Dr. Levy in May 1974, his office visit notes stated that he prescribed Depo-Provera, because "she didn't want to become pregnant."[179] In August 1974, she told Dr. Shapiro that she wanted an abortion if she were pregnant.[180] When she saw Dr. Levy in January 1975, he confirmed in his April 18, 1975, letter to Dr. Shapiro, that "she still wanted to have sterilization [so] we elected to do a hysterectomy."[181] Finally, as Anne MacMurdo admitted on cross examination, she did not consult another physician for a second medical opinion, but made a "snap decision" to have a hysterectomy and then knowingly signed a voluntary sterilization consent form.[182]

A second theme in David Covey's defense of Upjohn was Depo-Provera's 1974 package insert. The FDA-approved package insert clearly warned Drs. Levy and Shapiro that the drug's "use for contraception is investigational since there are unresolved questions relating to its safety for this indication. Therefore, this is not an approved use for this indication."[183] Under its "Adverse Reactions" heading, her physicians were alerted that use of the drug could produce "breakthrough bleeding, spotting, and change in menstrual flow."[184] Drs. Levy and Shapiro both testified that they were aware that the drug's package insert contained the warning and adverse reactions.[185] Granted the package insert did not quantify the bleeding, but Dr. Shapiro knew that prolonged bleeding was a possible, if rare side effect.[186] But Dr. Elizabeth Connell had no doubt: the package insert warnings were adequate to advise Anne MacMurdo's physicians about the drug's unapproved contraceptive use and its adverse effects, including bleeding.[187]

Since Upjohn had taken reasonable care to warn Anne MacMurdo's physicians about Depo-Provera's contraceptive use, David Covey turned to the third theme in his defense: Drs. Levy and Shapiro had disregarded the warnings in the drug's package insert in prescribing the drug for Anne MacMurdo and had instead been guided by their professional knowledge of its unapproved use. Dr. Levy testified that he had used Depo-Provera for contraception during his residency and at the Ochsner Clinic;[188] and Dr. Shapiro was aware that "there were family planning centers that were using Depo-Provera as a routine."[189] On cross examination, David Covey elicited from Dr. Roshan her opinion that this unapproved use of Depo-Provera was malpractice and a deviation from the "standard and accepted practice of the American College of Gynecologists and Obstetricians to prescribe Depo-Provera as a contraceptive."[190]

Drs. Levy and Shapiro, having disregarded Depo-Provera's package insert warnings, did not use the 150 milligram dose tested by Schwallie and Assenzo and specified by Upjohn in its New Drug Approval application as the amount to be used every three months for contraception. They chose instead a 250 milligram dose, because, as Dr. Shapiro acknowledged, it was the dosage "being recommended for contraceptive use . . . by most of the clinics."[191] Although he had read the Schwallie and Assenzo article, neither he nor Dr. Levy seemed to be aware that, as Drs. Benjamin and Roshan testified, a 250 milligram injection was 67 percent higher than the 150 milligram dose and that its contraceptive effect could last for at least five months.[192]

Anne MacMurdo's physicians also failed to provide her with the medical information necessary for her to give her knowing consent to Depo-Provera's use. They did not discuss the package insert with her, nor did they tell her that the drug was not FDA-approved for contraception and that its side effects could include prolonged bleeding.[193] Dr. Levy testified that, as a general rule, he did not discuss the package insert with patients;[194] and in Anne MacMurdo's case, he told her that the drug would have the opposite effect: it would result in the absence of bleeding.[195] Still, Dr. Levy's failure to provide her with any meaningful information about Depo-Provera could account for her believing that she was pregnant when she visited Dr. Shapiro and requested an abortion. Dr. Shapiro did not discuss the drug's side effects with Anne MacMurdo, but, as he testified, he had left that task to a counselor who, he further testified, had probably not informed her of the drug's side effects.[196]

When Anne MacMurdo returned to Dr. Levy on January 7, 1975, complaining of heavy and prolonged menstrual bleeding and dysmenorrhea from her second 250 milligram injection, his patient records stated that she requested sterilization and that he agreed to her request even though her complaint did not indicate a need for a hysterectomy.[197] In fact, Dr. Levy knew of other medical and surgical procedures, including hormone therapy and a D&C, to stop her menstrual bleeding, but he did not inform her of these options.[198] Dr. Roshan testified that his decision was "a deviation from accepted medical practice,"[199] and Dr. Shapiro, who agreed with Dr. Roshan that less drastic procedures were available to control bleeding, was much more explicit in criticizing Dr. Levy: "You can always sink a rowboat with a torpedo."[200]

In sum, David Covey presented evidence that Upjohn had fulfilled its duty to warn Drs. Levy and Shapiro by means of Depo-Provera's package insert that the drug was not approved for contraceptive use and that its use could cause bleeding problems. Upjohn was not responsible for Anne MacMurdo's use of Depo-Provera, her bleeding, and her hysterectomy; she and her physicians were. In risk management terms, Upjohn had assessed Depo-Provera's risks and found the drug unacceptable for contraceptive use. Drs. Levy and Shapiro had disregarded the drug's package insert and, without her informed consent, conducted their own risk assessment based on their professional knowledge of its unapproved contraceptive use and found that the risk was acceptable for her, because she had been unable to tolerate other contraceptive methods. Then Dr. Levy and Anne MacMurdo made a risk management decision to terminate her bleeding, not by a D&C, nor by allowing the drug to wear off, but with a hysterectomy.

Charge Conference

After the close of Anne MacMurdo's and Upjohn's cases, Judge Burnstein met with Michael Ericksen and David Covey to draw up the jury instructions: the law that the jury would follow to decide the case. She began by identifying the two legal issues for the jury to decide: whether Upjohn was negligent in marketing Depo-Provera and whether the company was negligent in failing to properly warn Anne MacMurdo's physicians.[201]

Although there was considerable discussion of these issues, Judge Burnstein's decision on a contributory negligence instruction was particularly significant. At first, she did not think there was a basis for Anne MacMurdo being contributorily negligent. It was only a question of whether or not Upjohn was negligent for its failure to warn.[202] After some discussion, she raised the issue of recreational drug use and referred to Dr. Connell's testimony that marijuana use could have contributed to Anne MacMurdo's bleeding.[203] Michael Ericksen disagreed and moved for a directed verdict, because there had been no testimony by any expert that marijuana use contributed to her bleeding problem while she was taking Depo-Provera.[204] Judge Burnstein denied his motion. Still he realized that her ruling "gave the jury the ability to compromise by giving a liability verdict to the plaintiff. Without the contributory negligence, the only option for those who were against her, would have been to hold out for a defense verdict."[205]

Closing Arguments

After hearing five days of evidence, the jury turned its attention to Michael Ericksen's and David Covey's closing arguments. Their task was to summarize the evidence for the jury by weaving it into a believable story, one that meshed with their theories of the case and asked the jury to make a decision about who had failed to manage Depo-Provera's contraceptive drug risk: Upjohn or Anne MacMurdo.

Michael Ericksen told the jury that the judge would give them negligence instructions and these would be the legal standard for them to apply in deciding the case.[206] Upjohn, he told the jury, had acted negligently in marketing Depo-Provera. The jury had heard evidence that Depo-Provera's unapproved use was a "national scandal," but that Upjohn had not acted as a reasonable drug company and controlled the drug's contraceptive use.[207] The jury had also heard evidence that physicians rely on the information provided by drug companies, but that Upjohn had also been negligent in failing to warn Anne MacMurdo's physicians, because Depo-Provera's package insert did not use language about bleeding that was strong enough to effectively deter her physicians from using the drug for contraception. "Why," he asked, "didn't Upjohn get serious about this? The answer is clear. . . . They were trying to get the FDA to approve this drug for contraception."[208] Anne MacMurdo's bleeding was not, as the evidence had shown, caused by her prescription and illicit drug use, as the defense counsel would have them believe. "The real reason for putting that stuff in is hoping that someone [on the jury] will not like the idea of marijuana and not listen to the rest of the evidence."[209] In closing, he would not, as is customary, suggest to the jury an amount of reasonable compensation. They had to decide the amount, but he did impress upon them that "no amount of money" would compensate Anne MacMurdo for her loss: she will never have the experience of having children.[210]

David Covey told the jury that the evidence did not support a verdict finding Upjohn negligent in marketing and labeling Depo-Provera. Upjohn had acted as a reasonably careful drug company by not permitting its sales personnel to discuss with physicians Depo-Provera's unapproved contraceptive use and by not selling the drug to family planning clinics and physicians for contraceptive use. The evidence clearly established that Drs. Levy and Shapiro had taken the initiative, without Upjohn's knowledge, to acquire the drug from their hospital pharmacies.[211] The evidence had also established that Upjohn had acted as a reasonably careful drug company in labeling Depo-Provera. The physicians knew from the drug's package insert that the drug was not recommended for contraception. All of the conflicting testimony over the labeling was "quibbling over words."[212] Clearly, Upjohn was not negligent in failing to warn the physicians because of its choice of words. In sum, there was a complete failure to prove that Upjohn's marketing and labeling of Depo-Provera were the legal causes of Anne MacMurdo's injuries.

What were the legal causes of her injuries? David Covey argued that the evidence established that Anne MacMurdo's and her physicians' decisions were the legal cause of her bleeding and hysterectomy, not Upjohn. The jury had heard evidence of her health problems, drug abuse, irregular menstrual periods, stillborn child, and suicide attempts, and her request for a hysterectomy, because "she did not want to have any more children."[213] The evidence also established that Drs. Levy and Shapiro had been warned that Depo-Provera could cause bleeding, but injected her with the drug anyway. Finally, the evidence established that Dr. Levy could have done a D&C instead of a hysterectomy if Depo-Provera had caused her bleeding.[214] Their verdict should not be influenced by sympathy for Anne MacMurdo. Justice required that they "weigh the evidence fairly and without sympathy, prejudice or bias."[215] The evidence, he concluded, was overwhelming: Upjohn was not negligent in marketing and failing to warn about Depo-Provera risks.

Michael Ericksen in his rebuttal argument agreed with David Covey that "Upjohn was not looking to make money" from the sale of Depo-Provera.[216] In 1974, the drug had produced only $2 million in sales. Upjohn's desire for FDA approval, he repeated, explained the company's negligent marketing of the drug.[217] Upjohn had created a program to monitor Depo-Provera's unapproved use because the "national scandal" threatened the drug's FDA approval, but the company's leadership was negligent in not executing the program, because it did not want to jeopardize FDA approval by alerting physicians to the drug's short-term side effects, including prolonged menstrual bleeding.

Upjohn was also negligent, because Depo-Provera's package insert failed to warn physicians about the bleeding problems by not including the evidence that the drug "causes excessive bleeding in 25 to 35 percent of patients."[218] Anne MacMurdo's hysterectomy did not cause her bleeding: "nobody says that."[219] Legal causation "require[s] you to find . . . that . . . Depo-Provera caused the bleeding leading to the hysterectomy . . . [and that] is enough legal causation."[220] Finally, he rebutted the contributory negligence claim by reminding the jury that "Anne Mac-Murdo had followed the recommendations of her physicians. She had a side effect which neither she nor her doctors perceived to be caused by that drug. . . . She didn't do anything wrong."[221]

In sum, the jury had not heard all the evidence, but only the evidence that fit each attorney's theory of the case, that was relevant to the legal issues as defined by the pretrial conference, and that was admissible during the trial as determined by the rules of evidence, the objections of the attorneys, and the rulings of the court. Still, Michael Ericksen had been able to politicize the trial by making the jury aware of the failure of Upjohn's marketing program to control the "national scandal" of Depo-Provera's unapproved contraceptive use and its failure to include more detailed evidence of menstrual bleeding in the drug's package insert, which could be explained by Upjohn's interest in the drug's FDA approval. David Covey had been able to personalize the trial by making the jury aware of Anne MacMurdo's use of birth control pills, two IUDs, and Depo-Provera, her use of illegal drugs and prescription medications for stress, sleeplessness, and suicide attempts, and her consent to a hysterectomy, because of her fear of having another stillborn acephalic child.

Jury Charge and Verdict

Once Michael Ericksen and David Covey completed their closing arguments, Judge Burnstein instructed the jury on the law of the case. It was their duty "to decide the disputed issues of fact and to apply the law to the facts."[222] She then identified the legal issues: whether Upjohn's negligent marketing and negligent failure to warn were the legal causes of Anne MacMurdo's loss and, if a preponderance of the evidence (51 percent) did not support her claims, whether she was negligent and, if she were, was it a "contributing legal cause to her injury."[223] Finally, "if the greater weight of the evidence shows that both . . . were negligent . . . you should determine the percentage . . . that is chargeable to each."[224] In risk management terms, her instructions required the jury to use the evidence to assess Depo-Provera's health risk and negligence law to determine whether it was an acceptable risk for Anne MacMurdo to bear.

At the conclusion of the five-day trial, how did the six-person jury decide the case? During its six-hour deliberation, the jury, like the two attorneys, created its theory of the case, a jointly-authored story "based on the evidence" and "then matche[d] . . . it against the jury instructions to provide a number of possible legal outcomes."[225] The jury's verdict for Upjohn on the issue of negligent marketing of Depo-Provera revealed that it was not persuaded by Michael Ericksen's story. On the issue of failure to warn, his story and David Covey's were almost evenly matched. By a mere preponderance of the evidence (51 percent), the jury found that Upjohn had negligently failed to provide adequate warnings in Depo-Provera's package insert, but that Anne MacMurdo had been 49 percent contributorily negligent.[226] The jury then assessed her total damages at $370,000,[227] a sum Judge Burnstein reduced by 49 percent in her final judgment of December 17, 1986, awarding Anne MacMurdo $188,700.[228]

As risk managers, the jury had used the evidence presented at trial to assess the drug's risk and its acceptability, not for a population of women, but for one woman, and not by using scientific criteria, but legal and personal ones: the jury instructions on negligence and, as Michael Ericksen had emphasized in his closing, "your common sense."[229] Using these criteria, the jury had decided that Upjohn's Depo-Provera marketing program was an acceptable means to manage the drug's unapproved contraceptive use, but on the failure to warn issue, both Upjohn and Anne MacMurdo shared responsibility for her injuries with a mere preponderance of the evidence supporting a verdict in her favor.

How may the jury's verdict be explained? First, the jury concluded without too much difficulty that Upjohn was not negligent in marketing Depo-Provera, because the evidence had established that the company had created a monitoring program to address the drug's unapproved contraceptive use, that it had sold the drug to the University of Miami Hospital pharmacy, not to the hospital's Family Planning Clinic nor to Dr. Shapiro, and that its sales representatives did not ask Dr. Shapiro about his use of Depo-Provera for contraception, because this inquiry was forbidden by company policy and federal law. Second, the jury found only by a mere preponderance of the evidence, that Depo-Provera's package insert had failed to warn Anne MacMurdo's physicians about heavy and prolonged menstrual bleeding. Michael Ericksen suggested that the jury liked her and viewed her as "a sparrow with a broken wing."[230] Why then mitigate Upjohn's liability by holding her 49 percent contributorily negligent? The jury could have been persuaded that her two physicians, though legally untouchable, still bore some responsibility for her injuries: Drs. Levy and Shapiro disregarded the drug's package insert and failed to inform her about its risks; and Dr. Levy knew, but failed to inform her about medical and surgical alternatives to a hysterectomy. The jury could also have been convinced that her marijuana use contributed to her bleeding and her "snap decision" to have a voluntary hysterectomy without seeking a second medical opinion could be explained by her desire to be sterilized.

Court of Appeals

Upjohn appealed to the Florida Court of Appeals from the trial court's judgment on the primary issue: its negligent failure to provide adequate warnings. Anne MacMurdo cross-appealed the trial court's verdict finding her 49 percent contributorily negligent. The court heard oral argument, rendered its decision on December 21, 1988, which affirmed the trial court's judgment on liability, reversed its judgment on contributory negligence, and remanded the case with instructions to enter a judgment for Anne MacMurdo for the full amount of her damages.[231]

The court of appeals' opinion first addressed Upjohn's argument that the evidence was insufficient to establish both the drug manufacturer's alleged failure to adequately warn the medical community that Depo-

Provera might cause heavy and prolonged bleeding and the existence of a causal connection between its failure to warn and Anne MacMurdo's hysterectomy. Judge Harry Anstead, speaking for a unanimous court, took as his starting point Judge Walden's reliance in *MacMurdo II* (1983) on the legal standard announced in *Lake v. Konstantinu* (1966):[232] the sufficiency of the manufacturer's warnings to physicians was a jury issue even where there was no conflicting evidence because "'Florida is committed to the 'slightest doubt' rule."[233]

Judge Anstead agreed with Upjohn that the court of appeals' *MacMurdo II* decision on summary judgment should not control the court's examination of the trial court's denial of Upjohn's directed verdict motion on failure to warn and its decision to submit the case to the jury, because

> substantially more evidence on the issue of liability was presented at trial than existed at the time this court reviewed and reversed the summary judgment. . . . Considerable evidence presented may have supported a verdict for Upjohn, [but] there was also substantial evidence presented that the drug . . . caused MacMurdo's bleeding problems, that the warnings were insufficient to alert her physicians of this risk, and that her hysterectomy was performed to treat the bleeding condition.[234]

Judge Anstead then turned to Anne MacMurdo's claim on cross-appeal that she was entitled to a directed verdict on the issue of contributory negligence. His analysis of her claim focused on Upjohn's arguments at trial that her history of casual drug use and/or her desire to be sterilized for treatment of her bleeding condition constituted contributory negligence.

He began by disposing of the so-called marijuana defense. At oral argument, he observed, Upjohn's counsel had conceded the lack of evidence connecting her drug use to her bleeding condition. His review of the record supported that concession. Then he examined at length and disposed of Upjohn's "snap decision" theory, because "the jury could have inferred MacMurdo was negligent by opting to proceed with a hysterectomy without considering available alternatives to treat her bleeding problem."[235] Anne MacMurdo, he held, had no legal duty to question her physician's advice nor seek a second medical opinion. Applying the holdings in *Mack v. Garcia* (1984)[236] and *Norman v. Mandarin Emergency Care Center, Inc.* (1986),[237] he found that "MacMurdo was not under a legal duty to determine whether a hysterectomy was the proper treatment and even if she were under *Piper* [*v. Moore* (1982)] . . . such a request would seem to be at most a contributing cause in fact, but not a legal cause of her injury."[238]

Since Anne MacMurdo had no legal duty, Judge Anstead held that it was legal error for Judge Burnstein to have submitted the contributory negligence issue to the jury. Upjohn had argued that she had a hysterectomy, not to stop her pain and bleeding, but because she wanted to be sterilized. However, Judge Anstead's review of Dr. Levy's testimony led him to conclude: "We do not believe that there was a sufficient basis in the evidence to hold that reasonable persons could differ on whether MacMurdo voluntarily had a hysterectomy outside the context of treatment for her bleeding condition or that she had treatment alternatives available to her at the time."[239]

Florida Supreme Court

Upjohn appealed the decision to the Florida Supreme Court. The court heard oral argument and then on May 31, 1990, by a vote of four to two with one justice abstaining, overturned the court of appeals' decision on negligent failure to warn and remanded the case with instructions for the trial court to enter a judgment for Upjohn.[240] Justice Stephen Grimes, speaking for the majority, first addressed the standard that the court had recently announced in *Felix v. Hoffman-LaRouche Inc.* (1989):[241] the adequacy of a manufacturer's warning about the dangers of a drug is "in many instances a question of fact, [but] we hold that it can become a question of law where the warning is accurate, clear, and unambiguous."[242] Using *Felix*, the court then overturned not only the court of appeals decision in *MacMurdo II* (1983),[243] but also its decisions *Lake v. Konstantinu* (1966)[244] and *Ricci v. Parke Davis & Co.* (1986)[245] which, he held, had misread its decision in *Tampa Drug Co. v. Wait* (1958)[246] "'to say that the adequacy of drug warnings is invariably a jury question.'"[247]

Justice Grimes then identified "the crucial question[:] . . . whether the warnings were adequate to warn the physicians of the possibility that Depo-Provera might be causing the condition experienced by Mac-Murdo."[248] Applying the *Felix* standard to the Depo-Provera package insert warnings, he rejected Anne MacMurdo's argument that Upjohn, aware of the Schwallie and Assenzo article's findings, should have provided a more specific description of the drug's adverse reactions and "characterized the bleeding as excessive, continuous or prolonged."[249] Since the insert had warned about breakthrough bleeding, spotting, and change in menstrual flow, he concluded, Upjohn had "warned of the possibility of abnormal bleeding outside of the menstrual period."[250]

The adequacy of the drug's package insert, which was directed at physicians, not patients, had to be proven by expert testimony.[251] Justice Grimes reported Dr. Elizabeth Connell as testifying that the insert was "adequate to warn physicians of all adverse bleeding reactions."[252] Dr. David Benjamin had disagreed with her, but Justice Grimes disqualified him because he was not a physician with an MD, but a pharmacologist with a PhD,[253] and, thereby, eliminated the evidence necessary for Anne MacMurdo to carry her burden of proof on the adequacy of Depo-Provera's package insert. With Dr. Benjamin disqualified, Justice Grimes concluded that "no medical expert . . . testified that the package insert was insufficient to put a doctor on notice that the symptoms displayed by MacMurdo in January 1975 could result from the use of Depo-Provera."[254] Justice Grimes did acknowledge that Dr. Levy's testimony came close to concluding that the package insert was insufficient to warn. As he reported, the physician testified that "MacMurdo was suffering from dysfunctional bleeding which he [Dr. Levy] characterized as anything other than normal bleeding while the package insert only referred to breakthrough bleeding and to change in menstrual flow."[255] Yet Justice Grimes added that Dr. Levy also testified that "if he had had the insert in front of him when Anne MacMurdo was describing her bleeding he might have concluded that the drug was causing her problem."[256]

Justice Leander Shaw dissented; he could not agree that Depo-Provera's package insert was "accurate, clear, and unambiguous" as required by *Felix v. Hoffman-LaRouche* (1989), because the package insert omitted any warning of prolonged bleeding.[257] Upjohn knew that the drug caused prolonged bleeding, because the Schwallie and Assenzo article, written by its researchers, disclosed that 27 percent of women experienced prolonged bleeding during the first three months.[258] Yet the court had rejected "contrary and competent substantial evidence" that the package insert was inadequate.[259] Dr. Benjamin, an expert in writing package inserts, had testified that the package insert was inadequate. Dr. Levy had testified that prolonged bleeding was not listed on the insert and "that he did not consider that Depo-Provera might be causing her problem because he expected the drug to have just the opposite effect: amenorrhea."[260] After rejecting this expert witness testimony, he argued that the court had invaded the province of the jury as the finder of fact by reweighing and reevaluating the evidence and then overturning its verdict based on conflicting evidence."[261]

In sum, the Florida Supreme Court held that the expert testimony on the inadequacy of the Depo-Provera package insert was insufficient to present a jury question. As a matter of law, it held, the warnings, per *Felix*, were accurate, clear, and unambiguous; even though the package insert did not specifically warn about excessive, continuous, or prolonged bleeding, "the insert [had] warned of the possibility of abnormal bleeding outside the menstrual period."[262] This holding does not mean that Depo-Provera's package insert will always be adequate as a matter of Florida law. In Anne MacMurdo's case, however, the court held that she did not present medical evidence that the insert was inadequate to warn her physicians about her prolonged bleeding, because the court held that the adequacy or inadequacy of a drug's labeling has to be based on a physician's testimony, not a pharmacologist's.

As Michael Ericksen observed, the ultimate arbiter of a drug's labeling will be the doctor who prescribes the medication.[263] If physician testimony establishes that the warnings are adequate, this evidence will provide Upjohn and other pharmaceutical companies with two defenses: first, the treating physician is the intervening cause who cuts the chain of causation to the manufacturer;[264] and second, the learned intermediary doctrine limits a drug manufacturer's duty to informing the physician about the drug by means of the package insert. If a physician, as the learned intermediary, fails to inform a patient about a drug's risks, then the patient's only legal recourse is a medical malpractice suit.[265]

As risk managers, the Florida Supreme Court narrowed the class of experts competent to evaluate Depo-Provera's package insert to physicians who could assess the drug's risk. Since the court held that no physician had testified that the warnings in the package insert were inadequate to warn physicians about excessive and prolonged menstrual bleeding, then the judge, as a risk manager, will decide whether the drug's risk is acceptable as a matter of law. If, however, in a future case, there is conflicting medical testimony by physicians about the adequacy of the warnings, the jury, as a risk manager, will have to assess the evidence and decide whether the risk was acceptable as a matter of law.

Summary

For thirty years, Depo-Provera was widely prescribed as a contraceptive in spite of serious questions about its safety. The drug was readily available because drug risk management was fragmented. The FDA, as a drug licensing agency, had limited authority to control the drug's non-approved use, Upjohn was unable to limit the drug's sale to its approved use, and physicians were free to make a professional judgment about the drug's safety and contraceptive uses, without informing women about the drug's FDA status and the risk that it could pose to their personal health. As a consequence, women were unable to make risk management judgments and then decide whether to give their informed consent to the drug's use. Some suffered the drug's adverse health effects in silence, but others took the initiative to involve the legal system and its courts in the management of contraceptive risk by filing products liability and medical malpractice suits to address the failure of two critical linkages in the pharmaceutical risk management system: the drug's package insert and physician informed consent.

Anne MacMurdo's story is a study in judicial risk management. There is no way to claim that her case is representative because no one knows how many women suffered adverse health reactions from the use of Depo-Provera and how many women brought products liability and medical malpractice suits to recover monetary damages based on their claims of Depo-Provera-induced injuries. Still, her story provides a window on judicial risk management: how Florida's legal system and its trial and appellate courts managed one of the drug's prominent short-term side effects: menstrual bleeding.

Anne MacMurdo had initiated the process of judicial risk management, but the Florida legal system imposed restrictions on her access to its courts. The state's statute of limitations did not allow her to sue her physicians, who could have been held liable for their failure to inform her about Depo-Provera's risk and for her injuries. The legal system also permitted the defendants to use the barrier of summary judgment multiple times to keep her case out of court. She survived these motions, but had to take a voluntary dismissal in her medical malpractice case.

Once her products liability case went to trial, her story became the subject of two contrary tellings of contraceptive risk and liability. In the pretrial conference, the judge edited the tellings of her story by her attorney and Upjohn to minimize politicizing and personalizing the trial. At trial, these edited tales were told to the jury, who did not hear all the available evidence, but only the evidence that fitted each attorney's theory of the case. To tell their stories, the attorneys used witnesses and documents, but their admissibility was defined by the rules of evidence and objections for relevance and hearsay.

In assessing this evidence, the jury wrote its own story and then applied the jury instructions on the law of negligence, written by the judge and attorneys, and used its "common sense." The jury found that Upjohn's monitoring program was an acceptable means to manage the drug's unapproved contraceptive use. Then by a mere preponderance of the evidence, it found that Upjohn had failed to warn Anne MacMurdo's physicians about the extent of the drug's risk of prolonged menstrual bleeding, while it also found her contributorily negligent.

The court of appeals overturned, as error, the trial court's contributory negligence verdict. No evidence supported the verdict that Anne MacMurdo's marijuana use contributed to her bleeding, nor could she be faulted under Florida law for accepting her physician's recommendation of a hysterectomy without a second medical opinion. With contributory negligence eliminated, the court found it acceptable to hold Upjohn solely liable for its failure to warn about excessive menstrual bleeding.

While the court of appeals found it unacceptable for the jury, as a risk manager, to render a verdict on contributory negligence without evidence to support it, the Florida Supreme Court, as a risk manager, created a new rule: only physicians could testify about the adequacy of a drug's package insert. Applying the rule, the court disqualified Anne MacMurdo's expert on drug package inserts and eliminated his testimony. With no evidence questioning the adequacy of Depo-Provera's package insert warnings, the court took the issue away from the jury, as a risk manager, and gave it to the judge to decide as a matter of law.

The Florida Supreme Court's decision angered Anne MacMurdo and surprised her attorneys. After her struggle to have her case heard; to sit through a six-day trial that exposed her personal life to public controversy; and to win full compensation on appeal only to have it taken away by a state supreme court decision. *Upjohn v. MacMurdo* changed the judicial rules of risk management, without explanation and without the opportunity for her to be granted a new trial at which she could present evidence in compliance with the court's new requirement that permitted only a physician to testify about the adequacy of Depo-Provera's package insert. This was a bitter end to her quest for justice.

In sum, Depo-Provera's unapproved contraceptive use for thirty years nationwide and Anne MacMurdo's state products liability case, involving one of the drug's short-term side effects, provides a counterpoint to Judith Weisz's story in Chapter 2 of the drug's national experience with the risk of cancer. In the next chapter her story will bring an end to the drug's twenty-five year contraceptive approval controversy with its FDA approval in 1992. Thereafter, Anne MacMurdo's story will continue to be told by other women who claim that their use of the drug caused their osteoporosis.

4

Marketing Approval and Litigation

Osteoporosis and the Realities of Medical Risk

Judith Weisz's story of the politics of drug risk management now returns to the Food and Drug Administration and its authority to decide whether to grant a pharmaceutical company a license to produce and market a drug.[1] A critical period for her story occurs after a company submits its New Drug Approval (NDA) application, the FDA reviews the company-supplied evidence of the drug's safety and effectiveness, and then decides whether to approve the drug. Up to this point in her story, Depo-Provera has been the subject of public debate for twenty-five years. Now the question of the drug's safety returns to be evaluated within the confines of the FDA in terms of the risk management criteria that will structure the agency's decision. There three future Fertility and Maternal Health Advisory Committee members—Drs. Janet Daling, Nancy Lee, and Jane Zones—will speak for Dr. Weisz when they question the agency's decision to cross the risk assessment boundary and allow risk acceptability policy arguments to influence its 1992 marketing approval decision with the condition that Upjohn conduct a post-approval study of a new risk: osteoporosis.[2]

Anne MacMurdo's story will continue to provide a window on the limits of the Food and Drug Administration's risk management authority when the use of a drug is removed from the hands of the agency and placed into those of physicians, who are authorized to prescribe a drug for a medical use approved by the FDA. In Depo-Provera's post-approval world, her story is told by four women who claimed that Depo-Provera caused their osteoporosis: Jamie Lorenzi, Cassandra Colville, Adrienne Oliver, and Melanie Montagnon. Unlike Anne MacMurdo's physicians, their physicians' knowledge of the drug was based on its FDA-approved labeling for contraceptive use. Still their stories, like hers, continue to raise medical malpractice and products liability issues, and they, like she,

faced formidable legal barriers when they decided to sue Upjohn, because, they claimed, the drug's package insert was inadequate to inform
their physicians of the risk of osteoporosis.

Judith Weisz's and Anne MacMurdo's stories draw together the two
levels of risk management based on the Federal Food, Drug, and Cosmetic Act and state civil law. Whether to make the drug publically available, the first level, is the legal responsibility of the FDA. Whether the
drug should be used by a patient, the second level, is the responsibility
of drug companies and physicians and is subject to state products liability and medical malpractice law. Together the two stories ask whether
a woman can make an informed decision to use Depo-Provera for
contraception.

Changing Research and Risk Environment

Judith Weisz's story traces its origins to The Upjohn Company's submission of Depo-Provera's New Drug Approval (NDA) application
in 1967,[3] In Chapter 2, her story explored the lengthy national public
debate over the drug's approval, which was defined by concerns that the
drug could cause breast, cervical, and endometrial cancer. In 1974, the
agency proposed to grant Depo-Provera limited marketing approval,[4]
but abandoned its proposal in the face of congressional opposition.[5]
The FDA then conducted a three-year review of the scientific evidence
and in 1978 disapproved the drug for general marketing because the
animal and human studies suggested that the drug could cause breast
and uterine cancer.[6] The FDA Public Board of Inquiry, chaired by Dr.
Weisz, reviewed the scientific evidence, and its 1984 report,[7] which concluded that Upjohn's research had serious flaws, served as the basis for
the FDA's decision in 1986 to allow Upjohn to voluntarily withdraw its
Depo-Provera New Drug Approval application.[8]

Judith Weisz's story now explores Depo-Provera's changing research
and risk environment, which led to the drug's contraceptive marketing approval in 1992. The FDA's 1978 disapproval of Depo-Provera had
awakened Upjohn to the need to conduct scientifically valid controlled
clinical studies of the drug's carcinogenic potential. The following year
the World Health Organization (WHO) took the first of two initiatives
that reshaped the debate over the assessment of the drug's risk, which

had been raised by the animal studies' breast and endometrial cancer findings and the uncontrolled human clinical studies' breast, endometrial, cervical, and ovarian cancer findings. WHO's first initiated a multi-center, hospital-based, case-control study with the principal objective of determining whether oral and injectable contraceptives, including Depo-Provera, increased the risk of breast, endometrial, and cervical cancer.[9]

WHO's second initiative addressed the controversy over the use of the beagle dog and rhesus monkey to assess the drug's risk of breast and endometrial cancer in women, a controversy that dated back to 1972 and played a prominent role in the FDA's decisions in 1974, 1978, and 1986 not to approve Depo-Provera for contraception. The WHO initiative began at meetings in 1976 and 1981, which raised concerns about the appropriateness of using the two animals in studying steroid contraceptives.[10] At a 1984 International Conference on Population, WHO authorized the development of new guidelines for testing of steroidal contraceptives in animals, because research had found that the dog and monkey studies had not been useful in predicting cancer in women.[11] Then, at its February 1987 symposium on "Improving the Safety Requirements for Contraceptive Steroids," WHO adopted guidelines that eliminated the use of the seven-year dog and ten-year monkey studies.[12]

At its August 1987 meeting, the FDA's Fertility and Maternal Health Advisory Committee responded to an agency request and recommended adoption of the WHO guidelines for elimination of the dog and monkey studies.[13] The FDA adopted the recommendation "with one exception that the beagle requirement was reduced from 7 to 3 years pending the completion of the WHO [clinical] studies on the association of Depo-Provera and breast cancer."[14] Now that the FDA had all but laid the "great beagle controversy" to rest,[15] the question was: Would the clinical studies provide the scientific evidence to dispel concerns about breast, cervical, and endometrial cancer?

The WHO study found that Depo-Provera had a protective effect against endometrial cancer, a minimal risk of cervical cancer and, did not substantially increase the overall risk of breast cancer.[16] Women under thirty-five years of age did, however, have an increased breast cancer risk, but the risk was not associated with the duration of contraceptive use.[17] Two Thailand studies found that low birth rate and infant mortality increased significantly the closer that conception occurred to an injection of the drug.[18] Finally, a New Zealand study, sponsored by the Auckland Hospital Department of Medicine, provided evidence for a new concern not previously part of the Depo-Provera debate: Were women who used the drug at risk of developing osteoporosis?[19] The results indicated the drug could lower the bone density of women, and those whose bone density was already lower than normal were at an added risk.

The final results of the cancer, osteoporosis, and fetal exposure studies appeared in major medical journals in 1991 and 1992: the breast cancer results in the *Lancet*, the endometrial cancer results in the *International Journal of Cancer*, the cervical cancer results in *Contraception*, the in utero cancer results in the *American Journal of Epidemiology*, and the osteoporosis results in the *British Medical Journal*.[20] After the WHO breast cancer findings were published in the *Lancet*, the FDA decided that the beagle dog was no longer a relevant model for the prediction of breast cancer in testing hormonal contraceptives and completely removed it as a requirement for the approval of Depo-Provera.[21]

1992 General Marketing Approval

Upjohn had already taken the initiative to submit a New Drug Approval application for Depo-Provera before these studies were in print. In December 1990, the company had formally requested a meeting with the FDA to discuss the requirements for an NDA.[22] At a November 12, 1991, meeting, the company and the agency explored the issues to be addressed in terms of the new clinical information, the proposed labeling, and a timetable for the submission of the NDA.[23] Thereafter, the application process proceeded swiftly. On April 29, 1992, Upjohn submitted NDA 20–246, which included the company's new research.[24] Within six months, the FDA obtained a favorable recommendation from its Fertility and Maternal Health Advisory Committee, negotiated with Upjohn over Depo-Provera's labeling, and approved the drug for general marketing as a contraceptive.

Advisory Committee Meeting

On May 14, 1992, Upjohn provided the FDA with an "Advisory Committee Brochure on Depo-Provera," a 117-page document that contained background information, summarized the technical, efficacy, and safety data, and concluded with a benefit to risk assessment.[25] On June 19, the Fertility and Maternal Health Advisory Committee met for one day to decide whether to recommend Depo-Provera's approval for contraceptive use.

The FDA did not intend for its advisory committee to serve as a forum for a thorough assessment of Depo-Provera's risk and to make an informed risk management recommendation.[26] From the outset, it was clear that the FDA intended to acquire only an endorsement of Depo-Provera from the advisory committee, because the agency limited the committee's public session to one hour and each of the fifteen speakers to four minutes, heard presentations only from FDA officials and Upjohn personnel, and concluded the meeting with a question session involving committee members and Upjohn personnel.[27]

Public Session

The public session, in spite of its brevity, did expose the major fault lines that had defined the twenty-five year controversy over Depo-Provera's approval. Like the Public Board of Inquiry and previous advisory committee and congressional hearings, the committee assessed the drug's carcinogenic risk and the acceptability of its use in order to increase contraceptive choice and serve the needs of special populations of women, but it gave little attention to short-term adverse side effects, including irregular menstrual bleeding, depression, and weight gain. Unlike prior public hearings, the advisory committee session was deeply influenced by the FDA's December 1990 approval of Norplant, a five year synthetic progesterone-based implant,[28] and was notable for its acknowledgement of Depo-Provera's possible link to osteoporosis.

The public session was heavily weighted in favor of speakers representing medical, family planning, and population control organizations. Representatives from the American Medical Association, the American College of Obstetricians and Gynecologists, the Alan Guttmacher

Institute, the International Planned Parenthood Federation, and the Population Crisis Committee all supported Depo-Provera's approval. Norplant's approval allowed them to argue that the FDA should approve the three-month injectable, because it had already assessed and accepted the risks of an even longer term progestogen contraceptive when it approved the five year implant. [29] In their limited time, the advocates of approval gave only passing attention to the World Health Organization research and other recent studies, but acknowledged that any risk of breast cancer and osteoporosis from Depo-Provera's use should be addressed by conducting further studies following the drug's approval.[30]

Depo-Provera's lengthy clinical experience and record of safety and effectiveness led the advocates of approval to conclude that any risks revealed by the recent research were acceptable. Depo-Provera was needed not only to increase contraceptive choice for women who found daily use of other contraceptives difficult to manage, who disliked or were unable to use other methods, who wanted a contraceptive unconnected to intercourse, and who had mental or physical disabilities.[31] Depo-Provera would also be less costly and easier to administer and involve a shorter delay in return to fertility and childbearing than Norplant, because it was a three-month injectable and not a five-year implant that required surgery.[32] Finally, they argued that monitoring Depo-Provera's use, counseling women, and assuring their informed choice with patient educational materials would minimize any risk to them.[33]

The National Women's Health Network, the National Black Women's Health Project, the National Latina Health Organization, and the Women's Economic Survival Summit were the only four organizations that opposed approval, because Depo-Provera's risk assessment had not changed. Recent controlled case studies confirmed that women using the drug experienced a loss of bone density and were at a statistically significant increased in risk of breast and cervical cancer. The breast cancer findings were troublesome for two reasons: they revealed an increased risk for young women[34] and they underestimated the risk to American women, becuase they were based on studies conducted in countries in which "breast cancer rates were far less than one half of the United States."[35] Cervical cancer results were also troublesome, because "African-American women are 2.5 times more likely to develop cervical cancer than white women."[36] Finally, they replied to Upjohn's dismissal of the bone density findings, because the New Zealand study was not well designed, with a question: "Well, why hasn't Upjohn done a better study?"[37]

The four women's health organizations viewed Depo-Provera not as a safe method for women to control their fertility, but as a contraceptive developed as a provider-dependent tool to control the reproductive lives of women. The drug had already been abused during the Grady Clinic study[38] and by the Indian Health Service, which used it for "custodial convenience" in managing mentally challenged Native American women.[39] For them, Norplant's coercive use provided a window into how Depo-Provera would be used to target young, poor, institutionalized, and imprisoned women.[40] Given the low literacy rates of these women, it was questionable whether they could give their informed consent any more than the women who participated in the Grady Clinic study.[41] With the great uncertainty surrounding Depo-Provera's assessment and potential for abuse, more testing was needed before approval, but if the drug were approved, it needed to be accompanied by mandates requiring "a registry of users. . . . [and] thorough informed consent."[42]

FDA and Upjohn Presentations

After the close of the one-hour open public session, the advisory committee listened to Dr. Ridgely Bennett, the FDA's Chief Medical Officer responsible for Depo-Provera, provide a historical overview of the drug, which included a summary of the most recent research: the WHO cancer studies, the New Zealand osteoporosis study, and the Thailand study of the drug's effect on the fetus and infants.[43] Now that Upjohn had submitted its new NDA, based on this research, he identified two options for the agency. The FDA "may either continue to support the decision of the Public Board of Inquiry or may decide the issue differently."[44] But first the agency asked its advisory committee for a risk management approval recommendation. Knowing that the FDA and Upjohn would develop the labeling "to identify any subgroups . . . that may be at increased risk," he framed the request for a recommendation as a question: "Should we or could we now blow away the cloud of controversy that has engulfed this drug?"[45]

Dr. Solomon Sobel, the Director of the FDA's Division of Metabolism and Endocrine Drug Products, objected to Dr. Bennett's options. In his view the FDA had a responsibility to make a decision consistent with the Public Board of Inquiry's risk assessment standards: The committee's task was to determine whether "these further studies meet the level of evidence for safety that the Public Board of Inquiry was seeking."[46] Dr. Philip Corfman, the FDA's Supervisory Medical Officer for Fertility and Maternal Health Drugs, also objected to Dr. Bennett's question. "We just received the NDA very recently, six weeks ago, so it is really too early for us to have a technical response to your question."[47] Why Dr. Corfman then concluded that "it is still appropriate for us to bring the issue to the Committee at this time" is baffling, because his initial statement revealed that the agency was not in a position to critique Upjohn's presentation and the advisory committee was not in a position to make a fully informed risk assessment and provide the agency with a risk management recommendation.[48]

After Dr. Bennett's remarks, the advisory committee listened to Upjohn's presentation, which was designed to address the safety issues that were the focus of the WHO cancer studies, the New Zealand osteoporosis study, and the Thailand study of the drug's effect on the fetus and infants. Dr. David Thomas, who coordinated the WHO studies, reported the principal findings on breast, cervical, endometrial, liver, and ovarian cancer. The WHO studies, he informed the committee, found no "causal relationship between DMPA and ovarian cancer."[49] Invasive cervical cancer's 10 percent increased risk, which was not statistically significant, had "no consistent trend of increasing risk with the duration of its use,"[50] but it was less than the 30 percent increased risk for oral contraceptives, which was statistically significant.[51] At the same time, Depo-Provera exerted an 80 percent "protective effect" on endometrial cancer, which was similar to the effect of oral contraceptives, and "appeared to persist for at least eight years"[52]

When Dr. Thomas turned to the WHO breast cancer study, he candidly informed the committee that he and his colleagues had "agonized a long time over the results," and then he provided his interpretation.[53] Women who had used Depo-Provera had a 20 percent increased risk of breast cancer; if, however, they were under thirty-five years of age, the risk rose to 40 percent and changed only minimally throughout the duration of the drug's use.[54] The highest increased risk, 119 percent, existed for premenopausal women who received a single injection although the risk declined to 45 percent with increasing use.[55] Dr. Thomas admitted that the currently available data were insufficient to explain the 119 percent increased risk. His own view was that Depo-Provera might be a "weak promoter," but it was more likely that the drug stimulated preexisting tumors, rather than promoting breast cancer, because its risk was greatest after the first injection and did not increase with longer use of the drug.[56]

When Dr. Thomas compared the WHO studies' Depo-Provera breast cancer results to oral contraceptive use in both the WHO's and Upjohn's New Zealand studies, he found comparable results.[57] In his review of sixteen studies of long-term use by young women, he found a 40 percent increased risk from oral contraceptives as compared to an increased risk of 45 percent from Depo-Provera.[58] In sum, the WHO study's principal breast cancer findings, along with those for endometrial and cervical cancer, led him to conclude that the "risks of cancer associated with using DMPA are low and no greater than cancer risks associated with the use of oral contraceptives."[59]

Questions from the advisory committee followed. Dr. Jane Zones, a future advisory committee member and currently Vice Chair of the National Women's Health Network, asked about an issue that had been raised in the open public session: How applicable were the low DMPA breast cancer risks in Thailand to the United States?[60] Dr. Thomas admitted that their domestic applicability was "a tricky one," but argued that results from the New Zealand study, "a relatively high risk country, . . . were remarkably consistent and comparable."[61] Since the committee had to make a risk-benefits recommendation, Dr. Zones also wanted to know what he considered to be "an acceptable increased risk of breast cancer" for American women.[62] Dr. Thomas returned to his WHO study conclusions and provided her with a comparative risk perspective to justify Depo-Provera approval: The injectable's "risks appear to be no greater than for [FDA-approved] oral contraceptives."[63]

The New Zealand osteoporosis study also raised risk assessment concerns. Dr. Tim Cundy, a University of Auckland medical researcher, explained to the advisory committee the primary finding of his study on Depo-Provera and osteoporosis, which had been published in the *British Medical Journal*: Premenopausal women were at a statistically significant increased risk of osteoporosis. The bone density in women twenty-five to fifty years of age who took Depo-Provera for five years, compared to the premenopausal control group, was 6.5 percent lower in the femoral neck (the region below the ball and socket hip joint) and 7.5 percent lower in the lumbar spine.[64] Bone loss tended to occur during early use and did not increase with continued use, but he acknowledged that the study included "women who had used DMPA for only a minimum of 5 years."[65]

Dr. Cundy also informed the advisory committee about the results of an as yet unpublished study of the effect on bone loss after discontinuing Depo-Provera, which found "no change at the femoral neck, but a significant increase in bone density at the lumbar spine."[66] Still, he argued, this did not alter the New Zealand study's risk assessment: "Long-term DMPA use was associated with significant reductions in mineral density of the lumbar spine and femoral neck which appear to correlate with the duration of DMPA use."[67] Use of Depo-Provera, as he concluded in his *British Medical Journal* article, "should therefore be considered a risk factor for osteoporosis."[68]

The final research issue was the effect of Depo-Provera on a fetus or infant of women who had been taking the drug while pregnant or post-partum while they were nursing. Dr. Ronald Gray addressed studies of low birth weight and of neonatal and infant mortality conducted in Thailand and published in the *American Journal of Epidemiology* with Dr. Tieng Pardthaisong. Their study of low birth weight from in utero exposure to Depo-Provera, due to an accidental pregnancy, reported a 90 percent increased risk when conception occurred within four weeks after an injection, a 50 percent increased risk for five to eight weeks, and a 20 percent increased risk beyond nine weeks.[69] Their study of neonatal and infant deaths due to accidental pregnancies reported an 80 percent increased risk of neonatal deaths and a 100 percent increased risk of infant deaths.[70] In fact, neonatal deaths increased to 150 percent when conception occurred within four weeks after injection.[71]

In his advisory committee presentation, Dr. Gray acknowledged "a two-fold increase in low birth weight . . . within the first 4 weeks after a Depo injection," but then he characterized the risk of mortality as "marginally increased" with both of these risks diminishing as the two studies had reported, with the increase of the interval between an injection and conception.[72] Still, these accidental pregnancies that led to low birth weight and death occurred in less than 1 percent of pregnancies and, he said, "constitute a small increased risk . . . which does not constitute an important problem with this drug"[73] and could be avoided by giving "the first injection of DMPA . . . within 5 days of the onset of the last regular menstrual period."[74]

After presenting the research studies on breast cancer, osteoporosis, and infant low birth weight and mortality, the Upjohn presentation closed with two brief clinical perspectives on the risk acceptability of the drug based on its unapproved domestic clinical use[75] and the contraceptive needs of young sexually active American women.[76] Then Dr. Bruce Stadel, Chief of the FDA's Epidemiology Branch, promised that his remarks would be "as swift as lightning," and in ten minutes, he stated that Depo-Provera breast cancer risk "fits the same pattern" as that of oral contraceptives[77] and that further studies of osteoporosis "would be desirable,"[78] but, otherwise he provided evidence for the view that FDA would offer no meaningful critique of Upjohn's clinical evidence of the drug's safety.

Committee Discussion and Recommendations

At the conclusion of Dr. Stadel's remarks, Dr. Susan McKay, an advisory committee member, expressed her displeasure with his brief remarks and with the narrow character of the hearing, which had addressed only the "physical outcomes," but not the "behavioral/ psychological parameters," including loss of libido and depression, which had been addressed in the public session. Were these of no importance, she asked? "You have not spoken about it. Upjohn did not speak about it; the clinicians did not speak about it."[79] Dr. Stadel quickly brushed aside her questions, saying "I have not studied those issues."[80]

The current advisory committee members, except Dr. Susan McKay, asked few critical questions about the research. By contrast, the future but currently non-voting members, who would replace several current members the following month, including Dr. Janet Daling, Dr. Nancy Lee, and Dr. Jane Zones, were critical of the FDA and Upjohn's presentations of the scientific evidence supporting approval.

When Dr. Barbara Hulka, the advisory committee chair, asked the committee for its evaluation of the research "findings on the possible effect of DMPA on osteoporosis and infant birth weight,"[81] Dr. Janet Daling raised the breast cancer issue. Would the committee have the option of approving Depo-Provera for women older than thirty-five, because the research had suggested that younger women were at increased risk of breast cancer?[82] Her question was disregarded, but not forgotten.

Dr. Nancy Lee returned to the breast cancer issue when she asked about the criteria for approval. Was the advisory committee to use the standard that Dr. Solomon Sobel had announced following Dr. Ridgely Bennett's presentation: whether the current research should meet "the level of evidence for safety that the Public Board of Inquiry was seeking?"[83] Dr. Sobel, abandoning his prior standard, informed her that the statutory basis for the approval of new drugs was "the presence of adequate and well-controlled studies that support the safety and efficacy of the drug."[84] Then he provided a narrow reading of the public board's report, when he said that its "centerpiece" was "an increased risk of breast cancer."[85] Since then, he added, the FDA had decided not to require the beagle and monkey studies "because we felt that . . . they were no longer predictive of risk" and that the WHO studies did not support an "appreciable risk" of breast cancer.[86] Now, he concluded, the committee's task was "to make an independent judgment on the WHO findings" and address "the osteoporosis risk and also the effect of inadvertent pregnancy on infant outcome[s]."[87]

Dr. Jane Zones deplored the committee's "rush to approval"[88] because of its lack of concern with the breast cancer risk of young women. She cited Dr. Samuel Shapiro's testimony during the public hearing, which emphasized that "the long-term use of Depo-Provera had not been adequately evaluated in any of the [recent] studies," and then concluded with a strong recommendation for long-term studies.[89] After Dr. Jennifer Niebyl, a current member, replied that any breast cancer concerns were a risk-benefit issue and other committee members expressed their confidence in Depo-Provera on the basis of its lengthy domestic and international use, the committee proceeded to unanimously approve the drug for contraception.[90]

Dr. Hulka then asked the advisory committee to address the labeling issue: What labeling did the committee recommend for infant birth weight and osteoporosis?[91] At this point, Dr. Nancy Lee asked whether the labeling would identify the breast cancer risk, but her brief discussion with Dr. Philip Corfman, the FDA Supervising Medical Officer, and Dr. Hulka revealed the narrow scope of the committee's task.

> DR. LEE: Do you all want us to talk about things that might go into the labeling right now? Because I would think we would want to also then discuss certainly the cancer issue.
>
> DR. CORFMAN: No.
>
> DR. LEE: No?
>
> DR. HULKA: Apparently what we are asked to speak about is infant birth weight and osteoporosis.
>
> DR. LEE: And what is the purpose of our discussion for that?
>
> DR. CORFMAN: What you might recommend for the labeling.
>
> DR. LEE: Then why would we not want to also discuss the cancer question for that?
>
> DR. CORFMAN: Because we have already decided about that?
>
> DR. LEE: We have?
>
> DR. CORFMAN: Well, the fact that we dropped the beagle requirement.
>
> DR. LEE: Okay.[92]

This colloquy ended any advisory committee consideration of the WHO and New Zealand breast cancer studies, nor would the committee consider the infant mortality research findings. When Committee member Dr. Ezra Davidson asked about labeling for infant mortality, Dr. Hulka replied that the committee's labeling recommendation would involve only low birth weight.[93]

The advisory committee then briefly discussed Dr. Ronald Gray's research on low infant birth weight,[94] and not "totally convinced of the validity of the data on . . . weight differences or effects of DMPA,"[95] recommended that the labeling be "very clear about the timing of the injection during the menstrual cycle so that no pregnant woman gets DMPA" and that the FDA "take opportunities to study the issue of infant birth rate in relation to DMPA."[96] Finally, the committee discussed the risk of osteoporosis even more briefly, and then recommended that the labeling include information on this risk and that the FDA conduct Phase IV post-approval studies to address the risk.[97]

In sum, the FDA Fertility and Maternal Health Advisory Committee's one-day meeting did not serve as forum for a thorough assessment of Depo-Provera's risk and an informed risk management recommendation. The FDA did not ask its advisory committee to assess any of the major short-term side effects of Depo-Provera use, including irregular menstrual bleeding, weight gain, and depression.[98] These risks had never seriously concerned the agency.[99] Cancer had been the risk that had dominated the agency's assessment of Depo-Provera's risk for over twenty years.[100] Still, the FDA did not ask its advisory committee to review the research on Depo-Provera's risk of breast, cervical, or endometrial cancer.[101] The agency had already eliminated the beagle studies when it received the WHO breast cancer study results and then made its approval and labeling decisions on all of the drug's carcinogenic risks solely on the basis of the WHO and New Zealand studies.[102] Then the FDA limited its advisory committee's task to making an approval recommendation based only on its assessment of the osteoporosis and low birth weight research and restricted its labeling recommendations to these two risks. All other labeling information, including the risks of breast and cervical cancer, had been decided by the FDA staff.[103]

FDA Marketing Approval

In the months following the Fertility and Maternal Drugs Advisory Committee meeting, events continued to move swiftly. On October 17, 1992, Upjohn submitted its draft labeling, which included physician prescribing information, patient labeling, and a patient brochure. Ten days later, Dr. Ridgely Bennett, the FDA Chief Medical Officer responsible for Depo-Provera, submitted his report, which adopted largely verbatim Upjohn's "FDA Advisory Committee Depo-Provera Brochure."[104] His report reviewed the drug's scientific studies and agency actions for the past thirty years. Then it described the findings of the new studies, including the breast and cervical cancer and the menstrual bleeding studies[105] that Upjohn had submitted with its April 29, 1992 NDA along with relevant earlier studies, but his evaluation of the drug's risks was limited to risks of breast cancer and osteoporosis.[106]

The WHO breast cancer study, he found, provided "the best available evidence"[107] that "the risks are well defined" and that "no additional data are necessary."[108] The Cundy study of bone mineral density loss had, however, become the subject of scientific criticism for "the inadequate matching of DMPA and control subjects on relevant risk factors; . . . the lack of bone density measurements in subjects before DMPA was begun; . . . and the potential for selection bias, particularly in the control groups."[109] In spite of these faults, Dr. Bennett recommended that Depo-Provera be approved for general marketing with a proposed five-year Phase IV study of bone mineral loss as a condition of approval.[110]

Dr. Philip Corfman concurred in Dr. Bennett's approval recommendation the same day he received his report. Breast cancer, the major approval issue, had been "adequately addressed" by the WHO study.[111] Only "two residual safety issues" remained. Osteoporosis would be addressed by a Phase IV study and low infant birth weight would be "prevented by assuring that the women are not pregnant when the drug is given."[112] Then on October 29, 1992, the FDA publically announced its marketing approval for Upjohn to market Depo-Provera for contraception, six months to the day after Upjohn had submitted its NDA.[113]

Dr. Solomon Sobel, Director of the FDA's Division of Metabolism and Endocrine Drug Products, wrote to Upjohn informing the company that the agency had completed its review of the NDA and had "concluded that adequate information has been presented to demonstrate that Depo-Provera . . . is safe and effective for use as recommended in the draft labeling."[114] His approval letter required the submission of the final labeling[115] and acknowledged Upjohn's commitment to a five-year Phase IV "bone mineral density study which examines the rate of bone mineral loss . . . and subsequent reversal of bone mineral loss following cessation of treatment."[116]

After twenty-five years of controversy over Depo-Provera, Dr. Sobel's letter announced, in effect, that the FDA had made a risk management decision to grant Upjohn a license to market the drug for contraceptive use. In 1974 and 1978, breast, cervical, and endometrial cancer had been the major issues preventing approval. By 1992, the FDA had been able to resolve the cancer issue and approve Depo-Provera by taking two steps: the agency had narrowed the basis for risk assessment by adopting the WHO recommendation to eliminate the use of animal studies, which had raised breast and endometrial cancer issues and frustrated marketing approval in 1974 and 1978; and then it had accepted WHO clinical research findings, which provided better assessments of the drug's carcinogenic risk, and used the data to decide that approving Depo-Provera would not create an unacceptable risk. After the FDA took these two steps, it assigned to its Fertility and Maternal Health Advisory Committee the narrow task of making a recommendation on only two post–Public Board of Inquiry risk issues: osteoporosis and low infant birth weight. Then the FDA, having already assessed Upjohn's human clinical trial data on Depo-Provera's contraceptive risks, decided that the risks of its use were acceptable. This risk management decision was, however, conditioned on the company conducting a Phase IV study of a new potential risk in the drug's use: osteoporosis.

1992 Depo-Provera Labeling

When the FDA approved Depo-Provera, it accepted Upjohn's final product labeling, which included the physician prescribing information, the patient labeling, and patient brochure. These materials were designed to provide physicians and patients with the information necessary to manage the drug's risk. Do these three documents adequately inform physicians and patients so that Depo-Provera can be safely and effectively used to prevent conception?

PHYSICIAN PRESCRIBING INFORMATION

The physician prescribing information provides an abbreviated summary of Depo-Provera's principal research findings. The most important findings appear under two headings. Under the "WARNINGS" heading is a description of the most significant risks: bleeding irregularities, bone mineral density changes, and breast cancer risks; and under the "INFORMATION FOR THE PATIENT" heading is an informed consent statement.[117]

The bleeding statement relies on the pivotal Upjohn study by Drs. Paul Schwallie and J. Robert Assenzo published in a 1973 *Fertility and Sterility* article.[118] The warning is brief: "Most women using DEPO-PROVERA . . . experience disruption of menstrual bleeding patterns. Altered menstrual bleeding patterns include irregular or unpredictable bleeding or spotting, or rarely, heavy or continuous bleeding."[119] The warning does not state, as the Schwallie and Assenzo article does, that 26.9 percent of the women in the study had continuous bleeding or spotting for eleven to thirty days in the first three months which the authors identified as excessive bleeding.[120] The warning does not distinguish between bleeding and spotting and the extent of heavy and continuous bleeding, but neither does the article. Nor does the warning state how long the continuous bleeding or spotting may persist, except to state that it will taper off the first year from 26.9 percent with the first injection to 11.9 percent with the fourth injection. At the same time, the warning does not mention that 40.6 percent of the women discontinued use in the first year.[121]

The bone mineral density warning, which relies exclusively on the New Zealand study of osteoporosis, is quite brief: "Use of DEPO-PROVERA may be considered among the risk factors for the development of osteoporosis. The rate of bone loss is greatest in the early years of use and then subsequently approaches the normal rate of age related fall."[122] The warning does not specify any of the risk factors of the New Zealand study that Dr. Cundy reported to the FDA advisory committee: Depo-Provera's use by women twenty-five to fifty years of age for a minimum of five years led to 6.5 percent lower bone density at the femoral neck and 7.5 percent lower bone density in the lumbar spine than in the control group of premenopausal women.[123]

The osteoporosis warning does not identify the scientific criticism of the Cundy study results identified by Dr. Ridgely Bennett in his October 27, 1992, Medical Officer's Original Summary of NDA 20–246.[124] Nor does the warning include Dr. Bennett's suggestion in his medical summary that a baseline bone mineral density scan be performed. "Perhaps," he said, "women with more than one risk factor for osteoporosis (family history, underweight, cigarette smoking, European or Asian origin) should have a bone density measurement if they are considering DMPA on a regular basis."[125] His suggestion is missing from the package insert and physician prescribing information, because Dr. Bennett did not include the bone density scan in his approval recommendations.

The breast cancer warning correctly reports the WHO findings about Depo-Provera use: a 20 percent overall increased risk and a 119 percent increased risk for women under thirty-five years of age who were first exposed within the four previous years.[126] The warning does not, however, report, as the WHO study does, that women under thirty-five years of age have a 40 percent increase in risk.[127] Nor does the warning say anything about long-term studies, because no long-term studies of

Depo-Provera and breast cancer had been conducted to evaluate the drug's use for twenty years. These omissions troubled Dr. Judith Weisz because the "published [WHO] studies provide insufficient long-term data for any conclusions to be drawn about Depo-Provera's effects."[128]

The cervical cancer warning does not provide any assessment of the risks of cervical cancer-in-situ, discussed in chapter 2,[129] but it does correctly report the WHO finding of an overall increased risk of invasive cervical cancer of 10 percent. Missing from the warning are the overall risk rates at each of the four WHO study centers, which ranged from a 70 percent increased risk at the Mexico center to a 40 percent protective effect at the Kenya center.[130] The warning reports only the 10 percent increased risk at the Chiang Mai, Thailand, center.[131] For women under thirty-five years of age, the warning reports that the increased risk varies from 22 to 28 percent, but it does not, as the WHO study does, report that the risk is inversely related to age: For women under twenty-five, the increased risk is 28 percent, while for those aged twenty-five to twenty-nine and those thirty to thirty-four, the increased risk is 22 to 23 percent, respectively.[132] Finally, the warning fails to report the overall risk of invasive cervical cancer.

The accidental pregnancies warning briefly summarizes the Gray and Pardthaisong finding that "accidental pregnancies that occur within 1–2 months after injection of DEPO-PROVERA . . . increased the risk of low birth rate which in turn is associated with neonatal death."[133] This warning does not, however, include the risk statistics from the Gray and Pardthaisong studies, nor does it reflect Dr. Gray's testimony before the advisory committee that a Depo-Provera injection within the first four weeks of conception would lead to "a two-fold increase in low birth rate."[134] The absence of these risk statistics may be accounted for, in part, by the advisory committee's failure "to be totally convinced of the validity of the data on infant birth weight,"[135] but it does not explain the absence of Gray and Pardthaisong neonatal and infant death statistics, which the FDA did not ask its advisory committee to evaluate. At the same time, the warning on accidental pregnancies did incorporate the advisory committee recommendation on the timing of the first Depo-Provera injection.[136]

The warning in the informed consent statement under the heading "Information for the Patient," recommends that physicians and health care professionals give their patients the patient labeling and inform them about "the drug's risks and benefits . . . as compared to other forms of contraception or no contraception at all."[137] This informed consent recommendation is, however, limited to informing the patient at her first visit about menstrual irregularities and bleeding. There is no recommendation to inform patients about any of the other warnings, including bone mineral density loss and breast and cervical cancer.

In sum, the physician prescribing information has flaws that impair the ability of physicians, as learned medical intermediaries, to provide their patients with the information about the drug necessary for them to make an informed contraceptive choice. As the foregoing analysis has revealed, the research studies on which the physician prescribing information is based, fail to provide sufficient risk information, but more seriously, these research studies suffer from both risk assessment and risk acceptability problems.

Serious risk assessment problems pervade the research on bleeding, bone mineral density loss, and cancer on which the FDA relied to make its drug marketing decision. The bleeding risks rely only on the Schwallie and Assenzo article; the bone mineral density loss risks rely only on the Cundy study, and all of the studies of cancer risks rely only on one WHO multinational, multi-center study, the first and only controlled case study of breast, cervical, endometrial, liver, and ovarian cancer.

All of these studies suffer from methodological problems, which have led other research scientists to question their validity. The risk of bleeding irregularities was based on the 1973 Schwallie and Assenzo article, which did not distinguish between bleeding and spotting and had a 40.6 percent dropout rate the first year.[138] The New Zealand osteoporosis study on which the physician prescribing information is based fails to provide sufficient risk assessment information, but more seriously, it fails to disclose the study's methodological problems identified in Dr. Ridgely Bennett's report, especially the study's limitation to bone density loss in the short term, five years or less, and the provision of no long-term data, of up to twenty years, on the risk of osteoporosis.[139] The WHO cancer studies were also short term. Dr. Shapiro told the advisory committee that there had been no long-term studies of Depo-Provera and breast cancer to evaluate the drug's use for twenty years.[140] Dr. Judith Weisz was also troubled, because the "published [WHO] studies provide[d] insufficient long-term data for any conclusions to be drawn about Depo-Provera's effects."[141]

The cancer risk assessments in these studies raise risk acceptability problems, because all the WHO studies were conducted in developing countries: Chile, Kenya, Mexico, and Thailand. None of these studies, which the FDA relied upon to approve Depo-Provera and which are listed in the physician prescribing information, involved domestic clinical studies. As a consequence, these studies raised a basic risk acceptability issue for Dr. Judith Weisz, who agreed with Cynthia Pearson's advisory committee testimony that the "breast cancer rates [in developing countries] were far less than one-half of the United States."[142]

Dr. Bennett's statement in his October 27 "Medical Officer's Original Summary," that breast cancer risks are "well defined [and that] no additional data are necessary"[143] and Dr. Corfman's letter the same day concluding that the breast cancer issue had been "adequately addressed by the WHO study"[144] are clearly at odds with a WHO background paper commissioned for its 1993 Special Programme in Human Reproduction meeting. In her paper, published the following year in *Contraception*, Dr. Clair Chilvers observed that "the amount of epidemiological data [on DMPA] related to its effect on breast cancer is very limited."[145] Given that breast cancer rates and risk/benefit evaluations are higher in developed countries than in developing countries, she concluded that "if we are to progress further in our assessment of breast cancer risk in relation to DMPA . . . more epidemiological studies [should] be planned and performed in developed countries."[146]

As a consequence of these risk assessment and risk acceptability faults, physicians will not be able to make a risk management decision based on an assessment of the drug's risk and then decide, knowing the patient and her personal circumstances and medical history, whether Depo-Provera will be an acceptable risk for her. Nor will she be able to know the risks and make a contraceptive choice, which would be right for her.

PATIENT LABELING AND PATIENT BROCHURE

Patients will be provided with two documents by their physicians. One is the patient labeling, which provides less detail than the physician prescribing information and is presented in non-technical language.[147] By contrast, the patient brochure, "Depo-Provera Contraceptive Injection Important Information for Patients" is based on the patient labeling, but is written in a reader-friendly manner.[148] The brochure emphasizes Depo-Provera's "unique benefits": its convenience and privacy and its safety, effectiveness, and reversibility. Then it briefly describes the drug's risks, including osteoporosis, and provides bulleted lists of its side effects, the personal health circumstances in which it should not be used, and the health problems to be reported to a physician.

The patient labeling and brochure have two similarities. First, their information about Depo-Provera's risks is substantially abbreviated and contains no risk statistics and no citations to the scientific literature. The patient labeling and brochure describe in almost identical terms the bone mineral loss risks. Depo-Provera "may be associated with a decrease in the amount of mineral stored in your bones" and may lead to bone fractures.[149] This loss is "greatest in the early years of . . . use, but begins to resemble the normal rate of age related bone mineral loss."[150]

Second, the labeling and brochure focus on the physician as a woman's learned medical intermediary. They instruct the woman to discuss the risks and benefits of Depo-Provera with her "health care provider [who] will help you to compare DEPO-PROVERA with other contraceptive methods as well as answer any questions."[151] The brochure provides a similarly worded instruction. The labeling and brochure also tell her that before a physician prescribes the drug, she will have a physical exam and will tell her physician about any medications she is taking along with her personal and family health history. The labeling does, however, go further than the brochure by informing her that if she experiences any of the list of specific warning signals "to call her health care provider immediately."[152] Her physician will not, however, be able to function as her learned medical intermediary, because of the faulted physician prescribing information, described above, and, as a consequence, she will find it difficult to make an informed contraceptive decision.

2004 Osteoporosis Black Box Warning

When the FDA approved Depo-Provera, the agency required two Phase IV post-approval studies of the drug's effect on bone mineral density loss in adolescents and young women (twelve to twenty-five years of age) and in adult women.[153] On the basis of these two studies, the FDA made substantial changes in 2004 to the physician prescribing information and the patient labeling and patient brochure by adding a black box warning highlighting the risk of osteoporosis.[154] The contents of the black box warning are repeated in the loss of bone mineral density warning (Loss of BMD warning) sections in all three documents, which appears as the first risk warning followed by the menstrual bleeding and breast cancer warnings.

The black box and Loss of BMD warnings have three principal features. First, physician prescribing information states that the use of Depo-Provera "is associated with the loss of significant bone mineral density."[155] This loss is a particular concern for adolescents and young women, because it is "a critical period of bone accretion."[156] The total loss of BMD after 4.6 years of Depo-Provera use is -8.04 at the hip, -8.51 at the femoral neck, and -9.29 at the lumbar spine.[157] It is, however, unknown whether "Depo-Provera CI use will reduce peak bone mass and increase the risk of osteoporotic fracture later in life."[158] BMD loss in adult women occurs at a less dramatic rate. The total loss after five years of use is -5.35 at the hip, -5.27 at the femoral neck, and -5.81 at the lumbar spine.[159] BMD loss continues for all women who use Depo-Provera, but the severity of this loss is also unknown. The Loss of BMD warning is cautious: "The decrease in BMD appears to be at least partially reversible."[160]

Second, the loss of bone mineral density warning reports that adult women who have taken Depo-Provera for five years and then have discontinued its use for two years experience a 61.03 percent recovery at the hip (-5.85 to -2.28), a 31.29 percent recovery at the femoral neck (-5.27 to -3.66), and a 10.33 percent recovery at the lumbar spine (-5.28 to -5.21).[161] No statistics are available for recovery of bone mineral density loss by adult women beyond those who have used it for five years and discontinued its use for two years. Nor are there any statistics for recovery of bone mineral density by adolescents and young women, because a study in progress of their BMD recovery had not been completed and reported at the time the warning was written.

Third, the black box and the Loss of BMD warnings state that Depo-Provera should be used for no more than two years and, thereafter, only "if other birth control methods are inadequate."[162] In determining the adequacy of other birth control methods, the Loss of BMD warning asks the physician and the woman to make a risk management decision by using risk-benefit analysis. The warning does not identify or discuss the benefits of various contraceptive methods, except in terms of their efficacy; nor does it identify specific risk factors for osteoporosis to be considered in making a contraceptive choice. The warning does state that if a woman wants to continue to take Depo-Provera, her "BMD should be evaluated" and in the case of "adolescents, interpretation of BMD results should take into account patient age and skeletal maturity."[163] This warning suggests, but does not explicitly state, that a BMD scan should be performed if a woman wants to continue Depo-Provera use, but says nothing about performing a baseline bone density scan before the first injection.

The patient labeling and patient brochure speak directly to the woman using nonmedical terminology: "Loss of calcium may cause weak, porous bones (osteoporosis) that could cause an increase in the risk that your bones might break after menopause."[164] When compared to the physician information, there are several important differences. Neither the patient labeling nor the brochure refers to the BMD loss as "significant." Unlike the physician prescribing information, both specifically inform the woman that "your health care provider . . . may ask you to have a test of your bones" if you have taken Depo-Provera for two years and want to continue its use.[165] But neither the patient labeling nor the brochure tells a woman before she receives her first injection to ask her physician to explain two risk factors that appear in the physician prescribing information: the amount of the bone loss she may suffer from using Depo-Provera and the reversibility of the bone loss, if she decides to discontinue the drug's use.

In sum, the 1992 Depo-Provera labeling—the physician prescribing information and the patient labeling and brochure—and the 2004 osteoporosis black box warning and the Loss of BMD warning are scientifically flawed documents, which pass to physicians the risk management task of making an individual patient decision. The labeling and warnings will also play a crucial role in products liability litigation. Courts will treat them as providing physicians and patients with adequate warnings of the drug's risks and require the woman to bear the burden of proving that the warnings are inadequate in order to avoid having her case dismissed on the basis of the drug company's summary judgment motion.

Osteoporosis Products Liability Litigation

After the FDA approved Depo-Provera in 1992, women who suffered a variety of adverse side effects from using the drug have sued their physicians and Upjohn in state and federal courts. This litigation has taken the form of individual lawsuits,[166] multi-district litigation,[167] class actions,[168] and mass tort cases,[169] but little is known about the outcome of these cases. Since the FDA revised the drug's labeling to include a black box warning in 2004, one issue has defined litigation over the drug's contraceptive use: osteoporosis.[170]

The largest post-2004 Depo-Provera litigation was a mass tort case in New Jersey's Bergen County Superior Court. *In re Depo-Provera Contraceptive Injection Litigation* involved 157 women who claimed to have suffered from osteoporosis, because Pfizer, Upjohn's corporate heir,[171] had failed to warn their physicians about this risk.[172] The case was settled on terms favorable to the plaintiffs for a confidential amount, but the case is subject to a protective order prohibiting the disclosure of documents related the litigation.[173] Aside from this mass tort case, only four federal cases provide the opportunity to tell the stories of women who, like Anne MacMurdo, have used Depo-Provera, suffered adverse side effects, and then sued Pfizer.[174]

These women face three formidable legal challenges that have defined Depo-Provera's approved contraceptive use as they did its unapproved use. What is Pfizer's legal duty in the sale of Depo-Provera? Does it meet its duty by providing accurate information in the FDA-approved package insert that accompanies the drug? What is the legal duty of physicians who prescribe the drug? Do they meet their duty when they use the physician prescribing information to inform women about the drug's known risks? What is the legal duty of the women who receive an injection of Depo-Provera? Do they meet their duty when they read and understand the patient labeling and brochure and then make an informed decision to receive the drug?

If a woman believes the physician has failed to provide her with information about the drug's known risks and she believes she has been injured by use of the drug, does she have a medical malpractice claim against her physician? If a woman believes that she has been injured by use of the drug, does she have a products liability claim against Pfizer for its negligent failure to warn her physician about the known risks of the drug's use? These two civil actions are her primary legal means to target the failure of two critical linkages in the pharmaceutical risk management system: the pharmaceutical company and the physician. If, however, the drug company has provided FDA-approved labeling to accompany the drug, her physician has provided her with the information about the drug's known risks, she has read and understood the patient labeling and brochure, and then she decides to receive the injection and is injured, these two legal means to manage contraceptive risk will not be available to her and she will be without a legal remedy.

Summary Judgment

Any woman who seeks legal redress for the harm that she claims to have suffered from the use of Depo-Provera will have to confront the rules and realities of the legal process. If her case is not settled, one reality is that a medical malpractice or products liability case will be dismissed on the physician's or on Pfizer's motion for summary judgment.[175] Anne MacMurdo survived three summary judgments. Since Depo-Provera was approved in 1992, no reported products liability case has gone to trial, because all have either been settled or defeated by Pfizer on motions for summary judgment.[176]

Four products liability cases—*Lorenzi v. Pfizer* (2007),[177] *Colville v. Pharmacia & Upjohn* (2008),[178] *Oliver v. Pharmacia & Upjohn* (2008),[179] and *Montagnon v. Pfizer* (2008)[180]—all testify to the difficulty of bringing a post-approval Depo-Provera products liability case and to the barrier that summary judgment erects to its trial.[181] In all four cases, the federal district courts granted summary judgments to Pfizer, because of two common factual weaknesses in the defendants' cases: None of the women had had a base-line bone mineral density scan before taking Depo-Provera and none of their expert witnesses was qualified to testify to the adequacy of the warnings or to the drug as a cause of osteopenia or osteoporosis.[182]

All of these summary judgment motions were heard in federal district courts, which applied Rule 56 of the Federal Rules of Civil Procedure. Rule 56 states that a party making the motion is entitled to have a judge dismiss a case if it is able to show that there is no genuine issue of material fact to be decided at trial.[183] The moving party, here the drug company defendant, can meet its burden by demonstrating that a plaintiff "cannot show an essential element of his case."[184] To survive a summary judgment motion, the plaintiff must provide "specific facts showing a genuine issue for trial" on each element of her products liability claim.[185]

In all these cases, the Depo-Provera plaintiffs brought products liability claims based on either state statutes or common law. The state laws usually require the plaintiffs to prove that the drug company's warnings were inadequate, that the plaintiff was injured by using the company's product, and that the company's failure to warn caused the plaintiff's injury. A drug company moving for summary judgment can meet its burden by demonstrating that the plaintiff's evidence is not sufficient to prove at trial all three elements of her products liability claim: inadequacy, causation, and injury. In deciding whether the plaintiff has provided sufficient evidence to survive summary judgment and allow a jury to decide the case, the court will determine "whether the evidence presents a sufficient disagreement to require the submission to a jury or whether it is so one-sided that one party must prevail as a matter of law."[186]

How the federal district courts have decided these four cases has depended on the facts of each case, the applicable federal and state law, and the plaintiff's and defendant's expert witnesses. These three elements will be briefly discussed and then used to explain the federal district court summary judgment decisions.

FACTS

Jamie Lorenzo, Cassandra Colville, Adrienne Oliver, and Melanie Montagnon, the four women in these cases, had received Depo-Provera injections for contraception between 1995 and 2005, and during this time had also received bone mineral density (BMD) scans revealing low BMD or osteopenia, but only after they had begun taking the drug.[187] All four filed suit in state court against Pfizer on products liability theories claiming that the drug company failed to give them adequate warning that one of the side effects of Depo-Provera was bone mineral loss amounting to either osteopenia or osteoporosis, that their use of the contraceptive directly caused their osteopenia[188] or osteoporosis,[189] and that they had been injured as a result of their bone mineral density loss. Pfizer removed all four cases to federal district court on the basis of diversity of citizenship jurisdiction,[190] and the federal courts decided the cases on motions for summary judgment by applying the products liability laws of the states in which they had jurisdiction.[191]

FEDERAL AND STATE LAW

The four cases involved both federal and state law. The 1992 FDA Depo-Provera labeling, the federal law, warned both physicians and patients about bone mineral density loss.[192] After the Phase IV post-approval clinical trials were reported, the product labeling was substantially revised in 2004 to include a black box warning and a much more detailed loss of bone mineral density warning for both physicians and patients.[193]

State products liability case law and statutes in these four cases recognized the learned intermediary doctrine, which provides that a pharmaceutical manufacturer's duty to warn a consumer about the risks of a prescription drug is satisfied when the prescribing physician receives adequate warning about the drug's risks.[194] Once the physician receives an adequate warning in the form of the drug's labeling, the learned intermediary doctrine provides a defense for pharmaceutical companies against patient suits.[195] As the federal district court in *Oliver v. Pharmacia & Upjohn* stated, citing *Stahl v. Novartis Pharmaceutical Corp.* (2002): "A drug's package insert will be considered adequate as a matter of law only if it (1) 'clearly and unambiguously' warns of the potential adverse effect and (2) the plaintiff's physician testifies that the warning adequately informed him/her of the risks associated with the drug."[196] If the physician fails to provide a patient with sufficient information about the drug's risks, then the patient's only legal recourse is a medical malpractice suit.

EXPERT WITNESS

In all four products liability cases, the use of expert witnesses was critical in deciding whether to grant summary judgment. The federal district courts first asked: Were the witnesses qualified to give an opinion on whether the warning labels were adequate, whether the drug caused the osteoporosis or osteopenia, and whether the plaintiff suffered a compensable injury? Then the courts asked: Was the expert's evidence sufficient to show that there were genuine issues of material fact on each of the three elements of the plaintiff's claim: inadequacy, causation, and injury? If there were, the case would go to trial and, if not, the case would be so one-sided that the judge could decide the case as a matter of law.

Depo-Provera Products Liability Cases

The Depo-Provera products liability cases had the three common elements described, but they also had unique features, each of which merits individual attention: the plaintiffs who brought them, their relationships with their physicians who gave them the injections and ordered the bone mineral density scans, and the attorneys and experts they retained.

LORENZI V. PFIZER (2007)

Jamie Lorenzi received Depo-Provera injections at Planned Parenthood of Mahoning Valley, Ohio, from March 1997 through January 2005. Prior to her first injection, when she was twenty-five years old, and at each subsequent injection, she received a Planned Parenthood four-page brochure, "Request for Examination, Treatment, and Injection of Depo-Provera Medroxyprogesterone (DMPA: Depo-Provera) for Contraception" and the "DMPA Patient Labeling Pamphlet," which included a statement she initialed acknowledging that she had "read the brochure, understood it and have had all my questions answered" and that she had been given the "DMPA Patient Labeling Pamphlet," which stated: "I know I should read and ask questions about anything I don't understand."[197] In October 2004, she received her first bone density scan, which revealed scores that her physician determined were in the osteopenia range. In July 2006, she filed a products liability suit against Pfizer claiming that the drug company failed to give her adequate warning that Depo-Provera's use would lower her bone mineral density, that the drug caused her injury, and that she was injured by her use of the drug.

The federal district court used the Ohio Products Liability Act (OPLA) to decide her case. The court relied upon OPLA's learned intermediary doctrine[198] to reject her claim that the Depo-Provera warnings were inadequate. Pfizer, the court held, had fulfilled its duty to warn her, because the company provided her physician with adequate warnings. Depo-Provera's 1992 and 2004 package inserts, the World Health Organization's bone mineral density categories, and Dr. Carolyn Westhoff's *Journal of Reproductive Medicine* article, summarizing the bone mineral density research literature,[199] clearly established that "the defendant gave warnings to both the physician and patient, . . . that these warnings meet the threshold test for adequacy set forth in the statute and case law . . . [, and that the] plaintiff, herself stated in her deposition that she had read the patient labeling."[200] In sum, the court's finding that the package insert warnings were adequate, as a matter of law, was sufficient to grant Pfizer summary judgment, but the court still proceeded to address the causation and injury issues.

On the causation issue, the court found that the expert testimony did not "establish a causal link" between her Depo-Provera use and her bone mineral density (BMD) loss. Dr. Anthony DeSalvo, the plaintiff's Planned Parenthood physician, testified at his deposition: "Without a baseline BMD measurement . . . one cannot know whether her BMD is naturally low or was caused or aggravated by the Depo-Provera."[201] Dr. Angelo Licata, a Cleveland Clinic endocrinologist and Pfizer expert witness, agreed. At his deposition, he stated that bone loss "is difficult to prove . . . [because] there are several reasons why she may have had a low peak bone mass . . . when she was first tested, including her gender, race (Caucasian), smoking, small stature, late puberty, lack of exercise, and diet."[202] Even if Depo-Provera had caused her bone loss, he "would have to ask how much,"[203] and if she had bone loss, he would have expected her to make "a nearly complete recovery after discontinuing it."[204] In sum, there was no issue of material fact, because both the plaintiff's and the defendant's witnesses agreed that it could not be proven that her bone loss was caused by her Depo-Provera use.

Finally, the court found that the expert testimony did not support Jamie Lorenzi's claim that her Depo-Provera use had injured her. In his deposition, Dr. DeSalvo stated: "There is no injury. Just to have a low bone mineral density means nothing. . . . Osteopenia is not a disease, it's a statistical score. And . . . [her] statistical score is well within the realm of patients in a normally distributed population."[205] Dr. Licata agreed and added that low bone density "doesn't imply a great deal about future fracture risk."[206] On the basis of their expert testimony, the court found as a matter of law that she had not shown that she had suffered a current injury, or that she would she suffer a future injury. In sum, the federal district court found that Jamie Lorenzi had failed to prove all three elements of her products liability claim and entered summary judgment in favor of Pfizer.

COLVILLE V. PHARMACIA & UPJOHN COMPANY (2008)

Cassandra Colville began using Depo-Provera in 1995, when she was twenty-five years old, and used the drug continuously until 2002, when she discontinued it to become pregnant. She received a bone density scan in 2003, which revealed osteopenia in her spine, but found that her left hip was normal. During these years, her physician, Dr. Zinnah Holmes, prescribed Depo-Provera without discussing with her its potential for bone density loss.[207] When Ms. Colville was no longer taking the contraceptive, Dr. Rutu Mahajan conducted a second bone scan in 2005, which revealed a bone density similar to her previous one, with some improvement.[208] Subsequently, she filed suit against Pharmacia & Upjohn alleging that "neither she nor her doctors were advised that the use of the medication for any extensive period of time would lead to the development of osteopenia" and that her use of the contraceptive directly caused her osteopenia, which was a compensable injury.[209]

When the Florida federal district court examined Cassandra Colville's two theories of liability, negligence and strict liability, instead of addressing each claim separately, it decided that "strict liability and negligent failure to warn cases boil down to three elements that the Plaintiff must prove: that Depo-Provera's warning was inadequate, its inadequacy proximately caused her injury, and she suffered an injury from using the contraceptive."[210]

The district court first addressed the adequacy of the osteoporosis warning in Depo-Provera's 1992 and 2004 FDA-approved package inserts. Florida's learned intermediary doctrine, the court said, limited Pharmacia & Upjohn's duty to warn to providing adequate warnings about the drug to the prescribing physician.[211] The Florida Supreme Court's decision in Upjohn v. MacMurdo (1990) provided the rule: "The adequacy of the warnings is determined by whether the warnings were adequate to warn a physician of the possibility that [the drug] might be causing the condition experienced by the Plaintiff."[212]

In deciding whether the osteoporosis warning was adequate, the court turned again to *MacMurdo*, which held that the warning in a package insert would be adequate, unless the plaintiff presented expert testimony supporting her claim that the warning was inadequate.[213] Like Anne MacMurdo, Cassandra Colville failed to offer expert testimony on the inadequacy of Depo-Provera's warnings. Her expert, Dr. Leon Terry, a neurologist, reviewed her medical records, including her bone scans and the Depo-Provera research on the risk of osteopenia, but the court decided that "none of this testimony or his opinion addressed the adequacy of the [Depo-Provera] warnings."[214] The testimony of her two physicians, though they were not presented as experts, provided no support in proving the inadequacy of the 1992 and 2004 package inserts. Dr. Holmes stated that the "language of the warning label . . . was adequate to advise her of the risk . . . of bone loss in using Depo-Provera."[215] Then Dr. Mahajan confirmed that the warnings identified osteoporosis as one of the drug's risk factors.[216] The district court then held, as the Florida Supreme Court did in *Upjohn v. MacMurdo* (1990), that "because Depo-Provera's warnings were 'accurate, clear, and unambiguous,' [they] . . . were indeed adequate to warn a physician that use of Depo-Provera could lead to osteoporosis."[217]

When the district court turned to the causation issue, its opinion, unlike the *Lorenzi* court's, did not include any expert testimony on the issue of whether Depo-Provera's use caused osteopenia, nor did it discuss the absence of a baseline bone mineral density score in rejecting her causation argument. Instead, the court directed its attention to Cassandra Colville's physician, Dr. Holmes, who, although she "understood the warnings and also had prior knowledge of the propensity of Depo-Provera to cause the low bone density," did not discuss this risk with her patients, including Ms. Colville.[218] This failure, the court decided, made it impossible for "the plaintiff to show that the inadequacy of the manufacturer's warnings was the proximate cause of her osteopenia diagnosis."[219]

The district court then quickly disposed of the injury issue with reference not only to her claim, but also to *Lorenzi*, which the court characterized as "a factually analogous case."[220] The *Lorenzi* expert's testimony, which established that osteopenia was neither an injury nor a disease, but "a slow process in the bone that could lead to an injury," led the court to find that the "plaintiff has not been able to establish a current or future injury as a result of a low bone density diagnosis."[221] In sum, the district court held that Cassandra Colville had failed to prove all three elements of her Florida products liability claim, based on theories of negligent failure to warn and strict liability theories, and entered summary judgment in favor of Pharmacia & Upjohn.

OLIVER V. PHARMACIA & UPJOHN COMPANY (2008)

Adrienne Oliver, the daughter of Cassandra Colville, had begun to use Depo-Provera for contraception in early 2004, when she was sixteen years old. She brought suit against Pharmacia & Upjohn for its failure to adequately warn her about Depo-Provera's use and that she had suffered osteopenia as a result of her use of the drug, but the drug company removed the case to federal district court, which entered summary judgment in its favor. When her attorney, who was also handling her mother's Depo-Provera case, failed to file a timely appeal of the adverse summary judgment, Adrienne Oliver, relying upon Rule 60(b) of the Federal Rules of Civil Procedure, requested the district court to grant her relief.[222] The district court decided that, even though she had not "demonstrated excusable neglect under Rule 60(b),"[223] it would decide, as a matter of equity, whether the Louisiana Products Liability Act (LPLA) provided her with a remedy.[224]

The district court began by rejecting her claim that "the warning labels should have mentioned Depo-Provera not only as a risk factor, but as a cause of osteopenia as well as the fact that bone density should be closely monitored while the patient is taking Depo-Provera."[225] The court refused to consider her broadly based claim, as the district would in *Montagnon v. Pfizer* (2008), because her claim "would circumvent the entire [FDA] drug approval process."[226] Instead, the court chose to decide only whether the warning labels were adequate under the Louisiana Products Liability Act, which stated that "the person to whom the adequate warning must be given is not the patient, but the prescribing physician."[227] If the drug company provides an adequate warning to the physician, "the learned intermediary doctrine discharges the drug company's duty to warn the patient."[228] Then the court, relying on *Oli-*

ver and *Stahl v. Pharmaceutical Co.* (2002),[229] held that Pharmacia & Upjohn had discharged its duty to warn, because "the Depo-Provera warning label contains specific references to bone mineral density loss as a risk factor. . . . [and] Oliver's treating physicians testified that they were adequately informed of the risks associated with the Depo-Provera warning label."[230]

The district court then turned to Adrienne Oliver's claim that Depo-Provera proximately or actually caused her osteopenia. The court first rejected her proximate cause claim because the LPLA's learned intermediary doctrine required her to show that "but for the inadequate warning, the treating physician would not have used or prescribed the product."[231] In fact, the court noted that her physician continued to prescribe Depo-Provera after the package insert was revised in 2004 to include the black box warning. Then, the court rejected her actual causation argument because she could not establish that her Depo-Provera use lowered her bone mineral density. As in *Lorenzi*, the plaintiff had "no original baseline bone mineral density score to compare with . . . [her] current bone density score."[232] In fact, her medical experts testified that without a baseline score, they could not offer an opinion that any bone mineral density loss she suffered was caused by her Depo-Provera use.[233]

Finally, the district court quickly dismissed the argument that Depo-Provera caused her a compensable injury. Citing the *Lorenzi* and *Colville* summary judgments, the court stated that her osteopenia was "virtually identical" to that of the plaintiffs in the other two cases and that "those federal courts held that osteopenia is not an injury for products liability purposes."[234]

MONTAGNON V. PFIZER (2008)

Melanie Montagnon received her first injection of Depo-Provera at Planned Parenthood of Connecticut in 1996 when she was eighteen years old and continued to receive injections until 2005. She had been told by a Planned Parenthood physician in December 2004, a month after the FDA added the black box warning to the Depo-Provera package insert, "to take a calcium supplement 'because of the risk of osteoporosis.'"[235] In August 2005, she was informed that Planned Parenthood would no longer provide her with Depo-Provera, because her bone density test earlier that month had reported a BMD score consistent with osteoporosis.[236] She subsequently sued Pfizer, claiming, pursuant to the Connecticut Products Liability Act (CPLA), actual and punitive damages for the harm she suffered from her use of Depo-Provera.

Of the four Depo-Provera summary judgment cases, hers is the most legally bold, but it was doomed for two reasons. First, she argued that the district court should not decide Pfizer's motion for summary judgment on the basis of whether the warnings in the 1992 and 2004 package inserts were adequate to inform her of the risk of osteoporosis. She argued instead that Pfizer should have had the FDA include in its 1992 labeling five additional warnings, derived from two studies of Depo-Provera and osteoporosis, which had been incorporated almost verbatim in its 2004 package labeling.[237] Second, she also argued that "no expert testimony is required to establish the inadequacy of the product warnings and that the . . . [two studies] are sufficient evidence to support a jury verdict that the Depo-Provera warnings are inadequate."[238] The district court rejected both arguments because "neither study recommends any change in the warnings and, if the court adopted these five additional warnings, it would demand of a lay jury a task for which it was not qualified and [would] invade the FDA's jurisdiction to assess scientific studies in making a drug approval decision and in writing package inserts."[239]

The district court then addressed Pfizer's summary judgment motion under the Connecticut Products Liability Act, as its standard of care had been modified by the learned intermediary doctrine, and granted Pfizer's motion, because Melanie Matagnon was unable to prove by expert testimony that Depo-Provera's package insert warnings were inadequate to notify a prescribing physician about the risk of osteoporosis. In fact, the court found that her expert, Dr. Erik Alexander, "was unable to offer an opinion as to the adequacy of the warnings . . . because he had not reviewed them."[240]

The federal district court, unlike the *Lorenzi* court, decided the case on the basis of Melanie Montagnon's failure to prove by expert testimony the inadequacy of Depo-Provera's package insert to warn. The court did not give any serious attention to the causation and injury elements of her products liability claim, except to note: "While Dr. Alexander testified as to causation between the drug and the plaintiff's injuries, there is no expert evidence . . . [to] assess the link between the warnings and the injuries suffered."[241] In sum, it is safe to conclude that the *Montagnon* court joined the other three district courts in properly granting Pfizer's summary judgment motions, because the conduct and testimony of the plaintiffs, along with the testimony of their physicians and expert witnesses, clearly demonstrated that there were no issues of material fact that required a jury trial, because the evidence was so one-sided that Pfizer was entitled to summary judgment as a matter of law.

Lessons for Osteoporosis Products Liability Litigation

Summary judgment is a formidable barrier to bringing a Depo-Provera products liability claim. Pfizer can easily meet its burden of proving that it is entitled to have its summary judgment motion granted for three reasons: its FDA-approved package insert, the state learned intermediary doctrine, and the plaintiff's burden of opposing the motion. All three limit the role of state and federal courts as risk managers.

Upjohn's 1992 and Pfizer's 2004 labeling warn of the risk of bone mineral density loss and osteoporosis. The 1992 FDA physician prescribing information contains a statement of this risk under the heading "WARNINGS," and the patient labeling identifies bone density loss as a risk factor under the heading "Risk of Using Depo-Provera."[242] The 2004 FDA physician and patient information contains a black box warning to alert them to the risk of osteoporosis. The *Oliver* and *Montagnon* courts, as risk managers, did not allow the plaintiffs to argue that the package inserts should have included additional information, because it is the FDA that has exclusive authority to assess scientific studies, determine pharmaceutical risks, and describe those risks in package inserts.

Whether the 2004 bone loss and osteoporosis warnings are adequate will be decided on the basis of state products liability statutes, which favor the drug company, because the statutes commonly include or recognize a learned intermediary doctrine that limits the company's duty to warn to the prescribing physician. The physicians in all four cases testified that the language of the warning in the FDA labeling was adequate to inform them of the risks of bone loss. All four district courts, in their limited role as risk managers, upheld the adequacy of the warnings: Three courts accepted physician testimony to establish their adequacy, while the Florida district court relied upon expert testimony.

Any woman who brings a Depo-Provera products liability case against Pfizer will have to confront the company's use of the learned intermediary doctrine. Legal scholars have argued for the abandonment of the doctrine, because pharmaceutical companies, including Pfizer, directly advertise their drugs to women and, thereby, "encroach on the doctor-patient relationship by encouraging consumers to ask for an advertised product."[243] Still, these scholarly arguments have not impressed state legislatures and judges, because forty-six states recognize the doctrine, and in these states, Pfizer can be expected to use the doctrine to shield itself from liability.

The plaintiffs in all four cases were unable to survive the barrier of summary judgment, because they failed to provide relevant expert testimony on the three elements of their products liability claims that would have entitled them to a jury trial: the inadequacy of the warnings, causation of harm, and injury. Their physicians testified that the warnings in the FDA labeling were adequate to inform them of the risks of bone loss. Even more troublesome, Jamie Lorenzi had read the patient insert, Cassandra Colville's expert did not address the adequacy of the warnings, and Melanie Montagnon's expert had not reviewed the warnings. The plaintiffs could not prove causation, because the *Lorenzi*, *Colville*, and *Oliver* courts accepted the testimony of Dr. DeSalvo, Lorenzi's physician, that without obtaining a baseline bone density scan prior to receiving the first Depo-Provera injection, no plaintiff could establish that the drug caused her bone loss, nor could she prove that her bone loss was a current or future injury. Once again, Dr. DeSalvo's testimony was crucial in the *Lorenzi*, *Colville*, and *Oliver* cases, because he testified that osteopenia was not an injury, but "a statistical score . . . well within the realm of patients in a normally distributed population."[244]

Any woman will find it difficult in responding to a Pfizer summary judgment motion to argue that the FDA-approved warnings were inadequate, that Depo-Provera caused her harm, and that her harm is a legally compensable injury. Pfizer will be able to rely on physician and medical expert testimony on Depo-Provera's FDA product labeling to argue that the drug's physician information is adequate to inform a doctor of the drug's risk of osteoporosis. Pfizer will also be assured that federal district courts, in making a risk management decision about the drug's adequacy, will be unlikely to look behind the language of the warnings in the drug's labeling and assess the uncertain science that supports them or to accept a plaintiff's proposal to supplement FDA warnings with her proposed warnings. Even if the FDA revised the black box and Loss of BMD warnings to recommend that physicians perform a baseline bone density scan before they provide women with their first injection of Depo-Provera, this revision, while likely to improve patient safety, will also further protect Pfizer from liability and potentially expose the woman's physician to medical malpractice liability for failure to conduct a baseline BMD scan.

Any woman will also have to confront the causation and injury issues. Once again, a federal district court, as a risk manager, would be likely to defer to the FDA-approved labeling, which does not state that the use of Depo-Provera causes osteoporosis, as Melanie Montagnon argued it should, but states only that the drug's use is associated with bone mineral density loss, which could lead to osteoporosis. The federal court would also be receptive to the arguments by Pfizer's experts that a woman's loss of bone mineral density could be associated with a woman's personal attributes and behavior, including "race (Caucasian), smoking, small stature, late puberty, lack of exercise, and diet."[245] Nor would she be likely to prevail on a claim that the bone density loss that she suffered from her use of Depo-Provera was an injury, because Pfizer medical experts would be likely to persuade a court that she has not suffered a legally compensable injury, because she has suffered no femoral neck, hip, or lumbar spine fractures.

As a consequence, if a woman is informed by her physician of the risks of using Depo-Provera, including osteoporosis, and she reads both the patient labeling and brochure, as Jamie Lorenzi did, she will have no products liability claim against Pfizer, nor even a medical malpractice claim against her physician. Only if she, like Cassandra Colville, is not informed by her physician about Depo-Provera's risks and is not provided with the patient labeling and brochure, will she have a medical malpractice claim against her physician.

Summary

The FDA's approval of Depo-Provera for contraception, a swift conclusion to a twenty-five-year controversy, is Judith Weisz's story of the national politics of drug risk management. The FDA's rush to approval, a mere six months from the submission of the New Drug Approval, to Depo-Provera's marketing approval, did not permit its Fertility and Maternal Health Advisory Committee to play a meaningful role in the assessment and acceptability of the drug's risk, nor did it permit the FDA staff to offer any meaningful critique of Upjohn's clinical studies. The FDA, having decided that Depo-Provera posed no significant risk of breast cancer, asked the committee to evaluate only the osteoporosis and low infant birth rate studies. So quickly did the FDA move that Dr. Ridgely Bennett's "Medical Officer's Report," supporting approval, did not engage in any independent critique of the Depo-Provera clinical studies, but adopted almost verbatim Upjohn's "FDA Advisory Committee Depo-Provera Brochure," which the company had submitted a month before the advisory committee's meeting.

Judith Weisz's story, as told by Drs. Janet Daling, Nancy Lee, Jane Zones, and other participants in the advisory committee meeting, questioned the clinical trial evidence from the WHO cancer studies and the New Zealand osteoporosis study, which the FDA disregarded in approving Depo-Provera. The WHO breast cancer study reported a statistically significant increased risk for young women, those most likely to be prescribed the drug, but the study was conducted in countries where the breast cancer rate is one-half that of American women. The New Zealand osteoporosis study found that women who took Depo-Provera lost bone mineral density and were at a statistically increased risk of osteoporosis, but the study was poorly designed, limited to five years, and involved a small number of women.

Clearly, the FDA made a risk management decision that rejected the risk assessment standards of the Public Board of Inquiry chaired by Dr. Judith Weisz, minimized the assessment of Depo-Provera's risk, and found it acceptable to market the drug, because the agency had recently approved Norplant, a long-acting progestogen, expressed its confidence that the drug's labeling could address groups of women who were at increased risk, and conditioned approval on a post-approval study of osteoporosis. When the agency approved Depo-Provera and revised its labeling by adding a black box warning, it alerted physicians to the risk of osteoporosis and transferred to them the task of making a risk management decision about the use of Depo-Provera when they prescribed the drug.

In Depo-Provera's post-approval world, Anne MacMurdo's story has been told by the women who suffered adverse side effects from the drug's use. Unlike her six day trial, little is known about their litigation, because their cases were settled for confidential amounts and the disclosure of documents prohibited by protective orders. The cases of Jamie Lorenzi, Cassandra Colville, Adrienne Oliver, and Melanie Montagnon are the exception. They, like Anne MacMurdo, initiated the process of judicial risk management by filing products liability suits against Upjohn corporate heirs, Pharmacia & Upjohn and Pfizer. While Anne MacMurdo survived Upjohn's summary judgment motion and had her case tried before a jury, they did not. Still, there are common features in their cases. The most important is the learned intermediary doctrine, which limited judicial risk management in these products liability cases, because the doctrine provides that Pharmacia & Upjohn and Pfizer have a legal duty to provide adequate warnings of the risk of using Depo-Provera not to the patient, but to the prescribing physician.

Were the warnings adequate? The courts in *MacMurdo* and *Lorenzi* found that the warnings met the threshold test for adequacy, because Upjohn and Pfizer had fulfilled their duty to provide physicians with Depo-Provera's FDA-approved labeling, which identified bleeding and bone mineral density loss as risk factors. As a consequence, Jamie Lorenzi and the other three women had the burden of proving by means of expert testimony that the warnings were inadequate. In *MacMurdo*, the Florida Supreme Court disqualified Anne MacMurdo's expert, and in *Colville*, the Florida federal district court found that Cassandra Colville's expert did not address the adequacy of the warnings. When Adrienne Oliver and Melanie Montagnon argued that the warnings were inadequate, because they failed to include additional warnings of the risk of osteoporosis and require monitoring of bone mineral density, the district courts declined to use this evidence to assess Depo-Provera's risk and rejected their challenges, because their assessment would invade the FDA's jurisdiction and circumvent its drug approval process.

At the same time, there are critical differences. Anne MacMurdo was able to prove at trial that Depo-Provera caused her bleeding, which was a compensable injury, but the four other women found it impossible to prove on summary judgment that the drug caused their low bone mass density and that this loss would lead to the future harm of fracture. Still, Anne MacMurdo's story, like those of the other four women who brought osteoporosis-osteopenia claims, document the difficulties of gaining access to state and federal courts and successfully using them to manage their contraceptive risk.

Judith Weisz's and Anne MacMurdo's stories of Depo-Provera's approval and its osteoporosis litigation provide a window on the assessment and acceptability of the drug's risk as they are governed by a dual system of risk management defined by federal and state law. Judith Weisz's story explains the FDA's risk management decision to approve the drug. After 1992, Anne MacMurdo's story provides a framework for understanding physician prescription decisions, the adverse effects women claim to have suffered from its use, and the legal remedies available to them. The four osteoporosis cases bind the two stories together and explore how federal and state law are interwoven in the context of litigation.

5

Chemical Castration

The Johns Hopkins Clinic and People v. Gauntlett

Judith Weisz's story of risk management has focused on the Food and Drug Administration's decisions throughout Depo-Provera's twenty-five-year contraceptive approval process. Now her story turns full circle to a subject introduced in Chapter 1: the FDA's limited control of the experimental use of Depo-Provera. For her, the FDA's drug risk management begins with the Claimed Investigational Exemption for a New Drug (IND), which creates a boundary between risk assessment and risk acceptability. Within this boundary, IND evidence is assessed using scientific criteria. Physicians and researchers, like those at the Grady Clinic, received an IND, but crossed this boundary when they used Depo-Provera for contraception. Judith Weisz's story, as told by Dr. Sidney Wolfe, Director of the Public Citizen Health Research Group, found that physicians at the Johns Hopkins Sexual Disorders Clinic who experimented with the drug's use on convicted sex offenders did not apply for, receive, or implement an IND, but operated outside the boundary for the conduct of scientific research.

In this setting, Depo-Provera's unapproved criminal justice use is Roger Gauntlett's story, which began at his 1984 trial, when the judge granted him probation on the condition that he use the drug as chemical castration, patterned on its use at the Johns Hopkins Clinic.[1] Since then, state legislatures have responded to the increase in child molestation by enacting chemical castration statutes that have either given courts the discretion to use the drug or mandated them to impose it. This new set of risk managers—state criminal court judges, legislators, and corrections officers—have operated outside the IND's boundary because they did not rely on any scientific assessment of Depo-Provera, but found it politically acceptable to impose the drug as a probation and parole condition on sex offenders convicted of child molestation. Roger Gauntlett's story is the tale of sex offenders who are compelled to use Depo-Provera as a condition of probation or parole, a story that provides them with the statutory and constitutional legal defenses he used to manage the drug's risk.[2]

Judith Weisz's and Roger Gauntlett's stories draw together two levels of risk management based on the Federal Food, Drug, and Cosmetic Act and state criminal statutes. Whether Depo-Provera research is required to comply with an IND research protocol is the risk management responsibility of the FDA. Whether the drug is used as a sentencing alternative is the risk management responsibility of state legislatures, courts, and parole boards. Together the two stories ask whether a convicted sex offender can make a knowing and informed decision to use Depo-Provera or is compelled to barter his body, at an unknown cost, for his freedom.

Depo-Provera's Sexual Disorders Research

Judith Weisz's story begins at the Johns Hospital's Sexual Disorders Clinic,[3] where Depo-Provera's use in the treatment of paraphilias began in 1966.[4] Dr. John Money found that the drug, as a steroid, reduced testosterone levels and consequently had a negative effect on genital functioning. "It was possible to show by calibrating the dosage, the frequency of ejaculation, erection, and erotic behavior could be calculated."[5] Dr. Pierre Gagne used doses varying from 100 to 600 milligrams per week (eight to forty-three times the dosage given to women for contraception every three months) and found that "patients become generally impotent as testosterone levels decreased to one-fourth of their initial levels."[6] Depo-Provera is also a psychotropic drug that can control paraphiliac behavior by reducing the brain's erotic imagery.[7] Drs. Dietrich Blumer and Claude Migeon reported that "the effects of MPA cannot be simply interpreted by its androgen depleting effect.[8] There is a direct effect on cerebral functions, as large doses of [this synthetic] progesterone administered intravenously have an anesthetic effect."[9]

Drs. John Money and Fred Berlin used Depo-Provera in conjunction with counseling in a program that included a one- or two-month hospital stay followed by outpatient treatment. Dr. Money found that his patients benefited from the drug, because it strengthened "the threshold or barrier to sexual arousal. . . . As a consequence, the individual is metaphorically on vacation from the demands of his sex drive and is so able to experience an erotic or psycho-sexual realignment in conjunction with counseling."[10]

Drs. Money and Berlin have acknowledged that Depo-Provera's use creates risks. The most common adverse short-term side effects include fatigue, weight gain, hot flashes, cold sweats, hypertension, headaches, and insomnia. They also found that Depo-Provera has to be continuously administered to be effective in controlling the paraphiliac's behavior, but their studies have not addressed the drug's long-term side effects, which, though unknown, may produce atypical sperm associated with fetal abnormalities.[11] In sum, they believed their discovery held out the promise that Depo-Provera could play a leading role in the pharmacological control of sexual deviation disorders and sex offender behavior.[12]

Depo-Provera's criminal justice use first came to public attention in 1983, when Joseph Frank Smith, the San Antonio ski mask rapist, was fined $10,000 and given ten years probation on the condition that he receive Depo-Provera injections at the Johns Hopkins Clinic. The case generated local protests and attracted national attention when Margaret Engle disclosed in a *Washington Post* article that "90 men from seven states are receiving treatment at Hopkins. Most are receiving or have received Depo-Provera. About 70 men are there under court order."[13]

The *Post* article attracted the attention of the Public Citizen Health Research Group and its director, Dr. Sidney Wolfe, who knew that Depo-Provera was not FDA-approved for criminal justice use. The *Post* article led him and Carey LaCheen, one of his assistants, to initiate an inquiry based on two risk management questions: Was the Johns Hopkins program experimentation or medical treatment? Was Dr. Berlin's use of Depo-Provera to treat convicted criminals approved by the FDA? The Health Research Group's answers revealed that the individuals and institutions, including the Food and Drug Administration, The Upjohn Company, the Johns Hopkins Institutional Review Board, and the Johns Hopkins Sexual Disorders Clinic, were operating in a fragmented system of risk management, that they failed to manage Depo-Provera's risk, and that these failures made Depo-Provera available for criminal justice use as a probation and parole condition for sex offenders.

The Food and Drug Administration

Pharmaceutical risk management is initially a matter for the FDA. The Federal Food, Drug, and Cosmetic Act grants the FDA authority to control the testing of potentially marketable drugs.[14] FDA approval of a Claimed Investigational Exemption for a New Drug (IND) permits a manufacturer to conduct preliminary tests. An IND is designed to ensure that investigators will "collect detailed information, adhere to informed consent requirements, make periodic reports to FDA, and obtain approval of an Institutional Review Board, by justifying the experimental use of a particular treatment and research design."[15]

Depo-Provera's odyssey began in 1963, when the FDA granted Upjohn IND approval to test the drug as a female contraceptive, and continued for thirty years until the agency granted Upjohn a marketing license. But the FDA has never approved Depo-Provera for any criminal justice use. As a drug approved for at least one medical purpose since 1960 and for contraception since 1992, it has been permissible for Upjohn to sell the drug, for physicians, exercising their informed medical judgment, to prescribe it to treat sexual deviation disorders, and for judges to condition probation and parole on its use. Depo-Provera's criminal justice use raises two questions: Can the drug be safe and effective for a criminal justice use that the FDA has not approved? What actions has the FDA taken with regard to Depo-Provera's unapproved criminal justice use?

The Health Research Group inquiry revealed that the FDA exercised limited control over the drug's non-approved experimental use. According to Dr. Harry Meyer, Director of the FDA's Center of Drugs and Biologics, agency regulations require drug manufacturers to submit an IND only when they sponsor clinical trials, but do not require "an individual physician independently treating patients."[16] A physician conducting a clinical investigation was, however, encouraged to submit an IND. "The Agency," he said, "has long held the position that the Federal Food, Drug and Cosmetic Act regulates investigation, not the 'practice of medicine,' and that once a drug product has been approved for marketing, a physician may, in treating patients prescribe the drug for uses not included in the drug's approved labeling."[17]

In reply to the Health Research Group's claim that Dr. Berlin's program was a research program and not the practice of medicine, Dr.

Meyer observed: "It is relatively easy to cite examples at each end of the practice-investigation spectrum on which there would be little disagreement," but for him, Dr. Berlin's situation was "less clear."[18] Nevertheless, he concluded: "We believe the treatment of these patients with Depo-Provera must in fact be considered part of the practice of medicine, primarily because there is no evidence that Dr. Berlin is doing anything other than providing what he believes to be appropriate patient care."[19]

The Health Research Group vigorously disagreed with the FDA's position. The Public Citizens Litigation Group attorneys asked the FDA to "reconsider its position that it does not have authority to regulate the widespread and increasing administration of Depo-Provera to male sex offenders."[20] They argued that the practice-of-medicine exemption is a narrow one. In *Chaney v. Heckler* (1983),[21] the District of Columbia Court of Appeals observed that "Congress intended to carve out only a limited practice-of-medicine exemption restricted to a physician's individualized treatment of his or her patient."[22] Dr. Berlin's program, the attorneys argued, was not the practice of medicine, but had "all the earmarks of a research program subject to FDA regulation," because the program involved:

> (1) the routine administration of Depo-Provera for an unapproved use for close to twenty years; (2) the provision of Depo-Provera to a large and apparently increasing number of persons; (3) the research . . . is being undertaken at an academic institution by a renowned research scientist, Dr. Fred Berlin, who has authored numerous articles regarding Depo-Provera's effects on sexual behavior. . . . ; (4) the administration of Depo-Provera to convicted sex offenders who are in an inherently coercive environment analogous to that involved with drug experimentation taking place in prisons; and (5) the use of Depo-Provera in a manner that is not in Dr. Meyer's own words, "widely recognized as effective" and which may have grave health consequences.[23]

The Health Research Group's inquiry met with limited success. In his reply to the Public Citizen attorneys, Dr. Mark Novitch, acting FDA Commissioner, told them that "Dr. Berlin of the Johns Hopkins Clinic filed an IND to cover the treatment program . . . [that] provides for adherence to a valid study protocol."[24] His statement must have displeased

Dr. Wolfe, because he had previously requested the protocol, but Dr. Berlin had refused saying that "the blind nature of this investigation can be best preserved at this time by keeping the details of our methodological protocol confidential."[25] Dr. Novitch also discouraged the Health Research Group from reading the FDA's acceptance of Dr. Berlin's IND broadly. "Our acceptance," he said, "is not to be viewed as a conclusion that all use of Depo-Provera to treat male sex offenders should be subject to an IND."[26]

The Upjohn Company

Pharmaceutical companies manage risk in physician use of their drugs by means of package inserts, which describe a drug and identify its FDA-approved uses, disapproved uses, warnings, precautions, and adverse reactions. A pharmaceutical company also meets its responsibility when its promotional materials make no reference to a drug's unapproved uses, and it is careful in monitoring its marketing of the drug. At the 1973 Senate hearings on Depo-Provera's unapproved contraceptive use, discussed in Chapter 2, Dr. William Hubbard, Executive Vice President at Upjohn, stated that "it would be inappropriate for the company to supply the drug directly to physicians who had declared their intention to use it for an unapproved use."[27]

At the same time, the Senate hearings also revealed that Upjohn's policy statement was at odds with the minimal control it had exercised over Depo-Provera's sale for unapproved contraceptive purposes. The FDA had disapproved the drug's contraceptive marketing in 1978 and 1986, in part, because its labeling would have limited value in controlling physician prescription practices and assuring patient consent. House hearings in 1987 on the "Use of Depo-Provera by the Indian Health Service" also disclosed that the company had continued to sell the drug for contraceptive use to private physicians and family planning clinics.[28]

Pharmaceutical companies also manage risk by sponsoring clinical trials, often conducted by university researchers, in conformity with an FDA-approved IND. Upjohn briefly had an IND for Depo-Provera's experimental use by men, but the extent of its research program and its authorization of Dr. Berlin's experiments is unclear.[29] Upjohn did, however, supply Dr. Berlin's program with Depo-Provera without cost, and he provided Upjohn with his research reports.[30] By October 1983, public attention to Depo-Provera's criminal justice use and the Health Research Group's investigation appears to have led Upjohn to discontinue its support of the Johns Hopkins program, withdraw its IND, and terminate its "plans to attempt to receive FDA approval of Depo-Provera for use in sex offenders."[31] In fact, Upjohn took further action to distance itself from the drug's use as a probation condition for sex offenders when it announced: "We have no plans to market [Depo-Provera] for sexually disturbed men."[32] Then, perhaps, referring to the San Antonio ski mask rapist case, it added: "Now juries are prescribing the drug. We consider that to be an inappropriate off-label use."[33]

The Johns Hopkins Institutional Review Board

University institutional review boards (IRBs) manage risk by requiring researchers to submit protocols to them and receive their approval before initiating their studies, by approving only studies with sound research designs that will assure that subjects are capable of giving their informed consent, by periodically reviewing research protocols, and by suspending or terminating protocols that violate accepted research practices, IRB standards, and FDA regulations.

The Johns Hopkins institutional review board exercised limited control over Depo-Provera's non-approved experimental use. According to Dr. N. Franklin Atkinson, Chair of the Johns Hopkins University Joint Committee on Clinical Investigation, the JCCI had, between 1976 and 1980, approved Dr. Berlin's protocol for Depo-Provera's use on convicted and incarcerated sex offenders. In 1976, he stated, "the JCCI approved (with some reservations) an RPN (research protocol) from Dr. Berlin in which patients . . . would be monitored by a variety of blood and psychological tests in an effort to profile the drug's effect on the endocrine system and behavioral traits."[34]

In 1979, however, the JCCI did not consider Dr. Berlin's use of the drug "ideal" and approved an extension of his protocol for only one year. "It was," Dr. Atkinson said, "strongly suggested . . . that a controlled study of the safety and efficacy of the form of therapy be undertaken."[35] Since

Dr. Berlin did not submit the suggested protocol, his subsequent Depo-Provera research on sex offenders was not based on a JCCI-approved research protocol, but "as the legal prerogative of a medical practitioner."[36]

Why did the JCCI take no action to suspend or terminate Dr. Berlin's research? Dr. Atkinson, like Dr. Meyer at the FDA, took refuge in the practice-of-medicine exception. "It is often difficult," he said, "for an IRB to clearly distinguish between what is 'accepted medical practice' from what may be 'experimental' especially in cases involving the unapproved use of drugs FDA approved for other purposes. Had we been dealing with an unlicensed drug, IRB approval would be mandatory, "[but in] this case," he argued, "because Depo-Provera is a licensed pharmaceutical, the physician involved had the option of continuing to treat patients based on his best clinical judgment without IRB approval or oversight."[37]

In response, Dr. Wolfe found that the JCCI's inability to distinguish the practice of medicine from research was specious, because the JCCI, prior to 1980, had regarded Dr. Berlin's program as experimental. Now, he concluded: "Although you no longer sanction this program and have insisted that a proper study be conducted, the former treatment program continues, now without your oversight."[38]

Johns Hopkins Sexual Disorders Clinic

Pharmaceutical researchers manage risk by employing a sound research design and assuring that their subjects are capable of and do, in fact, give both their voluntary and knowing consent to the use of drugs. The Health Research Group inquiry raised two basic informed consent questions about Depo-Provera's FDA unapproved criminal justice use at the Johns Hopkins Clinic: How can convicted sex offenders truly give informed consent to the drug's use? What is the duty of researchers to disclose the drug's risks to their subjects?

The Sexual Disorders Clinic's literature states that clients are first evaluated by a team of social workers, nurses, and physicians, and, if they are admitted to the program, they are given physical and psychiatric examinations, and possibly Depo-Provera.[39] In using the drug, Dr. Fred Berlin claimed that his was a treatment program, not an experimental one, and that it managed risk by providing the information necessary for his patients to give their informed consent. The clinic's consent form, obtained by the Health Research Group, disclosed, however, that Dr. Berlin's subjects/patients could not give their knowing consent.

The clinic's consent form tells the patient/subject that "Depo-Provera is a hormone which is similar to those contained in birth control pills . . . [but it] has not been approved by the FDA at this time for use as a 'sexual appetite suppressant,' although the FDA has deemed it to be effective for human use for other purposes."[40] Then the consent form states that "Depo-Provera is usually given once a week by means of two injections," and then it identifies the "most common" and "less common" side effects of Depo-Provera use.[41] The consent form acknowledges that Depo-Provera causes breast cancer in female beagle dogs, but then states: "There have been no reports of this drug causing cancer in men."[42] Finally, the consent form tells the patient/subject that "it is permissible for your doctor to prescribe this medication for you through this clinic with your consent" because it has been approved for other uses.[43]

All of these statements are misleading. The consent form does not disclose to the patients/subjects that no one has applied for FDA approval to use Depo-Provera as a "sexual appetite suppressant," nor does it reveal that the drug's only approved use in 1984 was as adjunctive therapy and palliative treatment of renal and endometrial cancer. The form does not identify Depo-Provera as a synthetic form of the hormone progesterone, nor does it disclose that the drug is an injectable female contraceptive approved for use in other countries, but not by the FDA, because the drug is a suspected carcinogen.

The consent form does not tell the patients/subjects the amount of Depo-Provera to be given with each injection, nor does it specify that this amount, on average 500 milligrams, may vary from eight to forty-three times the amount given to women for contraception every three months. The form does not identify the research reports on the drug's side effects or the amount of the drug administered to research subjects. Finally, the consent form does not tell the patients/subjects that no studies had reported the drug causing cancer in men, because none had been conducted. In fact, the form fails to state that no randomized controlled clinical studies on its use in men had been conducted. Instead, the form represents an uncontrolled research study as the practice of medicine, not only with the statement it is "permissible for your doctor to prescribe this medication for you through this clinic with your consent," but also with its constant use of the word "treatment."[44]

The Health Research Group's criticism of the Johns Hopkins Clinic's consent form revealed two basic flaws in the Johns Hopkins Clinic's program. First, Dr. Berlin was unable to make any scientifically valid statements about Depo-Provera's safety in the treatment of sexual disorders. Dr. Wolfe and Carey LaCheen, his research assistant, found that there was "no relevant information on the health effects in humans . . . [because] Upjohn [has] conducted its studies . . . without control groups to support the drug's approval as a female contraceptive. There is even less information on the safety of Depo-Provera for men . . . [because] there have been no controlled long-term studies to assess the risk of cancer, cardiovascular disease or permanent sterility."[45] For Dr. Berlin's patients/subjects, they concluded: "The real extent of Depo-Provera's risks are unknown."[46]

The Health Research Group's inquiry identified a second flaw in the Johns Hopkins Clinic program. Dr. Wolfe and Ms. LaChen found that "there is currently no good scientific evidence that Depo-Provera is effective for the treatment of male sex offenders,"[47] because Dr. Berlin's findings were based not on clinical studies, but on case reports and single-case experimental designs, which provided only anecdotal evidence. "There have been no double blind studies which compare the effectiveness of Depo-Provera plus counseling or psychotherapy to counseling and a saline injection . . . and no studies which compare the effect of Depo-Provera and counseling to Depo-Provera alone without the concomitant use of therapy."[48]

The Health Research Group then dismissed Dr. Berlin's claim that Depo-Provera acts as a "sexual appetite suppressant" by lowering testosterone levels, because "the relationship between testosterone levels and deviant compulsive sexual behavior has yet to be demonstrated. . . . [Furthermore,] Dr. Berlin's own data demonstrate that the relationship . . . is far from clear. . . . Not all of his patients [with deviant or compulsive sexual behavior] have high testosterone levels."[49] Dr. Wolfe and Ms. LaCheen also dismissed Dr. Berlin's claim, reported in three of his research publications, that Depo-Provera had an 85 percent success rate, because only three of twenty individuals had relapsed, but nine of the twenty were dropouts. "Patient dropouts," they concluded, "can hardly be counted as treatment successes. . . . When the dropouts are removed, there are only 11 remaining patients."[50]

In sum, the Health Research Group's inquiry into the Johns Hopkins program exposed the fragmented character of pharmaceutical risk management. The inquiry made clear that the FDA is a licensing agency with limited direct control over pharmaceutical marketing and research practices, that Upjohn had made Depo-Provera available for an IND unapproved research purpose, that Johns Hopkins institutional review board had failed to exercise meaningful oversight, that Dr. Berlin had failed to provide his research subjects/patients with information about the drug's FDA status and the risks its use posed to their personal health, and that they were unable to make an informed choice. The FDA, Upjohn, and the JCCI had, in fact, ceded the assessment and acceptability of Depo-Provera's risk to Dr. Berlin.

Depo-Provera's risk to sex offenders continues to be unregulated. The FDA has given no attention to the drug's criminal justice use. Upjohn continued to supply the drug to physicians who then used it to treat or experiment upon sex offenders. The Johns Hopkins University Joint Committee on Clinical Investigation has had no risk management role since 1991, when Dr. Berlin established the National Institute for the Study, Prevention, and Treatment of Sexual Trauma as a free-standing private clinic.[51] The National Institute continued to provide the clinical services of his university-affiliated clinic and use a consent form virtually identical to his Johns Hopkins Clinic form.[52] As a consequence, Dr. Berlin continued to provide Depo-Provera without disclosing its risks to his patients/subjects, who unknowingly consent to its use.

Sexual Disorders Research Continues

Judith Weisz's story of the Johns Hopkins Clinic, as told by Dr. Sidney Wolfe, is a tale of the clinic's failure to abide by the canons of scientific research. Thereafter, her story continues to be told by other medical researchers.Their critiques of the drug's use to treat men with sexual disorders and as a sentencing alternative for sexual offenders were defined by the Health Research Group's inquiry.

Dr. Berlin's studies and those conducted by other psychiatrists and clinical psychologists have not provided any scientifically valid basis for assessing the safety and effectiveness of using Depo-Provera to treat sex-ual deviates and sex offenders, including pedophiles, because they are case reports of the drug's use by several men and open trials of no more than fifty men. Case reports provide only anecdotal evidence detailing the patient's history, physical examination, diagnosis, administration of the drug, behavior outcomes, and follow-up for a short period of time.[53] Open trials allow both the researcher and subject to know the treat-ments being administered, but they and case reports fall short of the demanding requirements and statistical power of clinical trials, because of their "lack of control groups . . . non-random participant assignment, and small sample sizes."[54]

Even the three double-blind studies of Depo-Provera,[55] identified by Dr. Florence Thibaut, were based on nonequivalent control groups, small numbers of participants, and high dropout rates, which biased their results and undermined their statistical power to reliably measure the drug's effect on and assess its risk to human health.[56] In 2013, Dr. Thomas Douglas reported that "no randomized controlled trials have been published. Thus . . . evidence for . . . [the drug's] effectiveness is not robust"[57] With no clinical trials, one must add, evidence of its safety is also "not robust."

Without randomized controlled clinical trials, these studies suffer from several faults. First, they contain only passing references to sub-jects having signed informed consent forms, assuming the subjects had read them, and they may be as flawed as the consent forms the Health Research Group found Dr. Berlin provided to his research subjects. Without informed consent forms that fully disclose the study's pur-pose, duration, procedures, risks, and benefits, research subjects can-not knowingly and voluntarily consent, and investigators cannot assure them of their health and safety.

These studies have a second fault: They are not clinical trials. The studies that have been conducted suggest that Depo-Provera can be ef-fective in treating men with a variety of paraphilias, including pedo-philia,[58] that the drug is most effective when used in conjunction with psychotherapy, and that it must be continuously administered, otherwise the subject's "sexual appetite" will return.[59] At the same time, the studies have disclosed a lengthy alphabetical list of side effects first identified by Dr. John Money.[60] Long-term side effects have not been investigated, but, as documented by Depo-Provera's contraceptive research, they may include cancer and osteoporosis.[61] Since these studies of Depo-Provera are not clinical trials, but are case reports, open trials, and double blind studies with no statistical power,[62] the evidence of the drug's safety and effectiveness in treating sexual deviation disorders, or paraphilias, and their side effects is speculative.

These studies have a final fault: They were conducted to investigate not merely Depo-Provera's use in the treatment of sexual disorders, but also its use as a sentencing alternative with the goal of reducing the recidivism of sex offenders, particularly child molesters. This use introduces a new risk manager, the trial court judge, who will be confronted with two challenges in deciding whether to sentence a sex offender to use the drug as a probation condition. An individualized medical assessment by a psychiatrist trained in sexual disorders is a necessary first step, because sex offenders are a highly heterogeneous group who may suffer not only from pedophilia, but also from an antisocial personality disorder,[63] alcoholism, or drug abuse. If a defendant suffers from a sexual disorder, the judge's second step is to determine whether Depo-Provera can be used as a probation condition. There is, however, no scientifically credible research to support a judge ordering a defendant to use the drug: no reliable evidence that it is safe and effective and that its use reduces a defendant's risk of recidivism. Therefore, no defendant acting reasonably can give his informed consent to the judge's order, and his defense counsel has a duty to oppose the probation order on statutory and constitutional grounds.

People v. Gauntlett

People v. Gauntlett raised for the first time judicial competence to assess Depo-Provera's health risk and decide the drug's acceptability as a probation condition.[64] The case began when Roger Gauntlett, an Upjohn heir divorced from the mother of two children, was charged with five counts of sexual misconduct for the repeated rape of his fourteen-year-old stepdaughter and, after she left to live with her mother in Arizona, of turning his attention to his ten-year-old stepson.[65]

On July 12, 1983, when his trial was scheduled to begin, Roger Gauntlett entered a plea of *nolo contendere* to one charge of first degree criminal sexual conduct.[66] Judge John Fitzgerald proposed a sentence of one year in the county jail, five years probation, and a $2,000,000 donation from his trust fund to establish a rape counseling center.[67] In violation of Judge Fitzgerald's confidential order forbidding disclosure of the proposed sentence, the assistant prosecutor told the stepdaughter's natural father, who began a campaign against the plea bargain by sending letters to religious and community leaders protesting that the sentence had been influenced by Roger Gauntlett's money.[68] The public outcry and the assistant prosecutor's misconduct led Judge Fitzgerald to disqualify himself.[69]

On January 25, 1984, the case was transferred to Judge Robert Borsos, who five days later, sentenced Roger Gauntlett to five years probation with the first year to be served in the county jail.[70] As a condition of probation, the judge required him to submit himself "to castration by chemical means patterned after the research and treatment of the Johns Hopkin[s] Hospital" for five years.[71]

In deciding to impose a Depo-Provera condition, Judge Borsos had consulted two *American Journal of Psychiatry* articles on the use of the drug, a bibliography of articles on sexual deviation syndromes and the use of antiandrogen therapy,[72] a *Time* magazine article about a South Carolina trial judge who had imposed castration on three convicted rapists as a condition of their probation,[73] and a report by the defendant's psychiatrist, Dr. Mark W. Hinshaw, Executive Director of Psychiatric Consultation Services at Michigan State University.

This information was sufficient for Judge Borsos to reject the use of Depo-Provera as a probation condition. Why did he fail to assess the drug's health risk to Roger Gauntlett? Judge Borsos did not understand the limitations of the research reported in the two medical journal articles. Neither the articles by Drs. Fred Berlin and Carl Meinecke, nor the one by Dr. Pierre Gagne could have provided him with the scientific foundation to assess Depo-Provera's risk to the defendant.[74] If Judge Borsos relied upon these two articles, he ignored the importance of scientifically-based research. The Depo-Provera research, including the Berlin and Gagne articles, are clinical reports, not controlled case studies, which fail to provide the information essential to an assessment of the drug's risk. Even Dr. Berlin admitted that the three case studies reported in his journal article "were of limited research value."[75]

Judge Borsos also ignored Dr. Hinshaw's informed medical judgment about the risk that the drug posed to the defendant. In his report, Dr. Hinshaw had reached the following conclusions.

(1) The use of Depo-Provera in the Defendant's case "'is *medically and psychiatrically contraindicated.*"(2) Depo-Provera is authorized by the FDA in this country only for the treatment of "inoperable, recurrent, and metastic endometrial carcinoma and renal carcinoma." (3) The Defendant's conduct involved incest and incest is not one of the situations in which Depo-Provera has been used even on an experimental basis. (4) The Defendant is "at high risk" of having adverse medical and psychiatric reactions to the use of Depo-Provera. (5) The Defendant is under treatment for "heart spasms" for which he takes Paracardia. Progestogens such as Depo-Provera increase the incidence of cardiac dysfunction and pre-dispose individuals to thrombotic disorders. (6) The Defendant is receiving medication and psychotherapy for treatment of longstanding depression and because Depo-Provera has a potential side effect—psychic depression—the taking of Depo-Provera could be hazardous to his health. (7) The feminizing aspects of the drug would cause further problems and increase the existing depression. . . . [In conclusion,] there is absolutely no medical or psychiatric benefit that could occur from the use of Depo-Provera. On the contrary, its use would only interfere with the course of his current therapy and would expose him to needless medical and psychiatric risks.[76]

Without referring Roger Gauntlett for a professional diagnosis of his psychological and medical condition and hearing expert testimony, William Fette argued that Judge Borsos practiced medicine without a license by diagnosing Gauntlett as suffering from a "paraphiliac syndrome" and then prescribing Depo-Provera as a treatment, because the drug was "a highly effective working tool to reduce thoughts and urges about sex and [the] . . . ability to perform sex and thus to rehabilitate people in sex cases."[77] Judge Borsos also ignored Dr. Berlin's advice not to impose a Depo-Provera probation condition on a convicted sex offender, because it would "impinge upon human rights."[78] Instead, he sentenced Roger Gauntlett "to participate in a scientific experiment of an unproven drug, contrary to the rudimentary ethical and due process notions of informed consent, and under conditions even known researchers . . . [including Dr. Berlin] would not or could not accept."[79]

Roger Gauntlett challenged Judge Borsos's sentence before the Michigan Court of Appeals. William Fette, his attorney, prepared a 190-page brief to tell the court a story about the illegality of the judge's Depo-Provera probation condition on the grounds that it violated the state's common and statutory law and his client's federal constitutional rights. Judge Borsos's probation condition, he argued, violated the Michigan probation statute. The judge's use of the term "chemical castration," in his probation order, had no known medical or legal definition. If the judge were referring to Depo-Provera, it was a controversial drug that had not been licensed by the U.S. Food and Drug Administration for criminal justice use.[80]

The Depo-Provera condition was also a form of punishment disguised as a treatment that bore no relationship to Roger Gauntlett's offense or his rehabilitation. He had not been diagnosed with a "paraphiliac syn drome," which might, given the limited research data, be treatable with Depo-Provera; but the same data demonstrated that the drug was not effective in treating incest.[81] The probation condition was also impossible to perform, because it merely stated that Roger Gauntlett would "submit" to "chemical castration" at the Johns Hopkins Clinic,[82] but failed to anticipate what would happen if Dr. Berlin decided that the treatment was unsuitable, which was likely, because Roger Gauntlett had not been diagnosed as a pedophile and had not given his informed consent to Depo-Provera treatment.[83]

The probation condition had a final failure: It violated the doctrine of informed consent recognized in *Kaimowitz v. Michigan Department of Mental Health* (1973).[84] Judge Borsos's order had not allowed Roger Gauntlett to make a voluntary choice of accepting or declining probation or permitted him to make a knowing choice, because the judge had provided him with no information about the drug's risks, benefits, and alternatives. In sum, William Fette concluded that Judge Borsos's probation condition was invalid, because he had abused his discretion under the state's probation statute by issuing an order that "revealed a punitive interest and callous disregard for the Defendant's special needs" as described in Dr. Henshaw's report.[85]

William Fette then turned to the probation condition as a violation of Roger Gauntlett's federal constitutional rights. Unlike his thorough analysis of the statutory arguments he gave only passing attention to the probation condition's violation of the First, Fourth, and Fourteenth Amendments. Depo-Provera, he argued, is a psychotropic drug with a definite effect on cerebral functions, which violated Roger Gauntlett's First Amendment rights to mentation and freedom of thought.[86] The drug's use would also result in physical changes, including "an intended negative effect on genital functioning" and numerous side effects, including "weight gain of twenty to thirty pounds or more . . . [and] hypogonadism (shrinking in testicle size)" in violation of Gauntlett's Fourth Amendment "right to be free from bodily intrusions."[87] Finally, Depo-Provera would intrude upon the privacy of Roger Gauntlett's thoughts and emotions in violation of his right to privacy protected by the Due Process Clause of the Fourteenth Amendment.[88]

He gave particular attention to the Eighth Amendment, because of the impact of Depo-Provera on Roger Gauntlett's right to be free from a cruel punishment. Judge Borsos's use of the phrase "castration by chemical means" drew attention to the unacceptable penalty of surgical castration and his remarks that the drug would take away Roger Gauntlett's "manhood" indicated a punitive intent.[89] Turning to the U.S. Supreme Court's decision in *Estelle v. Gamble* (1976),[90] he found that the probation condition interfered with Roger Gauntlett's "existing medication or treatment . . . [and demonstrated] a deliberate indifference to the prisoner's serious medical needs" in violation of his right to be free from cruel and unusual punishments.[91]

The Michigan Court of Appeals decision in *People v. Gauntlett* (1984) found it unnecessary to examine arguments that a Depo-Provera probation condition violated a broad range of Roger Gauntlett's federal constitutional rights. The appellate court relied instead on four narrower grounds for its decision that Judge Borsos had imposed an illegal probation condition.[92]

First, the court found no statutory authorization for treating sex offenders with the drug and was unwilling to interpret the state probation statute, which granted trial courts the discretion to impose "other lawful conditions," to permit the use of Depo-Provera.[93] Michigan case law, along with the drug's experimental status and its "alphabet of adverse reactions from acne to cancer to weight gain," cast doubt on its validity as a probation condition.[94] Second, the court found that the professional literature demonstrated that Depo-Provera had not "gained acceptance in the medical community as a safe and reliable medical procedure."[95]

These two grounds, together with Depo-Provera's limited availability and the judge's order, made it virtually impossible for the defendant to perform the probation condition. A fourth and final ground was the court's displeasure with Roger Gauntlett's lack of informed consent, given that mentally incompetent persons and prison inmates "enjoy a greater degree of [statutory] protection from extraordinary procedures."[96] In sum, the Michigan Court of Appeals held that Judge Borsos had abused his discretion under state case law, because Roger Gauntlett's sentence was "so significantly disproportionate to sentences imposed on similarly situated defendants."[97]

In a terse decision, the Supreme Court of Michigan upheld the appellate court's finding that Depo-Provera was an unlawful probation condition, but it concluded that the appeals court had been premature in deciding that Judge Borsos had abused his sentencing discretion.[98] On remand, the trial court imposed a five- to fifteen-year prison sentence. Two appeals followed challenging the sentence. In the first, the Michigan Court of Appeals rejected Gauntlett's prison sentence and his due process, double jeopardy, and prosecutorial misconduct arguments.[99] The Michigan Supreme Court denied this appeal.[100] In the second appeal, Gauntlett challenged the sentence by petitioning the Michigan federal district court for a writ of habeas corpus,[101] but the court denied his petition[102] and the federal Court of Appeals for the Sixth Circuit affirmed.[103]

Roger Gauntlett's story, which began with his arrest in 1983 and ended with his release from prison in 1990, joins together the Johns Hopkins Clinic's use of Depo-Provera as an experimental drug and its first legally significant use as probation condition. His case also prominently introduced the trial court judge as a risk manager, who exercised the broad discretion granted by a state's probation statute to impose Depo-Provera as a probation condition, which was overruled on appeal, because of his failure to assess the drug's risk. Finally, Roger Gauntlett's case raised the ethical, medical, and legal issues that would continue to define Depo-Provera's criminal justice use.

State Chemical Castration Statutes

Judith Weisz's and Roger Gauntlett's stories were transformed in the years following his release from prison in 1990 and Depo-Provera's contraceptive approval in 1992 by a moral panic over child abduction, molestation, and murder.[104] National media attention, fear among parents, and political hostility toward those who harm children led to the enactment by the mid-1990s of national and state sexual predator statutes in an attempt to address the problem.[105] Judith Weisz's story is no longer one about the faulty science provided to support Depo-Provera's contraceptive approval and the drug's experimental use at the Johns Hopkins Clinic. Now it becomes the story of the drug's state legislatively mandated, but medically questionable use as a probation and parole condition for sex offenders. Roger Gauntlett's story is no longer one about an Upjohn heir's well-financed legal challenge to a judge's attempt to impose a Depo-Provera probation condition administered at the Johns Hopkins Clinic. Now his story becomes one told by convicted sex offenders with limited knowledge of the drug and without the benefit of his legal and financial resources to challenge the drug's criminal legal use.

State Parole Statutes: A Response to Moral Panic

The moral panic of the 1990s altered the risk management role of state trial court judges in making Depo-Provera probation and parole decisions. Until 1996, state probation and parole statutes, including Michigan's, granted judges, like Robert Borsos, the broad discretion to determine the probation conditions best suited to the defendant and to impose any lawful conditions.[106] Michigan and forty-three states still grant their judges this discretion, limited only by statutorily enumerated provisions governing eligibility and the term of probation.[107] Otherwise, state statutes provide no guidance for judges.

California became the first state to enact a chemical castration statute expressly using Depo-Provera as a parole condition to address the problem of child sex offenders. The 1996 statute vests risk management authority in its trial court judges and gives them the discretion to order Depo-Provera's use as a parole condition for first-time sexual offenders convicted of sodomy, oral copulation, sexual action with force, and bodily injury committed against children.[108] For second offenders, the statute mandates that judges order sex offenders to begin using the drug one week prior to release on parole, unless they choose surgical castration.[109] After release, the parolee is required to continue the drug's use under the supervision of the Department of Corrections until the Board of Prison Terms decides that the drug's use is no longer necessary.[110]

Fifteen other states proposed chemical castration legislation within the next two years, but only eight enacted statutes with five currently in force, four of which follow the California model.[111] Iowa, Louisiana, and Montana, like California, provide for Depo-Provera's use by persons who have been convicted of a sexual offense, variously defined,[112] against a child victim below a specified age[113] while Florida does the same, but without imposing an age limit. None of the four states requires the offender to be diagnosed with a paraphilia or sexual deviation disorder. The judges in these states, as in California, are granted limited risk management discretion. Only Louisiana mandates Depo-Provera's use on the first offense, while the other three states follow California in giving their judges the discretion to order the drug's use.[114] On the second offense, judges have no discretion. In California and the four states, they are required to order Depo-Provera's use.[115] California, Florida, Iowa, and Louisiana, but not Montana, permit their convicted sex offenders to choose between using the drug and surgical castration.[116]

The Departments of Corrections in California and the four states also have risk management authority to initiate Depo-Provera use in prison.[117] Florida courts determine the length of the drug's use, possibly for the life of the offender, while the corrections agencies in the other three states have discretionary authority to determine the duration of its use.[118] There is, however, no agreement among California and the four states on the consequences of a sex offender's failure to comply with an order to continue Depo-Provera injections. Iowa follows California in not specifying a penalty; Louisiana revokes parole for noncompliance; Florida makes a sex offender's failure to continue Depo-Provera's use a second-degree felony; and Montana imposes a sentence of criminal contempt of court with incarceration for ten to one hundred years.[119]

Among the six states, Wisconsin is the outlier, because it vests sole authority to make risk management decisions about Depo-Provera's use not in trial court judges, but in its Department of Corrections and its Parole Commission. These agencies are required to determine whether a convicted child sex offender will use Depo-Provera as a condition of parole.[120] Otherwise, the statute says nothing about the duration of the drug's use and the consequences of noncompliance. In sum, Wisconsin's is the broadest and most standardless of all six statutes.[121]

Together these six state statutes mark a sharp break with the use of Depo-Provera by individual trial court judges, like Judge Borsos, who exercise their statutory discretion in ordering sex offenders to take the drug as a probation condition. In enacting these statutes, state legislatures created two new roles for themselves. They authorized themselves to engage in the practice of medicine by prescribing a specific medication for everyone found guilty of the sexual offenses defined in their criminal codes.[122] They also authorized uncontrolled scientific experiments by mandating that all sexual offenders receive "weekly injections regardless of effectiveness . . . [and] regardless of whether individuals can tolerate the drug."[123]

In practicing medicine and authorizing the experimental use of Depo-Provera, these legislatures were not interested in managing Depo-Provera's risk for sex offenders, because they did not consult with, nor hear testimony from medical experts, including Dr. Fred Berlin. If he had testified, it is likely that he would have repeated for them his five criticisms of chemical castration statutes published in the *New England Journal of Medicine*: they disregarded the limited medical knowledge of Depo-Provera's criminal justice use by not restricting the drug to persons with pedophilia; they did not require an individual medical and psychiatric assessment to determine the drug's effectiveness; they did not provide any "collateral psychological therapies and support"; they did not administer it voluntarily; and they did not make any provision to "systematically track clinical outcomes and criminal recidivism."[124]

Instead, these legislatures responded to the public clamor to protect children by using Depo-Provera to reduce sex offender recidivism. Without any assessment of the drug's risk to sex offenders, the legislatures decided that any health risk to the sex offender was acceptable given the crimes committed and harms inflicted, because the drug promised to protect children by incapacitating their predators. To this end, the legislatures wrote statutes that "exhibit[ed] the classic signs of panic legislation, namely poor drafting, overly broad scope, and inadequate consideration of the likely consequences."[125] As a result, the statutes do not provide state courts and corrections agencies with the health risk assessment and acceptability standards to manage the risks of Depo-Provera's discretionary and mandatory use, because they contain the following risk management faults.

The state statutes fail to provide for a qualified medical professional to assess the risks of Depo-Provera use. The California, Iowa, Montana, and Wisconsin statutes do not provide for the appointment of a physician with the medical psychiatric expertise to evaluate the sex offender and determine whether he has a diagnosable sexual disorder. Florida requires only a court appointed "medical expert."[126] Louisiana alone specifies the appointment of a "qualified mental health professional with experience in treating sex offenders," but, like Florida, it does not require the health professional to be a physician.[127]

The statutes do not contain the criteria for assessing whether the sex offender is an appropriate candidate for Depo-Provera. The Iowa statute requires "an appropriate assessment to determine whether treatment would be effective," and the Montana statute requires a "medically safe treatment," but they do not specify who will make the diagnosis. Florida requires that the sex offender be "an appropriate candidate for treatment," but, like Louisiana, it does not ensure a valid diagnosis of a sexual disorder that may be treatable with the drug, because it does not identify any criteria for determining an "appropriate candidate."[128] Only Louisiana provides psychological counseling in conjunction with Depo-Provera, but only if it is a component of a treatment plan.

None of the statutes permits the sexual offender to make a risk management decision, because they fail to provide him with informed consent to Depo-Provera's use. Florida, Iowa, and Wisconsin do not address the subject. California, Louisiana, and Montana require only that their courts inform the sex offender of the drug's side effects, but they do not give him the right to consent or refuse to use the drug. In all, the statutes do not provide the sex offender with any meaningful right to a knowing and voluntary consent to a Depo-Provera parole condition.

The state statutes suffer from a final failure by giving their courts and corrections agencies the standardless discretion to implement a Depo-Provera parole condition. None of the statutes specifies any criteria for making an initial decision and its periodic review. None of the statutes identifies a termination date. Instead, they contain open-ended provisions that permit the drug to be used until "no longer necessary" with the possibility that the drug's use may be required for life.[129] The correction agencies in five states will make this decision, while in Florida a judge decides.[130] The statutes do not identify who will provide the injections, require the participation of a physician knowledgeable about the drug and its use by sex offenders, or immunize those who will provide Depo-Provera injections from civil and criminal liability, except in Louisiana, and then, only if the drug's use is a component of an individualized treatment plan.[131] Who will pay for the treatment, which may be required for life? Here the states are split. In California, Florida, and Montana, the state will pay, but in Iowa and Louisiana, it is the offender's responsibility.[132] Wisconsin is, once again, the outlier by not identifying who will pay.

In sum, these six states listened to the siren song of moral panic and enacted punitive chemical castration statutes that dehumanized sex offenders and treated them like "animals who prey upon vulnerable children."[133] Now their song has ended. Since 1999, no state has enacted a chemical castration statute. In 2008, Louisiana amended its statute[134] in direct response to the U.S. Supreme Court decision in *Kennedy v. Louisiana* (2008),[135] which barred the death penalty for sex offenders. At the same time, two states, Georgia in 2006[136] and Oregon in 2011,[137] repealed their statutes. The song has ended, but the haunting malady of the legislation's lyrics in six states lingers on.[138]

State Court Enforcement

State courts have the opportunity to manage risk, but state appellate courts have heard very few cases involving a Depo-Provera parole condition. Anecdotal evidence suggests two explanations. Sex offenders who have pled out their cases, as 95 percent of criminal defendants do, and been sentenced to incarceration with a Depo-Provera parole condition have waived their right to appeal by accepting a plea agreement.[139] In *People v. Foster* (2000), for example, a California court of appeals affirmed the defendant's thirty-year prison sentence with a Depo-Provera parole condition, because he had agreed in his plea bargain to waive his right to appeal.[140]

At the same time, trial court judges have not used their discretionary authority nor enforced Depo-Provera mandatory use as a parole condition. As of 2005, Florida trial court judges had sentenced only 3 of 107 sexual offenders who qualified for the drug's mandatory use as a parole condition, because they were "unaware of the statute or the defendant's triggering qualifications."[141] As of 2009, the California statute was not being enforced,[142] because judges have the discretion for public policy reasons to refuse to impose a sentence approved by the legislature, including a Depo-Provera parole condition, that "involves weekly injections . . . which alter the physiology and psychology of the convict."[143]

When state appellate courts have heard Depo-Provera parole cases, they have limited their review to requiring trial courts to comply with the provisions in their state's chemical castration statutes. In *Houston v. State* (2003)[144] and *Jackson v. State* (2005),[145] Florida courts of appeal reversed sentences mandating Depo-Provera's use on the grounds that the trial courts had failed to comply with the statute's requirements to appoint a "medical expert" to determine if the defendant would be "an appropriate candidate for treatment within 60 days," and to specify the duration of treatment for a term of years.

State appellate courts have not heard any challenges to the legality of the chemical castration statutes, including a legislature's authority to mandate the criminal legal use of a specific medication, the judicial authority to refuse to comply with Depo-Provera's statutorily mandated use, and the legal issues raised by the four risk management flaws discussed above. At the same time, state appellate courts have avoided federal constitutional challenges to a Depo-Provera parole condition. In *People v. Steele* (2004), a California court of appeals avoided an Eighth Amendment challenge, because it found that the defendant had "failed to preserve the issue for [appellate] review by not challenging the constitutionality of the [parole] order at trial."[146]

In sum, state legislatures have not managed Depo-Provera's health risk in writing their chemical castration statutes; nor have they provided their courts and corrections agencies with the guidance to implement these statutes. State appellate court review of Depo-Provera parole conditions has been limited to requiring trial courts to comply with vaguely worded statutory provisions. In no instance has a state appellate court had or taken the opportunity to engage in a substantive review of these statutes.

Since *People v. Gauntlett* (1984) and the enactment of the six chemical castration statutes now in force, state appellate courts have not decided cases that together examine the statutory and constitutional legal arguments that address the risk management issues raised by Depo-Provera's criminal justice use. They are, however, the arguments that William Fette made for Roger Gauntlett. Now they are the arguments that convicted sex offenders can make to manage the drug's risk. If they do, state appellate courts will have to address the following question: Is Depo-Provera's use a violation of state statutes and a sex offender's constitutional rights?

State Statutory Issues

Probation and parole are "creatures of statute,"[147] but generally they provide little guidance for judges, except in the six states with chemical castration parole statutes. Probation and parole may be viewed in contractual terms: The defendant contracts with the court to abide by the specific conditions as an alternative to or release from incarceration. Judges provide the conditions, but the defendant usually has the choice of accepting or rejecting them. If a convicted sex offender rejects them, he will by default have chosen incarceration as Roger Gauntlett did.[148] In the six chemical castration states, however, judges are specifically granted the discretion or mandated to impose a Depo-Provera parole condition that will permit the convicted sex offender to be released from prison. He may reject the condition, but then he will have chosen either continued incarceration or surgical castration.

The convicted sex offender, like Roger Gauntlett, will have another choice: He can begin serving his prison sentence and then appeal the judge's sentence or challenge the parole statute by addressing three questions. Is a Depo-Provera probation or parole condition a legitimate use of a trial judge's discretionary sentencing authority or is it an abuse of discretion? Is a Depo-Provera parole condition a legitimate use of a state's legislature's power? Can a sex offender give his knowing and voluntary consent to Depo-Provera probation and parole conditions, or is he coerced into using his reproductive capacity as a bargaining chip to avoid or to be released from incarceration? Together, these three questions will provide the convicted sex offender with a risk management defense by their attention to the assessment of the drug's risk and the acceptability of its use as a probation and parole condition.

Depo-Provera Probation and Parole Conditions

Medical and psychiatric treatment are two conditions a trial judge may include in a convicted sex offender's sentence.[149] Any condition must, however, be reasonably related to the offense and be capable of performance within the term of probation or parole.[150] Can a statute that permits or requires a judge to include a Depo-Provera probation and parole condition in a sex offender's sentence be challenged on the ground that the condition is unreasonable and incapable of performance?

A Depo-Provera condition must be reasonably related to the offender's crime and his rehabilitation.[151] A condition is unreasonable, according to *In re Manino* (1968), if it "has no relation to the crime of which the offender was convicted. . . . [and] requires or forbids conduct . . . not reasonably related to future criminality."[152] The Depo-Provera parole condition in the six state chemical castration statutes will fail both parts of the *Manino* test of reasonableness. As a discretionary or mandatory parole condition, the drug has no relationship to the offender's criminal behavior if he, like Roger Gauntlett, is not a pedophile.[153] For the same reason, Depo-Provera is unlikely to bear any relationship to his future criminality.[154] The drug will reduce his sex drive temporarily and, thereby, interfere with the privacy of his family life and his right to procreate, but it is not at all clear it will reduce his impulse to molest children.[155]

A treatment must also be capable of performance within the term of probation or parole.[156] To be capable of performance, a condition must be available to the convicted sex offender. Depo-Provera is actually available nationwide. Three of the six chemical castration parole statutes provide for the state to pay the cost of treatment,[157] but otherwise the drug is practically unavailable to almost all sex offenders, because they will be unable to afford the cost of the treatment.

Whether Depo-Provera is available in all six states will also depend on the willingness of medical personnel to administer the drug and the medical advisability of its use.[158] Some physicians will be reluctant to use Depo-Provera, because its criminal justice use is still experimental. As Dr. Berlin has acknowledged, medical studies of Depo-Provera are largely anecdotal and do not establish its safety and effectiveness. These studies have, however, documented that the drug's use produces an "alphabet of adverse reactions," which are as detrimental to a sex offender's mental and physical health as Dr. Henshaw claimed they would be to Roger Gauntlett's.[159] Physicians may also be persuaded by the American Medical Association's declaration in 1998 that Depo-Provera's use is unethical when it is imposed by a judge rather than being prescribed by a physician.[160] Physicians may also be reluctant to administer the drug for a final reason: They could be held criminally or civilly liable.[161]

Probation and parole conditions that are capable of performance must also be possible of fulfillment within the term of probation or parole. Most states limit felony probation and parole from five to ten years.[162] As a probation or parole condition, however, Depo-Provera does not permanently eliminate sexual potency; but must be used continually, because it produces only a temporary reduction in testosterone and the suppression of sexual arousal. Once the drug is discontinued, sexual potency and arousal return to pre-injection levels.[163] The six state statutes with a Depo-Provera parole condition will, therefore, violate the fulfillment test, because none of them sets a termination date, but permit the drug to be used until "no longer necessary," with the duration of its use dependent on the discretion of state courts and correction authorities. As a consequence, Depo-Provera's use as a parole condition could require life parole, which will make it difficult to enforce and will violate a state's probation statute.[164] A Depo-Provera life probation and parole condition that requires the continued use of the drug will also be subject to challenge on grounds of unreasonableness, because the drug's long-term use may lead to cancer and osteoporosis.

Acceptance of a Depo-Provera Probation and Parole Condition

Probation and parole are usually granted only if the defendant accepts, but his acceptance has to be based on his informed consent: It has to be both knowing and voluntary.[165] Informed consent depends on his knowledge of his diagnosis, the nature, purpose, and duration of the treatment,[166] and four factors identified in *Canterbury v. Spence* (1972): the known risks of the contemplated treatment, the expected benefit, the possible disadvantages without any treatment, and the alternative methods of treatment available.[167]

Judge Borsos did not provide Roger Gauntlett with any information required by the *Canterbury* test.[168] The Florida, Iowa, and Wisconsin chemical castration statutes say nothing about informed consent, apparently leaving the task to the discretion of the sentencing judge. California, Louisiana, and Montana provide the convicted sex offender with information about only one *Canterbury* criterion: Depo-Provera side effects.[169] Even if a trial judge imposed a Depo-Provera probation or parole condition, it will not be possible to provide the sex offender with information about all of the *Canterbury* criteria, because the Depo-Provera research is based on case reports, open trials, and three double-blind studies,[170] and their results are often contradictory and anecdotal.[171]

Voluntary consent depends upon the ability to freely choose. Consent by convicted defendants, prisoners, and institutionalized mental patients to psychosurgery or psychoactive drugs, given as a condition of probation or parole, is coerced.[172] In *Kaimowitz v. Department of Mental Health* (1973), the court held that when a mental patient's release depends upon his consent to experimental surgery, coercion exists and voluntary consent cannot be given.[173] Judge Borsos did not give Roger Gauntlett the opportunity to consent; nor do the six state chemical castration statutes give a convicted sex offender that opportunity. Even if the statutes were to provide him with the opportunity, an offender's decision could not be voluntary, because the sex offender, when faced with two options, a lengthy prison sentence or release from incarceration with a Depo-Provera condition, cannot be said to have the capacity to act freely in making a choice.[174] Freedom of choice is impossible, because his loss of liberty constitutes a deprivation of such a magnitude that he cannot choose freely and voluntarily, but is forced to give his consent to an alternative he would not otherwise choose.

In sum, a convicted sex offender can manage the drug's risk by arguing that a judge cannot make him an offer of probation, because the judge has no basis on which to make an assessment of the drug's risk and its acceptability, because Depo-Provera research is based primarily on case reports and not randomized controlled clinical trials. The sex offender will next argue that he cannot accept a parole condition, or any similar probation condition, because the condition is neither reasonably related to his crime or rehabilitation, nor is it capable of performance. Finally, he will argue that he cannot give his informed consent, because a judge cannot provide him with the information about the drug that will to allow him to give his knowing consent; nor will he be able to choose freely if the choice will be made for him by the judge.

Federal Constitutional Issues

Sentencing sex offenders to probation or granting them parole must be consistent with their federal constitutional rights.[175] A convicted sex offender will be able to manage Depo-Provera's risk by arguing that a probation or parole condition containing the drug, which is not reasonably related to his crime or rehabilitation and is impossible for him to perform, will violate his substantive and procedural constitutional rights as, William Fette argued, they violated Roger Gauntlett's.[176]

The federal constitutional rights implicated by a Depo-Provera condition are based on positive and negative conceptions of the constitutional liberty of mind and body and on two kinds of freedom—freedom to (autonomy) and freedom from (integrity)—related to the body and mind.[177] The constitutional right of personal autonomy protects one's freedom to engage in mental and bodily behaviors, and the constitutional right of personal integrity protects one's freedom from government intrusions on mind and body. The intersection of these concepts produces four areas of freedom that will serve as the vehicle to evaluate the specific constitutional rights at issue.

The First Amendment's Free Speech Clause confers a personal right to both mental autonomy and integrity: the freedom to receive, generate, and express one's thoughts and to be free from government thought control. The Eighth Amendment's Cruel and Unusual Punishment Clause bestows a right to mental and bodily integrity free from government invasions. The Fourteenth Amendment's Due Process Clause contains the guarantees of procedural due process and substantive limits on government invasions of bodily integrity, "the freedom to generate behaviors," and bodily autonomy.[178] Finally, the Fourteenth Amendment's Equal Protection Clause grants a right to bodily integrity, which limits government from discriminating.

How do probation and parole conditions that permit or require Depo-Provera's use intrude upon a sex offender's four personal freedoms in a manner that violate his First, Eighth, and Fourteenth Amendment rights? A sex offender's attorney can argue, as William Fette did for Roger Gauntlett, that a Depo-Provera condition is unacceptable, because it is not based on any meaningful medical assessment of the drug's risk to his client's personal health and it intrudes upon his fundamental First, Eighth, and Fourteenth Amendments freedoms.

First Amendment Freedom of Speech

Depo-Provera conditions are subject to First Amendment scrutiny because they intrude upon mental autonomy and integrity.[179] The amendment's fundamental right to freedom of expression includes the guarantee of mental autonomy that protects the right to mentation, the ability to receive, generate, and communicate ideas, and within its penumbras, as *Griswold v. Connecticut* (1965) held, a right to privacy.[180] The First Amendment also contains a guarantee of mental integrity. In *Stanley v. Georgia* (1969), the Supreme Court proclaimed: "It is wholly inconsistent with the philosophy of the First Amendment to grant government the power to control a person's thoughts," including loathsome, noxious, and immoral thoughts.[181] *Kaimowitz v. Department of Mental Health* (1973) specifically recognized that psychotherapy intrudes upon a person's mental processes and generation of ideas, which come within the bounds of the First Amendment and a right to privacy.[182]

Depo-Provera intrudes upon a sex offender's ability to think about sex. As a psychotropic drug, "the effects of MPA cannot simply be interpreted by its androgen-depleting effect. There is a direct effect on cerebral functions as large doses of [this synthetic] progesterone administered intravenously have an anesthetic effect."[183] Studies at John Hopkins and elsewhere agree: The use of Depo-Provera diminishes sexual fantasies. Dr. John Money found that the drug reduces imagistic eroticism, including "sexual or erotic sleeping dreams, day dreams, and copulation fantasies."[184]

The First Amendment does not prohibit all intrusions on mental autonomy. *Rennie v. Klein* (1978), a case involving the involuntary administration of psychotropic drugs to a mental patient, held that the First Amendment does not prohibit all intrusions on freedom of thought.[185]

Whether a drug impermissibly intrudes upon a person's freedom to think and right to privacy in thoughts about sex, the *Rennie* court said, will depend on the length and permanency of their effects on a person's senses and ability to think and speak.[186] Measured by the *Rennie* effects test, a Depo-Provera condition and its involuntary administration will violate a sex offender's First Amendment rights, because the effect of a single injection may be temporary and reversible, but its effectiveness as a probation and parole condition will require its continuous use.[187]

A First Amendment fundamental rights analysis will also condemn the use of a Depo-Provera condition if it is imposed by a judge in the exercise of his statutory discretion or mandated for him to impose by state statute. The sex offender's fundamental right to generate sexually deviant ideas will be subject to strict scrutiny, which will permit a state to limit or forbid conduct based on those thoughts only if it can first demonstrate a compelling interest.[188] Clearly, a state will be able to demonstrate that it has a compelling interest in preventing child molestation. Then the government will have to establish that a Depo-Provera condition is necessary to achieve this compelling interest. Here the state's argument is likely to fail, because there are other means more narrowly tailored to and less burdensome on a sex offender's fundamental right to mentation. Instead of being probated, the sex offender can be incarcerated and, if incarcerated, be denied parole and required to serve the entirety of his sentence.

Even if a court were to decide that a Depo-Provera condition did not intrude upon a sex offender's fundamental right to mentation, the condition must comply with the requirements of the usually less demanding rational basis review: The condition must advance a legitimate government interest in the prevention of sexual offenses against children and must be a means reasonably related to the advancement of that goal.[189] Clearly, the state has a legitimate interest in preventing child molestation, but a Depo-Provera condition cannot rationally advance that goal, because the experimental research has documented that the drug is not effective in reducing the incidence of sex offenses, including child molestation.

Eighth Amendment Cruel and Unusual Punishment

Probation and parole conditions are subject to the Eighth Amendment's limitation on cruel and unusual punishment, which protects mental and bodily integrity.[190] Whether these conditions violate a sexual offender's Eighth Amendment right will depend upon the answers to two questions: Do these conditions result in treatment or punishment? Are these conditions cruel and unusual punishment?

Depo-Provera is not exempt from Eighth Amendment scrutiny merely because it is characterized as treatment.[191] William Fette argued in the *Gauntlett* case that the drug was a form of punishment disguised as treatment.[192] *Rennie v. Klein* established a four-part test to determine if a therapy is treatment or punishment, which the U.S. Supreme Court adopted in *Washington v. Harper* (1990): Does it have any therapeutic value? Is its use recognized as accepted medical practice? Is it part of an ongoing psychotherapeutic program? And, even though it may have long-term benefits, are its adverse effects unreasonably harsh?[193]

The *Rennie* test will condemn the chemical castration statutes, first of all, because case studies have found that Depo-Provera may have therapeutic value for individual men, but these findings are highly questionable, because they are not based on randomized clinical trials. The statutes will fail the second *Rennie* test element because the Michigan Court of Appeals, agreeing with William Fette, found that Depo-Provera's use was not accepted medical practice; nor is it today.[194] Furthermore, the American Medical Association has declared that it is unethical for physicians to administer the drug under court order.[195] The six state statutes, except for Louisiana's, will fail the third *Rennie* test element, because they do not require the drug's use in conjunction with a psychotherapeutic program. Yet, even Louisiana's statute is suspect, because the studies that use the drug in conjunction with psychotherapy have found that its effectiveness depends on a sex offender's voluntary consent, not his compelled use by court order.

State castration statutes will also fail the final *Rennie* test element, because Depo-Provera has no benefits for men, only adverse side effects that can be unreasonably harsh. The drug's short-term side effects include those associated with its contraceptive use: weight gain, hot flashes, and headaches. The drug's long-term use may deprive them of their manhood, because its feminizing effects include the growth of breast tissue, a higher register voice, and less body hair. It may also impair their ability to procreate and produce atypical sperm, which are associated with congenital abnormalities. The drug's use also causes phlebitis, hypoglycemia, dyspnea, hypogonadism, and cerebrovascular disorders, and may aggravate existing conditions such as epilepsy, asthma, and cardiac and renal dysfunction.[196] Finally, the contraceptive research has documented that the drug can lead to cancer and osteoporosis,[197] a risk for men that would be substantially enhanced, because its weekly use in amounts range from eight to forty-three times the 150 milligram dose used by women every three months for contraception.

The legislative history of these chemical castration statutes confirms that they were enacted not to provide treatment to sex offenders, but to punish them. The California statute, for example, has, as its primary purpose, the imposition of "the penalty of chemical castration" for specific sex crimes identified in the state's penal code.[198] The governor's message approving the legislation reflected the public perception of sex offenders as sick and evil people when it stated that use of Depo-Provera would treat "their sexual compulsions while enacting a particularly severe kind of retribution."[199]

Since Depo-Provera does not qualify as a treatment for rapists and child molesters, then its use raises a second question: Is the use of the drug cruel and unusual punishment? William Fette asserted in the *Gauntlett* case that a cruel punishment is one that is "so severe as to be degrading to the dignity of man."[200] Justice Brennan elaborated this concept in *Furman v. Georgia* (1972) when he observed that "the fundamental premise of the Clause is that even the vilest criminal remains a human being possessed of human dignity."[201] The Supreme Court has not, however, settled on a specific test for human dignity or on one theory of Eighth Amendment interpretation, but has instead enunciated three separate tests to answer the question.

The *Tropp v. Dulles* (1958) test asks if the punishment is inherently cruel.[202] None of the chemical castration statutes will pass the *Tropp* test. Their legislative histories document that their purpose is the imposition of a "severe kind of retribution."[203] A Depo-Provera parole condition, like Judge Borsos's probation condition, is "doubly cruel" because it is "designed to both shackle the mind and cripple the body of sex offend-

202 | CHEMICAL CASTRATION

ers."[204] The drug will rob him of his manhood by impairing his mind of the ability to conceive erotic images and his body of the physical ability to procreate. The statutes also inflict gratuitous suffering on non-paraphiliacs whose mandatory use will not diminish the incidence of child molestation.[205]

The *Weems v. U.S.* (1910) test asks if the punishment is grossly disproportionate to the offense for which it is imposed,[206] while the *Furman v. Georgia* (1972) test asks if the punishment exceeds what is necessary to accomplish the state's legitimate aims.[207] Together, these two tests identify three common faults with the chemical castration statutes. First, they impose a Depo-Provera condition on all sex offenders, as defined by their respective statutes. The drug's condition is, however, a grossly disproportionate punishment for non-paraphiliac sex offenders, because the existing research documents that the drug will not change their behavior, but will cruelly impose upon them all the adverse effects already described while not accomplishing the state's legitimate goal of reducing the incidence of child molestation.

The statutes have a second fault: The research studies suffer from design flaws, already discussed, which have reported contradictory results of both increased and decreased recidivism with Depo-Provera's use,[208] while one study has found no difference in recidivism between prisoners who used the drug and those who did not.[209] Other studies have reported that cognitive behavior therapy is at least as effective as Depo-Provera in preventing recidivism, with both treatments producing a 30 percent recidivism rate.[210] The statutes have a final fault: Depo-Provera, with all its reported adverse effects and its ineffectiveness in reducing recidivism, is grossly disproportionate to a prison sentence in achieving the government's objective of reducing the incidence of child molestation.

In sum, Depo-Provera probation and parole conditions are in constitutional jeopardy. The *Rennie v. Kline's* test confirms that the drug's condition is punishment, not therapy. As punishment, all three Eighth Amendment tests agree that the condition violates the amendment's core concept of human dignity. The *Tropp* test condemns the condition as cruel, *Weems* as grossly disproportionate to other penalties, and *Furman* as unlikely to succeed in accomplishing the state's objective of protecting children from their molesters. The medical evidence, sparse though it is, condemns the use of this experimental drug, because it "treats an offender as though he . . . were not a human person . . . but as a mere animal or a thing lacking in human dignity."[211]

Fourteenth Amendment Due Process Clause

Probation and parole conditions must conform to the Fourteenth Amendment's guarantees of procedural and substantive due process, which protect bodily autonomy and integrity.[212] A Due Process Clause analysis asks two procedural questions relevant to the sex offender's decision about a Depo-Provera probation or parole condition. First, is there sufficient liberty interest involved? A choice for a sex offender between serving a lengthy prison term or accepting probation or parole conditioned on the continual use of an experimental drug certainly involves a sufficient liberty interest that due process requires a hearing. As the Supreme Court announced in *Washington v. Harper* (1990): "The forcible injection of a medication into a non-consenting person's body represents a substantial interference with that person's liberty."[213] The chemical castration statutes will also fail to satisfy this due process requirement, because they do not provide for a hearing at sentencing, prior to release from prison on parole, or periodically during the post-release period to monitor the sex offender's use of Depo-Provera.

Since a probation and parole decision involves a sufficient liberty interest, the second question is: What kind of hearing is required? For sentencing, parole, and post-parole hearings, *Rennie v. Klein* requires a lawyer to deal with substantive legal issues and ensure that proper procedures are followed,[214] and an "outside psychiatrist of . . . [the defendant's] choice to evaluate the need for medication."[215] *Rennie* would require a psychiatrist to determine that the sex offender is suffering from a mental illness or abnormality and that a medical treatment is in his best interest. *Harper* would require a psychiatrist to also determine that the medical treatment is necessary for the safety of the sex offender and others and to confirm that there are no less intrusive alternatives to the medical treatment. *Rennie* would suggest that if Depo-Provera is prescribed, a psychiatrist needs to be involved in the parolee's ongoing medical supervision, because of the drug's adverse side effects.

The six chemical castration statutes will fail to comply with these *Rennie-Harper* criteria. The California, Iowa, Montana and Wisconsin statutes do not identify who, if anyone, will conduct the psychiatric evaluation; nor do they address the ongoing need for medical supervision. The Florida statute identifies a "medical expert," while the Louisiana statute is more specific in requiring "a qualified mental health professional with experience in treating sex offenders,"[216] but neither statute requires a physician, let alone a psychiatrist of the sex offender's choice. Only two statutes mention medical assessment. Florida requires a determination that the sex offender is "an appropriate candidate for treatment," and the Iowa statute provides for "an appropriate assessment to determine whether the treatment will be effective,"[217] but neither statute specifies the criteria for the "appropriate candidate" and "appropriate assessment."

Even if these states complied with the *Rennie-Harper* criteria and provided a psychiatrist of the sex offender's choice and even if the psychiatrist identified the sex offender as a paraphiliac, the experimental studies suggest that Depo-Provera's use would not be in the sex offender's best interests, nor would its use keep children safe. Even a hearing that complied with the *Rennie-Harper* criteria would still not be fair unless it addressed two substantive legal issues: the sex offender's right to make a knowing and voluntary choice to receive or reject a Depo-Provera condition, and, if he rejected the condition, to choose by default the lesser evil of incarceration. Yet none of these six statutes satisfies the *Canterbury* four-factor test to assure that he makes a decision knowingly, nor can they overcome the conclusion of *Kaimowitz* that his decision cannot be voluntary, because he is coerced to bartering his body for his freedom, in spite of his knowledge of the drug's present and future risks.

The Fourteenth Amendment's Due Process Clause has a substantive component that protects bodily autonomy and integrity by guaranteeing people the liberty to make personal decisions free from government control. Whether to accept or decline a Depo-Provera condition involves an intensely personal medical choice. The U.S. Supreme Court in *In re Quinlan* (1976) and *Cruzan v. Missouri* (1990) recognized that the due process right to privacy includes personal decisions about medical treatment.[218]

A Depo-Provera condition requires sex offenders to make a personal sexual choice. The U.S. Supreme Court has recognized that the right to privacy includes the freedom to make personal decisions about procreation, contraception, marriage, the termination of pregnancy, and the maintenance of family relationships.[219] This sexual privacy right can be traced to *Skinner v. Oklahoma* (1942), where the Supreme Court held that government-enforced sterilization in the form of a vasectomy intruded upon a person's right to privacy in marriage and procreation.[220] The use of Depo-Provera intrudes upon the personal right to procreate, because its effect on testosterone levels may leave men sexually impotent.[221] If the drug's use does not, some studies suggest that its use in high doses produces atypical sperm, which are associated with congenital abnormalities.[222] As a result, a Depo-Provera condition will impermissibly involve state government in the regulation and enjoyment of the marital relationship and procreation.

The Fourteenth Amendment does not prohibit all government intrusions on personal rights to make personal medical and sexual decisions, but here Depo-Provera's use intrudes upon "marriage and procreation [, which] are fundamental to the very existence of the race."[223] As with the First Amendment's guarantee of mental autonomy and integrity, government actions that place substantive limits on personal choices in matters involving a Fourteenth Amendment fundamental right also are subject to the strict scrutiny standard: The government may not intrude without a compelling interest.[224] The government will easily demonstrate a compelling interest in protecting society from child molestation, but it will find it difficult to establish that a Depo-Provera condition is a necessary means to achieve the state's compelling interest, because psychotherapy and incarceration are less burdensome on the offender's fundamental rights.

Even if a Depo-Provera condition did not intrude upon a sex offender's fundamental right to make personal medical and sexual decisions, the government would still have to confront the usually less demanding requirements of rational basis review.[225] Here the government is no more likely to prevail than it did with rational basis review of the offender's First Amendment guarantee of mental autonomy and integrity. A Depo-Provera condition cannot rationally advance the legitimate government interest in the prevention of child molestation, because the research studies demonstrate that the drug is not effective in reducing the incidence of the offense.

Fourteenth Amendment Equal Protection

Sentencing sex offenders to probation as an alternative to incarceration or granting them parole must occur in a manner that not only respects their mental and bodily autonomy and integrity, but also complies with the Fourteenth Amendment's Equal Protection Clause. William Fette did not make an equal protection argument on Roger Gauntlett's behalf, because his Depo-Provera probation condition was one judge's discretionary exercise of his sentencing authority. The state chemical castration statutes have, however, created a class of convicted felons and granted trial court judges discretionary authority or mandated them to impose a Depo-Provera parole condition on this class of felons.

These legislative classifications raise a spectrum of Equal Protection Clause concerns that involve all three levels of judicial review, which range from strict scrutiny (the least deferential to legislation) to intermediate scrutiny to rational basis review (the most deferential to legislation). In spite of the range in judicial scrutiny of state legislation, all six statutes will violate all three standards of equal protection review.

Strict scrutiny will condemn these statutes because they create a class of felons, sex offenders, and then impose upon them harsher sentences than for other felons and trammel their fundamental right to procreate, first recognized in *Skinner v. Oklahoma* (1942).[226] Clearly, these six statutes single out sex offenders and authorize courts to deprive them of their right to procreate by imposing a Depo-Provera parole condition that will require the drug to be taken in perpetuity. Strict scrutiny review will recognize the states' compelling interest in preventing child molestation, but will condemn the statutes for the same reasons that they violate due process privacy.

These statutes will violate the Equal Protection Clause for a second reason: They discriminate on the basis of sex.[227] Even though written in facially neutral language, they discriminate in their practical effects. Studies of Depo-Provera suggest that the drug reduces sexual imagery and testosterone levels in men and diminishes their impulse to molest children. As an FDA-approved contraceptive, the drug does reduce sexual drive, but only for a small percentage of women.[228] The drug's continuous use will have a disparate sexual impact, constituting state-imposed sterilization of women, while not effecting their molestation

of children. Whether men become sterile will depend on their testosterone levels and the amount of Depo-Provera required to reduce their
testosterone and sexual fantasies to a level that eliminates their impulse
to molest children.

An equal protection analysis will condemn these statutes because
gender is a quasi-suspect classification subject to intermediate judicial
scrutiny, which requires statutes to be substantially related to an important governmental interest.[229] Protecting society from child molesters is
clearly an important governmental interest, but a Depo-Provera parole
condition, imposed on both men and women, is not a means substantially related to the achievement of this objective, because it will not reduce the incidence of these offenses by women, but it will deprive them
of their fundamental right to procreate. At the same time, depending on
the amount of the drug used, it may reduce sexual offenses by men, but
not necessarily deprive them of sexual activity and the ability to procreate. Of course, this gender-based disparity relies on clinical trials of
women; but for men, there are only experimental case studies, open trials, and double-blind studies.

The state statutes will violate the Equal Protection Clause for a final
reason: They fail rational basis review.[230] The statutes treat all sex offenders alike regardless of whether they are diagnosed with a paraphilia
and, if diagnosed with pedophilia, also suffer from schizophrenia, substance abuse, or an antisocial personality disorder.[231] The statutes then
subject all these sex offenders to the same parole condition even though
Depo-Provera will not deter pedophiles with associated mental disorders from molesting children. None of the statutes, except for Louisiana's, cures this overinclusiveness, because none requires their courts
to conduct an individual psychiatric examination of convicted sex offenders.[232] These statutes will, of course, serve a legitimate purpose of
reducing recidivism, but their Depo-Provera conditions are not rationally related to this purpose, because their overinclusiveness will not
permit courts to reduce child molester recidivism and because the drug's
experimental studies of men have documented that it is not effective in
reducing the incidence of pedophiles who molest children.

Rational basis review will condemn these statutes because they create a class of felons, sex offenders, and then impose upon them harsher
sentences than on other felons. Unlike other felons, sex offenders have

been the object of intentional unequal treatment, because their victims have been children. The California statute, like those of the other five states, clearly reveals a legislative response to a transitory public hysteria over the menace of child molestation by the enactment of legislation that has a disparate impact on sex offenders and punishes them as a despised minority with an experimental drug.[233] These statutes were enacted to serve a legitimate governmental interest in reducing the recidivism of sex offenders who molest children, but Depo-Provera is not a means rationally related to this purpose, because there are other medical means that burden the sex offender's mind and body less, including psychotherapy.

Constitutional Summary

A convicted sex offender has the risk management task to use his constitutional rights to defend himself from the discretionary and mandatory use of Depo-Provera as a probation or parole condition by arguing that this condition violates his First and Fourteenth Amendment due process rights to mental and bodily autonomy and integrity, because it is neither the least restrictive means to achieve the state's compelling interest in protecting society against child molestation, nor is it rationally related to legitimate state interests. The Depo-Provera condition violates his Eighth Amendment right to mental and bodily integrity, because the drug is not a treatment, but a cruel punishment, one that denies him human dignity, is grossly disproportionate to other penalties, and is incapable of accomplishing the state's goal of protecting children. Finally, the condition violates his Fourteenth Amendment right to equal protection, because it discriminates on the basis of gender and against sex offenders as a class of felons and because it fails to distinguish among sex offenders by imposing on all of them the same parole condition when nondiscriminatory alternative means are available to serve the government's interest in protecting children.

Summary

Depo-Provera continues to be used as a probation and parole condition in spite of serious ethical, medical, and legal questions about its safety and effectiveness. For Judith Weisz, it is a story of the politics of risk management, which focuses on the FDA's limited exercise of its authority to regulate the experimental use of Depo-Provera. Limited as this authority is by the practice of medicine standard, it allowed the Grady Clinic and Johns Hopkins Clinic to operate outside the boundaries of scientific research. As told by Dr. Sidney Wolfe, her story is a tale of the FDA's, Upjohn's, and the Johns Hopkins Institutional Review Board's collective failure to manage Depo-Provera's risk and permit Dr. Berlin to conduct his experimental research under the guise of the practice of medicine without obtaining from his subjects their informed consent to use the drug. Since then, her story has been told by medical researchers who have criticized Dr. Berlin's studies and those conducted by others for their lack of scientific rigor and the limited value of their findings. Even Dr. Berlin has recognized that these studies have only anecdotal value, because they are case reports, open trials, and double-blind studies, not randomized case-controlled clinical trials.

Judith Weisz's story was transformed when these studies were taken out of their clinical setting and used for criminal justice purposes. Trial court judges, such as Judge Borsos, exercised their broad statutory discretion to deal with sex offenders by practicing medicine and mandating that they participate in a scientific experiment. Judith Weisz's story of the drug's criminal justice use was transformed again by the politics of child abduction, molestation, and murder and by state legislatures that enacted panic legislation. The legislators, like the judges, paid no heed to Dr. Berlin's concern about the drug's mandated use. As scientific amateurs, the state legislators conducted no assessment of Depo-Provera's risk for sex offenders and then practiced medicine by finding that the risk of the drug's use was acceptable as a parole condition in order to protect children from their molesters.

Yet this state government use of Depo-Provera as a probation and parole condition is not beyond the FDA's control. The Health Research Group argued that the practice-of-medicine exception was a narrow one restricted to individual physicians treating their patients and did not extend to state government actions involving the use of a drug for criminal justice purposes. The Supreme Court disagreed and held in *Heckler v. Chaney* (1985) that the FDA's decision not to take enforcement action to prevent state government criminal justice use of a medication was committed to the agency's discretion by the Federal Food, Drug, and Cosmetic Act.[234] In sum, Depo-Provera is available to cruelly punish sex offenders, because the FDA has decided not to exercise its risk management authority to regulate the drug's medical experimental use and its state government use as a probation and parole condition.

Roger Gauntlett's story of Depo-Provera's use as a probation and parole condition is deeply interwoven with Judith Weisz's story of the FDA's failure to manage the drug's experimental research, which provided the medical studies for Judge Borsos to use in imposing on Roger Gauntlett a Depo-Provera probation condition. The FDA's failure to manage the drug's risk also gave state legislatures, bewitched by the drug's promise of a medical solution to the moral panic over child molestation, the opportunity to grant judges the discretion or mandate them to use the drug as a parole condition.

Roger Gauntlett's own story of risk management, one that used medical studies and state statutory and federal constitutional law to successfully challenge his probation condition, also provides a legal-medical paradigm for sex offenders to challenge state chemical castration statutes. As William Fette's defense of Roger Gauntlett makes clear, statutory and constitutional law are two legal tools that are intertwined with the medical evidence to manage the drug's risk for even the vilest criminal. This evidence clearly exposes Depo-Provera's unacceptable risk to a sex offender when judges use the wide discretion granted by probation statutes to mandate the drug's use and when state statutes specifically permit or require them to use the drug as a parole condition. This evidence establishes that a Depo-Provera condition is not reasonably related to his crime and rehabilitation, is impossible for the sex offender to perform, and fails to provide him with the opportunity to give his informed consent.

These statutes, ethically and legally deficient on their own terms, also violate the sex offender's constitutional rights. The medical evidence documents that Depo-Provera intrudes upon his First Amendment right to receive, generate, and express his thoughts; his Eighth Amendment right to be free from cruel punishment; and his Fourteenth Amendment procedural right to a fair hearing, its substantive right to sexual privacy, and its guarantee of equal protection. A state legislature can justly claim a need to protect children from their molesters, but the medical evidence documents that Depo-Provera's cruel side effects mean that the state will have to choose other methods that are less burdensome on a sex offender's fundamental constitutional rights.

William Fette successfully joined these statutory and constitutional arguments with Depo-Provera's medical evidence to challenge Roger Gauntlett's probation condition. There have, however, been no statutory and constitutional challenges to the chemical castration statutes in state or federal court. This analysis provides the framework for such an appeal.

Conclusion

Contraceptive Drug Risk Failure, Human Dignity,
and a Duty to Act

The odyssey of Depo-Provera has been told as three stories of the politics of contraceptive drug risk management. The stories have joined the national struggle over Upjohn's FDA application to have the drug licensed as a female contraceptive to the state medical malpractice and products liability issues raised by its contraceptive use and the criminal justice issues raised by its use as a probation and parole condition for sex offenders.

Three Stories of Contraceptive Risk

The three stories of this odyssey have been told by Judith Weisz, Anne MacMurdo, and Roger Gauntlett, whose personal encounters with Depo-Provera joined the national controversy to its state civil and criminal experience. At the center of each story has been a trial in which each played a central role: Judith Weisz chaired the FDA's Public Board of Inquiry, a science court; Anne MacMurdo was the plaintiff in a state products liability suit against The Upjohn Company; and Roger Gauntlett was the defendant in a state statutory rape trial. Their personal encounters with Depo-Provera involved a wider audience: FDA officials who have critiqued it as an experimental drug, women who have used it as a contraceptive, and men who have been ordered to take it as a criminal sanction.

At the same time, they have not been the sole tellers of their tales. Judith Weisz's story of scientific integrity in the assessment of Depo-Provera's risk has been told by Dr. Alan Lissok, who authored the FDA's IND Audit Report on the Grady Clinic, which found "severe deficiencies" in its research program and exposed its failure to produce any scientifically credible evidence about the drug's contraceptive use. Before Upjohn submitted Depo-Provera for limited contraceptive approval in 1974, the FDA's Dr. Michael Popkin, who had critiqued Upjohn's clinical studies, found four cases of breast cancer, sixteen cases of cervical cancer, and a 65 percent dropout rate. At the Public Board of Inquiry hearings, Dr. Sidney Wolfe critiqued the Schwallie and Assenzo study's methods and menstrual bleeding findings and stated that the use of the drug would create "menstrual chaos."[1] When the FDA asked its Fertility and Maternal Health Advisory Committee in 1992 for an approval recommendation, Drs. Janet Daling, Nancy Lee, and Jane Zones questioned whether the breast cancer research supported approval. Together they and women's rights activists have told a story of scientific integrity in the assessment of contraceptive drug risk.

Anne MacMurdo's story has been told by other women who have suffered substantial short-term side effects from Depo-Provera's use. At Senator Kennedy's 1973 hearings, it was Anna Burgess who first told the world of her coerced use of the drug at a Tennessee family planning clinic. The National Women's Health Network reported in its National Registry the stories of hundreds of women who used the drug without giving their informed consent and litigated, without success, the claims of the women who were subjects in the Grady Clinic experiments. At Anne MacMurdo's trial, Michael Ericksen, her attorney, used her story to create a theory of her case, a story that marshaled the evidence of her heavy and continuous menstrual bleeding and subsequent hysterectomy and that won a jury verdict in her favor, later reversed on appeal. Her personal story is a cautionary tale told by other women before and after the drug's contraceptive approval whose cases did not go to trial, but were settled for confidential amounts or dismissed when courts granted Upjohn's and Pfizer's summary judgment motions. Together they tell a story of the failure of the courts to assess the drug's risk and judge its acceptability as a female contraceptive.

Roger Gauntlett's story began at the Johns Hopkins Clinic where Dr. Sidney Wolfe's Health Research Group, telling Judith Weisz's story, discovered that the clinic's program to treat convicted sex offenders with Depo-Provera was based on faulty research techniques and provided only anecdotal evidence of the drug's safety and effectiveness, but was nonetheless used by trial court judges as a probation condition for convicted offenders. Roger Gauntlett, like Anne MacMurdo, had his story told by his attorney, William Fette, who opposed the drug's use, because of the mental and physical health risks it posed to his client, and had the drug's probation condition overturned on appeal. His arguments on appeal defined for future defendants the statutory and constitutional grounds for challenging the criminal justice use of the drug. Since the mid-1990s, Roger Gauntlett's story took on increased importance when state legislatures enacted statutes either granting their trial judges the discretion or mandating them to order Depo-Provera's use as a parole condition without the defendant's informed consent. His story is told by other sex offenders who have been ordered by judges, as he was by Judge Borsos, to use Depo-Provera. Together, they tell a story of the judicial failure to assess the drug's risk and determine its acceptability as a criminal sanction.

Of the three stories, Judith Weisz's is the dominant one. Hers defines the scientific standards for the conduct of animal and human studies and sets the risk assessment criteria for FDA approval of Depo-Provera, for litigating products liability and medical malpractice cases, and for imposing Depo-Provera as a criminal sanction. Her story reminds us that risk acceptability judgments are political and legal matters, which are properly the subject of public debate and policy-making by the FDA, Congress, and state legislatures, subject to judicial review, but the touchstone of any sound contraceptive drug policy is the quality of scientific evidence.

Depo-Provera's Domestic Odyssey

Depo-Provera's three stories of risk management have focused almost exclusively on the drug's domestic odyssey. The twenty-five year risk management controversy was defined by the 1962 Kefauver Harris Amendments to the Federal Food, Drug, and Cosmetic Act, which created a more powerful FDA and a more detailed and lengthy drug approval process that placed on pharmaceutical companies the burden of providing the agency with scientific proof that a drug is both safe and effective for its proposed medical use. The amendments also created an agency more open to criticism by its own scientists, members of Congress, and health and population organizations. At the same time, the

1962 amendments left untouched the power of pharmaceutical companies to conduct research, of physicians to prescribe Depo-Provera, and of state legislatures and courts to impose the drug as a criminal sanction.

In 1967, the Food and Drug Administration expanded its contraceptive drug policy-making environment by creating the Obstetrics and Gynecology Advisory Committee (later the Fertility and Maternal Health Advisory Committee) to furnish the agency with advice from physicians and researchers with expertise in women's health and by requiring the advisory committee to hold hearings open to the public.[2] Drug policy-making was no longer limited to the FDA and pharmaceutical companies, but included politically active consumer rights and women's health organizations and international population control organizations that challenged the agency's decisions and advisory committee recommendations by taking their case to the media and to Congress, where they found sympathetic senators and representatives.

In this transformed drug risk management setting, the advocates and opponents of Depo-Provera's approval made risk assessment and risk acceptability arguments in hearings held by FDA advisory committees, congressional committees, and the Public Board of Inquiry. Upjohn, the International Planned Parenthood Foundation, the United Nations Fund for Population Activities, and other international population control organizations argued that a large body of research demonstrated the drug's safety and provided not only a contraceptive alternative for women who, like Anne MacMurdo, were unable to use the Pill or an IUD, but also a long-acting birth-control method for women in developing countries. The Health Research Group, the National Women's Health Network, and other health and feminist activists challenged these arguments. For them, the animal and human studies supporting approval were flawed and nationwide evidence documented that the drug was being abused, had serious short-term side effects, and raised concerns about its long-term risk of breast cancer and osteoporosis.

Consumer and women's organizations and activists were successful in delaying FDA approval of Depo-Provera. With congressional intervention, they forced the FDA to retreat and disapprove the drug's limited contraceptive marketing in 1974, to disapprove the drug for general marketing in 1978, and to follow the Public Board of Inquiry's recommendation to, once again, disapprove the drug for general marketing in

1986 because of Upjohn's shoddy research. They were, however, unable to delay its general marketing in 1992. At the World Health Organization's request, the FDA had eliminated the use of animal studies and accepted the results of improved WHO and New Zealand clinical trials, even though they revealed an increased risk of breast cancer and osteoporosis, two risks that have not disappeared with further research, but continue to haunt the drug's approved contraceptive use.

In sum, Depo-Provera's contraceptive risk over the past half century has been defined primarily by the national debate over its long-term risk of cancer and osteoporosis. Its subtext has been the many short-term side effects suffered by women nationwide and the medical malpractice and products liability litigation its use has provoked, but the drug's criminal justice use has not been part of the controversy. Together, the stories of the drug's approval and its impact on the personal health of women and men are the story of multiple failures to manage the drug's risk.

Risk Management Failures

This collective story told by Judith Weisz, Anne MacMurdo, and Roger Gauntlett identifies the individuals and institutions who failed to manage Depo-Provera's contraceptive and criminal justice uses and why. Together their stories define the three relatively independent legal stages on which this risk management drama has been enacted and principal players who have influenced the action on their own stage and on the other two stages in ways that together make them collectively responsible for the failure to manage the risk of using Depo-Provera as a contraceptive and as a criminal justice sanction.

The Food and Drug Administration

The FDA failed to manage Depo-Provera's risk in regulating its experimental use, in approving its contraceptive marketing, and in responding to its post-approval studies. The FDA allowed the Grady Clinic to operate under its IND from 1967 to 1978 without submitting annual reports and terminated its IND only when the agency's data audit revealed the severe shortcomings of the clinic's program. At the same time, the FDA never required the Johns Hopkins Clinic to obtain an IND for its experimental use of Depo-Provera on sex offenders, because Dr. Berlin's treatment of these men fell within the practice of medicine.

Throughout Depo-Provera's twenty-five-year approval history, the FDA knew that its medical officers had doubts about the drug's long-term cancer risk from the monkey and beagle studies and that they knew about the drug's short-term side effects from the Schwallie and Assenzo study, but approved the drug for limited contraceptive use in 1974. Then the agency retreated in the face of congressional opposition, engaged in thorough intra-agency review, and disapproved the drug for general marketing license in 1978, a decision it reaffirmed in 1986 by relying on the Public Board of Inquiry's report. During these years, the agency knew, but did nothing about the drug's unapproved contraceptive use even though Senator Edward Kennedy's 1973 hearings, the 1983 Board of Inquiry hearings, and the 1987 Indian Health Service hearings exposed the drug's widespread unapproved use by physicians and family planning clinics.

After Upjohn withdrew its NDA for Depo-Provera in 1986, the FDA eliminated the use of animal studies, which had frustrated the company's previous approvals, and, knowing from its Fertility and Maternal Advisory Committee hearings that there were scientific doubts about the drug's breast cancer and osteoporosis studies, approved Depo-Provera for general marketing in 1992 conditioned only on the conduct of a post-approval osteoporosis study. So hurried was the approval process, taking only six months, that one medical officer complained that there had not been enough time to thoroughly analyze the studies; and another medical officer failed to engage in an independent review, because he adopted almost verbatim Upjohn's Advisory Committee Brochure. Then the FDA took twelve years to respond to the drug's post-approval osteoporosis study by placing a black box warning in the drug's labeling and recommended restricting its use to two years.

The Upjohn Company and Pfizer, Inc.

The FDA is not solely responsible for the failure to manage Depo-Provera's risk. The Upjohn Company knew about the poor quality of its animal and human studies, the drug's cancer risk, and its numerous short-term side effects, but continued to seek FDA approval. Denied limited approval in 1974, Upjohn did not become serious about conducting scientifically valid research until it was denied general marketing approval in 1978. Following the Public Board of Inquiry's review of Upjohn's shoddy scientific evidence, the company objected to the board's disapproval recommendation, but voluntarily withdrew Depo-Provera's drug application in 1986.

During these years, Upjohn was unable or unwilling to limit the drug's sale to its approved uses. In 1973, the Kennedy "Quality of Health Care" hearings revealed that the Tennessee Department of Health purchased the drug as a general order from Upjohn and then made it available to family planning clinics. In 1986, Anne MacMurdo's trial revealed that the University of Miami Hospital's pharmacy had ordered the drug from Upjohn and dispensed it to Dr. Shapiro, who had used it for contraception. Her trial also revealed that Upjohn limited its oversight to monitoring the drug's sales. Federal law did not permit Upjohn sales representatives to ask physicians about their prescribing of Depo-Provera for contraception, because it was an FDA unapproved use.

When Depo-Provera was approved, Upjohn knew its breast cancer and osteoporosis research was scientifically suspect. Upjohn and perhaps Pfizer, its corporate heir, have supplied Depo-Provera to research centers and their physicians to use the drug to control sexual offender behavior without an FDA-approved IND. If Pfizer supplies Depo-Provera to carry out court probation and parole orders imposing the drug on convicted sex offenders, the company has to know that the drug is not FDA-approved for that purpose and that the American Medical Association has declared that the drug's use is unethical when it is imposed by court order.

Physicians

Physicians in private practice, family planning clinics, and research centers failed to manage Depo-Provera risk. In two research settings, Drs. Fred Berlin and Robert Hatcher failed to manage Depo-Provera's criminal justice and contraceptive uses. At the Johns Hopkins Clinic and thereafter at his National Center for the Study, Prevention, and Treatment of Sexual Disorders, Dr. Berlin took refuge in the practice-of-medicine exception to an FDA-required IND and prescribed the drug for his patients, because it had been FDA approved for other medical purposes. The exception permitted him to conduct experiments on convicted sex offenders, identify Depo-Provera's short-term health risks, and conclude that the drug was an acceptable means of controlling paraphiliac behavior of men who "voluntarily" consented to its use, but without being fully informed its risks. Since Dr. Berlin's research, published in professional journals, was based on clinical reports, it provides only anecdotal evidence of little scientific value.

Dr. Robert Hatcher, who was responsible for conducting the Grady Clinic study, did not hide behind the practice-of-medicine exception, but behind an IND while providing Depo-Provera to as many as 11,400 women. He, like Dr. Berlin, crossed the boundary between research science and the practice of medicine and in the process behaved unethically toward his subjects/patients and the scientific community. The Grady Clinic, like the Johns Hopkins Clinic, failed to provide its subjects/patients with the information about the drug necessary for them to give their informed consent, failed to abide by its IND and use a well-designed protocol for selecting subjects and collecting, analyzing, and reporting data, and failed to provide periodic reports to its institutional review board and the FDA. These failures to observe clinical study standards compromised the quality of the clinic's research and made the articles it published in professional journals medically and scientifically worthless.

Outside Depo-Provera's research setting, physicians in private practice and family planning clinics across the country were able to take shelter, as Dr. Berlin did, in the practice-of-medicine exception and to prescribe the drug during the thirty-two years before it was approved for contraceptive use. Drs. Levy and Shapiro were also able to prescribe the drug for Anne MacMurdo without informing her about its FDA-unapproved contraceptive status and the risks it might pose to her health, because the FDA had approved Depo-Provera for another medical purpose. Since Depo-Provera's approval, physicians, as in Cassandra Colville's case, still fail to inform women about the drug's risk.

Courts

Courts became involved in Depo-Provera's risk management at the initiative of private parties and governments. All three stories of the drug's contraceptive risk have had a defining moment in the form of a trial. The FDA's Depo-Provera Public Board of Inquiry, a science court, evaluated the drug's scientific evidence in support of Upjohn's application for the drug's contraceptive marketing approval. In *Upjohn v. MacMurdo*, a state trial court heard a products liability complaint that Upjohn negligently marketed and labeled the drug. In *People v. Gauntlett*, a state trial court imposed a Depo-Provera probation condition for statutory rape. The conduct of each trial was based on a separate body of law—federal administrative law, state negligence law, and state criminal law—but each trial was confronted with the same task: managing Depo-Provera's contraceptive risk.

The Public Board of Inquiry functioned as an intra-agency appellate court convened to review the scientific evidence supporting the FDA's 1978 decision to deny the drug contraceptive approval. Dr. Judith Weisz and her fellow board members reviewed the scientific evidence and held a pre-conference hearing to establish hearing procedures. Then the board's five-day hearing was conducted as an impartial scientific inquiry restricted to risk assessment questions provided by the FDA, but risk acceptability issues were a subtext. The board's report confined its analysis to an assessment of the animal and human research and, distinguishing science from policy, provided only very brief answers to the FDA's risk acceptability questions, because they were beyond the board's competence and within the agency's domain. Upjohn challenged the board's disapproval recommendation, but the FDA rejected the challenge and then accepted Upjohn's voluntary withdrawal of its Depo-Provera drug application.

The board's report did not, however, serve as a precedent for the FDA's 1992 approval of Depo-Provera, because the agency had adopted WHO guidelines and eliminated the use of animal studies to evaluate the drug's safety. Then the agency decided that the criteria for approval, as Dr. Solomon Sobel announced at the Fertility and Maternal Health Advisory Committee, would not be "the level of evidence for safety that the Public Board of Inquiry was seeking," but the Food, Drug, and Cosmetic Act's requirement of "adequate and well-controlled studies."[3]

In Anne MacMurdo's products liability case, the state's legal system encouraged the parties to use the rules of discovery to obtain evidence from each other and then to avoid a trial by either settling their case or having a court grant one party's motion for summary judgment. In this way, courts avoid being directly involved in making risk management decisions. In Depo-Provera post-approval osteoporosis cases, a mass tort lawsuit involving 157 women was settled, but the individual cases brought by Jamie Lorenzi, Cassandra Colville, Adrienne Oliver, and Melanie Montagnon were dismissed on Pfizer's motions for summary judgment.

Anne MacMurdo's products liability case survived summary judgment motions and went to trial, but her trial provided an inadequate forum to manage her risk. The jurors were scientific amateurs who knew nothing about her, Upjohn, and Depo-Provera until they heard the attorneys' opening statements. During the trial, they did not hear all the evidence. At the pretrial conference, the judge excluded evidence that did not directly focus on two legal theories: negligent marketing and failure to warn. At the trial, the jurors heard only the evidence defined by each attorney's theory of the case: two opposing risk management stories. In reaching a verdict, a risk management decision, the jurors relied upon their state's negligence law, the evidence they had heard, and their "common sense" to assess the drug's risk and then decide whether its risk was an acceptable one for Anne MacMurdo to bear and, if not, to find that Upjohn was negligent in failing to warn her physicians about the drug's risk.

In reviewing the evidence and expert witness testimony, the appellate judges were also scientific amateurs, who did not assess the drug's scientific merits. The Court of Appeals merely decided that the evidence did not support the jury's contributory negligence verdict. The Florida Supreme Court, reversing the appellate court decision, held that Anne MacMurdo's expert was not qualified to testify about the adequacy of the drug's labeling. In sum, her products liability trial and appeals reveal the substantial limitations of jurors and judges functioning as risk managers.

Since Anne MacMurdo's case, it is unlikely that any woman who claims that Depo-Provera has harmed her health will have her claim heard in a trial court. Pfizer will be able to avoid a jury trial by settling a case or having a court grant its summary judgment motions as it did in the four osteoporosis cases. Pfizer will also protect itself with Depo-Provera's labeling, which warns women about the drug's risks, and with the learned intermediary doctrine, which imposes on the physicians the duty to inform their patients of the drug's risks. Pfizer and women will also be inclined to settle their cases, as they did in the osteoporosis mass tort lawsuit. Settlement avoids the uncertainties and public exposure of a trial, and any appeals. Settlement for Pfizer means that the company avoids public knowledge of Depo-Provera's risk, maintains its FDA approval to market the drug, and facilitates its overseas use by U.S. aid programs and foreign governments. Settlement for women avoids the exposure of their personal lives to public scrutiny during a trial and the prospect of appellate court review if a jury decides a case in their favor.

Roger Gauntlett's trial provided an inadequate forum to manage Depo-Provera's risk. Judge Borsos was a scientific amateur who did not know that Depo-Provera was not FDA-approved as a probation condition and who had relied upon two articles based on anecdotal evidence of its safety and effectiveness. Judge Borsos also practiced medicine without a license, because he was unqualified to conduct a medical examination of Roger Gauntlett and prescribe Depo-Provera without knowing its risks for him. The Michigan Court of Appeals overturned the judge's probation order, because the drug's use had no statutory authorization, its use was not accepted by the medical community as safe and effective, and its use by the defendant was not based on his informed consent.

Six state legislatures provide the statutory authorization for trial court judges to use Depo-Provera as a parole condition for convicted sex offenders. In enacting these statutes, state legislators failed to manage Depo-Provera's risk. As scientific amateurs, they did not know or care that the FDA had not approved Depo-Provera's use by sex offenders and that the studies of its use by pedophiles were not based on scientifically valid research methods, but on case studies that yielded only anecdotal evidence of the drug's safety and effectiveness. All these legislators cared about was responding to the public demand that they provide a solution to the problem of child molestation. As a result, their statutes did not provide judges with any guidance in assessing the drug's risk and the acceptability of its use by a convicted sex offender, but granted judges the authority to impose Depo-Provera as a parole condition without a psychiatric and medical examination of the defendant and without his informed consent.

Since this Depo-Provera legislation was enacted, there have been very few sex offenders required to use the drug. Judges, functioning as risk managers, have refused to impose the drug, because they have the discretion for public policy reasons not to comply with a legislatively mandated sentence. When judges have imposed a Depo-Provera parole condition, corrections officials have encountered difficulties in finding physicians to administer the drug, because they may be persuaded by the American Medical Association guidelines that it is unethical to comply with a court-ordered use of the drug. State appellate courts have limited their review of Depo-Provera parole conditions to requiring trial courts to comply with the parole statute's requirements, but have not heard any federal constitutional challenges to these state statutes.

A New Risk Management Agenda

These failures by the FDA, Upjohn and Pfizer, physicians, and courts have made it difficult for women to decide whether to give their informed consent to the drug's use. These failures, along with those of state legislatures, have also meant that men convicted of sexual offenses have been compelled to accept a Depo-Provera probation or parole condition without their informed consent. What can be done to protect these women and men from Depo-Provera's risk to their health? All the principal participants should change their management of the drug's risk, beginning with the FDA.

The Food and Drug Administration should hold hearings and promulgate five new rules governing Depo-Provera's contraceptive and criminal justice uses. Depo-Provera's contraceptive use can be addressed by two new rules. One would control the drug's sale and require that Pfizer will no longer be permitted to take refuge in a middleman defense, as Upjohn did at the 1973 Kennedy hearings and at the Mac-Murdo trial, claiming, in effect, "We were selling the drug to a state health department or to a hospital as part of a bulk order." This new rule would require Depo-Provera sales to be tracked to the physicians who use the drug for contraceptive purposes and criminal justice purposes. A second rule would control the drug's use by amending its labeling to require that all women have a baseline bone mineral density scan prior to their first Depo-Provera injection, complete an FDA-designed consent form when they are given their first injection, and have periodic follow up exams. These two rules would protect women from the drug's impact on their health and their physicians from a state medical malpractice suit.

Depo-Provera's criminal justice misuse could be curbed by three new rules. One would narrow the practice-of-medicine exception to a physician's individualized treatment of his or her patient. A second rule would require research centers to obtain an FDA-approved IND to test Depo-Provera for criminal justice use. A third rule would reverse the FDA's position, accepted by the Supreme Court in *Heckler v. Chaney* (1985), and permit the agency to exercise its discretion and prohibit state government use of Depo-Provera as a probation and parole condition until IND research, based on randomized case-controlled clinical trials, demonstrates the drug's safety and effectiveness and until the FDA has granted Pfizer a license to market the drug for use as a probation and parole condition.

If the FDA fails to take the initiative to make these needed rule changes, then congressional hearings would provide a public forum, as they did in the 1970s and 1980s, for consumer and health activists and organizations to testify to the FDA's failure to manage Depo-Provera's contraceptive and criminal justice risk. Senate and House hearings could encourage the agency to take the initiative to hold its own hearings and make the five proposed new rules or congressional hearings could lead to legislation directing the FDA to make these rule changes.

Other parties responsible for Depo-Provera's risk management should not wait for the FDA to act. Pfizer can take the initiative and refuse to fill any orders to use Depo-Provera as a probation and parole condition. Pfizer can also support the proposed rules that would serve the health interests of women and men who use Depo-Provera, often without their informed consent. These rules would also serve the company's interests. Depo-Provera's domestic sales for contraception and criminal justice have been relatively small compared to its international sales, currently facilitated by FDA approval.

Supporting these rules could change the public perception of Pfizer as an unethical pharmaceutical company. Upjohn, its corporate ancestor, had taken advantage of Depo-Provera's FDA approval as a palliative cancer treatment to sell the drug to physicians who then prescribed it as an FDA-unapproved contraceptive. Since 1992, Upjohn, and then Pfizer have relied upon Depo-Provera's approved use as a cancer treatment and contraceptive to permit judges to order its FDA-unapproved use as a probation and parole condition and physicians and health professionals to administer the drug in amounts from eight to forty-three times the dose given to women every three months for contraception and, thereby, permit states to treat sex offenders like the animals used to test the drug's contraception use.

Physicians since the 1960s have administered Depo-Provera to women for social, economic, and political reasons, frequently without their informed consent. Instead of valuing women as patients and caring about the impact of the drug on their health, physicians have treated them as producers to be regulated. Now physicians should require women to have a baseline bone mineral density scan and follow-up scans, to read the drug's patient information and patient brochure, and then to sign an FDA-approved informed consent form. Physicians at research centers should end the charade of hiding behind the practice of medicine exception and apply for, receive, and comply with an IND to conduct human clinical trials of Depo-Provera's criminal justice use and provide their subjects with FDA-approved informed consent forms for them to read and sign. Physicians should also refuse, as Oregon physicians did, to administer Depo-Provera to paroled sex offenders and follow instead the American Medical Association's ethical guidelines.

Judges responsible for products liability cases have a limited risk management role, because state legal systems prefer that negligence claims be settled privately, as most are. Only if a case is not settled or dismissed does it go to trial. In pretrial conferences, in controlling the conduct of trials, and in deciding on jury instructions, judges need to avoid the twin perils of allowing a trial to be either politicized or personalized by the evidence presented by the plaintiff's and defendant's attorneys. Judges should also be aware that there are substantial differences between the meaning of scientific evidence based on the studies of populations of women and the legal evidence that applies to one woman's case against a pharmaceutical company. Finally, judges should be sensitive to the fact that a case is not being decided by a panel of scientific experts, but a lay jury using its common sense.

Judges in criminal cases should be more aware of the ethical and legal limits to their authority to parole and probate convicted sex offenders. No matter how vile the man who stands before them, there are statutory and constitutional limits to a judge's authority. The sex offender has a First Amendment right to receive, generate, and express his thoughts free from state control, an Eighth Amendment right to be free from a cruel punishment, and a Fourteenth Amendment right to due process entitling him to a hearing attended by his attorney and a psychiatrist. A judge, using his own discretion or mandated state law, must balance the state's interest in protecting children against the defendant's federal constitutional rights and refuse to impose a Depo-Provera probation or parole condition, because the state must use other means to promote its interest in protecting children.

Women who use Depo-Provera should not be reluctant to ask, but insist on a baseline bone mineral density scan and periodic follow-up exams. They should also make an informed choice by reading the patient information and patient brochure and discussing this information with their physicians, before deciding whether to sign an FDA-designed consent form. Otherwise, women will have no legal recourse if they are injured by the drug. Unlike women who may choose Depo-Provera as a contraceptive, men have the drug imposed upon them as probation or parole condition. To protect themselves from the physical and mental ravages the drug may inflict upon them, they must insist on their Fourteenth Amendment due process right to have their attorney and a psychiatrist of their choice present at the sentencing hearing and refuse to sign a plea agreement that denies them the right to challenge their Depo-Provera probation or parole condition on state statutory and federal constitutional grounds.

A Duty to Act

Judith Weisz's, Anne MacMurdo's, and Roger Gauntlett's stories of Depo-Provera's contraceptive risk are about the failure to respect human dignity, which is the highest value of civil society and the duty of all citizens and the state to respect and protect. All managers of risk have an ethical duty to the women who choose to take Depo-Provera for contraception and the men who are ordered to take it as a condition of probation or parole to treat them with dignity.

When The Upjohn Company continually sought the Food and Drug Administration's approval for Depo-Provera's contraceptive use, when the FDA authorized the drug's contraceptive use, when Upjohn and Pfizer marketed the drug, and when physicians used the drug for contraceptive and criminal justice purposes, all of them failed in their duty to manage Depo-Provera's risk and behaved unethically. They now have a duty to acknowledge the harm they have caused and continue to cause, to adopt the rules I have proposed, and to seriously consider banning the drug.

GLOSSARY OF LEGAL AND MEDICAL TERMS

ASSUMPTION OF RISK. Assumption of risk is a claim that a plaintiff should have known a situation was inherently or obviously dangerous, but took the chance of being injured, was injured, and is not entitled to recover damages.[1]

BREACH OF WARRANTY. A breach of warranty is a broken promise about a product by a manufacturer or seller. Warranty protection is provided by the Uniform Commercial Code (UCC), which has been adopted in part by all states.[2]

CIVIL LAW. Civil law is a body of rules separate from criminal and public law, which delineate private rights and remedies and govern disputes between individuals in such areas as contracts, property, and torts.[3]

CLASS ACTION LAWSUIT. A class action lawsuit, a form of complex litigation, aggregates many plaintiffs' claims into a single lawsuit filed on behalf of all potential plaintiffs to be heard in a single court. The class must be certified by the court which determines whether all of the plaintiffs have been harmed in a similar manner and whether the lawsuit represents the interests of all potential plaintiffs. Federal class actions are governed by Federal Rule of Civil Procedure 23.

CODE OF FEDERAL REGULATIONS. The CFR "is an annual codification of the . . . rules published in the *Federal Register* by the executive departments and agencies of the Federal Government. . . . The CFR is keyed to and kept up-to-date by the daily *Federal Register* . . . . When a Federal agency publishes a regulation in the *Federal Register*, that regulation usually is an amendment to the existing CFR."[4]

COMPENSATORY DAMAGES. Compensatory damages are a monetary award for an actual injury or economic loss.[5]

COMMON LAW. The common law is a body of law established by court decisions rather then by statute.[6]

CONCURRING OPINION. A concurring opinion is "a separate opinion delivered by one or more judges which agrees with the decision of the majority of the court, but offering its own reasons for reaching that decision."[7]

CONTRIBUTORY NEGLIGENCE. Contributory negligence is a doctrine that states that a person injured in part due to his or her own negligence is barred from recovering damages from another party who was claimed to have caused the injury.[8]

COUNTERCLAIM. A counterclaim is "a claim presented by a defendant in opposition to . . . a claim of the plaintiff. If established, it will defeat or diminish the plaintiff's claim."[9]

DEPOSITION. A deposition is an out-of-court sworn testimony of a witness for use in court. At a deposition, the parties are represented by attorneys who question the witness. A court reporter records the testimony and then creates a written transcript of the deposition for the parties. Depositions are taken to gather evidence, to provide a record of the witness's testimony so the witness may be impeached if his/her testimony at trial deviates from the deposition testimony, and to have the testimony available as evidence if a witness is not able to attend the trial.[10]

DIRECTED VERDICT. A directed verdict is a ruling by a trial judge, often based on a motion of one of the parties, that there is no legally sufficient evidence for a reasonable jury to reach a different conclusion and judgment is entered on behalf of the party who has made the motion.[11]

DISCOVERY. Discovery is the fact-finding process that takes place after a lawsuit has been filed and before trial in order to allow the parties to prepare for settlement or trial by obtaining evidence from the opposing party using depositions, interrogatories, admissions, and request for documents.[12]

DIVERSITY JURISDICTION. U.S. Constitution, Article 3, Section 2, grants Congress the power to allow federal courts to hear civil cases when the parties (persons and corporations) are citizens of different states. Congress has exercised this Article 3 power, currently codified in 28 U.S. C. §1332, to limit diversity jurisdiction to cases involving claims of at least $75,000.

EQUITY. Equity is justice administered according to fairness as contrasted with the rules of law.[13]

FEDERAL REGISTER. The *Federal Register* is "a legal newspaper [of the Federal Government] published every business day. . . . The *Federal Register* contains: federal agency regulations, proposed rules and public notices, executive orders, and proclamations."[14]

FEDERAL RULE OF CIVIL PROCEDURE 60(B). This rule "permits relief of a judgment or order on the grounds of mistake, inadvertence, surprise, or neglect."[15]

HABEAS CORPUS. Habeas corpus (Latin for "you have the body") is "a court order or writ which directs law enforcement officials (prison administrators or police) who have custody of a prisoner to appear in court to determine whether the prisoner is lawfully in prison. . . . The writ is employed procedurally in federal district courts to challenge the constitutionality of a state court conviction."[16]

INTERROGATORIES. Interrogatories are specific written questions submitted by a party to the other party who must respond under oath and in writing.[17]

LEARNED INTERMEDIARY DOCTRINE. The learned intermediary doctrine is an exception to the common law rule that a manufacturer has a duty to warn the ultimate consumer about the risks of using its products. The doctrine is a defense, used by pharmaceutical companies in products liability cases, which states that the company has fulfilled its duty of care when it has provided all of the necessary information about a drug to physicians who serve as learned intermediaries for the manufacturer in communicating that information to their patients and in weighing the risks and benefits of the drug in prescribing it for their patients who are the ultimate consumers. First used in *Sterling Drug v. Cornish*, 370 F.2d 82, 83 (8th Cir. 1966) and later adopted by forty-six states, the doctrine requires plaintiffs to prove that the manufacturer's drug package insert information was inadequate to warn his or her physician and that this failure to warn caused the plaintiff's injuries.[18]

MASS TORT LAWSUIT. A mass tort lawsuit, a form of complex litigation, aggregates numerous plaintiffs who claim to have suffered a harm from a single wrongful act caused by a corporate defendant and whose cases are tried in a single court. Like a class action, the plaintiffs pool their resources to obtain more information and build stronger cases without incurring large expenses alone. But unlike a class action, the plaintiffs maintain their own lawsuits, because a single act can cause a multitude of harms and individual plaintiffs may suffer in different ways or deserve more damages than others.[19]

MOTION TO DISMISS. A motion to dismiss is an application by a defendant requesting a judge to rule that a plaintiff has not and cannot prove his or her case and the defendant cannot lose.[20]

MULTI-DISTRICT LITIGATION. Multi-district litigation, a form of complex litigation, "arises when civil litigation involving one or more common questions of fact is pending in different federal judicial districts and such actions are transferred to any district for coordinated or consolidated pre-trial proceedings. . . . Such transfers are made by the Judicial Panel on Multidistrict Litigation."[21]

NOLO CONTENDERE. *Nolo contendere* (Latin for "I do not wish to contend") is "a plea . . . to a criminal complaint or indictment by which the defendant does not admit or deny the charges, though a fine or sentence may be imposed. . . . Unlike a guilty plea, a *nolo contendere* plea may not be used against the defendant in a civil action based on the same acts."[22]

OVERINCLUSIVE CLASSIFICATION. An "overinclusive classification by definition burdens some not similarly situated with respect to a rule . . . [and] may, of course, be challenged as denying equal protection."[23]

PRODUCTION OF DOCUMENTS. The production of documents is a request made by one party to another party to provide documents in their possession or control that pertain to the subject matter of the lawsuit.[24]

PROTECTIVE ORDER. A protective order in mass tort litigation insures the confidentiality of documents, including the contents of depositions.[25]

PUNITIVE DAMAGES. Punitive damages are a monetary award beyond that necessary to compensate a person for losses and are intended to punish outrageous misconduct and to deter a defendant from similar misbehavior in the future.[26]

RULES DECISION ACT. The Rules Decision Act, 28 U.S.C §1652, provides that state law, including state statutes and judicial decisions, is the substantive law federal courts will apply in diversity cases.

RULES ENABLING ACT. Rules Enabling Act, 28 U.S.C. §2072, provides that the federal courts will apply federal procedural and evidentiary rules (Federal Rules of Civil Procedure and Federal Rules of Evidence) in diversity cases.

SETTLEMENT. A settlement is "an agreement by which the parties having disputed matters between them avoid a trial."[27]

STATUTE OF LIMITATIONS. A statute of limitations is a defense asserted to defeat a legal action brought against a party after the specified time has elapsed.[28]

STRICT LIABILITY. Strict liability is legal responsibility for an injury without proof of fault by the defendant. In products liability cases, a plaintiff has the burden to prove that an item was defective, the defect caused the injury, and the defect rendered the product unreasonably dangerous, but does not have to prove that the manufacturer was negligent.[29]

SUMMARY JUDGMENT. A summary judgment is a court order based on a motion of one party to dispose of a case without a trial when there is no dispute as to the material facts of the case and when the party who makes the motion is entitled to judgment as a matter of law. The motion for summary judgment may be granted against all or part of a claim or defense.[30]

TITLE XX. The Social Security Act, Title XX, Section 2001, is an entitlement program referred to as the Social Services Block Grant. Block grant funds are given to states to help them achieve a wide range of social policy goals, which include preventing child abuse, increasing the availability of child care, and providing community-based care for the elderly and disabled.[31]

TORT LAW. Tort law is "a body of private rights, obligations, and remedies applied by courts in civil proceedings to provide relief for persons who have suffered harm from the wrongful acts of others. . . . Three elements of every tort action are: Existence of a legal duty from the defendant to the plaintiff, a breach of the duty, and damages as a proximate result. Tort law includes negligence, products liability, and strict liability law."[32]

UNIFORM COMMERCIAL CODE. The Uniform Commercial Code (UCC) is a set of proposed laws for commercial transactions created by the American Law Institute. The UCC's Article 2 contains provisions governing the sale of goods.[33]

VOLUNTARY DISMISSAL. A voluntary dismissal is the termination of a lawsuit at the request of the plaintiff and the loss of the right to bring a same legal action again.[34]

MEDICAL GLOSSARY

ADJUNCTIVE THERAPY. Adjunctive therapy is any treatment used in conjunction with another treatment to increase the chances of a cure.[35]

ANDROGEN. An androgen is "a male sex hormone that promotes the development and maintenance of the male sex characteristics. The major androgen is testosterone. . . . An antiandrogen [such as Depo-Provera] blocks the action of androgens."[36]

ANENCEPHALY. Anencephaly is the absence at birth of a major portion of the brain, skull, and scalp.[37]

ANTISOCIAL PERSONALITY DISORDER. An antisocial personality disorder is a chronic mental condition characterized by dysfunctional and destructive thinking and perception of others. A person with this disorder has no regard for right and wrong, often disregards the rights, wishes, and feelings of others, has drug and alcohol use problems, behaves violently, and is likely to violate the law.[38]

ATHEROSCLEROSIS. Atherosclerosis is "a progressive thickening and hardening of the walls of medium-sized and large arteries as a result of fat deposits on their inner lining."[39]

BLACK BOX WARNING. The FDA black box warning, or boxed warning, appears on the label of "drugs that have special problems, particularly ones that may lead to death or serious injury. . . . This warning information displayed within a box in the prescribing information . . . is . . . referred to as a 'boxed' or 'black box' warning."[40]

CEREBROVASCULAR DISEASE. Cerebrovascular disease is "a disease of the blood vessels, especially arteries that supply the brain, usually caused by atherosclerosis and can lead to a stroke."[41]

CERVICAL CANCER. Cervical cancer occurs in the cells of the cervix, the lower part of the uterus (womb) that connects to the vagina, and can be detected with a Pap test.[42]

CERVICAL CANCER IN SITU. Cervical cancer in situ is a noninvasive form in which cancerous cells are confined to the surface of the cervix.[43]

CERVICAL NEOPLASIA. Cervical neoplasia is the abnormal growth of cells on the surface of the cervix. The cells are not cancerous, but they can lead to cancer of the cervix if not treated.[44]

CHEMICAL CASTRATION. Using Depo-Provera to suppress the production of testosterone and erotic imagery is inaccurately identified as chemical castration, because of its supposed similarity to surgical castration, a sterilization procedure that removes the testicles.[45]

CHRONIC RENAL FAILURE. Chronic renal failure is a chronic kidney disease, which signifies loss of kidney function. People with permanent kidney failure need dialysis or a kidney transplant.[46]

CONTRAINDICATION. A contraindication is a condition that makes the administration of a drug or the carrying out of a medical procedure inadvisable.[47]

DALKON SHIELD. The Dalkon Shield is a contraceptive intrauterine device (IUD) developed by the Dalkon Corporation and marketed by the A. H. Robins Company. Questions about the IUD's efficacy in preventing pregnancy, its expulsion rate, and its tendency to cause septic abortions and pelvic inflammatory disease led to lawsuits in which juries made multimillion dollar awards to women harmed by the device. Robins declared bankruptcy and sold the company to American Home Products, now owned by Wyeth Pharmaceuticals.

DEPO-PROVERA. Depo-Provera's generic name is Depo-medroxyprogesterone acetate, which is abbreviated as DMPA. The trade name is Depo-Provera Contraceptive Injection, which is abbreviated as Depo-Provera CI or DPCI. Colloquially, it is known as "the Shot."

DES. Diethylstilbestrol (DES) is a synthetic estrogen given to pregnant women to reduce the risk of pregnancy complications. In 1971, DES was shown to cause clear cell carcinoma, a rare vaginal tumor in girls and women who had been exposed to this drug in utero. The FDA subsequently withdrew the use of DES for pregnant women.

DIAGNOSTIC AND STATISTICAL MANUAL OF MENTAL DISORDERS. The *Diagnostic and Statistical Manual of Mental Disorders* (DSM) provides a common language and standard criteria for the classification of mental disorders. The fifth edition of the DSM, DSM-5, was published in 2013 by the American Psychiatric Association.

DILATION AND CURETTAGE. Dilation and curettage (D&C) is "a procedure to remove tissue from inside the uterus. Doctors perform dilation and curettage to diagnose and treat certain uterine conditions, such as heavy bleeding, or to clear the uterine lining after a miscarriage or abortion."[48]

DOUBLE-BLIND STUDY. "A double-blind study is an experimental procedure in which neither the subjects of the experiment nor the persons administering the experiment know the critical aspects of the experiment [and thereby] . . . guard against both experimenter bias and placebo effects."[49]

DYSPNEA. Dyspnea is "difficult or labored breathing, shortness of breath, and a sign of a serious disease of the airway, lungs, or heart."[50]

ENDOMETRIAL BIOPSY. An endometrial biopsy samples the inner lining of the uterus (the endometrium) to determine the cause of abnormal uterine bleeding.[51]

ENDOMETRIAL CANCER. Endometrial cancer (uterine cancer), begins in the layer of cells that form the lining (endometrium) of the uterus (womb), the organ where fetal development occurs.[52]

ENDOMETRIOSIS. Endometriosis is "an often painful disorder in which tissue that lines the inside of the uterus, the endometrium, grows outside the uterus. Displaced endometrial tissue continues to act as it normally would: it thickens, breaks down and bleeds with each menstrual cycle. Because this tissue has no way to exit the body, it becomes trapped and surrounding tissue becomes irritated eventually developing cysts."[53]

EPIDEMIOLOGY. Epidemiology is the study of health in a population to understand the causes and patterns of health and illness. An epidemiological study compares two groups of people who are alike except for one factor, such as exposure to a chemical or the presence of a health effect. The purpose of the study is to determine if a factor is associated with the health effect.[54]

FEMORAL NECK. The femoral neck is the neck of the thigh bone (femur). When a femoral neck fracture occurs, the ball of the femur is disconnected from the rest of the thigh bone.[55]

FIBROID TUMORS. Fibroid tumors are benign growths in the uterus.[56]

GLUCOSE. Glucose is a simple sugar, known as dextrose, which the body produces from protein, fat, and carbohydrates. Glucose intolerance, the inability to properly metabolize glucose, is a pre-diabetic state. Pregnant mothers who are untreated are at an increased risk of developing Type 2 diabetes, and their babies are at an increased risk of having low blood sugar and jaundice.[57]

HABITUAL ABORTION. A habitual abortion, also termed "recurrent abortion," is the occurrence of three or more miscarriages (spontaneous abortions) with no intervening pregnancies.[58]

HYPOGLYCEMIA. Hypoglycemia, "low blood sugar, may be associated with anxiety, sweating, tremor, palpitations, nausea, and pallor. Hypoglycemia starves the brain of glucose energy essential for brain function. Lack of glucose energy to the brain can cause headache, mild confusion, abnormal behavior, loss of consciousness, seizure, coma, and death."[59]

HYPOGONADISM. Hypogonadism is "a condition in which decreased production of gonadal hormones leads to below-normal function of the gonads and to retardation of sexual growth and development in children. The gonads are the ovaries and testes and the hormones they normally produce include estrogen, progesterone, and testosterone."[60]

HYSTERECTOMY. A hysterectomy is an operation to remove a woman's uterus. A woman may have a hysterectomy for different reasons, including uterine fibroids that cause pain and bleeding; cancer of the uterus, cervix, or ovaries; endometriosis; abnormal vaginal bleeding; and chronic pelvic pain. A hysterectomy for noncancerous reasons is usually considered only after all other treatment approaches have been tried without success.[61]

IND (NOTICE OF CLAIMED INVESTIGATIONAL EXEMPTION FOR A NEW DRUG). The IND protocol contains a set of questions to be answered and the research design to be followed; the criteria for selecting the subjects and receiving their informed consent; the resources needed and the methods to be used to collect the data; and the means to be used to analyze and report the data. The IND includes a description of the drug, reports of its animal tests that indicate human testing is justified and reasonably safe, and the company's plans for human and further animal tests.[62]

LUMBAR SPINE. The lumbar spine is the five vertebrae situated between the thoracic vertebrae and the sacral vertebrae in the spinal column.[63]

MENSES. Menses, also known as menstruation, is the periodic shedding of the uterine lining (endometrium), which is released through the vagina.[64]

MENORRHAGIA. Menorrhagia is a menstrual period with abnormally heavy or prolonged bleeding, which causes enough blood loss and cramping that it is difficult to maintain usual activities.[65]

MESCALINE. Mescaline is "a psychoactive agent with effects similar to LSD. A Schedule I substance, the drug produces visual hallucinations, such as color patterns and spatial distortions."[66]

METABOLIC STUDIES. Metabolic studies examine the body's chemical processes that digest food, transform it into energy to satisfy bodily needs, and eliminate the waste. Studies of Depo-Provera found metabolic side effects from using the drug, including weight gain, glucose intolerance, and changes in serum cholesterol concentrations.[67]

MISCARRIAGE. A miscarriage is a spontaneous abortion that occurs before twenty weeks of gestation.[68]

MPA. Medroxyprogesterone Acetate (MPA) is the generic name of Depo-Provera.

NEMBUTAL. Nembutal is a sedative.[69]

NORPLANT. Norplant is a hormone-based contraceptive composed of six small silicone rods containing the progestogen Levonorgestrel and is implanted under the skin of the upper arm; it is effective for up to five years. Approved by the FDA in 1990, the drug became the subject of substantial litigation and was withdrawn from the domestic market in 2002 by its manufacturer, Wyeth Pharmaceuticals.

OSTEOPENIA. Osteopenia is defined as low bone mass. See: Osteoporosis.

OSTEOPOROSIS. Osteoporosis is a disorder in which the bones become increasingly porous, brittle, and subject to fracture because of the loss of calcium and other minerals. The World Health Organization defines the following bone density values. "Normal Bone Density: A value for BMD [bone mineral density] . . . within 1 SD [standard deviation] of the young adult mean. Low Bone Mass: (osteopenia). A value for BMD more than 1 SD but less than 2.5 SD below the young adult mean. Osteoporosis: A value for BMD . . . 2.5 or more below the young adult mean in the presence of one or more fragility fractures."[70]

OVARIAN CYSTS. Ovarian cysts are fluid-filled sacs within or on the surface of an ovary, one of which is located on each side of the uterus. Eggs (ova) develop and mature in the ovaries and are released in monthly cycles during a woman's childbearing years. While most ovarian cysts disappear without treatment, some can become cancerous.[71]

PALLIATIVE TREATMENT. Palliative treatment is a treatment of a terminally ill patient intended to alleviate pain and suffering.[72]

PAP SMEAR. A Pap smear is a test for cervical cancer which is divided into five classes based on what the cells look like to the pathologist. Class I is normal; Class II cells appear a little irregular, usually representing bacterial infection; Class III and IV Pap smears suggest that dysplastic (abnormally developed) cells are present and further testing is needed; and Class V usually means cancer.[73]

PARAPHILIAS. "Paraphilias are a diagnosable psychosexual disorder [that] . . . result from recurrent, intense sexual urges, fantasies, or behaviors."[74] The paraphilias described in the *Diagnostic and Statistical Manual of Disorders* (DSM-5) are fetishism, transvestism, zoophilia, pedophilia, exhibitionism, voyeurism, sexual masochism, and sexual sadism.

PEDOPHILIA. Pedophilia, one of the eight paraphilias, is defined by "recurrent, intense erotic fantasies, urges or behaviors involving a prepubescent (13 years of age or younger) child. . . . [This] is a psychosexual affliction that only becomes criminal if the person engages in the illegal act of sexual behavior with a child."[75]

PELVIC INFLAMMATORY DISEASE. Pelvic inflammatory disease, commonly called PID, is "an infection of the female reproductive organs. PID is one of the most serious complications of a sexually transmitted disease in women: It can lead to irreversible damage to the uterus, ovaries, and fallopian tubes; and is the primary preventable cause of infertility in women."[76]

PHLEBITIS. Phlebitis is "an inflammation of a vein and, usually, the formation of a clot in the vein. In the leg, phlebitis causes the leg to swell with fluid and can carry the potential for dislodging blood clots to the lungs."[77]

POSTPARTUM. Postpartum is the period immediately after childbirth and extending for about six weeks.[78]

PREMENSTRUAL SYNDROME. Premenstrual syndrome (PMS) has a variety of symptoms, including mood swings, tender breasts, food cravings, fatigue, irritability, and depression.[79]

PROGESTERONE. Progesterone is the principal female hormone that prepares the uterus to receive and sustain a fertilized egg.[80]

PROGESTOGEN. Progestogen is a "synthetic derivative form . . . of progesterone which has some of the physiologic activity and pharmacologic effects of progesterone." Depo-Provera is a progestogen.[81]

PROSPECTIVE STUDY. A prospective study takes a group of subjects and watches for outcomes, such as the development of a disease, during the study period and relates this to other factors such as a suspected risk or protective factor.[82]

PSYCHOTROPIC DRUG. A psychotropic drug is "any drug capable of affecting the mind, emotions, and behavior. Legal drugs, such as lithium for bipolar disorder, and illicit drugs, such as cocaine, are psychotropic."[83]

QUAALUDE. Quaalude is a sedative and hypnotic drug.[84]

RANDOMIZED DOUBLE BLIND PLACEBO CONTROLLED STUDY. A randomized double blind placebo controlled study is the best experimental design for testing the effectiveness of a new medication. Subjects are assigned randomly to a treatment group that receives the new medication and to a control group that receives a placebo. The results are then compared. The experiment is double-blinded to eliminate researcher bias and placebo effects, because neither the researcher nor the subjects know critical aspects of the experiment, such as the assignment of the subjects to experimental and control groups.[85]

RETROSPECTIVE STUDY. A retrospective study classifies subjects as either having some outcome (specific disease) or lacking it (controls) and then examines the subjects' personal histories and medical records for specific factors that might be associated with that disease.[86]

RUBELLA VACCINATION. A rubella vaccination prevents rubella, also called "German measles" or "three day measles." Rubella can have severe complications in the first trimester of pregnancy, including birth defects or death of the fetus.[87]

SCHIZOPHRENIA. Schizophrenia is a brain disorder characterized by abnormal social behavior and failure to recognize reality. Schizophrenia may result in hallucinations, delusions, and extremely disordered thinking and behavior.[88]

SECONAL. Seconal is a sedative used to calm a patient before surgery.[89]

SICKLE CELL DISEASE. Sickle cell disease is a genetic and life-long blood disorder that can cause attacks of sudden and severe pain.[90]

STELAZINE. Stelazine is a drug used to treat anxiety.[91]

SUBSTANCE ABUSE. Substance abuse is the use of a drug, including alcohol, amphetamines, barbiturates, cocaine, cannabis, and morphine, in amounts harmful to the person and others and may result in criminal or antisocial behavior, and long-term personality changes.[92]

TERATOGEN. A teratogen is an agent that can halt pregnancy, disturb the development of an embryo or fetus, and cause a birth defect in the child.[93]

TERATOGENIC EFFECT. A teratogenic effect is the consequence of a pregnant woman consuming a harmful substance that manifests itself as mental or growth deficiencies in the developing fetus.[94]

THALIDOMIDE. Thalidomide is a drug that was marketed overseas as a sedative and for morning sickness, a purpose for which it was not government approved. Its use by pregnant women interfered with a child's normal development and caused them to be born with phocomelia, resulting in shortened or absent limbs. This tragedy was averted in the United States because Dr. Frances Kelsey of the U.S. Food and Drug Administration refused to approve the drug's application, which contained incomplete and insufficient data on its safety and effectiveness.[95]

THREATENED ABORTION. A threatened abortion is a condition before the twentieth week of pregnancy characterized by uterine bleeding and cramping sufficient to suggest that a miscarriage may result.[96]

THROMBOEMBOLIC DISORDER. A thromboembolic disorder is a condition in which a blood clot forms inside a blood vessel, breaks loose, and, if carried by the blood to plug the lungs, results in a pulmonary embolism, or if carried by the blood to plug the brain, results in a stroke.[97]

THROMBOPHLEBITIS. Thrombophlebitis usually occurs when a blood clot blocks a vein, typically in the legs with the possibility of dislodging and being carried by the blood to lungs and brain and blocking an artery.[98]

THORAZINE. Thorazine is a sedative and tranquilizing drug.[99]

TUBAL LIGATION. Tubal ligation is a permanent form of birth control in which a woman's fallopian tubes are surgically cut or blocked to prevent pregnancy.[100]

NOTES

PREFACE AND ACKNOWLEDGEMENTS

1 William Green, "Depo-Provera, Castration, and the Probation of Rape Offenders: Statutory and Constitutional Issues," *University of Dayton Law Review* 12(1): 1–26 (Fall 1986).

INTRODUCTON

1 Depo-Provera's generic name is Depo-medroxyprogesterone acetate, which is abbreviated DMPA or MPA. The trade name is Depo-Provera Contraceptive Injection, which is abbreviated Depo-Provera CI or DPCI. Colloquially, it is known as "The Shot."

2 For studies of risk management and regulation, *see, e.g.*, Stephen Breyer, *Breaking the Vicious Circle: Toward Effective Risk Regulation* (Cambridge, MA: Harvard University Press, 1993); Thomas Burke, *Regulating Risk: The Science and Politics of Risk* (Washington, DC: International Life Sciences Institute, 1993); Mary Douglas and Aaron Wildavsky, *Risk and Culture* (Berkeley: University of California Press, 1982); John Graham and Jonathan Wiener, *Risk vs. Risk* (Cambridge, MA: Harvard University Press, 1997); Sheila Jasanoff, *Risk Management and Culture* (New York: Russell Sage Foundation, 1986); and William Wardell and Louis Lasagna, *Regulating Drug Development* (Washington, DC: American Enterprise Institute, 1976).

3 National Academy of Sciences, *Risk Assessment in the Federal Government: Managing the Process* (Washington, DC: National Academy Press, 1983), 3.

4 *Ibid.*

5 Susan G. Hadden, "Generic Regulations and Generic Critics," *Politics and Life Sciences* 4:48–49 (Aug. 1985).

6 Civil law is a body of rules, distinct from criminal or public law, which delineate private rights and remedies and govern disputes between individuals in such areas as contracts, property, and torts. Tort law governs private wrongs and, for this study, includes negligence, products liability, and strict liability law. Henry Campbell Black, *Black's Law Dictionary* (St. Paul, MN: West Publishing, 1979), 233 and 1335.

7 Using Depo-Provera to suppress the production of testosterone and erotic imagery is inaccurately identified as chemical castration, because of its supposed similarity to surgical castration, a sterilization procedure that removes the testicles.

William Green, "Chemical Castration," 31–33, in Robert H. Blank and Jenna C. Merrick, eds., *Encyclopedia of U.S. Biomedical Policy* (Westport, CT: Greenwood Press, 1995).

8 Federal Food, Drug, and Cosmetic Act, 21 U.S.C. 301–399 (2014).

9 Black, *supra* note 6.

10 Discovery is the pretrial phase in a lawsuit during which each party obtains evidence from the opposing party by means of requests for answers to interrogatories, the production of documents, admissions, and depositions. *Ibid.*, 418–19.

A directed verdict is a ruling by a trial judge, often based on a motion of one of the parties, that there is no legally sufficient evidence for a reasonable jury to reach a different conclusion, and thus judgment is entered on behalf of the moving party. *Ibid.*, 413.

A settlement is "an agreement by which the parties having disputed matters between them" can avoid a trial. *Ibid.*, 1231.

11 A counterclaim is "a claim presented by a defendant in opposition to . . . a claim of the plaintiff. If established, it will defeat or diminish the plaintiff's claim." *Ibid.*, 315.

12 The 1962 Food, Drug, and Cosmetic Act Amendments, 21 U.S. ch. 9, are known as the 1962 Kefauver-Harris Amendments and 1962 Drug Efficacy Amendments.

13 Philip J. Hilts, *Protecting America's Health: The FDA, Business and One Hundred Years of Regulation* (New York: Alfred A. Knopf, 2003), 162.

14 Thalidomide is a drug that was marketed overseas as a sedative and for morning sickness, a purpose for which it was not government approved. Its use by pregnant women interfered with a child's normal development and caused them to be born with phocomelia, resulting in shortened or absent limbs. This tragedy was averted in the United States because Dr Frances Kelsey of the U.S. Food and Drug Administration refused to approve the drug's application, because it contained incomplete and insufficient data on its safety and effectiveness. *Ibid.*, 144–61.

15 *Supra* note 8, at 21 U.S.C. 312 (2014).

16 A randomized double-blind placebo controlled study is the best experimental design for testing the effectiveness of a new medication. Subjects are assigned randomly to a treatment group that receives the new medication and to a control group that receives a placebo. The results are then compared. The experiment is double-blinded to eliminate researcher bias and placebo effects, because neither the researcher, nor the subjects know critical aspects of the experiment, such as the assignment of the subjects to experimental and control groups. *Mosby's Medical Dictionary*, 7th ed. (St. Louis, MO: Mosby, Elsevier, 2006), 1589.

17 *Supra* note 8, at 21 U.S.C. 355(a) (2014).

18 Bernard Asbell, *The Pill: A Biography of the Drug that Changed the World* (New York: Random House, 1995), 156–69.

19 Betty Friedan, *The Feminine Mystique* (New York: W. W. Norton, 1963).

20 Contemporary feminism has been defined in terms of three phases. Second-wave feminism, which defined feminist activism from the 1960s through the early

1990s, focused on sexuality, family, education, workplace, reproductive rights, and the effort to amend the Constitution to include an Equal Rights Amendment. *See, e.g.*, Charlotte Krolokke and Anne Scott Sorensen, "The Three Waves of Feminism," 1–24, in their *Gender Communication Theories and Analyses: From Silence to Performance* (Thousand Oaks, CA: Sage, 2005).

21 Barbara Seaman, *The Doctor's Case against the Pill* (New York: R. H. Wyden, 1969).
22 Boston Women's Health Book Collective, *Our Bodies, Ourselves* (New York: Simon and Schuster, 1973). Known by various names until it was incorporated in 1972 as the Boston Women's Health Book Collective, it is now known as Our Bodies Ourselves. Its founders include Miriam Hawley, Judy Norsigian, and Norma Swenson. *Our Bodies, Ourselves* was first published in 1970 by the New England Free Press as *Women and Their Bodies*. Sandra Morgan, *Into Our Own Hands: The Woman's Health Movement in the United States* (New Brunswick, NJ: Rutgers University Press, 2002), 16–22.
23 Morgan, *supra* note 22, at 29 (quoting Sandra Morgan's interview of Belita Cowan, Washington, DC, June 1992).
24 *Ibid.* (quoting National Women's Health Network, *Network News*, 1–2 (Oct. 1976)).
25 Cynthia Pearson, "National Women's Health Network and the FDA: Two Decades of Activism," *Reproductive Health Matters* 6:132–41 (Nov. 1995).
26 Betsy Hartmann, *Reproductive Rights and Wrongs: The Global Politics of Population Control*, rev. ed. (Boston: South End Press, 1995), 201.
27 Kim Yanoshik and Judy Norsigian, "Contraception, Control, and Choice," 71, in Kathryn Ratliff et al., eds., *Healing Technology: Feminist Perspectives* (Ann Arbor: University of Michigan Press, 1989).
28 Stephen Minkin, "Nine Thai Women Had Cancer . . . None of Them Took Depo-Provera: Therefore Depo-Provera Is Safe. This Is Science?," *Mother Jones* 36 (Nov. 1981).
29 The FDA black box warning or boxed warning appears in the labeling of "drugs that have special problems, particularly ones that may lead to death or serious injury. . . . This warning information is displayed within a box in the prescribing information [and] . . . is referred to as a 'boxed' or 'black box' warning." www.fda.gov.
30 A summary judgment is a court order based on a motion of one party to dispose of a case without a trial when there is no dispute as to the material facts of the case and one party is entitled to judgment as a matter of law. Black, *supra* note 6, at 1287.
31 The learned intermediary doctrine is a defense used by pharmaceutical companies in products liability cases. It states that the company has fulfilled its duty of care when it provides all of the necessary information about a drug to physicians who act as learned intermediaries in communicating that information to their patients. Richard C. Goetz and Karen R. Growdon, "A Defense of the Learned Intermediary Doctrine," *Food and Drug Law Journal* 63(2): 422–243 (2008).

CHAPTER 1. THE GRADY HOSPITAL STUDY

1 Federal Food, Drug, and Cosmetic Act, 21 U.S.C. 312 (2014).

2 The IND (Notice of Claimed Investigational Exemption for a New Drug) includes a description of the drug, reports of its animal tests that indicate human testing is justified and reasonably safe, and the company's plans for human and further animal tests. *Ibid*. See also David A. Kessler, "Regulation of Investigational New Drugs," *New England Journal of Medicine* 32(5): 281–88 (Feb. 2, 1989).

3 The New Drug Application (NDA) includes reports of a drug's animal and human studies and the drug's proposed labeling and advertising. If the FDA approves a drug's NDA, it will permit a pharmaceutical company to market the drug and physicians to prescribe it for its labeled use. Federal Food, Drug, and Cosmetic Act, 21 U.S.C. 355(a) (2014).

4 The IND protocol contains a set of questions to be answered and the research design to be followed, the criteria for selecting the subjects and receiving their informed consent, the resources needed and the methods to be used to collect the data, and the means to be used to analyze and report the data. *Ibid.*, 21 U.S.C. 312 (2014).

5 Depo-Provera has also been used to treat men with sexual deviation disorders, beginning in 1965, but without an FDA-approved IND. Chapter 5 explores the drug's use by physicians at the Johns Hopkins Hospital. Dr. Fred Berlin used the drug on male sex offenders who received weekly injections from 100 to 800 milligrams, which is the equivalent of eight to forty-three times the amount given to women every three months for contraception. State court judges, relying on their discretion, state sexual offense statutes, and Dr. Berlin's journal articles, have conditioned the grant of probation or parole on the use of the drug.

6 The Upjohn Co., NDA 12–541, "Depo-Provera Sterile Aqueous Suspension C-150 for Treatment of Endometriosis and Habitual and Threatened Abortion" (Nov. 1, 1960). Withdrawn Sept. 17, 1974, and June 26, 1974, respectively.

   A miscarriage is a spontaneous abortion that occurs before twenty weeks of gestation. A threatened abortion is a condition in pregnancy that occurs before the twentieth week and is defined by uterine bleeding and cramping sufficient to suggest that a miscarriage may result. *Mosby's Medical Dictionary*, 7th ed. (St. Louis, MO: Mosby, Elsevier, 2006), 1756. A habitual abortion is "a spontaneous termination of three successive pregnancies before the twentieth week of gestation." *Ibid.*, 842.

   Endometriosis is "an often painful disorder in which tissue that lines the inside of the uterus, the endometrium, grows outside the uterus. Displaced endometrial tissue continues to act as it normally would: it thickens, breaks down and bleeds with each menstrual cycle. Because this tissue has no way to exit the body, it becomes trapped and, as surrounding tissue becomes irritated, eventually develops cysts." *Ibid.*, 644.

7 The Upjohn Co., IND 1086, "Depo-Provera Sterile Aqueous Suspension C-150 for Contraception" (July 12, 1963). Discontinued Aug. 15, 1988.

8 W. Newton Long, IND 9693, "Depo-Provera Sterile Aqueous Suspension C-150 for Contraception" (1967).

9 "Patient Labeling of Medroxyprogesterone Acetate Injectable Contraceptive; Stay of Effective Date of Final Order," *Federal Register* 39:38226 (Oct 30, 1974).

10 U.S. Food and Drug Administration. "Upjohn Company, Depo-Provera Sterile Acqueous Suspension," *Federal Register* 43:28555 (June 30, 1978).

11 U.S. Food and Drug Administration, "Depo-Provera: Hearing on Proposal to Refuse Approval of Supplemental New Drug Application," *Federal Register* 44:44274 (July 27, 1979).

12 Endometrial cancer (uterine cancer), begins in the layer of cells that form the lining (endometrium) of the uterus (womb), the organ where fetal development occurs. *Mosby's, supra* note 6, at 643–44.

   Cervical cancer occurs in the cells of the cervix, the lower part of the uterus that connects to the vagina, and can be detected with a Pap test. *Ibid.,* 345–46.

13 Long, *supra* note 8, at 9.

14 Michael Spindel, "Characteristics of the Population of Depo-Provera Patients within the Grady Memorial Hospital System," 45, in Robert A. Hatcher et al., eds., *Depo-Medroxyprogesterone Acetate: Experience at the Grady Memorial Hospital Family Planning Program in Atlanta, Georgia: 1967–1979* (Atlanta: Department of Gynecology and Obstetrics, Emory University School of Medicine, 1980).

   The Social Security Act, Title XX, Section 2001, is an entitlement program referred to as the Social Services Block Grant (SSBG). Block grant funds are given to states to help them achieve a wide range of social policy goals, which include preventing child abuse, increasing the availability of child care, and providing community-based care for the elderly and disabled. 42 U.S.C. 1397.

15 Robert A. Hatcher and Aliza Greenspan, "A Descriptive Analysis of the Women Using Depo-Provera at the Grady Memorial Hospital Family Planning Clinic, 1974 and 1978," in Hatcher et al., *supra* note 14, at 23.

   Menses, also known as menstruation, is the periodic shedding of the uterine lining (endometrium) that is released through the vagina. *Mosby's, supra* note 6, at 1179.

   Sickle cell disease is a genetic and life-long blood disorder that can cause attacks of sudden and severe pain. *Ibid.,* 1704.

   Menorrhagia is a menstrual period with abnormally heavy or prolonged bleeding, which causes enough blood loss and cramping that it is difficult to maintain usual activities. *Ibid.,* 1179.

16 Hatcher et al., *supra* note 14, at 24.

   Teratogenic effect is the consequence a woman consuming a harmful substance that causes a mental or growth deficiency in the developing fetus. *Mosby's, supra* note 6, at 1831.

A rubella vaccination prevents rubella, also called "German measles" or "three day measles." Rubella can have severe complications in the first trimester of pregnancy, including birth defects or death of the fetus. *Ibid.*, 1654–55.

Postpartum is the period immediately following childbirth that lasts for about six weeks. *Ibid.*, 1502.

17 A Pap smear is a screening test for cervical cancer. See *supra* note 12.

18 Melvin Williams, Jacob Adams, and Robert Hatcher, "Policies and Procedures Which Have Guided the Grady Memorial Hospital Family Planning Clinic in Providing Depo-Medroxyprogesterone Acetate 1967–1978," in Hatcher et al., *supra* note 14, at 11–13.

19 The Grady Clinic study of Depo-Provera discontinuation rates appears in F. Douglas Scutchfield and W. Newton Long, "Parenteral Medroxyprogesterone as a Contraceptive Agent," *Public Health Reports* 84(12): 1059–62 (1969); in Hatcher et al., *supra* note 14, at 115–18; in F. Douglas Scutchfield et al., "Medroxyprogesterone Acetate as an Injectable Female Contraceptive," *Contraception* 3(1): 21–34 (1970); and in Hatcher, *supra* note 14, at 119–33.

The Grady Clinic study of breast cancer appears in Aliza Greenspan et al., "Association of Depo-Medroxyprogesterone Acetate and Breast Cancer," in Hatcher et al., *supra* note 14, at 70–76.

The Grady study of estrogen use to manage bleeding appears in Aliza Greenspan and Robert A. Hatcher, "The Prevalence of Estrogen Use and Pregnancy in Women Using Depo-Medroxyprogesterone Acetate for Contraception at the Grady Memorial Hospital Family Planning Clinic," in Hatcher et al., *supra* note 14, at 77–86.

The Grady Clinic study of breast, uterine, and ovarian cancer appears in Arthur P. Liang et al., "Risk of Breast, Uterine Corpus, and Ovarian Cancer in Women Receiving Medroxyprogesterone Acetate," *Journal of the American Medical Association* 249(21): 2909–12 (June 3, 1983).

The Grady Clinic study of mortality among African-American women appears in Howard Ory, "Mortality among Black Contraceptive Users," *Journal of the American Medical Association* 251(8): 1044–48 (Feb. 24, 1983).

20 Scutchfield and Long, *supra* note 19, and in Hatcher et al., *supra* note 14, at 115–18; Scutchfield et al., *supra* note 19, and in Hatcher, *supra* note 14, at 119–33; Greenspan et al., in Hatcher et al., *supra* note 14, at 70–76; Greenspan and Hatcher, in Hatcher et al., *supra* note 14, at 77–86; and Liang et al., *supra* note 19.

21 Grady Memorial Hospital, Family Planning Clinic, "DEPO-PROVERA CONSENT," in Hatcher et al., *supra* note 14.

22 Thrombophlebitis usually occurs when a blood clot blocks a vein, typically in the legs, with the possibility of dislodging and being carried by the blood to lungs and brain and blocking an artery. *Mosby's, supra* note 6, at 1849.

A contraindication is a condition that makes the administration of a drug or the carrying out of a medical procedure inadvisable. *Ibid.*, 454.

A thromboembolic disorder is a condition in which a blood clot forms inside a blood vessel, breaks loose, and, if carried by the blood to plug the lungs, results in a pulmonary embolism, or if carried by the blood to plug the brain, results in a stroke. *Ibid.*, 1849.

Cerebrovascular disease is a group of brain dysfunctions related to disease of the blood vessels supplying the brain, which can cause a stroke. *Ibid.*, 343.

23 National Women's Health Network, "Women's Health Group Establishes Registry for Birth Control Shot," Press Conference (June 3, 1979).

24 National Women's Health Network, "Depo-Provera Registry Questionnaire," Rosa H., (Mar. 14, 1983). A Grady patient's full name is withheld because all responses to the questionnaire are confidential.

25 *Ibid.*, Sandra N. (n.d.).

26 U.S. Food and Drug Administration, *Official Transcript of Proceedings. Report of the Public Board of Inquiry on Depo-Provera* 4:28–29 (Jan. 13, 1983).

27 Charles E. Edwards, Commissioner of Food and Drugs, U.S. Food and Drug Administration, testimony before the US. Congress, Senate, Committee on Labor and Public Welfare, *Quality of Health Care—Human Experimentation: Hearings before the Subcommittee on Health*, 93rd Cong., 1st Sess., 21 (Feb. 21, 1973).

F. X. Wazeter, International Research and Development Corporation (IRDC), "Depo-Provera: Long-Term Intramuscular Study in Beagle Dogs— Twenty-Four Month Interim Report" (unpublished, Sept. 1970). A second dog study was undertaken with a significantly modified protocol. *See*: D. E. Longe-necker, "Pharmacology Supplemental Review," U.S. Food and Drug Adminis-tration (unpublished, Apr. 19, 1977 and Jan. 28, 1978). *See also*: Stephen Minkin, "Depo-Provera: A Critical Analysis," *Women and Health* 5(2): 49 (1980), for an analysis of the animal studies.

28 Robert J. Temple, Acting Director, Office of New Drug Evaluation, Center for Drugs and Biologics, testimony before the FDA Public Board of Inquiry, *supra* note 26, at 2:7–8 (Jan. 11, 1983).

29 Victor Berliner, MD, FDA staff member, testimony before the U.S. Food and Drug Administration, Obstetrics and Gynecology Advisory Committee, *Transcript of Twenty-Third Meeting*, 59 (June 2, 1972).

30 *Ibid.* (FDA OB/GYN Advisory Committee discussion), 33–56 *passim*.

31 U.S. Food and Drug Administration, statement submitted to the U.S. Congress, House of Representatives, Select Committee on Population, 95th Cong, 1st Sess., 350 (Aug. 8, 1978).

32 J. W. Armistad, "Medical Officer's Summary of NDA No. 12, 541," U.S. Food and Drug Administration, 4 (Jan. 21, 1971) in U.S. Congress, House Committee on Government Operations, "Use of Advisory Committees by the Food and Drug Administration: Hearings before the Subcommittee on Intergovernmental Rela-tions, House Committee on Government Operations, Part I," 93rd Cong., 2nd Sess., 356–57 (Apr. 30, 1974).

33 Marion J. Finkel, FDA Staff Member, testimony before the U.S. Food and Drug Administration. Obstetrics and Gynecology Advisory Committee, *Minutes of Twentieth Meeting*, 8 (July 2, 1971).

34 Metabolic studies examine the body's chemical processes that digest food, transform it into energy to satisfy bodily needs, and eliminate waste. Studies of Depo-Provera found that metabolic side effects from using the drug include weight gain, glucose intolerance, and changes in serum cholesterol concentrations. *Mosby's, supra* note 6, at 1186.

35 FDA OB/GYN Advisory Committee Meeting, *supra* note 29, at 22–24.

36 *Ibid.*, 29.

37 *Ibid.*

38 *Ibid.*, 29–30.

39 *Ibid.*, 30.

40 *Ibid.*, 31.

41 *Ibid.*, 34.

42 *Ibid.*, 37. The International Research Development Corporation conducted a ten-year monkey study, beginning in 1968, and reported non-malignant mammary modules in the monkeys and, unexpectedly, the development of uterine cancer. IRDC, Long-Term Depo-Provera Study in Monkeys, Final Report, 1979, summarized in Judith Weisz, Griff T. Ross, and Paul Stolley, *Report of the Public Board of Inquiry on Depo-Provera*, U.S. Food and Drug Administration, 29–31 (Oct. 17, 1984).

43 FDA OB/GYN Advisory Committee Meeting, *supra* note 29, at 44–45.

44 *Ibid.*, 45.

45 *Ibid.*, 45–51.

46 *Ibid.*, 50–51 and 54–56.

47 *Ibid.*, 60.

48 Michael Popkin, "Medical Officer's Review of IND 1086—Progress Report, July 20, 1972," in House Committee on Government Operations, *supra* note 32, at 361.

49 Paul C. Schwallie and J. Robert Assenzo, "Contraceptive Use Efficacy Study Utilizing Medroxyprogesterone Acetate Administered as an Intramuscular Injection Once Every 90 Days," *Fertility and Sterility* 24:331–39 (1973).

50 House Committee on Government Operations, *supra* note 32, at 359.

51 *Ibid.*, 361.

52 *Ibid.*, 363.

53 *Ibid.* U.S. Food and Drug Administration, Bureau of Drugs, "Postscript to Medical Officer's Summary of NDA No. 12, 541" (Aug. 9, 1972).

54 House Committee on Government Operations, *supra* note 32, at 362.

55 Senate Health and Human Experimentation Hearings, *supra* note 27.

56 House Committee on Government Operations,, *supra* note 32.

57 *Ibid.*, 363.

58 *Ibid.*, 363–65.

59 Hatcher et al., *supra* note 14, at 150–51. The FDA issued its redesigned consent form on Sept. 10, 1972.

60 *Ibid.*, 13.

61 "Informed Consent Form for Depo-Provera," in Hatcher et al., *supra* note 14, at 150–51.

62 *Ibid.*, 151.

63 *Ibid.*, 150.

64 *Ibid.*, 151.

65 "Certification by Physician," in Hatcher et al., *supra* note 14, at 152.

66 Robert A. Hatcher, Grady Memorial Hospital Family Planning Clinic, testimony before the U.S. Congress, House of Representatives, Select Committee on Population, "The Depo-Provera Debate: Hearings before the House Select Committee on Population," 95th Cong., 2nd Sess., 212 (Aug. 8, 9, and 10, 1978).

67 Melvin Williams, Jacob Adams, and Robert Hatcher, "Policies and Procedures which Have Guided the Grady Memorial Hospital Family Planning Clinic in Providing Depo-Medroxyprogesterone Acetate 1967–1978," in Hatcher et al., *supra* note 14, at 15–16.

68 U.S. Food and Drug Administration, *Data Audit of IND #9693: Depo-Provera as an Injectable Contraceptive at the Grady Memorial Hospital*, 1 (Jan. 3, 1979).

69 *Ibid.*, 3.

70 *Ibid.*

71 *Ibid.*

72 Hatcher et al., *supra* note 14, at 10.

73 *Ibid.*, 10–11.

74 A Pap smear is a test for cervical cancer and is divided into five classes based on what the cells look like to the pathologist. Class I is normal; Class II cells appear a little irregular, usually representing bacterial infection; Class III and IV Pap smears suggest that dysplastic (abnormally developed) cells are present and further testing is needed; and Class V usually means cancer. *Mosby's*, *supra* note 6, at 1388.

75 Popkin, *supra* note 48; and Schwallie and Assenzo, *supra* note 49.

76 Hatcher et al., *supra* note 14, at 11.

77 *Ibid.*

78 FDA Public Board of Inquiry, *supra* note 26, at 4:10–11 (Jan. 13, 1983).

79 House Select Committee on Population, *supra* note 66, at 12 (Aug. 8, 1978). *See also*: FDA Public Board of Inquiry, *supra* note 26, at 4:11 (Jan. 13, 1978).

Cervical cancer occurs in the cells of the cervix (the lower part of the uterus that connects to the vagina) and can be detected with a Pap test. *Mosby's*, *supra* note 6, at 345–46.

Glucose is a simple sugar, known as dextrose, which the body produces from protein, fat, and carbohydrates. Glucose intolerance, the inability to properly metabolize glucose, is a prediabetic state. Pregnant mothers who are untreated are at an increased risk of developing Type 2 diabetes; their babies have increased risk of low blood sugar and jaundice. *Ibid.,* 815–16.

80 Hatcher et al., *supra* note 14, at 1.
81 Hatcher, testimony before the House Select Committee on Population, *supra* note 14, at 15.
82 Hatcher, *ibid.*, 220.
83 Hatcher et al., *supra* note 14, at 7.
84 FDA Grady Audit, *supra* note 68, at 4.
85 Hatcher, Statement, in House Select Committee on Population, *supra* note 66, at 216–18.
86 *Ibid.*, 7.
87 *Ibid.*
88 *Ibid.*
89 *Ibid.*
90 *Ibid.*
91 *Ibid.*, 4–5.
92 National Women's Health Network, *supra* note 24; author's analysis of fifty-six questionnaire responses submitted on various dates in 1983.
93 *Ibid.*
94 *Ibid.*, Thelma G. (Mar. 18, 1983).
95 FDA Grady Audit, *supra* note 68, at 5.
96 *Ibid.*, 6.
97 *Ibid.*
98 *Ibid.*, 7.
99 *Ibid.*, 5.
100 Hatcher, testimony, in House Select Committee on Population, *supra* note 66, at 11.
101 FDA Grady Audit, *supra* note 68, at 5.
102 *Ibid.*
103 *Ibid.*
104 *Ibid.*, 6.
105 *Ibid.*
106 *Ibid.*, 8.
107 *Ibid.*, 7.
108 *Ibid.*
109 *Ibid.*
110 *Ibid.*
111 *Ibid.*, 4.
112 FDA Board of Inquiry, *supra* note 26, at 4:25 (Jan. 13, 1983).
113 FDA Grady Audit, *supra* note 68, at 8.
114 The Bureau of Drugs was merged with the Bureau of Biologics in 1982 to form the Center for Drugs and Biologics.
115 FDA Public Board of Inquiry, *supra* note 26, at 5:14 (Jan. 14, 1983).

116 FDA Grady Audit *supra* note 68, at 8.

117 *Ibid.*

118 *Ibid.*

119 *Ibid.*, 9.

120 Letter to Hon. Ted Weiss, Chairman, Intergovernmental Relations and Human Resources Subcommittee, Committee on Government Operations, House of Representatives, U.S. Congress, from Robert C. Wetherell, Associate Commissioner for Legislation and Information, U.S. Food and Drug Administration, 2 (Sept. 29, 1983).

121 Hatcher et al., *supra* note 14, at 6.

122 George Tucker, "Depo-Provera (DMPA): An Assessment of the Contraceptive Methods Chosen Following Its Discontinuation in Our Grady Population," Resident Research Day Paper (June 5, 1980), Emory University School of Medicine, in Hatcher et al., *supra* note 14, at 56.

123 *Ibid.*

124 Grady Memorial Hospital, Family Planning Clinic Program, "Why Are You Stopping the Birth Control Shot at the Grady Hospital" (a patient education pamphlet distributed to all patients using DMPA at the time the Grady Family Planning Clinic discontinued its use), in Hatcher et al., *supra* note 14, at 157 (emphasis in original).

125 *Ibid.*

126 *Ibid.*, 157–58 (emphasis in original).

127 *Ibid.*, 157.

128 *Ibid.*

129 *Ibid.*, (emphasis in original).

130 *Ibid.*

131 *Ibid.*, 158.

132 *Ibid.*, 158–59.

133 Tucker, *supra* note 122, at 59.

134 FDA Public Board of Inquiry, *supra* note 26, at 4:32 (Jan. 13, 1983).

135 Hatcher et al., *supra* note 14, at 7.

136 U.S. Food and Drug Administration. "Depo-Provera; Hearing on Proposal to Refuse Approval of Supplemental New Drug Application," *Federal Register* 44:44274 (July 27, 1979).

137 The Commissioner of Food and Drugs appointed the three-member board on Sept. 10, 1981, pursuant to 21 C.F.R. 13.10(C). *Federal Register* 47:36470 (Aug. 20, 1982).

138 FDA Public Board of Inquiry, *supra* note 26. For two analyses of the Public Board of Inquiry, *see*: Wendy Kline, "Bodies of Evidence: Activists, Patients, and the FDA Regulation of Depo-Provera," *Journal of Women's History* 22(3): 64–87 (2010); and Sidney A. Shapiro, "Scientific Issues and the Function of Hearing Procedures: Evaluating the FDA's Public Board of Inquiry," *Duke Law Journal* 46(2): 288–345 (1986).

139 FDA Public Board of Inquiry, *supra* note 26, at 2:21 (Jan. 11, 1983).

140 *Ibid.*

141 *Ibid.*, 23.

142 *Ibid.*, 22–23.

143 *Ibid.*, 4–5 (Jan. 13, 1983).

144 *Ibid.*, 7, 8–23.

145 *Ibid.*, 24–26.

146 *Ibid.*, 25.

147 *Ibid.*, 27.

148 *Ibid.*

149 *Ibid.*, 27–28.

150 *Ibid.*, 28–29.

151 *Ibid.*, 31–32.

152 *Ibid.*, 31–32.

153 *Ibid.*, 5:15 (Jan. 14, 1983).

154 *Ibid.*, 16.

155 *Ibid.*, 17.

156 Hatcher et al., *supra* note 14.

157 See articles cited *supra* note 19.

158 FDA Public Board of Inquiry, *supra* note 26, at 2:192 (Jan. 11, 1983).

159 *Ibid.*, 192–93.

160 *Ibid.*, 193.

161 *Ibid.*

162 *Ibid.*, 5:27–28 (Jan. 14, 1983).

163 *Ibid.*, 80.

164 *Ibid.*, 81.

165 *Ibid.*, 4:39 (Jan. 13, 1983).

166 *Ibid.*

167 Weisz, *supra* note 42, at 172.

168 *Ibid.*, 87. *See*: Aliza R. Greenspan, "A Follow-Up Study of D&C or Endometrial Biopsy in Depo-Provera Users," 189–91 (1978), in Hatcher et al., *supra* note 14.

169 Weisz, *supra* note 42, at 99.

170 *Ibid.*, 91–92.

171 *Ibid.*, 92–93.

172 *Ibid.*, 175.

173 Letter to Frank E. Young, MD, Commissioner, Food and Drug Administration, from Kenneth M. Cyrus, Assistant Secretary and Associate General Counsel, Food and Drug Administration, The Upjohn Co. (Sept. 29, 1986).

174 "Human Subjects; Depo-Provera Sterile Aqueous Suspension," *Federal Register* 51: 37651 (October 17, 1986).

175 Weisz, *supra* note 42, at 161–62.

176 *Ibid.*, 5.

177 Letter to Arthur Hull Hayes, MD, Commissioner, U.S. Food and Drug Administration, from Ted Weiss, Chairman, Intergovernmental Relations and Human Resources Subcommittee, Committee on Government Operations, House of Representatives, U.S. Congress, 1 (June 13, 1983).

178 Letter to Hon. Ted Weiss, Chairman, Intergovernmental Relations and Human Resources Subcommittee, Committee on Government Operations, House of Representatives, U.S. Congress, from Robert C. Wetherell, Jr., Associate Commissioner for Legislation and Information, U.S. Food and Drug Administration, 2 (Sept. 29, 1983).

179 National Women's Health Network, "Women's Health Group Establishes Registry for Birth Control Shot," Press Conference Notice (June 5, 1979).

180 National Women's Health Network, "Request for Emergency Grant," Stop Depo-Provera Campaign, 4 (1979).

181 National Women's Health Network, *supra* note 24.

182 Cynthia A. Pearson, "National Women's Health Network and the U.S. FDA: Two Decades of Activism," *Reproductive Health Matters* 6:135 (Nov. 1995).

183 Office Memorandum to Belita Cowan, Executive Director, National Women's Health Network, from Laura Negin, National Women's Health Network (Oct. 28, 1980).

184 "Depo-Provera: FDA Hearings Raise Questions," *off our backs*, 5 (Feb. 1983).

185 FDA Public Board of Inquiry, supra note 26, at Helen Holmes, 4:158–61, 5:38–45; Stephen Minkin 4:144–64, 5:49–53; Judy Norsigian 4:114–36; Dr. Sidney Wolfe at 4:37–77, 5:75–83 (Jan. 13 and 14, 1983).

186 National Women's Health Network of Georgia, Black Women's Health Project, "Atlanta Women in 'Depo-Provera Experiment' Asked to Join Class Action Suit," Press Release (Feb. 2, 1983).

187 Letter to Depo-Provera Registry Member, from Cary LaCheen, Researcher, and Sidney M. Wolfe, MD, Public Citizen Health Research Group, 1 (Dec. 6, 1983).

188 Author's analysis of the National Women's Health Network Registry questionnaire forms.

189 *Ibid.*

190 National Women's Health Network, National Women's Health Network Registry, Question 13 (1979).

191 Letter to Susan Seidler, National Women's Health Network, from Cary LaCheen, Researcher, Public Citizen Health Research Group, 1 (Dec. 6, 1983).

192 Susan Seidler, "Grady Class Action Update" Memorandum (Feb. 8, 1984).

193 The Upjohn Co. Defendant Upjohn Company's Notice of Motion to Dismiss for Delay in Prosecution, Civil Action No. 82/245, Superior Court of City and County of San Francisco, State of California, 2 (Mar. 31, 1988). Motion granted (May 31, 1988).

194 *Ibid.*, 2–3.

195 Maryanne Galante, "Depo-Provera, Cancer Link Alleged in California Action," *National Law Journal*, n.p. (Apr. 2, 1984).

196 Letter to Sibyl Shainwald, Esq., Fuchsberg & Fuchsberg, and Arthur Bryant, Esq.,
Trial Lawyers for Public Justice, from James P. Kreindler, Kreindler & Kreindler, 1
(Sept. 19, 1985).
197 *Ibid.*
198 National Women's Health Network, Motion for Reconsideration of Order Granting Withdrawal of Counsels in *National Women's Health Network v. The Upjohn
Company*, Civil Action No. 8212345 (Dec. 30, 1985).
199 The Upjohn Co. Defendant Upjohn Company's Notice of Motion to Dismiss for
Delay in Prosecution. Civil Action No. 82/245, Superior Court of City and County
of San Francisco, State of California, 2 (Mar. 31, 1988). Motion granted (May 31,
1988).

CHAPTER 2. THE TWENTY-FIVE YEAR FDA APPROVAL
CONTROVERSY
1 21 U.S.C. 355(a) (2014).
2 Upjohn's animal studies were criticized, because the beagle dog and rhesus monkey were seen as inappropriate test models in evaluating the drug's human safety.
Upjohn's human clinical studies are faulted for their design, sample sizes, control
groups, length of exposure, loss of their subjects to follow-up, and lack of statistical power.
3 Depo-Provera's unique features are its privacy, convenience, and availability to
women unable to use other methods and for whom other methods failed.
4 Progesterone is the principal female hormone that prepares the uterus to receive
and sustain a fertilized egg. *Black's Medical Dictionary*, 41st ed., Dr. Harvey
Marchvitch, ed. (Lanham, MD: Scarecrow Press, 2006), 583.
    Progestogen is a "synthetic derivative form . . . of progesterone which has some
of the physiologic activity and pharmacologic effects of progesterone." Depo-
Provera is a progestogen. *Stedman's Medical Dictionary for the Health Professional
and Nursing*, 6th ed. (Philadelphia: Lippincott Williams & Wilkins, 2008), 1272.
5 F. X. Wazeter, International Research and Development Corporation (IRDC),
"Depo-Provera: Long-Term Intramuscular Study in Beagle Dogs—Twenty-Four
Month Interim Report" (unpublished, Sept. 1970); F. X. Wazeter, International
Research and Development Corporation (IRDC), "Depo-Provera: Long-Term
Intramuscular Study in the Monkey—Twenty-Four Month Interim Report" (unpublished, Sept. 1970). A second dog study was undertaken with a significantly
modified protocol. *See*: D. E. Longenecker, "Pharmacology Supplemental Review,"
U.S. Food and Drug Administration (unpublished, Apr. 19, 1977 and Jan. 28,
1978). *See also*: Stephen Minkin, "Depo-Provera: A Critical Analysis," *Women and
Health* 5(2): 49 (1980), for an analysis of the animal studies.
6 Metabolic studies examine the body's chemical processes that digest food, transform it into energy to satisfy bodily needs, and eliminate the waste. Studies of
Depo-Provera found that metabolic side effects from using the drug include weight

gain, glucose intolerance, and changes in serum cholesterol concentrations. *Mosby's Medical Dictionary*, 7th ed. (St. Louis, MO: Mosby, Elsevier, 2008), 1186.

7 U.S. Food and Drug Administration, Obstetrics and Gynecology Advisory Committee, *Transcript of Twenty-Third Meeting*, 29, 60 (June 2, 1972).

8 *Ibid.*, 37, 45–53 *passim*.

9 Letter to Lewis M. Hellman, Deputy Assistant Secretary for Population Affairs, Department of Health, Education, and Welfare, from Philander P. Claxton, Jr., Special Assistant to the Secretary for Population Matters, Department of State, 1 (July 1, 1971).

10 FDA Advisory Committee, *supra* note 7, at 45–47.

11 U.S. Congress, Senate, Subcommittee on Health, Committee on Public Welfare, "Hearings on Quality of Health Care—Human Experimentation," 93rd Cong., 1st Sess. (Feb. 21 and 22, 1973).

12 U.S. Food and Drug Administration, Obstetrics and Gynecology Advisory Committee, *Transcript of Twenty-Seventh Meeting*, 6–7 (Feb. 22, 1973).

13 *Ibid.*, 4.

14 Paul C. Schwallie and J. Robert Assenzo, "Contraceptive Use—Efficacy Study Utilizing Medroxyprogesterone Acetate Administered as an Intramuscular Injection Once Every 90 Days," *Fertility and Sterility* 24:331–39 (1973).

15 Paul C. Schwallie, The Upjohn Co., testimony before the FDA Advisory Committee, *supra* note 12, at 35–59.

16 R. G. Carlson, The Upjohn Co., testimony before the FDA Advisory Committee, *ibid.*, 59–65.

17 Michael Popkin, "Medical Officer's Review of IND 1086—Progress Report, July 20, 1972," U.S. Food and Drug Administration, 361, in U. S. Congress, House of Representatives, Committee on Governmental Operations, Subcommittee on Intergovernmental Relations, "Hearings on Use of Advisory Committees by the Food and Drug Administration," 93rd Cong., 2nd Sess. (Apr. 30, 1974).

Cervical cancer occurs in the cells of the cervix (the lower part of the uterus that connects to the vagina) and can be detected with a Pap test. *Mosby's, supra* note 6, at 345–46.

18 Sheldon J. Segal, Population Council, J. J. Speidel, Agency for International Development, Malcolm Potts, International Planned Parenthood Foundation, and Mary Lane, Margaret Sanger Research Bureau, testimony before the FDA OB/GYN Advisory Committee, *supra* note 12, at 65–90.

19 *Ibid.*, 66.

20 *Ibid.*, 106–09.

21 *Ibid.*, 109.

22 *Ibid.*, 110.

23 *Ibid.*, 111–12.

24 *Ibid.*, 136.

25 *Ibid.*, 142.

26 *Ibid.*, 150 (referencing F. Douglas Scutchfield et al., "Medroxyprogesterone Acetate as an Injectable Female Contraceptive," *Contraception* 3[1]: 21–34 (1970)).

27 *Ibid.*, 149.

28 *Ibid.*, 48.

29 *Ibid.*, 132.

30 *Ibid.*, 130, 134.

31 *Ibid.*, 129.

32 *Ibid.*, 137.

33 *Ibid.*, 156.

34 *Ibid.*

35 The *Federal Register* is "a legal newspaper [of the Federal government] published every business day. . . . The *Federal Register* contains: federal agency regulations, proposed rules and public notices, executive orders, and proclamations." www.archives.gov.

36 "Medroxyprogesterone Acetate Injectable Contraceptive: Proposed Patient Labeling." *Federal Register* 38:27940 (Oct. 9, 1973).

37 *Ibid.*

38 *Ibid.*

39 *Ibid.*

40 *Ibid.*

41 *Ibid.*, 27941.

42 *Ibid.*, 27940–42.

43 *Ibid.*, 27940.

44 Applications for FDA Approval to Market a New Drug, Refusal to Approve an Application, 21 CFR 314.125 (b) (1–16).

   The Code of Federal Regulations "is an annual codification of the . . . rules published in the *Federal Register* by the executive departments and agencies of the Federal Government. . . . The CFR is keyed to and kept up-to-date by the daily *Federal Register* . . . . When a Federal agency publishes a regulation in the *Federal Register*, that regulation usually is an amendment to the existing CFR." www.archives.gov.

45 Applications for FDA Approval to Market a New Drug, Approval of an Application and Abbreviated Application, 21 CFR 314.105 (a).

46 *Ibid.*, (a) (2, 3, 4).

47 U. S. Congress, House of Representatives, Committee on Governmental Relations, Subcommittee on Intergovernmental Relations, "Hearings on Use of Advisory Committees by the Food and Drug Administration," 93rd Cong., 2nd Sess., 323 (Apr. 30, 1974).

48 *Ibid.*, 340.

49 *Ibid.*, 341.

50 *Ibid.*, 343.

51 *Ibid.*, 356–63. Includes J. W. Armistad, "Medical Officer's Summary of NDA No. 12, 541," U.S. Food and Drug Administration, 4 (Jan. 21, 1971), and 2 (May 5, 1971),

and the text of Michael Popkin, "Medical Officer's Review of IND 1086—Progress Report, July 20, 1972," U.S. Food and Drug Administration (July 20, 1972).

The principal source for research findings of excessive cervical cancer rates in clinical studies is L. C. Powell and R. J. Seymour, "Effects of Depo-Medroxyprogesterone Acetate as a Contraceptive Agent," *American Journal of Obstetrics and Gynecology* 10:36 (1971).

52 House Hearings on FDA Use of Advisory Committees, *supra* note 47, at 361–63 (discussing the 1973 Schwallie and Assenzo study, *supra* note 14).

53 *Ibid.*, 368–69.

54 *Ibid.*, 369. *See*: National Cancer Institute, "Third National Cancer Survey: An Overview of Available Information," *Journal of the National Cancer Institute* 53(6): 1565–75 (1974).

55 *House Hearings* on FDA Use of Advisory Committees, *supra* note 47, at 374.

56 *Ibid.*

57 *Ibid.*

58 *Ibid.*

59 *Ibid.*, 380. Cervical cancer in situ is a noninvasive form in which cancerous cells are confined to the surface of the cervix. *Mosby's, supra* note 6, at 345–46.

60 House Hearings on FDA Use of Advisory Committees, *supra* note 47, at 381.

61 *Ibid.*

62 *Ibid.*

63 "Patient Labeling for Medroxyprogesterone Acetate Contraceptive Injection," *Federal Register* 39:32907 (Sept. 12, 1974).

64 *Ibid.*

65 *Ibid.*

66 *Ibid.*, 32909.

67 *Ibid.*, 32908.

68 *Ibid.*, 32909.

69 Letter to Caspar Weinberger, Secretary, Department of Health, Education, and Welfare, from L. H. Fountain, Chair, Intergovernmental Relations Subcommittee, Committee on Government Operations, U.S. House of Representatives, 11 (Oct. 2, 1974).

70 *Ibid.*, 5–6.

71 *Ibid.*, 4.

72 *Ibid.*, 7.

73 *Ibid.*, 9.

74 *Ibid.*, 9–10.

75 *Ibid.*, 8.

76 *Ibid.* (citing Memorandum to Marion J. Finkel, Director of Office of Scientific Evaluation, from Bertram D. Litt, Mathematical Statistician, Division of Biometrics, Food and Drug Administration, 2 (June 17, 1974)).

77 *Ibid.*, 7–8.

78 *Ibid.*, 8–9.

79 *Ibid.*, 5 (citing Bertram D. Litt memorandum, *supra* note 76, at 2).

80 *Ibid.*, 5.

81 *Ibid.*, 11.

82 *Ibid.*, 9–10.

83 Federal Food, Drug, and Cosmetic Act, 21 U.S.C. 505(d).

84 Letter to Caspar Weinberger from L. H. Fountain, *supra* note 69, at 11.

85 *Ibid.*

86 Letter to L.H. Fountain, Chairman, Subcommittee on Intergovernmental Relations, Committee on Governmental Operations, House of Representatives, from Caspar Weinberger, Secretary, Department of Health Education and Welfare (Oct. 9, 1974).

87 Letter to L. H. Fountain, Chairman, Subcommittee on Intergovernmental Relations, Committee on Governmental Operations, House of Representatives, from Alexander M. Schmidt, Commissioner, U. S. Food and Drug Administration (Oct. 9, 1974). Subsequently, the FDA stayed Depo-Provera's final approval order. *See*: "Patient Labeling for Medroxyprogesterone Acetate Contraceptive Injection," *Federal Register* 39:36472 (Oct. 22, 1974).

88 U.S. Food and Drug Administration, Obstetrics and Gynecology and Biometric and Epidemiological Methodology Advisory Committees (Apr. 7, 1975), 6.

89 *Ibid.*, 4. The Biometrics and Epidemiology Methodology Advisory Committee (BEM) was created in 1969 and composed of statistical and epidemiological experts who provided statistical advice to the FDA, including the quality of data in clinical trials. The committee was disbanded in 1977, and its members were placed on each of the FDA's subject matter advisory committees.

90 Powell and Seymour, *supra* note 51, at 36.

91 FDA OBGYN & BEM Advisory Committees, *supra* note 88, at 101.

92 *Ibid.*, 80.

93 *Ibid.*, 142–43, 149–51.

94 *Ibid.*, 163 and 168.

95 *Ibid.*, 168–69.

96 *Ibid.*, 165–66.

97 *Ibid.*, 173–74.

98 *Ibid.*, 175–76.

99 *Ibid.*, 175, 177.

100 *Ibid.*, 164.

101 *Ibid.*, 183 (referencing Anita Johnson, at 164).

102 *Ibid.*, 183–84.

103 U.S. Food and Drug Administration, Obstetrics and Gynecology and Biometric and Epidemiological Methodology Advisory Committees, "Depo-Provera, Injectable, as a Contraceptive. Report to the Obstetrics and Gynecology Advisory Committee," 7–8 (Apr. 30, 1975).

104 *Ibid.*, 9.

105 *Ibid.*, 11.

106 Osteoporosis is a disorder in which the bones become increasingly porous, brittle, and subject to fracture because of the loss of calcium and other minerals. Osteoporosis is a bone density (BMD) value of more than a 2.5 standard deviation below the young adult mean in the presence of fragility fractures. WHO Study Group, "WHO Technical Report 843: Assessment of Fracture Risk and Its Application to Screening for Postmenopausal Osteoporosis," *World Health Organization*, 5–6 (1994).

107 Epidemiology is the study of health in a population to understand the causes and patterns of health and illness. An epidemiological study compares two groups of people who are alike except for one factor, such as exposure to a chemical or the presence of a health effect. The purpose of the study is to determine if a factor is associated with the health effect. www.who.int.

108 "The Upjohn Co., Depo-Provera Sterile Aqueous Suspension," *Federal Register* 43:28555 (June 22, 1978).

109 21 CFR 314.126 (a-d). The CFR specifically excludes as inadequate "uncontrolled or partially controlled studies" as well as "case reports and random experience," because they do not permit scientific evaluation of a drug's safety (21 CFR 314.126 (e)). Otherwise, the CFR permits the agency to define "reasonably applicable tests" of contraceptive drugs, such as Depo-Provera, to include epidemiological studies of breast, cervical, and endometrial cancer and "safe for its intended use" to mean that "the risks of treatment are outweighed by its benefits when the drug is used as labeled" (Robert Temple, MD, testimony before the U.S. Food and Drug Administration, Public Board of Inquiry on Depo-Provera, *Official Transcript of Proceedings*, 3:15 (Jan. 11, 1983), www.archives.gov).

110 Applications for FDA Approval to Market a New Drug, Approval of an Application, 21 CFR 314.105 (c). The CFR grants the FDA considerable flexibility in applying these standards and in exercising "its scientific judgment to determine the kind and quality of data and information . . . required to meet them." 21 CFR 314.105 (c).

111 FDA Federal Register Notice, *supra* note 108, at 28556 (citing 21 CFR 314.125 (a)(3) & (4)).

112 Lester Lave, *The Strategy of Social Regulation: Decision Frameworks for Policy* (Washington, DC: Brookings Institution, 1981), 8–28.

113 U.S. Congress, House of Representatives, Select Committee on Population, "The Depo-Provera Debate: Hearings before the House Select Committee on Population," 95th Cong., 2nd Sess., 58 (Aug. 9, 1978).

114 FDA Federal Register Notice, *supra* note 108, at 28556.

115 Donald Kennedy, statement submitted to the House Select Committee on Population, *supra* note 113, at 308 (Aug. 8, 1978).

116 FDA Federal Register Notice, *supra* note 108, at 28556.

117 Bruce Silverglade, "The Risks of Risk Assessment and Risk-Benefit Analysis," *Food, Drug, and Cosmetic Law Journal* 38:318, 323 (1981).

118 FDA Federal Register Notice, *supra* note 108.

119 FDA Federal Register Notice, *supra* note 36.

120 *Ibid.*

121 FDA Federal Register Notice, *supra* note 63, at 32909–10.

122 FDA Federal Register Notice, *supra* note 108, at 28556.

123 *Ibid.*

124 *Ibid.*

125 National Academy of Sciences, *Risk Assessment in the Federal Government: Managing the Process* (Washington, DC: National Academy Press, 1983), 3.

126 FDA Federal Register Notice, *supra* note 108, at 28556.

127 *Ibid.*

128 *Ibid.*

129 *Ibid.*

130 *Ibid.*

131 Allan M. Allard and Nicholas W. Allard, "Exporting United States Pharmaceuticals in the 1980s," *Food, Drug, and Cosmetic Law Journal*, 39:411 (1984).

132 The countries are Egypt, Jordan, Korea, Taiwan, and Yemen.

133 House Select Committee on Population, *supra* note 113, at 60.

134 *Ibid.*, 58–60.

135 *Ibid.*, 73.

136 *Ibid.*, 183–84.

137 *Ibid.*, 184.

138 Anita Johnson, "Depo-Provera: A Contraceptive for Poor People," Public Citizen Health Research Group (Dec. 1976); and Letter to Theodore Cooper, Assistant Secretary for Health, Department of Health, Education, and Welfare, from Anita Johnson, Researcher, and Sidney Wolfe, MD, Director, Health Research Group, 9 (Dec. 16, 1976).

139 House Select Committee on Population, *supra* note 113, at 186.

140 *Ibid.*

141 *Ibid.*, 70.

142 *Ibid.*

143 *Ibid.*

144 Deborah Maine, "Depo: The Debate Continues," *Family Planning Perspectives* 10:342 (1981).

145 Formal Public Evidentiary Hearings, 21 CFR 12.

146 The first public board of inquiry had been established to review the FDA's approval of Aspartame. *Federal Register* 44:31716 (June 1, 1979).

147 Public Hearing before a Public Board of Inquiry, Proceedings of a Board, 21 CFR 13.30 (e).

148 *Ibid.*

149 Public Hearing before a Public Board of Inquiry, Administrative Record of a Board, 21 CFR 13.40 (d).

150 *Ibid.*, 21 CFR 13.40.

151 Depo-Provera; Hearing on Proposal to Refuse Approval of Supplementary New Drug Application, *Federal Register* 44:44274 (July 27, 1979).

152 Dr. Judith Weisz, Head, Division of Reproductive Biology, Department of Obstetrics and Gynecology, Hershey Medical Center, Pennsylvania State University; Dr. Griff T. Ross, Associate Dean, Clinical Affairs, University of Texas at Houston; and Dr. Paul Stolley, Professor of Medicine and Research Medicine, School of Medicine, University of Pennsylvania.

153 Rachel B. Gold and Peters D. Willson, "Depo-Provera: New Developments in a Decade-Old Controversy," *Family Planning Perspectives* 13:37 (1981).

154 U.S. Agency for International Development, "Report of the Ad-Hoc Panel on Depo Medroxyprogesterone Acetate" (1980); International Planned Parenthood Federation, "Statement of the International Medical Advisory Panel on Depo-Provera" (1980); and World Health Organization, Special Programme of Research, Development and Research Training in Human Reproduction, "Statement on Safety of the Long-Acting Injectable Contraceptive Depo-Provera" (1978).

155 U.S. Agency for International Development, "Report of the Ad-Hoc Panel," *supra* note 154, at 5–6.

156 *Ibid.*, 13–17, 24–25.

157 *Ibid.*, 12–13, 24.

158 *Ibid.*, 11–12, 23.

159 *Ibid.*, 10–11, 23.

160 *Ibid.*, 8–10, 22.

161 *Ibid.*, 7–8, 22.

162 *Ibid.*, 25.

163 National Women's Health Network, "Stop Depo-Provera Campaign: Request for Emergency Grant," (Oct. 1979). *See*: Cynthia A. Pearson, "National Women's Health Network and the U.S. FDA: Two Decades of Activism," *Reproductive Health Matters* 5:132–41 (Nov. 1995).

164 Gold and Willson, *supra* 153, at 37–38.

165 *Ibid.*

166 *Ibid.*

167 *Ibid.*

168 *Federal Register* 47:36470 (1982).

169 The Bureau of Drugs was merged with the Bureau of Biologics in 1982 to form the Center for Drugs and Biologics.

170 FDA Federal Register Notice, *supra* note 151, at 44275.

171 *Ibid.*

172 *Ibid.*

173 *Ibid.* A teratogen is a substance, agent, or process that interferes with normal prenatal development, causing the formation of one or more developmental abnormalities of the fetus. *Mosby's, supra* note 6, at 1831.

174 FDA Federal Register Notice, *supra* note 108, at 28555. Estrogen therapy is most commonly used to treat the symptoms of menopause. It reduces or stops the short-term changes of menopause. *Mosby's, supra* note 6 at 174.

175 FDA Federal Register Notice, *supra* note 151, at 44275.
176 *Ibid.*
177 *Ibid.*
178 U.S. Food and Drug Administration, Public Board of Inquiry on Depo-Provera, *Official Transcript of Proceedings*, 1:5 (Jan. 10, 1983).
179 *Ibid.*, 1:4.
180 *Ibid.*, 1:26.
181 *Ibid.*, 1:27–28.
182 *Ibid.*, 1:20.
183 *Ibid.*, 1:31.
184 *Ibid.*, 1:120.
185 *Ibid.*, 1:110.
186 *Ibid.*, 2:7 (Jan. 11, 1983).
187 *Ibid.*, 2:9.
188 *Ibid.*, 2:190.
189 *Ibid.*, 2:212.
190 *Ibid.*, 4:43 (Jan. 13, 1983).
191 *Ibid.*, 4:44.
192 *Ibid.*, 1:11 (Jan. 10, 1983).
193 *Ibid.*, 1:12.
194 *Ibid.*
195 *Ibid.*, 1:12–13.
196 *Ibid.*, 1:12.
197 *Ibid.*, 2:14 (Jan. 11, 1983).
198 *Ibid.*, 5:92 (Jan. 14, 1983).
199 *Ibid.*, 1:15–16 (Jan. 10, 1983).
200 *Ibid.*, 5:58 (Jan. 14, 1983).
201 *Ibid.*, 1:84–85 (Jan. 10, 1983).
202 *Ibid.*, 5:84–85 (Jan. 14, 1983).
203 *Ibid.*, 2:16, testimony. Robert Temple, M.D., FDA Acting Director of the Office of New Drug Evaluation, U.S. Food and Drug Administration (Jan. 11, 1983).
204 *Ibid.*, 5:86 (Jan. 14, 1983).
205 *Ibid.*, 5:89.
206 *Ibid.*, 5:91.
207 *Ibid.*, 5:49.
208 Judith Weisz, Griff Ross, and Paul Stolley, *Report of the Public Board of Inquiry on Depo-Provera*, U.S. Food and Drug Administration (Oct. 17, 1984). *Federal Register* 49:43507 (Oct. 29, 1984).
209 Weisz, *supra* note 208, at 5.
210 Public Hearing before a Public Board of Inquiry, Submissions to a Board, 21 CFR 12:20, Administrative Record of a Board, 13.40 c) (1).
211 Weisz, *supra* note 208, at 5.
212 *Ibid.*, 7.

213 *Ibid.*, 2, 22.

214 *Ibid.*, 22–23.

215 *Ibid.*, 64.

216 *Ibid.*, 30.

217 *Ibid.*, 31.

218 U.S. Food and Drug Administration, Public Board of Inquiry, Report of Group of Pathology Consultants Designated by the Depo-Provera Board of Inquiry to Evaluate and Determine the Nature of Upjohn Company's Rhesus Monkey's Uterine Tumors Observed in the Long-Term IRDC Study (1983).

219 *Federal Register* 48:31910 (July 12, 1983).

220 Weisz, *supra* note 208, at 33.

221 *Ibid.*, 32.

222 *Ibid.*, 174.

223 *Ibid.*, 54.

224 *Ibid.*, 64.

225 *Ibid.*, 175.

226 *Ibid.*, 175–76.

227 *Ibid.*, 88.

228 *Ibid.*

229 *Ibid.*, 89.

230 *Ibid.*, 85–86. A prospective study identifies a group of subjects and then watches them for outcomes, such as the development of diseases. *Mosby's, supra* note 6, at 1540. A retrospective study examines the subject's personal history and medical records for specific factors associated with a disease. *Ibid.*, 1629.

231 Weisz, *supra* note 208, at 94.

232 *Ibid.*, 102.

233 *Ibid.*, 103.

234 *Ibid.*, 106. Cervical neoplasia is the abnormal growth of cells on the surface of the cervix. The changes are not cancerous, but they can lead to cancer of the cervix if not treated. *Mosby's, supra* note 6, at 346.

235 Weisz, *supra* note 208, at 95. An endometrial biopsy samples the inner lining of the uterus (the endometrium) to determine the cause of abnormal uterine bleeding. *Mosby's, supra* note 6, at 235.

236 Weisz, *supra* note 208.

237 *Ibid.*, 95–96.

238 *Ibid.*, 98.

239 *Ibid.*, 100.

240 *Ibid.*, 84–85.

241 *Ibid.*

242 *Ibid.*, 145.

243 *Ibid.*, 160.

244 *Ibid.*, 161.

245 *Ibid.*, 162.

246 *Ibid.*, 160.

247 *Ibid.*, 165.

248 *Ibid.*, 166.

249 *Ibid.*, 167.

250 *Ibid.*, 170, 181.

251 *Ibid.*, 169.

252 *Ibid.*

253 *Ibid.*, 169–70.

254 *Ibid.*, 170.

255 *Ibid.*, 172.

256 *Ibid.*, 179.

257 Public Hearing before a Public Board of Inquiry, Administrative Record of a Board, 21 CFR 13.40 (c) (4).

258 Kenneth M. Cyrus, Assistant Secretary and Associate General Counsel, The Upjohn Co., and Richard F. Kingham, Covington and Burling, "Exceptions to Report of the Public Board of Inquiry and Brief for the Upjohn Company," The Upjohn Co., 2, 12–65 (Jan. 24, 1985).

259 *Ibid.*, 3, 73–76.

260 *Ibid.*, 4, 73–76.

261 *Ibid.*

262 Fletcher E. Campbell and Catherine L. Copp, Counsel, Center for Drugs and Biologics, U.S. Food and Drug Administration, "Response of the Center for Drugs and Biologics to the Exceptions of the Upjohn Company," U.S. Food and Drug Administration (Apr. 24, 1985), 13–14.

263 *Ibid.*, 17.

264 *Ibid.*, 25.

265 *Ibid.*, 38–39 (citing Weisz, *supra* note 208, at 169–70).

266 Letter to Dr. J. Barzelatto, Director, Special Programme of Research in Human Reproduction, World Health Organization, from Frank E. Young, Commissioner, U.S. Food and Drug Administration (Feb. 8, 1985).

267 Frank E. Young, Commissioner, U.S. Food and Drug Administration, "Order Denying Request to Reopen Record and for Oral Argument," U.S. Food and Drug Administration (Sept. 19, 1986).

268 *Ibid.*, 6.

269 Letter to Frank E. Young, Commissioner, U.S. Food and Drug Administration, from Paul D. Stolley, Professor, School of Medicine, University of Pennsylvania (Mar. 1, 1985). Letter to Frank E. Young, Commissioner, U.S. Food and Drug Administration, from Judith Weisz, Professor, Milton S. Hershey Medical Center, Pennsylvania State University (Apr. 10, 1985).

270 Young, *supra* note 267, at 4, n.5.

271 Letter to Frank E. Young, Commissioner, U.S. Food and Drug Administration, from Kenneth Cyrus, Assistant Secretary and Associate General Counsel, The Upjohn Co. (Sept. 29, 1986).

272 Letter to Kenneth Cyrus, Assistant Secretary and General Counsel, The Upjohn Co., from Frank E. Young, Commissioner, Food and Drug Administration (Oct. 10, 1986). *See also*: "Human Drugs; Depo-Provera Sterile Aqueous Suspension," *Federal Register* 51:37651 (Oct. 23, 1986).

CHAPTER 3. CONTRACEPTIVE CHAOS

1 *See*: Richard C. Ausness, "'There's Danger Here, Cherie': Liability for the Promotion and Marketing of Drugs and Medical Devices for Off-Label Uses," *Brooklyn Law Review* 73(4): 1253 (Summer 2009); and Steven R. Salbu, "Off-Label Use, Prescription, and Marketing of FDA Approved Drugs: An Assessment of Legislative and Regulatory Policy," *Florida Law Review* 51:181 (1999).

2 U.S. Congress, House of Representatives, Committee on Interior Insular Affairs, *Use of the Drug Depo-Provera by the Indian Health Service: Oversight Hearings before the Subcommittee on General Oversight and Investigations*, 100th Cong., 1st Sess. (Aug. 6, 1987).

3 U.S. Food and Drug Administration, "Use of Approved Drugs for Unlabeled Indications," *FDA Drug Bulletin*, 4–5 (June 1982).

4 *Ibid.*, 5.

5 U.S. Congress, Senate, Committee on Labor and Public Welfare, *Quality of Health Care—Human Experimentation: Hearings before the Subcommittee on Health*, 93rd Cong. 1st Sess. (Feb. 21–22, 1973).

6 *Ibid.*, 79.

7 National Women's Health Network, *Depo-Provera Registry* (1982).

8 The Upjohn Co., Depo-Provera, Package Insert (June 1974).

9 *Ibid.*

10 Senate, *supra* note 5, at 105.

11 *Ibid.*

12 *Ibid.*, 108.

13 Upjohn Co., "Depo-Provera Sterile Aqueous Suspension," *Federal Register* 43:28556 (June 22, 1978).

14 Judith Weisz, Griff T. Ross, and Paul Stolley, *Report of the Public Board of Inquiry*, U.S. Food and Drug Administration, 169–70 (Oct. 17, 1984).

15 House, *supra* note 2.

16 Weisz, *supra* note 14, at 11–15.
Palliative treatment is intended to alleviate pain and suffering of a terminally ill patient. *Mosby's Medical Dictionary*, 7th ed., (St. Louis, MO: Mosby, Elsevier, 2006), 1381.
Adjunctive therapy is any treatment used in conjunction with another treatment to increase the chances of a cure. *Ibid.*, 44–45.

17 Network, *supra* note 7.

18 Weisz, *supra* note 14, at 12.
A threatened abortion is "a condition in which vaginal bleeding is less than an inevitable abortion and the cervix is not dilated, and abortion may or may not occur." *Mosby's, supra* note 16, at 1847.

An habitual abortion, also termed recurrent abortion, is the occurrence of three or more miscarriages (spontaneous abortions) with no intervening pregnancies. *Ibid.*, 842.

A teratogen is an agent that can halt pregnancy, disturb the development of an embryo or fetus, and cause a birth defect in the child. *Ibid.*, 1831.

19 Network, *supra* note 7.

Ovarian cysts are fluid-filled sacs within or on the surface of an ovary. One ovary is located on each side of the uterus. Eggs (ova) develop and mature in the ovaries and are released in monthly cycles during a woman's childbearing years. While most ovarian cysts disappear without treatment, some can become cancerous. *Mosby's*, *supra* note 16, at 1366.

Fibroid tumors are benign growths in the uterus. *Ibid.*, 733.

Premenstrual syndrome (PMS) has a variety of symptoms, including mood swings, tender breasts, food cravings, fatigue, irritability, and depression. *Ibid.*, 1516.

20 Senate, *supra* note 5, at 78–79, 83.

21 *Ibid.*, 83.

22 *Ibid.*

23 Letter from Faith P. to the National Women's Health Network (Mar. 20, 1980), in Network, *supra* note 7. A person's full name is withheld because Network Registry correspondence is confidential.

24 Mike Masterson, "Taking the Shot: Pioneer Cool to Debate about Drug," *Arizona Republic*, A1 (Nov. 9, 1986).

25 Senate, *supra* note 5, at 83.

26 Weisz, *supra* note 14, at 172.

27 Senate, *supra* note 5, at 59.

Tubal ligation is a permanent form of birth control in which a woman's fallopian tubes are surgically cut or blocked off to prevent pregnancy. *Mosby's*, *supra* note 16, at 1903.

28 Senate, *supra* note 5, at 61, 108.

29 *Ibid.*, 87.

30 *Ibid.*, 90.

31 Kathleen Kerr, "A Long Shot for the '80s," *Newsday*, n.p. (June 12, 1984); and Mike Masterson, "Taking the Shot: Problem Drug 'Affects' So Many Aspects of Your Life," *Arizona Republic*, A1 (Nov. 12, 1986).

32 Network, *supra* note 7.

33 Betsy Veith, "Statistical Analysis of the National Women's Health Network Depo-Provera Registry, 1979–1982," in Network, *supra* note 7.

34 Letter from Kay C. to the National Women's Health Network (Dec. 16, 1981), in Network, *supra* note 7.

35 Karen Branan and Bill Turnley, "The Ultimate Test Animal: A New Documentary," video, 1985. *See also*: Masterson, *supra* note 24; and House, *supra* note 2, at 211.

36 Discovery is a fact-finding process that takes place after a lawsuit has been filed and before trial in order to allow the parties in the case to prepare for settlement or trial. Discovery methods include depositions, interrogatories, and requests for the production of documents. Henry Campbell Black, *Black's Law Dictionary*, 5th ed. , 418–19 (St. Paul, MN: West Publishing, 1979).

A deposition is an out-of-court sworn testimony of a witness for use in court. At a deposition, the parties are represented by an attorneys who question the witness. A court reporter records the testimony and then creates a written transcript of the deposition for the parties. Depositions are taken to gather evidence, to create a record of a witness's testimony so that the witness may be impeached if his or her testimony at trial deviates from the deposition testimony, and to have the testimony available as evidence if witness is not able to attend the trial. *Ibid.*, 396.

Interrogatories are specific written questions submitted by a party to the other party who must respond under oath and in writing. *Ibid.*, 735

The production of documents is a request made by one party to another party to provide documents that are in his or her possession or control and that pertain to the subject matter of the lawsuit. *Ibid.*, 418.

A summary judgment is a court order granted when there are no disputed material facts for a court to decide, and the moving party is entitled to prevail as a matter of law. The motion for summary judgment may be granted against all or part of a claim or defense. *Ibid.*, 1287

37 *Perez v. Mount Sinai Hospital*, 509 A.2d 552 (1986); *Popham v. Reyner*, 503 N.Y.S. 645 (1986).

38 A hysterectomy is an operation to remove a woman's uterus. A woman may have a hysterectomy for various reasons, including uterine fibroids that cause pain and bleeding; cancer of the uterus, cervix, or ovaries; endometriosis; abnormal vaginal bleeding; and chronic pelvic pain. A hysterectomy for noncancerous reasons is usually considered only after all other treatment approaches have been tried without success. *Mosby's, supra* note 16, at 937.

39 *MacMurdo v. Upjohn*, Amended Complaint, at 4, No. 78–8487-CL (Broward Cir. Ct., 17th Jud. Cir., Broward County, Fla., Jan. 11, 1979).

40 Letter to Sen. Edward M. Kennedy from Anne MacMurdo, 1–2 (Dec. 6, 1975); and Letter to Rep. L. H. Fountain from Anne MacMurdo, 1–2 (Dec. 9. 1975). Copies of these two letters and others cited in this note were supplied by Anne MacMurdo.

Senator Kennedy wrote informing Anne MacMurdo about pending legislation on the protection of human subjects. Letter to Anne MacMurdo from Edward M. Kennedy, Senator, U.S. Senate, (Mar. 17, 1976).

Representative Fountain supplied her with copies of his 1974 hearings and correspondence with Secretary Caspar Weinberger objecting to the FDA's proposal to approve Depo-Provera for limited marketing. Letter to Anne MacMurdo from D. C. Goldberg, Professional Staff Member for L. H. Fountain, Member, U.S. House of Representatives, (Dec. 16, 1975).

Subsequently, Mr. Fountain wrote to Anne MacMurdo informing her that even though the FDA's Obstetrics and Gynecology Advisory Committee had recommended limited marketing approval, "FDA had not made a decision in the matter" and that he would send her letter to the agency, because "I am sure they would be interested in knowing about your experience." Letter to Anne MacMurdo from D. C. Goldberg. Professional Staff Member for L. H. Fountain, Member, U.S. House of Representatives (Dec. 18, 1975).

41 MacMurdo Letters to Kennedy and Fountain, 1.

42 *Ibid.*, 2.

43 *Ibid.*

44 *MacMurdo v. Upjohn*, Complaint, No. 78–8487-CL (Broward Cir. Ct., 17th Jud. Cir., Broward County, Fla., May 19, 1978); *MacMurdo v. Upjohn*, Amended Complaint, No. 78–8487-CL (Broward Cir. Ct., 17th Jud. Cir., Broward County, Fla., Jan. 11, 1979).

A breach of warranty is a broken promise about a product by a manufacturer or seller. Warranty protection is provided by the Uniform Commercial Code (UCC), which has been adopted in part by all states. Black, *supra* note 36, at 171.

Strict liability is legal responsibility for an injury without proof of fault by the defendant. In a products liability case, the plaintiff has the burden to prove that an item was defective, that the defect caused the injury, and that the defect rendered the product unreasonably dangerous, but does not have to prove that the manufacturer was negligent. *Ibid.*, 1275.

Compensatory damages are a monetary award for an actual injury or economic loss. *Ibid.*, 352. Punitive damages are a monetary award beyond that necessary to compensate a person for losses and are intended to punish outrageous misconduct and to deter a defendant from similar misbehavior in the future. *Ibid.*, 362.

45 *MacMurdo v. Upjohn*, Answer to Amended Complaint, No. 78–8487-CL (Broward Cir. Ct., 17th Jud. Cir., Broward County, Fla., Apr. 29, 1991).

Contributory negligence is a doctrine that states if a person were injured due in part to his or her own negligence, he or she is barred from recovering damages from another party who is claimed to have caused the accident. Black, *supra* note 36, at 931.

46 *MacMurdo v. Upjohn*, Answer to Amended Complaint, No. 78–8487-CL (Broward Cir. Ct., 17th Jud. Cir., Broward County, Fla., Feb. 23, 1979).

Assumption of risk is a claim that a plaintiff should have known a situation was inherently or obviously dangerous, but took the chance of being injured, was injured, and is not entitled to recover damages. Black, *supra* note 36, at 113.

47 A statute of limitations is a defense asserted to defeat a legal action brought by the plaintiff after the statutorily specified time has elapsed. Black, *supra* note 36, at 835. For the Florida statute of limitations, *see*: Florida Laws: Fla. Statutes—Title 8, Ch. 95, §11(4) (a) and (b).

48 *MacMurdo v. Upjohn*, 388 So.2d 1103 (Fla. 4th DCA 1980).

49 *Ibid.*, citing *Adana v. Holub*, 381 So.2d 231 (Fla. 1980).

50 *Ibid.*

51 *Ibid.*, 1104.

52 *MacMurdo v. Upjohn*, Summary Judgment, No. 78–8487-CL (Broward Cir. Ct., 17th Jud. Cir., Broward County, Fla., Oct. 1,1981).

53 A motion to dismiss is an application by a defendant requesting a judge to rule that a plaintiff has not and cannot prove his or her case and the defendant cannot lose. Black, *supra* note 36, at 914.

54 *MacMurdo v. Upjohn*, Memorandum of Law in Support of Defendant's Motion to Dismiss Memo, at 1, No. 78–8487-CL (Broward Cir. Ct., 17th Jud. Cir., Broward County, Fla., Sept. 20, 1985).

55 *Ibid.*, 4.

56 *Ibid.* The Uniform Commercial Code (UCC) is a set of proposed laws for commercial transactions created by the American Law Institute. The UCC's Article 2 contains provisions governing the sale of goods. Black, *supra* note 36, at 1373.

57 *Charmichael v. Reitz*, 17 Cal.App. 958, 95 Cal. Rptr. 381 (Cal. 2d 1971).

58 *MacMurdo v. Upjohn*, Motion to Dismiss Memo, at 5, No. 78–8487-CL (Broward Cir. Ct., 17th Jud. Cir., Broward County, Fla., Sept. 20, 1985).

59 *MacMurdo v. Upjohn*, Notice of Voluntary Dismissal, at 1, No. 78–8487-CL (Broward Cir. Ct., 17th Jud. Cir., Broward County, Fla., Dec. 1985).

   A voluntary dismissal is the termination of a lawsuit at the request of the plaintiff and the loss of the right to bring the same legal action again. Black, *supra* note 36, at 421.

60 *MacMurdo v. Upjohn*, Motion for Summary Final Judgment, at 1, No. 78–8487-CL (Broward Cir. Ct., 17th Jud. Cir., Broward County, Fla., Oct. 14, 1981).

61 *MacMurdo v. Upjohn*, 444 So.2d 119, 450 (Fla. 4th DCA 1983).

62 *Ibid.*, 450–51.

63 103 So.2d 603 (Fla. 1958).

64 189 So.2d 171 (Fla. 2d DCA 1966).

65 *MacMurdo v. Upjohn*, 444 So.2d 449, 450 (Fla. 4th DCA 1983) (emphasis in original).

66 *Ibid.*, 451.

67 443 F.Supp. 121 (W.D. Tenn. 1977).

68 *MacMurdo v. Upjohn*, 444 So.2d 449, 451 (Fla. 4th DCA 1983).

69 *Ibid.*, 452.

70 *Dunkin v. Syntex Laboratories*, 443 F.Supp. 121 (W.D. Tenn. 1977); *Chambers v. G.D. Searle & Co.*, 441 F.Supp. 377 (D.Md. 1975).

71 *MacMurdo v. Upjohn*, Motion for Summary Judgment, No. 78–8487-CL (Broward Cir. Ct., 17th Jud. Cir., Broward County, Fla., July 25, 1986).

72 *MacMurdo v. Upjohn*, Plaintiff's Motion for Continuance and Plaintiff's Motion to Extend Time to File Responses to Expert Interrogatories, No. 78–8487-CL (Broward Cir. Ct., 17th Jud. Cir., Broward County, Fla., Aug. 5, 1986).

73 *MacMurdo v. Upjohn*, Order on Plaintiff's Motion for Extension of Time, No. 78–8487-CL (Broward Cir. Ct., 17th Jud. Cir., Broward County, Fla., Aug. 14, 1986).

74 *MacMurdo v. Upjohn*, Upjohn's Motion to Compel Better Answers to Interrogatories and to Produce Expert Witness Reports, No. 78–8487-CL (Broward Cir. Ct., 17th Jud. Cir., Broward County, Fla., Aug. 22, 1986).

75 *MacMurdo v. Upjohn*, Affidavit, No. 78–8487-CL (Broward Cir. Ct., 17th Jud. Cir., Broward County, Fla., Aug. 27, 1986).

76 Interview with Michael Ericksen, attorney, West Palm Beach, Fla. (Jan. 3, 1991).

77 *MacMurdo v. Upjohn*, Depositions of Dr. Sorosh Roshan, an obstetrician and gynecologist (Nov. 22, 1986), and two Upjohn employees: Dr. Paul C. Schwallie (Nov. 19, 1986) and Frank Fletcher (Nov. 19, 1986), No. 78–8487-CL (Broward Cir. Ct., 17th Jud. Cir., Broward County, Fla., 1986).

78 *MacMurdo v. Upjohn*, Trial Transcript, at 53–54, No. 78–8487-CL (Broward Cir. Ct., 17th Jud. Cir., Broward County, Fla., 1986).

79 *Ibid.*

80 James McWhinney, *Trial Notebook* (Washington, DC: American Bar Association Section on Litigation, 1981), 4.

81 Willard Gaylin, *The Killing of Bonnie Garland* (New York: Penguin, 1983), 111–13.

82 *MacMurdo v. Upjohn*, Trial Transcript, at 57, No. 78–8487-CL (Broward Cir. Ct., 17th Jud. Cir., Broward County, Fla. 1986).

83 *Ibid.*, 69.

84 *Ibid.*, 70–71.

85 *Ibid.*, 79.

86 *Ibid.*, 34.

87 *Ibid.*, 35.

88 *Ibid.*, 93, 94.

89 *Ibid.*, 93.

90 *Ibid.*, 94.

91 *Ibid.*, 95.

92 *Ibid.*

93 *Ibid.*, 73.

94 *Ibid.*, 76.

95 *Ibid.*, 108.

96 *Ibid.*, 103.

97 *Ibid.*, 113.

98 *Ibid.*, 103.

99 *Ibid.*, 117–20.

100 *Ibid.*, 138–39.

101 *Ibid.*, 127–28.

102 *Ibid.*, 126.

103 *Ibid.*, 136. Anencephaly is the absence at birth of a major portion of the brain, skull, and scalp. *Mosby's*, *supra* note 16, at 96.

104 *MacMurdo v. Upjohn*, Trial Transcript, *supra* note 82, at 137.

105 *Ibid.*
106 *Ibid.*, 140.
107 *Ibid.*, 306.
108 *Ibid.*, 717.
109 *Ibid.*, 735.
110 *Ibid.*, 736.
111 *Ibid.*
112 *Ibid.*, 739. Dr. Connell incorrectly identified Senator Kennedy as Senator Fountain.
113 *Ibid.*, 455–56.
114 *Ibid.*, 456–57 (Nov. 19, 1986, deposition testimony at 22). Mr. Fletcher quoted from The Upjohn Company, Memorandum to Sales Managers from R. E. Peterson, Domestic Sales Department, The Upjohn Co. (Oct. 25, 1973).
115 *MacMurdo v. Upjohn*, Trial Transcript, *supra* note 82, at 933, 935.
116 *Ibid.*, 934.
117 *Ibid.*, 228.
118 *Ibid.*, 208–09.
119 *Ibid.*, 470–71.
120 *Ibid.*, 470.
121 *Ibid.*, 454 (Nov. 19, 1986, deposition testimony, at 22).
122 *Ibid.*
123 *Ibid.*, 20.
124 *Ibid.*, 946.
125 *Ibid.*, 210, 213.
126 *Ibid.*, 217.
127 *Ibid.*, 544 (Nov. 22, 1986, deposition testimony, at 66).
     Pelvic inflammatory disease, commonly called PID, is an infection of the female reproductive organs. PID is one of the most serious complications of a sexually transmitted disease in women: It can lead to irreversible damage to the uterus, ovaries, and fallopian tubes and is the primary preventable cause of infertility in women. *Mosby's*, *supra* note 16, at 1420.
128 *MacMurdo v. Upjohn*, Trial Transcript, *supra* note 82, at 770.
129 *Ibid.*, 776. Dilation and curettage (D&C) is "a procedure to remove tissue from inside the uterus. Doctors perform dilation and curettage to diagnose and treat certain uterine conditions, such as heavy bleeding, or to clear the uterine lining after a miscarriage or abortion." *Mosby's*, *supra* note 16, at 566.
130 *MacMurdo v. Upjohn*, Trial Transcript, *supra* note 82, at 776–77.
131 *Ibid.*, 784.
132 *Ibid.*, 783.
133 *Ibid.*, 787.
134 *Ibid.*, 298–99.
135 *Ibid.*, 277, 322–29 (Dr. Benjamin testimony about Paul C. Schwallie and J. Robert Assenzo, "Contraceptive Use—Efficacy Study Utilizing Medroxyprogesterone Ac-

etate Administered as an Intramuscular Injection Once Every 90 Days," *Fertility and Sterility* 24:331–39 [1973]).

136 *MacMurdo v. Upjohn*, Trial Transcript, *supra* note 82, at 326.
137 *Ibid.*, 327.
138 *Ibid.*, 329–30.
139 *Ibid.*, 376.
140 *Ibid.*, 408.
141 *Ibid.*, 410.
142 *Ibid.*, 544 (Aug. 15, 1978, deposition testimony, at 40).
143 *Ibid.*, 552–53.
144 *Ibid.*, 696.
145 *Ibid.*, 503–4.
146 *Ibid.*, 555 (Aug. 11, 1978, deposition testimony, at 67).
147 *Ibid.*, 544 (Nov. 22, 1986, deposition testimony, at 51).
148 *Ibid.*, 544 (Aug. 15, 1986, deposition testimony, at 41–42).
149 *Ibid.*, 552–53 (referencing Aug. 11, 1978, deposition testimony, at 77).
150 *Ibid.*, 590, 607.
151 Upjohn, *supra* note 8; and *MacMurdo v. Upjohn*, Trial Transcript, *supra* note 82, at 544 (Aug. 15, 1978 deposition testimony, at 59–61).
152 *MacMurdo v. Upjohn*, Trial Transcript, *supra* note 82, at 544 (Aug. 15, 1978, deposition testimony, at 57–58).
153 *Ibid.*, 544 (Aug. 15, 1978, deposition testimony, at 46–47, 56).
154 *Ibid.*, 607 (referencing Aug. 26, 1981, deposition testimony, at 27).
155 *Ibid.*, 559–60.
156 *Ibid.*, 544 (Nov. 22, 1986, deposition testimony, at 16).
157 *Ibid.*, 615.
158 *Ibid.*, 567–74.
159 *Ibid.*, 601–2.
160 *Ibid.*, 604.
161 *Ibid.*, 691.
162 *Ibid.*, 544 (Nov. 22, 1986, deposition testimony, at 40–41).
163 *Ibid.*, 706.
164 *Ibid.*, 544 (Nov. 22, 1986, deposition testimony, at 66).
165 *Ibid.* (Nov. 22, 1986, deposition testimony, at 64).
166 *Ibid.*, 16.
167 *Ibid.*, 352.
    LSD is a powerful psychedelic drug that produces temporary hallucinations. *Mosby's*, *supra* note 16, at 1117, 1130.
    Mescaline is "a psychoactive agent with effects similar to LSD. A Schedule I substance, the drug produces visual hallucinations, such as color patterns and spatial distortions." *Ibid.*, 1183.
168 *MacMurdo v. Upjohn*, Trial Transcript, *supra* note 82, at 582–83.
    Thorazine is a drug that used as a sedative and tranquilizer. *Mosby's*, *supra* note 16, at 1846.
    Stelazine is a drug used to treat anxiety. *Ibid.*, 1766.

169 *MacMurdo v. Upjohn*, Trial Transcript, *supra* note 82, at 589.
    Quaalude is a sedative and hypnotic drug. *Mosby's, supra* note 16, at 1575.
170 *MacMurdo v. Upjohn*, Trial Transcript, *supra* note 82, at 606.
    Nembutal is a sedative. *Mosby's, supra* note 16, at 1270. Seconal is a sedative
    used to calm a patient before surgery. *Ibid.*, 1683.
171 *MacMurdo v. Upjohn*, Trial Transcript, *supra* note 82, at 544 (Nov. 22, 1986, depo-
    sition testimony, at 43–44).
172 *Ibid.*, 709–11.
173 *Ibid.*, 809 (Connell testimony), and 544 (Roshan testimony) (Nov. 22, 1986, depo-
    sition testimony, at 58–59).
174 *Ibid.*, 544 (Nov. 22, 1986, deposition testimony, at 47).
175 *Ibid.*, 710.
176 *Ibid.*, 811.
177 *Ibid.*, 575.
178 *Ibid.*, 606.
179 *Ibid.*, 619.
180 *Ibid.*, 576.
181 *Ibid.*, 622.
182 *Ibid.*, 613, 616–17.
183 Upjohn, *supra* note 8.
184 *Ibid.*
185 *MacMurdo v. Upjohn*, Trial Transcript, *supra* note 82, at 544 (Aug. 15, 1978, deposi-
    tion testimony, at 25 and 526).
186 *Ibid.*, 503.
187 *Ibid.*, 725–26.
188 *Ibid.*, 544 (Aug. 15, 1978, deposition testimony, at 20).
189 *Ibid.*, 552–53.
190 *Ibid.*, 544 (Nov. 22, 1986, deposition testimony, at 28).
191 *Ibid.*, 513–14.
192 *Ibid.*, 395–96 (Benjamin); 544 (Roshan) (Nov. 22, 1986, deposition testimony, at
    87).
193 *Ibid.*, 544 (Levy), (Aug. 15, 1978, deposition testimony, at 22, 25, 47, 50); and
    517 (Shapiro), (Aug. 20, 1978, deposition testimony, at 20, 28–29, 35–35, 62–
    63).
194 *Ibid.*, 544 (Levy) (Aug. 15, 1978, deposition testimony, at 20).
195 *Ibid.*, 25.
196 *Ibid.*, 517 (referencing Aug. 20, 1978, deposition testimony, at 62).
197 *Ibid.*, 544 (Aug. 15, 1978, deposition testimony, at 42, 47, 86).
198 *Ibid.*, (Aug. 15, 1978, deposition testimony, at 56).
199 *Ibid.*, 544 (Nov. 22, 1986, deposition testimony, at 52).
200 *Ibid.*, 492.
201 *Ibid.*, 876.
202 *Ibid.*, 881, 883.
203 *Ibid.*, 888.

204 *Ibid.* A directed verdict is an order from a judge when he or she finds that no reasonable jury could reach a decision it has reached. Black, *supra* note 36, at 413.

205 Interview with Michael Ericksen, attorney, West Palm Beach, Fla. (Jan. 3, 1991).

206 *MacMurdo v. Upjohn*, Trial Transcript, *supra* note 82, at at 982, No. 78–8487-CL (Broward Cir. Ct., 17th Jud. Cir., Broward County, Fla., 1986).

207 *Ibid.*

208 *Ibid.*, 984.

209 *Ibid.*, 991.

210 *Ibid.*, 993–94.

211 *Ibid.*, 1012–13.

212 *Ibid.*, 1011.

213 *Ibid.*, 1009.

214 *Ibid.*, 1008.

215 *Ibid.*, 1019.

216 *Ibid.*, 1025.

217 *Ibid.*, 1026.

218 *Ibid.*, 1024.

219 *Ibid.*, 1025.

220 *Ibid.*

221 *Ibid.*, 1028.

222 *Ibid.*, 1030.

223 *Ibid.*, 1031.

224 *Ibid.*, 1031–32.

225 Joseph Sanders, *Bendectin on Trial* (Ann Arbor: University of. Michigan Press, 1998), 130.

226 *MacMurdo v. Upjohn*, Trial Transcript, *supra* note 82, at 1046, No. 78–8487-CL (Broward Cir. Ct., 17th Jud. Cir., Broward County, Fla., 1986). *See also*: *MacMurdo v. Upjohn*, Verdict. No. 78–8487-CL (Broward Cir. Ct., 17th Jud. Cir., Broward County, Fla., Dec. 6, 1986).

227 *MacMurdo v. Upjohn*, Trial Transcript, *supra* note 82, at 1045–46.

228 *MacMurdo v. Upjohn*, Final Judgment, No. 78–8487-CL (Broward Cir. Ct., 17th Jud. Cir., Broward County, Fla., Dec. 16, 1986).

229 *Ibid.*, 976–77.

230 Ericksen, *supra* note 205.

231 536 So.2d 337 (4th DCA 1988).

232 189 So.2d 171 (2d DCA 1966).

233 *Upjohn v. MacMurdo*, 536 So.2d, 337, 339 (Fla. 4th DCA, 1988), citing *MacMurdo v. Upjohn*, 444 So.2d 449, 461 (Fla. 4th DCA 1983).

234 *Ibid.*, 340. Upjohn moved for a directed verdict on failure to warn, MacMurdo moved for a directed verdict on contributory negligence, and Judge Burnstein denied both motions.

235 *Ibid.*

236 433 So.2d 17 (Fla. 1st DCA, 1984).

237 490 So.2d 76 (Fla. 1st DCA, 1986).

238 *Upjohn v. MacMurdo*, 536 So.2d, 337, 340 (Fla. 4th DCA, 1988).

239 *Ibid.*, 341.

240 562 So.2d 680, 683 (Fla. 1990).

241 540 So.2d 102 (Fla. 1989).

242 562 So.2d 680, 681–82 (Fla. 1990).

243 *MacMurdo v. Upjohn*, 444 So.2d 449 (Fla. 4th DCA 1983).

244 189 So.2d 171 (Fla. 2d DCA 1966).

245 491 So.2 1182 (Fla. 4th DCA 1986).

246 103 So.2d. 603 (Fla. 1958).

247 562 So.2d 680, 681–82 (Fla. 1990), citing *Felix v. Hoffman-LaRouche*, 540 So.2d 102 (Fla., 1989).

248 *Ibid.*, 683.

249 *Ibid.*

250 *Ibid.*

251 *Ibid.*

252 *Ibid.*, n.1.

253 *Ibid.*, n.3.

254 *Ibid.*

255 *Ibid.*

256 *Ibid.*

257 *Ibid.*, 684.

258 *Ibid.*

259 *Ibid.*, 683.

260 *Ibid.*, 684.

261 *Ibid.*

262 *Ibid.*, 683.

263 Ericksen, *supra* note 205.

264 *Ibid.*

265 Interview with Richard Kupfer, attorney, West Palm Beach, Fla. (Jan. 3, 1991).

CHAPTER 4. MARKETING APPROVAL AND LITIGATION

1 21 U.S.C. 355(a) (2014).

2 The World Health Organization defines osteoporosis and osteopenia based on the following bone density values: "Normal: Bone Density: A value for BMD . . . within 1 SD [standard deviation] of the young adult mean. Low Bone Mass: (osteopenia). A value for BMD more than 1 SD but less than 2.5 SD below the young adult mean. Osteoporosis: A value for BMD . . . 2.5 or more below the young adult mean. Severe osteoporosis (established osteoporosis): A value for BMD more than 2.5 SD below the young adult mean in the presence of one or more fragility fractures." WHO Study Group, "WHO Technical Report 843: Assessment of Fracture Risk and Its Application to Screening for Postmenopausal Osteoporosis," *World Health Organization*, 5–6 (1994).

"A person's bone mineral density [BMD] is composed of two norms," one of which is "young normal. . . . Young normal, known as your T-score, compares your BMD to the optimal or peak density of a 30 year old healthy adult and determines your fracture risk which increases as BMD falls below young normal levels . . . The difference between your BMD and that of a healthy young adult is referred to as a standard deviation (SD). . . . For most tests 1 SD equals a 10–12 percent decrease in bone density." *Ibid.*

3 The Upjohn Co., "NDA 12–541-S-004. Depo-Provera Sterile Acqueous Suspension for Contraception" (Feb. 27, 1967). Withdrawn Sept. 29, 1986.

4 "Patient Labeling of Medroxyprogesterone Acetate Injectable Contraceptive, *Federal Register* 39:32907 (Sept. 12, 1974).

5 "Patient Labeling of Medroxyprogesterone Acetate Injectable Contraceptive, Stay of Effective Date of Final Order," *Federal Register* 39:36472 (Oct. 30, 1974).

6 The Upjohn Co., "Depo-Provera Sterile Acqueous Suspension," *Federal Register* 43:28555 (June 30, 1978).

7 Judith Weisz, Griff T. Ross, and Paul Stolley, *Report of the Public Board of Inquiry on Depo-Provera* (Oct. 17, 1984).

8 "Human Drugs. Depo-Provera Sterile Aqueous Suspension," *Federal Register* 51:37651 (Oct. 23, 1986).

9 Michael Klitsch, "Injectable Hormones and Regulatory Controversy: An End to the Long-Running Story?," *Family Planning Perspectives* 25(1): 37–40 (Jan.–Feb. 1993).

10 World Health Organization, Special Programme of Research, Development and Research Training in Human Reproduction, "Guidelines for Toxicological and Clinical Assessment and Post-Registration Surveillance of Steroidal Contraceptives," WHO/HRP/SP.REP 87.1 (1987).

11 "Steroid Contraceptives Stress Postmarketing Surveillance to Better Protect Users," *Family Planning Perspectives* 19(2): 270–72 (1993). *See also*: K. C. Jacobs and K. P. Hatfield, "A History of Chronic Toxicity and Animal Carcinogenic Studies for Pharmaceuticals," *Veterinary Pathology* 50(2): 328 (2013).

12 WHO Guidelines, *supra* note 10; Jacobs and Hatfield, *supra* note 11, at 328. *See also*: Basil E. McKenzie, "Guidelines and Requirements for the Evaluation of Contraceptive Steroids," *Toxicology Pathology*, 17(2): 377–84 (1989).

13 Ridgely Bennett, MD, "Medical Officer's Original Summary of NDA 20,246," U.S. Food and Drug Administration, 7 (Oct. 27, 1982); Jacobs and Hatfield, *supra* note 11, at 328.

14 Bennett, *supra* note 13, at 7; Jacobs and Hatfield, *supra* note 11.

15 Bennett, *supra* note 13, at 3.

16 David B. Thomas and Robert A. Ray, "Depot-Medtoxyprogesterone Acetate (DMPA) and Risk of Endometrial Cancer," *International Journal of Cancer* 49:186–90 (1991); David B. Thomas et al., "Depot-Medtoxyprogesterone Acetate (DMPA) and Risk of Squamous Cell Cervical Cancer," *Contraception* 45:299–312 (1992); and David B. Thomas and Elizabeth Noonan, "Breast Cancer and Depot-

Medtoxyprogesterone Acetate: A Multinational Study," *Lancet*, 833–38 (Oct. 5, 1991).

17 Thomas and Noonan, *supra* note 16.

18 Teng Pardthaisong and Ronald H. Gray, "In Utero Exposure to Steroid Contraceptives and Outcome of Pregnancy," *American Journal of Epidemiology* 134(8): 795–803 (Oct. 15, 1991); and Ronald H. Gray and Teng Pardthaisong, "In Utero Exposure to Steroid Contraceptives and Survival during Infancy," *American Journal of Epidemiology* 134(8): 804–11 (Oct. 15, 1991).

19 Tim Cundy et al., "Bone Density in Women Receiving Depot Medroxyprogesterone Acetate for Contraception," *British Medical Journal* 30:13 (July 6, 1991).

20 *Supra* notes 16, 18 and 19.

21 *Infra* note 26, at 74–75 (presentation of Ridgely Bennett, MD).

22 The Upjohn Co., "FDA Advisory Committee Depo-Provera Brochure," 10 (May 14, 1992).

23 Letter to Division of Metabolism and Endocrine Drug Products, Center for Drug Evaluation and Research, U.S. Food and Drug Administration, "Depo-Provera Clinical Summary Information for Nov. 12, 1991, Strategy Meeting," from J. R. Assenzo, MD, U.S. Pharmaceutical Affairs, The Upjohn Co. (Nov. 5, 1991).

   Letter to Division of Metabolism and Endocrine Drug Products, Center for Drug Evaluation and Research, U.S. Food and Drug Administration, "Depo-Provera, Nov. 12, 1991, Meeting Minutes," from J. R. Assenzo, MD, U.S. Pharmaceutical Affairs, The Upjohn Co. (Nov. 25, 1991).

   Letter to J. R. Assenzo, MD, U.S. Pharmaceutical Affairs, The Upjohn Co., "Comments on Information to be Submitted in NDA 20–246," from Solomon Sobel, MD, Director, Division of Metabolism and Endocrine Drug Products, Center for Drug Evaluation and Research, U.S. Food and Drug Administration (Nov. 29, 1991).

24 Letter to Division of Metabolism and Endocrine Drug Products, Center for Drug Evaluation and Research, U.S. Food and Drug Administration, "Submission of NDA 20–246 for Depo-Provera," from J. R. Assenzo, MD, U.S. Pharmaceutical Affairs, The Upjohn Co. (Apr. 29, 1992).

25 Letter to Division of Metabolism and Endocrine Drug Products, Center for Drug Evaluation and Research, U.S. Food and Drug Administration, "FDA Advisory Committee Brochure," from J. R. Assenzo, MD, U.S. Pharmaceutical Affairs, The Upjohn Co. (May 14, 1992).

26 U.S. Food and Drug Administration, Fertility and Maternal Health Advisory Committee, Transcript of Meeting (June 19, 1992).

27 The FDA limited the advisory committee's public session to one hour and the fifteen speakers to four minutes each. Eleven of the speakers favored approval. After the public session, Dr. Philip Corfman, the FDA's Supervisory Medical Officer for Fertility and Maternal Health Drugs, observed: "We just received the NDA very recently, six weeks ago, so it is really too early for us to have a technical

response . . . because so many people have to review it—the chemists, all the various units within FDA." *Ibid.*, 78.

28 Norplant was approved by the FDA on Dec. 10, 1990.

29 *Supra* note 26, at 27 (presentation by Dr. Tom Houston, American Medical Association) and 38 (presentation by Dr. Eileen McGrath, American Women's Medical Association).

30 *Ibid.*, 53 (presentation by Dr. Samuel Shapiro, Boston University School of Medicine) and 37 (presentation by Dr. Eileen McGrath, American Medical Women's Association).

   Even though Dr. Shapiro supported the drug's approval, he was not persuaded that the WHO Costa Rica and New Zealand studies had shown that "short-term . . . or long-term use of Depo-Provera increases breast cancer at a young age." *Ibid.*, 53. For him, it was not "biologically possible that short duration use could increase risk," and "no long-term studies had been conducted to evaluate the drug's use for up to twenty years." *Ibid*, 53, 56. In line with his critique, Dr. Shapiro suggested that the Advisory Committee include in its risk management recommendation a statement that the breast cancer studies had not evaluated the drug's long-term use and that it strongly recommended that long-term studies be conducted. *Ibid.*, 56.

31 *Ibid.*, 31 and 34 (presentation by Lisa Kaeser, Allen Gutmacher Institute), 39–40 (presentation by Elaine Locke, American College of Obstetricians and Gynecologists), and 60 (presentation by Susan Wysocki, National Association of Nurse Practitioners).

32 *Ibid.*, 26 (presentation by Dr. Tom Huston, American Medical Association), 34 (presentation by Lisa Kaeser, Allen Guttmacher Institute), 39–40 (presentation by Elaine Locke, American College of Obstetricians and Gynecologists), and 59 (presentation by Dr. Louise B. Tyrer, Association of Reproductive Health Professionals).

33 *Ibid.*, 29 (presentation of Dr. Carlos Huezo, International Planned Parenthood Federation), 34 (presentation by Linda Kaeser, Allan Guttmacher Institute), and 59, (presentation by Dr. Louise Tryer, Association of Reproductive Health Professionals).

34 *Ibid.*, 45 (presentation by Cynthia Pearson, National Women's Health Network) and 49 (presentation by Julia Scott, National Black Women's Health Project).

35 *Ibid.*, 46 (Cynthia Pearson presentation).

36 *Ibid.*, 49 (Julia Scott presentation).

37 *Ibid.*, 48 (Cynthia Pearson presentation).

38 *Ibid.*, 50 (Julia Scott presentation).

39 *Ibid.*, 42 (presentation by Luz Alvarez Martinez, National Latina Health Organization).

40 *Ibid.*, 52 (Julia Scott presentation).

41 *Ibid.*

42 *Ibid.*, 49 (Cynthia Pearson presentation).

43 *Ibid.*, 76.

44 *Ibid.*

45 *Ibid.*, 77.

46 *Ibid.*, 78.

47 *Ibid.*

48 *Ibid.*

49 *Ibid.*, 115. The generic name of Depo-Provera is Depo-medroxyprogesterone acetate, which is abbreviated DMPA or MPA. Depo-Provera is also know by its trade name, Depo-Provera Contraceptive Injection, which is abbreviated Depo-Provera CI or DPCI.

50 *Ibid.* The Thomas study reports increased risk as relative risk. Relative risk is a comparison of the risk levels of two different groups of people. Relative risk is used to determine whether belonging to one group (women who receive injections of Depo-Provera) increases or decreases the risk of developing a disease (breast cancer) compared to (relative to) women in another group (women who do not receive an injection). If, for example, a woman user of Depo-Provera has a 1.5 relative risk of breast cancer, she has a 50% increased risk compared to (relative to) women who do not use the drug. www.medicalbiostatistics.com.

51 FDA Advisory Committee, Meeting Transcript, *supra* note 26, at 116. A 30% increased risk is a 1.3 relative risk.

52 *Ibid.*, 118. An 80% protective effect is a .20 relative risk.

53 *Ibid.*, 120.

54 *Ibid.*, 120–21. A 20% increased risk is a 1.20 relative risk, and a 40% increased risk is a 1.40 relative risk.

55 *Ibid.*, 120–21. A 119% increased risk is a 2.19 relative risk, and a 45% increased risk is a 1.45 relative risk.

56 *Ibid.*, 125.

57 *Ibid.*, 128–29.

58 *Ibid.*, 129. A 40% increased risk is a 1.40 relative risk, and a 45% increased risk is a 1.45 relative risk.

59 *Ibid.*, 130.

60 *Ibid.*, 135.

61 *Ibid.*

62 *Ibid.*, 139.

63 *Ibid.*,

64 *Ibid.*, 148 (presentation by Dr. Tim Cundy).

The femoral neck is the neck of the thigh bone (femur). When a femoral neck fracture occurs, the ball is disconnected from the rest of the thigh bone or femur. *Mosby's Medical Dictionary*, 7th ed. (St. Louis, MO: Mosby, Elsevier, 2006), 724.

The lumbar spine is the five vertebrae situated between the thoracic vertebrae and the sacral vertebrae in the spinal column. *Black's Medical Dictionary*, 41st ed., Dr. Harvey Marchvitch, ed. (Lanham, MD: Scarecrow Press, 2006), 662–63.

65 Cundy, *supra* note 26, at 149. DMPA is Depo-Provera's generic abbreviation.

66 *Ibid.*, 153.

67 *Ibid.*, 150.

68 Cundy et al., *supra* note 19, at 16.

69 Pardthaisong and Gray, *supra* note 18, at 795. The authors' report increased risk as relative risk. A 1.9 relative risk within 4 weeks, a 1.5 relative risk for 5 to 8 weeks, and a 1.2 relative risk beyond risk 9 weeks.

70 *Ibid.*, 804. An 80% increased risk is a 1.8 relative risk, and a 100% increased risk is a 2.0 relative risk.

71 *Ibid.* A 150% increased risk is a 2.5 relative risk.

72 *Supra* note 26, at 173–74.

73 *Ibid.*, 178.

74 *Ibid.*, 179.

75 *Ibid.*, 181–90 (presentation by Dr. Andrew Kaunitz, University of Florida Health Services Center, Jacksonville).

76 *Ibid.*, 190–95 (presentation of Dr. Amy Pollack, Engender Health).

77 *Ibid.*, 205.

78 *Ibid.*, 201.

79 *Ibid.*, 206.

80 *Ibid.*

81 *Ibid.*, 209.

82 *Ibid.*, 212.

83 *Ibid.*, 213 (quoting Dr. Solomon Sobel, at 78).

84 *Ibid.*, 214.

85 *Ibid.*

86 *Ibid.*

87 *Ibid.*

88 *Ibid.*, 215.

89 *Ibid.* (quoting Dr. Samuel Shapiro, at 53).

90 *Ibid.*, 217.

91 *Ibid.*

92 *Ibid.*, 217–18.

93 *Ibid.*, 218.

94 *Ibid.*, 218–21.

95 *Ibid.*, 219.

96 *Ibid.*, 221.

97 *Ibid.*, 222.

98 *Ibid.*, 205–6 (discussion by Drs. Susan McKay and Bruce Stadel).

99 Klitsch, *supra* note 9.

100 *Ibid.*

101 *Supra*, note 26, at 209–18 (discussion by Drs. Barbara Hulka, Janet Daling, Nancy Lee, Solomon Sobel, and Jane Zones).

102 *Ibid.*, 218 (discussion by Dr. Philip Corfman).

103 *Ibid.* (discussion by Dr. Barbara Hulka, advisory committee chair).
104 Bennett, *supra* note 13, at 8–10. Dr. Bennett's summary adopts, largely verbatim, the content of the Upjohn's "FDA Advisory Committee Depo-Provera Brochure."
105 *Ibid.*, 24–25.
106 *Ibid.*, 9–29.
107 *Ibid.*, 25.
108 *Ibid.*, 27.
109 *Ibid.*, at 19 (citing H. Hinchley, "Letter, DMPA and Bone Density," *British Medical Journal* 303:467 [1991]; S. F. Lane, "Bone Density in Women Receiving Depot Medroxyprogesterone Acetate for Contraception," *British Medical Journal* 303:467 [1991]; and A. Szarewski and J. Billebaud, "DMPA and Bone Density," *British Medical Journal* 303:467 [1991]).
110 This was not the first time that the FDA had proposed a Phase IV post-marketing study for osteoporosis. The agency had been aware of and concerned about Depo-Provera's risk of osteoporosis as early as 1974, when it approved the drug for limited contraceptive use. *Ibid.*, 29. As Dr. Ridgely Bennett told the Fertility and Maternal Health Advisory Committee at its June 19, 1992, meeting: "The agency believed that Phase IV post-marketing studies should be conducted in order to more adequately define the effect, if any, of Depo-Provera on . . . bone density." *Supra* note 26, at 69.
111 Philip A. Corfman, MD, "Letter to the Record, Action on NDA 20–246," U.S. Food and Drug Administration (Oct. 27, 1992).
112 *Ibid.*
113 Warren Leary, "U.S. Approves Drug Used by Injection for Birth Control," *New York Times*, A1 (Oct. 29, 1992).
114 Letter to J. R. Assenzo, MD, The Upjohn Company, "Approval of NDA 20–246," from Solomon Sobel, MD, Director, Division of Metabolism and Endocrine Drug Products, Center for New Drug Evaluation, U.S. Food and Drug Administration (Oct. 29, 1992).
115 *Ibid.*, 3.
116 *Ibid.*, 1.
117 The Upjohn Co., "Depo-Provera Physician Information," 2–3 (Oct. 1992).
118 Paul Schwallie and J. Robert Assenzo, "Contraceptive Use—Efficacy Study Utilizing Medroxyprogersterone Acetate Administered as an Intramuscular Injection One Every 90 Days," *Fertility and Sterility* 24:33–39 (1973). The Schwallie and Assenzo article is the principal publication of Upjohn's pivotal study: Study 144. The Upjohn Co., "Depo-Provera. C-150. NDA 20–246, Item 8: Clinical Data, Section E. Integral Summary of Safety Information, 4: Effects on Menstrual Cycle, 8.2/0011–15" (1992).
119 The Upjohn Co,, *supra*, note 117, at 2–3.
120 Schwallie and Assenzo, *supra*, note 118, at 334–35.
121 *Ibid.*, 333.
122 The Upjohn Co., *supra*, note 117, at 2.

123 Cundy et al., *supra* note 19 at 148.

124 Bennett, *supra* note 104 at 19.

125 *Ibid.*, 21.

126 A 20% overall increased risk is a1.2 relative risk, and a 119% percent increased risk is a 2.19 relative risk.

127 A 40% increase in a 1.4 relative risk.

128 Klitsch, *supra* note 9, at 38.

129 The risk of cervical cancer-in-situ first came to light in 1974, when Dr. Michael Popkin, an FDA researcher, reviewed the Schwallie and Assenzo study and found sixteen cases of cervical cancer-in-situ that, along with his bleeding and breast cancer findings, led him to recommend that Upjohn's IND be terminated. U. S. House of Representatives, Committee on Governmental Operations, Subcommittee on Intergovernmental Relations, "Hearings on Use of Advisory Committees by the Food and Drug Administration," 93rd Cong., 2nd Sess., 356–63 (Apr. 30, 1974). The hearings include the text of Michael Popkin, "Medical Officer's Review of IND 1086—Progress Report" (July 20, 1972). Ignored by the FDA, Dr. Popkin's review led Representative L. H. Fountain to hold a hearing and then to have the FDA stay its limited approval of Depo-Provera.

130 An increased risk of 10 % is a 1.1 relative risk, an increased risk of 70% is a 1.7 relative risk, and a decreased risk of -40% is a .60 relative risk.

131 Thomas and Ray, *supra* note 16, at 304. An increased risk of 10% is a 1.1 relative risk.

132 An increased risk from 22% to 28% is a 1.22 to 1.28 relative risk, a 28% increased risk is a 1.28 relative risk, and a 22% to 23% increased risk is a 1.22 to 1.23 relative risk.

133 Pardthaisong and Gray, *supra* note 18, at 795; and Gray and Pardthaisong, *supra* note 18, at 804.

134 Gray, *supra* note 26, at 173–74 (FDA FMHA Committee testimony).

135 *Ibid.*, 219 (discussion by Barbara S. Hulka, advisory committee chair).

136 *Ibid.*, 221.

137 The Upjohn Co., *supra* note 117, at 3.

138 The Schwallie and Assenzo article, *supra* note 118, first attracted attention when Dr. Michael Popkin, an FDA researcher, reviewed the research and found that 32% of the women reported unpredictable and prolonged bleeding or spotting, which contributed to the highest percentage of all the reasons for the 65% dropout rate. This finding led him to question the validity of the study's findings. *Supra* note 129.

In 1978, Dr. Ridgely Bennett revealed the dubious value of the Schwallie and Assenzo study when he testified before the House Select Committee on Population and characterized the study as "just an observational report." U.S. House of Representatives, Select Committee on Population, 95th Cong., 2nd Sess., 73 (Aug. 9, 1978).

The Schwallie and Assenzo study has two basic problems. First, it does not distinguish between bleeding and spotting, define heavy bleeding, or identify the amount of heavy and continuous bleeding per month. Second, the article raises a self-selection bias, because it reports the bleeding or spotting as tapering off during the first year from 26.9% with the first injection to 11.9% with the fourth injection, to 5.8% over two years, to 5% over three years. At the same time, it reports an increase in the percentage of women who dropped out of the study from 40.6% the first year to 58% the second year and 69.8% the third year. As Dr. Sidney Wolfe told the Public Board of Inquiry, "Women who experience the heaviest and most prolonged bleeding are probably more likely to discontinue use of the drug, and will not be included in the analysis of bleeding that follows." U.S. Food and Drug Administration, Depo-Provera Public Board of Inquiry, Transcript of Hearing, 4:43 (Jan. 13, 1983) (statement by Dr. Sidney Wolfe, Director of the Public Citizen Health Research Group).

139 Bennett, *supra* note 13, at 19; and Hinchley and Lane, *supra* note 109.
140 Shapiro, *supra* note 26, at 53.
141 Klitsch, *supra* note 9, at 38.
142 Pearson, *supra* note 26, at 45.
143 Bennett, *supra* note 13, at 27.
144 Corfman, *supra* note 111.
145 Clair Chilvers, "Breast Cancer and Depo-Medroxiprogesterone Acetate: A Review," *Contraception* 49(9): 220 (1996).
146 *Ibid.*, 220–21.
147 The Upjohn Co., "Depo-Provera Contraceptive Injection. Patient Labeling" (Oct. 1992).
148 The Upjohn Co., "Depo-Provera Contraceptive Injection. Important Information for Patients" (Oct. 16, 1992).
149 Upjohn, *supra* note 147, at 1; and, Upjohn, supra note 148, at 6–7.
150 Upjohn, Patient Labeling, *supra* note 147, at 1; and Upjohn, Patient Information, *supra* note 148, at 6.
151 The Upjohn Co., *supra* note 147, at 1.
152 *Ibid.*, 2.
153 Letter to The Upjohn Co., "Attention: R. J. Assenzo, M.D., NDA 20–246," from Solomon Sobel, MD, Director, Division of Metabolism and Endocrine Drugs, Center for New Drug Evaluation, U.S. Food and Drug Administration, 1 (Oct. 29, 1992).
154 Pharmacia & Upjohn Co., "Depo-Provera Contraceptive Injection. Physician Information" (2004); and Pharmacia & Upjohn, "Depo-Provera Contraceptive Injection. Patient Labeling" (2004).
     The FDA updated its bone mineral density and breast cancer warnings in the physicians' prescribing information and patient labeling. *See*: U.S. Food and Drug Administration, "Depo-Provera Contraceptive Injection Injectable

Suspension. Safety Labeling Changes Approved by the FDA Center for Drug Evaluation and Research (CDER), October 2010," www.fda.gov.

155 Pharmacia & Upjohn, *supra* note 154, at 1, 4.

156 *Ibid.*, 4.

157 *Ibid.*, 6.

158 *Ibid.*, 4. Depo-Provera CI is an abbreviation for Depo-Provera Contraceptive Injection.

159 *Ibid.*, 5. The total bone mineral density loss was calculated by adding the bone density loss incurred by the group using Depo-Provera to the bone density gained by the control group.

160 *Ibid.*, 4.

161 *Ibid.*, 5. The total bone mineral density loss was calculated by adding the bone density loss incurred by the group using Depo-Provera to the bone density gained by the control group.

162 *Ibid.*, 1, 4.

163 *Ibid.*, 4.

164 The Upjohn Co., "Depo-Provera Contraceptive Injection. Patient Labeling" (Oct. 2004).

165 *Ibid.*, 4. The patient brochure has the same statement. *See*: The Upjohn Co., "Depo-Provera Contraceptive Injection. Patient Information" (May, 2, 2006).

166 A complete list of individual Depo-Provera lawsuits is unlikely, because there is no readily available record of all the cases that have been settled. The reported individual osteoporosis lawsuits include the four discussed in this chapter: *Lorenzi v. Pfizer Inc.* (2007), *Colville v. Pharmacia & Upjohn* (2008), *Oliver v. Pharmacia & Upjohn Co.* (2008), and *Montagnon v. Pfizer Inc.* (2008).

   Other individual cases include one products liability osteoporosis case (*Bachelor v. Pfizer, Inc.*, No. 2:12-CV-908-WKW (M.D. Miss. (July 25, 2013), two medical malpractice birth defect cases (*Terrabone v. Floyd*, 767 So.2d (La. Ct. App. 2000); and *Webster v. Desai*, No. A10A0556 (Geo. Ct. App. 2010); and one products liability case involving twelve plaintiffs alleging various adverse effects (*Taylor, et al. v. Pharmacia-Upjohn Co.*, No. CIV A.4:03CV148LN (S.D. Miss. 2005).

167 Multidistrict litigation, one form of complex litigation, "arises when civil litigation involving one or more common questions of fact is pending in different federal judicial districts and such actions are transferred to any district for coordinated or consolidated pre-trial proceedings. . . . Such transfers are made by the Judicial Panel on Multidistrict Litigation." Brian R. Martinotti, "Complex Litigation in the New Jersey and Federal Courts: An Overview of the Current State of Affairs and a Glimpse of What Lies Ahead," *Loyola University of Chicago Law Journal* 44:562, n. 4 (2012).

   The one reported multidistrict litigation post-approval case is *In re Depo-Provera Products Liability Litigation*, 499 F.Supp. 1348 (Jud.Pan.Multi.Lit. 2007). The case involved three federal osteoporosis products liability cases: two individual California cases (*Windward v. Pfizer Inc.*, C.A. No.4:07–878 (2007); and *Cable v. Pfizer Inc.*, C.A. No.4:04–879 (2007); and one New Jersey putative class action case (*Riddell v. Pfizer*, C.A. No.3:06–5418 (2007). The California cases sought monetary damages while the New Jersey case sought "to have Pfizer pay for a program to monitor bone mass density of everyone in the United States who had used Depo-Provera for more than two years and to recover the cost of treatment." Jacqueline Bell, "Depo-Provera Case Must Stay in California: MDL Panel," *Law 360* (Aug. 24, 2007), www.law360.com. The California plaintiffs moved to consolidate their cases with the New Jersey case and have them transferred to the New Jersey federal district court. The MDL panel denied consolidation. *In re Depo-Provera Products Liability Litigation*, U.S. Judicial Panel on Multidistrict Litigation, No. MDL-1856 (Aug. 6, 2007).

168 A class action lawsuit, another form of complex litigation, aggregates many plaintiffs' claims into a single lawsuit that is filed on behalf of all potential plaintiffs and is heard in a single court. The class must be certified by the court, which determines whether all of the plaintiffs have been harmed in a similar manner and whether the lawsuit represents the interests of all potential plaintiffs. Federal class actions are governed by Federal Rule of Civil Procedure 23. F. R. Civ. Pro. 23.

There are two reported Depo-Provera post-approval class actions: *Riddell v. Pfizer Inc.* (2007) discussed in *supra*, note 167, and *Whitaker v. Upjohn Co.*, 1996 WL 371501 (E.D. La. 1996). *Whitaker* was filed as a class action in a Louisiana trial court claiming various Depo-Provera-related injuries. Pfizer and Upjohn removed to federal court where the class action was dismissed and the action then proceeded as a mass joinder case. The Federal Rule of Civil Procedure 42 permits a court to join multiple plaintiffs if their cases involve a common questions of law or fact. Fed. R. Civ. P. 42.

169 A mass tort lawsuit, a form of complex litigation, aggregates numerous plaintiffs who claim to have suffered a harm from a single wrongful act caused by a corporate defendant and whose cases are tried in a single court. Unlike the plaintiffs in a class action, those in a mass tort lawsuit maintain their own suits, because a single act can cause a multitude of harms, and individual plaintiffs may suffer in different ways or deserve more damages than others. Like class actions, mass tort suits involve plaitiffs' pooling their resources to obtain more information and build stronger cases without incurring large expenses alone. Martinotti, *supra* note 167, at 562, n.4. The major post-approval mass tort case, involving 157 plaintiffs and one defendant, Pfizer, is *In re Depo-Provera Contraceptive Injection Litigation*, Case No. 276. N.J. Sup. Ct, Law Div., Bergen County (2007), which was settled for a confidential amount.

170 *Supra* note 2 for a definition of osteoporosis.

171 The Upjohn Company was established in 1886. In 1995, Upjohn merged with Pharmacia AB to form Pharmacia & Upjohn Co.. In 2000, Pharmacia & Upjohn Co. merged with G. D. Searle & Co. to create Pharmacia Corp. In 2003, Pharmacia Corp. merged with Pfizer, Inc.

172 *In re Depo-Provera Contraceptive Injection Litigation*, Case No. 276, N.J. Sup. Ct. Law Div., Bergen County (2007).

173 Protective orders in mass tort litigation insure the confidentiality of documents, including the contents of depositions. Henry Campbell Black, *Black's Law Dictionary*, 5th ed. (St. Paul, MN: West Publishing, 1979), 1101. *See, e.g.*, William G. Childs, "When the Bell Can't Be Unrung: Document Leaks and Protective Orders in Mass Tort Litigation," *Review of Litigation* 27:565–78 (2008).

174 In all four summary judgment cases, the defendant is identified in the text as Pfizer even though in the *Colville* and *Oliver* cases the defendant is Pharmacia & Upjohn Co., because Pfizer is the company created by the mergers described *supra* note 171.

175 Summary judgment is a court order granted when there are no disputed material facts for a court to decide, and the moving party is entitled to prevail as a matter of law. The motion for summary judgment may be granted against all or part of a claim or defense. Black, *supra* note 173, at 1287.

176 *Supra* notes 166–169.

177 *Lorenzi v. Pfizer, Inc.*, 519 F.Supp.2d 742 (N.D. Ohio 2007).

178 *Colville v. Pharmacia & Upjohn Co.*, 565 F.Supp.2d 1314 (N.D. Fla. 2008).

179 *Oliver v.Pharmacia & Upjohn Co.*, 2008 WL 4691626 (E.D. La. 2008).

180 *Montagnon v. Pfizer Inc.*, 584 F.Supp. 2d 459 (D.Conn. 2008).

181 *Supra* note 171 for Upjohn's corporate history.

182 *Supra* note 2 for definitions of osteoporosis and osteopenia.

183 Federal Rules of Civil Procedure, Rule 56.

184 *Colville v. Pharmacia & Upjohn Co.*, 565 F.Supp.2d 1314, 1219 (N.D. Fla. 2008) (citing *Riley v. Newton*, 94 F.3d 632, 638–39 [11th Cir. 1996]).

185 *Lorenzi v. Pfizer, Inc.*, 519 F.Supp.2d 742, 744 (N.D. Ohio 2007) (citing *Anderson v. Liberty Lobby*, 477 U.S. 256 [1986]).

186 *Ibid.*, 744 (quoting *Anderson v. Liberty Lobby*, 477 U.S. 250, 251–52 [1986]).

187 *Ibid.*, 745. *See: supra* note 2 for bone mass definitions: normal, osteopenia, and osteoporosis.

188 *See: Lorenzi v. Pfizer, Inc.*, 519 F.Supp.2d 742 (N.D. Ohio 2007); *Colville v. Pharmacia & Upjohn Co.*, 565 F.Supp.2d 1314 (N.D. Fla. 2008); and *Oliver v.Pharmacia & Upjohn Co.*, 2008 WL 4691626 (E.D. La. 2008).

189 *See: Montagnon v. Pfizer Inc.*, 584 F.Supp. 2d 459 (D.Conn. 2008).

190 U.S. Constitution, Article 3, Section 2, grants Congress the power to allow federal courts to hear civil cases when the parties (persons and corporations) are diverse—that is, they are citizens of different states. Congress has exercised this Article 3 power, currently codified in 28 U.S. C. §1332, to limit diversity jurisdiction to cases involving claims of at least $75,000.

191 The Rules Decision Act, 28 U.S.C §1652, provides that state law, including state statutes and judicial decisions, is the substantive law federal courts will apply in diversity cases. The Rules Enabling Act, 28 U.S.C. §2072, provides that the federal

courts will apply federal procedural and evidentiary rules (Federal Rules of Civil Procedure and Federal Rules of Evidence) in diversity cases.

192 *Colville v. Pharmacia & Upjohn Co.*, 565 F.Supp.2d 1314 (N.D. Fla. 2008). *See: supra* notes 117, 147, and 148 for the 1992 physician information, patient labeling, and patient brochure.

193 *Colville v. Pharmacia & Upjohn Co.*, 565 F.Supp.2d 1314, 1317 (N.D. Fla. 2008). See *supra* note 154 for the 2004 physician information and patient labeling.

194 All four states recognize the learned intermediary doctrine. *See:* for Ohio, *Howland v. Purdue Pharyna L.P.*, Ohio St.3d 584 N.E. 141 (2004); for Florida, *Upjohn Co. v. MacMurdo*, 562 So.2d 680, 683 (Fla. 1990); for Louisiana, *Stahl v. Novartis Pharmaceutical Corp.*, 283 F.3d 254, 268 (5th Cir. 2002); and for Connecticut, *Vitanza v. Upjohn Co.*, 778 A.2d 829, 839 (2001).

195 The learned intermediary doctrine is an exception to the common law rule that a manufacturer has a duty to warn the ultimate consumer about the risks of using its products. Where the learned intermediary doctrine applies, a manufacturer of a pharmaceutical drug will fulfill its duty of care when it provides all of the necessary drug information to a physician who is expected to serve as a learned intermediary for the manufacturer by weighing the risks and benefits of the drug in prescribing it to a patient who is the ultimate consumer.

First used in *Sterling Drug v. Cornish*, 370 F.2d 82, 83 (8th Cir. 1966), and later adopted by forty-six states, the doctrine requires the plaintiff to prove that the manufacturer's drug package insert information was inadequate to warn his or her physician and that this failure to warn caused his or her injuries. *See, e.g.*: Allen Wong, "Products Liability: The Fate of the Learned Intermediary Doctrine," *Journal of Law, Medicine and Ethics* 30(3) 471–72 (2002); and William Green, "Consumer-Directed Advertising of Contraceptive Drugs: The FDA, Depo-Provera, and Products Liability," *Food and Drug Law Journal* 50(4): 553–57 (1995).

196 *Oliver v.Pharmacia & Upjohn Co.*, 2008 WL 4691626, 6 (E.D. La. 2008) (citing *Stahl v. Novartis Pharmaceutical Corp.*, 283 F.3d 254, 268 [5th Cir. 2002]).

197 *Lorenzi v. Pfizer, Inc.*, 519 F.Supp.2d 742, 747 (N.D. Ohio 2007).

198 Ohio Revised Code §2307(C).

199 Carolyn Westhoff, "Bone Mineral Density and DMPA," *Journal of Reproductive Medicine* 47:795 (2002).

200 *Lorenzi v. Pfizer, Inc.*, 519 F.Supp.2d 742, 749 (N.D. Ohio 2007).

201 *Ibid.*, 748.

202 *Ibid.*, 752 (quoting Licata deposition, at 4).

203 *Ibid.* (quoting Licata deposition, at 3).

204 *Ibid.* (quoting Licata deposition, at 4).

205 *Ibid.*, 749 (quoting DeSalvo deposition, at 29–30).

206 *Ibid.*, 750 (quoting Licata deposition, at 26).

207 *Colville v. Pharmacia & Upjohn Co.*, 565 F.Supp.2d 1314, 1322 (N.D. Fla. 2008).

208 *Ibid.*, 1318.

209 *Ibid.*, 1317.

210 *Ibid.*, 1320.

211 *Ibid.*, 1321. *See, e.g.*, Carol Rooney, "The Learned Intermediary Doctrine: An Update," *Trial Advocate Quarterly* 29(1): 6–12 (2010).

212 *Colville v. Pharmacia & Upjohn Co.*, 565 F.Supp.2d 1314, 1322 (N.D. Fla. 2008), (quoting *Upjohn Co. v. MacMurdo*, 562 So.2d 680, 683 (Fla. 1990). *See, e.g.*, William Green, "Miscarriage of Justice: Depo-Provera Case May Insulate Drug Makers," *Trial* 27(7): 61–65 (July 1991).

213 *Ibid.*

214 *Ibid.* (citing *Upjohn Co. v. MacMurdo*, 562 So.2d 680, 683 (Fla. 1990).

215 *Ibid.*

216 *Ibid.*

217 *Ibid.*, 1321–22 (quoting, in part, *Felix v. Hoffman-LaRouche, Inc.*, 540 So.2d. 102, 105 [Fla. 1989]).

218 *Ibid.*, 1322.

219 *Ibid.*

220 *Ibid.*, 1321.

221 *Ibid.*, 1322–23.

222 Federal Rule of Civil Procedure 60(b) "permits relief of a judgment or order on the grounds of mistake, inadvertence, surprise, or neglect." Fed. R. Civil Pro. 60(b). *Oliver v. Pharmacia & Upjohn Co.*, 2008 WL 4691626, 1 (E.D. La. 2008).

223 *Ibid.*, 13.

224 Equity is justice administered according to fairness as contrasted with rules of law. Black, *supra* note 173, at 484.

225 *Oliver v. Pharmacia & Upjohn Co.*, 2008 WL 4691626, 15 (E.D. La. 2008).

226 *Montagnon v. Pfizer, Inc.*, 584 F.Supp.2d 459 (D.Conn. 2008).

227 *Oliver v. Pharmacia & Upjohn Co.*, 2008 WL 4691626, 6 (E.D. La. 2008).

228 *Ibid.*, 16.

229 83 F.3d 254, 266 (5th Cir. 2002).

230 *Oliver v. Pharmacia & Upjohn Co.*, 2008 WL 4691626, 18–19 (E.D. La. 2008).

231 *Ibid.*, 21.

232 *Ibid.*, 23, citing *Lorenzi v. Pfizer, Inc.*, 519 F.Supp.2d 742, 742 (N.D. Ohio 2007).

233 *Ibid.*, 24.

234 *Ibid.*, 26, citing *Lorenzi v. Pfizer, Inc.*, 519 F.Supp.2d 742 (N.D. Ohio 2007); and *Colville v. Pharmacia & Upjohn Co.*, 565 F.Supp.2d 1314 (N.D. Fla. 2008).

235 *Montagnon v. Pfizer Inc.*, 584 F.Supp.2d 459, 461 (D. Conn. 2008).

236 *Ibid.*

237 *Ibid.*, 461–62. The five warnings were based on the two articles—Cundy et al., *supra* note 19; and Delia Scholes et al., "Bone Mineral Density in Women Using Depot Medroxyprogesterone Acetate for Contraception," *Obstetrics and Gynecology* 93(2): 233 (Feb. 1999)—and would require the FDA to warn physicians that: "(1) bone loss is greater with increasing duration of use and may not be completely

reversible, (2) use of DPCI in adolescents or early adulthood will reduce peak bone mass and increase the risk of osteoporosis in later life, (3) DPCI should be used for more than two years only if other birth control methods are inadequate, (4) use of DPCI may cause loss of calcium stored in bones, and the longer DPCI is used, the more calcium is likely to be lost, and (5) loss of calcium may cause weak, porous bones (osteoporosis), that could increase the risk of bone breakage especially after menopause (the 'proposed warnings')." Quoting Plaintiff's Document #46, at 7. *Compare*, 1992 and 2004 "Physician Information," *supra* notes 117 and 154.

238 *Montagnon, supra* note 235, at 462.
239 *Ibid.,* 463.
240 *Ibid.,* 462.
241 *Ibid.,* 463.
242 *Supra* note 117.
243 Wong, *supra* note 195.
244 *Lorenzi v. Pfizer, Inc.,* 519 F.Supp.2d 742, 749 (N.D. Ohio 2007).
245 *Lorenzi v. Pfizer, Inc.,* 519 F.Supp.2d 742, 752 (N.D. Ohio 2007), (quoting Licata deposition, at 4).

CHAPTER 5. CHEMICAL CASTRATION

1 Depo-Provera has been identified as chemical castration because of its supposed similarity to surgical castration, a procedure for sterilizing men. Surgical castration will not be discussed in this chapter. There is a substantial literature on the subject. The following three articles explore the ethical, legal, and medical literature: William Green, "Depo-Provera, Castration, and the Probation of Rape Offenders," *University of Dayton Law Review* 12(1): 1–26 (1986); Pamela K. Hicks, "Castration of Sexual Offenders: Legal and Ethical Issues," *Journal of Legal Medicine* 14:641–67 (1993); and Charles L. Scott and Trent Holmberg, "Castration of Sex Offenders: Prisoner's Rights Versus Public Safety," *Journal of the American Academy of Psychiatry and the Law* 31:502–9 (2003).

2 Depo-Provera, along with Norplant, the IUD, and the Pill, have been imposed as probation conditions on women who have been convicted of child abuse and neglect. *See, e.g., People v. Walsh*, 593 N.W.2d 558 (Mich. 1999) (use of Depo-Provera or Norplant found unlawful on appeal); *In re I.N.G.* [Renee Gamez], 2003 WL 222997795 (Mich. 2003) (use of Depo-Provera rescinded on appeal); *People v. Johnson*, 1992 WL 685375 (Cal.Ct.App. 1992) (Norplant probation condition mooted on appeal). The use of these procreation restrictions violate a woman's Fourteenth Amendment Due Process Clause rights, but they will not be discussed in this study. For studies of the use of Norplant as a probation condition and the constitutional issues raised by its use, *see, e.g.,* Catherine Albiston, "The Social Meaning of the Norplant Condition: Constitutional Considerations of Race, Class, and Gender," *Berkeley Journal of Gender, Law & Justice* 9(1): 9–41 (Sept. 2013); and Kristyn M. Walker "Note: Judicial Control of Reproductive Freedom:

The Use of Norplant as a Condition of Probation," *Iowa Law Review* 78:779 (Mar. 1993).

3 The Sexual Disorders Clinic was established in 1980. At the time of the Public Citizen Health Research Group inquiry, the clinic was identified as the Biosexual Psychohormonal Clinic in Dr. Fred Berlin's correspondence with the Health Research Group. In 1991, Dr. Berlin established a free-standing private clinic, the National Center for the Study, Prevention, and Treatment of Sexual Trauma, which offers the same services as the Johns Hopkins Clinic. *See*: National Institute for the Study, Prevention, and Treatment of Sexual Trauma (n.d.).

4 "Paraphilias are a diagnosable psychosexual disorder [that] . . . results from recurrent, intense sexual urges, fantasies, or behaviors." Cynthia S. Osborne and Thomas N. Wise, "Paraphilias," 294–95, in Richard Balon and R. Taylor Segraves, *Handbook of Sexual Dysfunctions* (New York: Taylor & Francis, 2005), referencing American Psychological Association, *Diagnostic and Statistical Manual of Mental Disorders*, 4th text revision (Arlington, VA: American Psychological Association, 2000). The paraphilias described in *DSM IV-TR* are fetishism, transvestism, zoophilia, pedophilia, exhibitionism, voyeurism, sexual masochism, and sexual sadism. See also: American Psychological Association, *Diagnostic and Statistical Manual of Mental Disorders*, 5th ed. (Arlington, VA: American Psychological Association, 2013).

5 John Money, Claus Wiedking, Paul A. Walker, and Dean Gain, "Combined Antiandrogenic and Counseling Program for Treatment of 46,XY and 47,XYY Sex Offenders," 116, in Edward Sachar, ed., *Hormones, Behavior, and Psychotherapy* (New York: Raven Press, 1976).

6 Pierre Gagne, "Treatment of Sex Offenders with Medroxyprogesterone Acetate," *American Journal of Psychiatry* 131:646 (1981).

7 A psychotropic drug is "any drug capable of affecting the mind, emotions, and behavior. Legal drugs, such as lithium for bipolar disorder, and illicit drugs, such as cocaine, are psychotropic. *Mosby's Medical Dictionary*, 7th ed. (St. Louis, MO: Elsevier, 2006), 1556.

8 Androgen is "a male sex hormone that promotes the development and maintenance of the male sex characteristics. The major androgen is testosterone." *Ibid.*, 1556. "An antiandrogen [such as Depo-Provera] blocks the action of androgens." *Ibid.*

9 Dietrich Blumer and Claude Migeon, "Hormone and Hormonal Agents in the Treatment of Aggression," *Journal of Nervous and Mental Disease* 160:128 (1976).

10 Money et al. *supra* note 5, at 119.

11 Connecticut Department of Corrections, *Report of the Depo-Provera Study Group*, 5 (1983).

12 The medical-psychiatric literature has established that Depo-Provera is an experimental drug. *See, e.g.,* Florence Thibaut, Flora de la Barra, Harvey Gordon, Paul Cosyns, John M.W. Bradford, and the WFSBP Task Force on Sexual Disorders, "The World Federation of Societies of Biological Psychiatry (WFSBP) Guidelines

for the Biological Treatment of Paraphilias," *World Journal of Biological Psychiatry* 11:622 (2010).

13 Margaret Engel, "Giving Sex Offenders Drug Spurs Concern," *Washington Post*, A1 (July 18, 1983).

14 Federal Food, Drug, and Cosmetic Act, 21 U.S.C. 312 (2014).

15 Letter to Robert Temple, MD, Director, Office of New Drug Evaluation, Center for Drugs and Biologics, Food and Drug Administration, from Sidney Wolfe, MD, and Carey LaCheen, Public Citizen Health Research Group (Aug. 16, 1983), 2.

16 Letter to Sidney M. Wolfe, MD, and Carey LaCheen, Public Citizen Health Research Group, from Dr. Harry Meyer, Director, Center for Drugs and Biologics, Food and Drug Administration (Dec. 16, 1983), 1.

17 *Ibid.*, 1.

18 *Ibid.*, 2.

19 *Ibid.*, 2.

20 Letter to Mark Novitch, MD, Acting Commissioner, Food and Drug Administration, from Eric R. Glitzenstein, William B. Schultz, and Alan B. Morrison, Public Citizen Litigation Group (Mar. 15, 1984), 1.

21 *Chaney v. Heckler*, 718 F.2d 1174 (DC. Cir, 1983), vacated and remanded, *Heckler v. Chaney*, 470 U.S. 821 (1985). In *Chaney*, the Supreme Court held that the FDA's decision not to take enforcement action to prevent the use of drugs by state governments for capital punishment purposes was unreviewable under the Administrative Procedure Act § 701(A)(2), because the agency's decision has traditionally been "committed to agency discretion" and Congress did not intend to alter that tradition.

22 Letter to Mark Novitch, MD, Acting Commissioner, Food and Drug Administration, from Eric R. Glitzenstein, William B. Schultz, and Alan B. Morrison, Public Citizen Litigation Group (Mar. 15, 1984), 2.

23 *Ibid.*, 3.

24 Letter to Eric R. Glitzenstein, William B. Schultz, and Alan B. Morrison, Public Citizen Litigation Group, from Mark Novitch, MD, Acting Commissioner, Food and Drug Administration (June 5, 1984), 1. Note: The author found no entry in FDA IND files for Depo-Provera criminal justice use by Dr. Fred Berlin, Dr. John Money, or the Johns Hopkins Social Disorders Clinic.

25 Letter to Sidney M. Wolfe, MD, Public Citizen Health Research Group, from Fred S. Berlin, MD, PhD, Assistant Professor, Co-Director, Biosexual Psychohormonal Clinic, Johns Hopkins University School of Medicine (Apr. 23, 1984), 1.

26 Letter to Eric R. Glitzenstein, William B. Schultz, and Alan B. Morrison, Public Citizen Litigation Group, from Mark Novitch, MD, Acting Commissioner, Food and Drug Administration (June 5, 1984), 1.

27 U.S. Congress, Senate, Committee on Labor and Public Welfare, "Quality of Health Care-Human Experimentation: Hearings before the Subcommittee on Health," 93rd Cong. 1st Sess., 105 (Feb. 21, 1973).

28 U.S. Congress, House of Representatives, Committee on Interior and Insular Affairs, "Use of the Drug Depo-Provera by the Indian Health Service: Oversight Hearings before the Subcommittee on Health," 100th Cong., 1st Sess. (Aug. 6, 1987).

29 The Upjohn Co., IND 3256, "Depo-Provera Aqueous Suspension C-150 for Male Sex Offenders" (July 20, 1966). Withdrawn Apr. 3, 1968.

30 Upjohn also provided Depo-Provera to "private physicians on the staff in the General Research Center at the University of Texas Medical Branch." Walter J. Meyer III, Collier Cole, and Evangeline Emory, "Depo-Provera Treatment for Sex Offending Behavior: An Evaluation of Outcomes," *Bulletin of the American Academy of Psychiatry and the Law* 20(2): 250 (1992).

31 Letter to Ronald Powell, Commissioner, Department of Correction, State of New Hampshire, from Sidney M. Wolfe, MD, and Carey LaCheen, Public Citizen Health Research Group (Mar. 27, 1984), 2. *See*: Upjohn, *supra* note 29.

32 Ruth Shereff, "Some Drugs Have Another Side," *Chemical Business*, 37 (Mar. 1984).

33 *Ibid.*

34 Letter to Sidney M. Wolfe, MD, Public Citizen Health Research Group, from N. Franklin Adkinson, Jr., MD, Chair, Joint Committee on Clinical Investigations, Johns Hopkins School of Medicine (July 26, 1983), 3.

35 *Ibid.*

36 *Ibid.*, 2–3.

37 *Ibid.*, 3.

38 Letter to N. Franklin Adkinson, Jr., MD, Chair, Joint Committee on Clinical Investigations, Johns Hopkins School of Medicine, from Sidney M. Wolfe, MD, Public Citizen Health Research Group (Aug. 12, 1983), 1.

39 Biosexual Psychohormonal Clinic, Johns Hopkins University of School of Medicine, "Biosexual Psychohormonal Clinic," (n.d.), 1.

40 *Ibid.*, "Consent Form" (n.d.), 1–2.

41 *Ibid.*, 2.

42 *Ibid.*

43 *Ibid.*

44 *Ibid.*

45 Letter to Robert J. Brooks, Chief, Program Development, Department of Correction, State of Connecticut, from Sidney M. Wolfe, MD, and Carey LaCheen, Public Citizen Health Research Group (Oct. 17, 1983), 3.

46 *Ibid.*, 4.

47 *Ibid.*

48 *Ibid.*

49 *Ibid.*, 5.

50 *Ibid.*

51 Dr. Berlin left the Johns Hopkins Sexual Disorders Clinic because "he earned the scorn of many [including child advocates] with his position that therapists specializing in the treatment of pedophiles . . . should not have to report sexual offenders to law enforcement authorities." To avoid the strain negative publicity

had on the clinic's relationship with Johns Hopkins Medical Center, he established his own private clinic. Jonathan Bor, "Sexual-Disorders Clinic Is Severed from Hopkins; Often-Criticized Director Takes His Operation Private," *Baltimore Sun,* July 3, 1992, articles.baltimoresun.com.

52 National Institute, *supra* note 2. National Institute for the Study, Prevention, and Treatment of Sexual Trauma, "Consent Form: Depo-Provera" (n.d.).

53 J. K. Aronson, "Anecdotes as Evidence," *British Medical Journal* 326:7403 (2003).

54 Thomas Douglas, Pieter Bonta, Farah Foquaert, Katrien Devolder, and Sigrid Sterchx, "Coercion, Incarceration, and Chemical Castration: An Argument from Autonomy," *Journal of Bioethical Inquiry* 10(3): 393–405, at 395 (2013).

55 "A double-blind study is an experimental procedure in which neither the subjects of the experiment nor the persons administering the experiment know the critical aspects of the experiment. A double-blind procedure is used to guard against both experimenter bias and placebo effects." *Mosby's, supra* note 7, at 586–87.

56 Thibaut et al., *supra* note 12, at 622.

57 Douglas et al., *supra* note 54, at 395.

58 Pedophilia, one of the eight paraphilias, is defined by "recurrent, intense erotic fantasies, urges or behaviors involving a prepubescent (13 years of age or younger) child." Osborne and Wise, *supra* note 4, at 305. As Osborne and Wise explain, "Pedophilia is a psychosexual affliction that only becomes criminal if the person engages in the illegal act of sexual behavior with a child." *Ibid.*

59 Fred S. Berlin and Carl F. Meinecke, "Treatment of Sex Offenders with Antiandrogenic Medication: Conceptualization, Review of Treatment Modalities, and Preliminary Findings," *American Journal of Psychiatry* 138:606 (1981). *See also:* Linda S. Grossman, Brian Martin, and Christopher Fichtner, "Are Sex Offenders Treatable? A Research Overview," *Psychiatric Services* 50(3): 353 (1999).

60 A longer list of side effects is provided by Blumer and Migeon, *supra* note 9, at 136; Thibaut et al., *supra* note 12, at 622; and Meyer, Cole, and Emory, *supra* note 30, at 254.

61 Christopher I. Li, Elizabeth F. Baeber, Mei Tzu Tang, Peggy L. Porter, Janet L. Daling, and Katherine E. Malone, "Effect of Depo-Medroxyprogesterone Acetate on Breast Cancer Risk among Women 20 to 44," *Cancer Research* 72: 2028–35 (2012). Susan Flinn, "Depo-Provera and Bone Mineral Density," National Women's Health Network, 1–7 (Feb. 2011, updated 2015), nwhn.org.

62 Thibaut et al., *supra* note 12, at 621–22; and Grossman, Martin, and Fichtner, *supra* note 59, at 350–53.

63 "Antisocial personality disorder is a type of chronic mental condition in which a person's ways of thinking, perceiving situations and relating to others are dysfunctional—and destructive. People with an antisocial personality disorder typically have no regard for right and wrong and often disregard the rights, wishes and feelings of others." *Mosby's, supra* note 7, at 121.

64 The use of Depo-Provera was also raised incidentally in two previous appellate cases. *Dennis v. State* involved a question of the quality of psychiatric testimony in

a rape case where the defendant had pled not guilty by reason of insanity. 28 A.2d 284 (Md.App. 1971). *State v. Christopher* involved the revocation of a defendant's probation for child molestation and sentencing of the defendant on his guilty pleas to six additional charges of child molestation, which occurred during the probationary period. 652 P.2d 1031 (Ariz. 1982).

65 Defendant-Appellant's Brief on Appeal, 2, *People v. Gauntlett*, 352 N.W.2d 311 (Mich.App. 1984).

66 *Nolo contendere* is "a plea . . . to a criminal complaint or indictment by which the defendant does not admit or deny the charges, though a fine or sentence may be imposed. . . . Unlike a guilty plea, a *nolo contendere* plea may not be used against the defendant in a civil action based on the same acts." Henry Campbell Black, *Black's Law Dictionary*, 5th ed. (St. Paul, MN: West Publishing, 1979), 645.

67 Defendant-Appellant's Brief on Appeal, *supra* note 65, at 4, and Exhibit 19, *People v. Gauntlett*, 352 N.W.2d 311 (Mich.App. 1984).

68 *Ibid.*, 4, 150–51, and Exhibit 10, at 3.

69 *Ibid.*, 5, and Exhibit 10, at 5.

70 *Ibid.*, 10. *See*: Order of Probation, *People v. Gauntlett*, No. D 824–00–076 FY (Mich.Cir.Ct. Kalamazoo County, Jan. 30, 1984).

71 Defendant-Appellant's Appeal Brief, *supra*, note 65, at 11. A week after Roger Gauntlett began serving his one-year jail sentence, Judge Borsos amended his sentence to give him a choice between complying with the Depo-Provera probation condition and being resentenced. The amended sentence stated that if Roger Gauntlett were unable "for any reason . . . to carry out the course of treatment . . . the entire probation shall be set aside . . . and the Defendant then resentenced." Supplement to Sentencing Remarks and Amendment to Order of Probation, *People v. Gauntlett*, No. D 824–00–076 FY (Mich.Cir.Ct. Kalamazoo County, Feb. 6, 1984). *See*: Exhibit 8.

After Roger Gauntlett's appeal struck down the five-year probation with the Depo-Provera condition, Judge Jack Warren resentenced him to a five-year prison term. *People v. Gauntlett*, 658 F.Supp. 1488 (W.D. Mich. 1987).

The Superior Court of Pennsylvania, however, reversed a trial court order that a juvenile, having been found guilty of assault and admitting, while incarcerated, to having cravings to assault girls, undergo chemical castration.. The court relied, in part, on Green, *supra* note 1. *In the Matter of R.B.*, 765 A.2d 398 (2000).

72 Berlin and Meinecke, *supra* note 59, at 606; and Gagne, *supra* note 6, at 646.

73 M. S. Sherrill, "Castration or Incarceration," 122:70 *Time* (Dec. 12, 1983), discussing *State v. Brown*, 326 S.W.2d 411 (S.C. 1985), the South Carolina castration case.

74 Gagne, *supra* note 6; and Berlin and Meinecke, *supra* note 59.

75 Berlin and Meinecke, *supra* note 59, at 605.

76 Defendant-Appellant's Brief on Appeal, *supra* note 65, at 12, Exhibit 15 (letter to William Fette from Dr. Mark W. Hinshaw), *People v. Gauntlett*, 352 N.W.2d 311 (Mich.App. 1984).

77 *Ibid.*, 91.

78 Berlin and Meinecke, *supra* note 59, at 606. Dr. Berlin, referring to the *Gauntlett* case, stated that he "would be opposed to the imposition of Depo-Provera treatment upon an unwilling individual." Fred S. Berlin, "The Paraphilias and Depo-Provera: Some Medical, Ethical, and Legal Considerations," *Bulletin of the American Academy of Psychiatry and the Law* 17(3): 233–39, 236 (1989).

79 Defendant-Appellant's Brief on Appeal, *supra* note 65, at 102. *People v. Gauntlett*, 352 N.W.2d 311 (Mich.App. 1984).

80 *Ibid.*, 96.

81 *Ibid.*, 133.

82 *Ibid.*, 10.

83 *Ibid.*, 121.

84 *Kaimowitz v. Michigan Department of Mental Health*, Civil No. 73-19434-Aw (Mich.Cir.Ct. Wayne County, July 10, 1973), summarized at 42 U.S.L.W. 2063 (July 31, 1973) and reprinted in full in Samuel I. Shuman, *Psychosurgery and the Medical Control of Violence: Autonomy and Deviance* [Detroit: Wayne State University Press, 1977], 214–15).

85 Defendant-Appellant's Brief on Appeal, *supra* note 65, at 90, *People v. Gauntlett*, 352 N.W.2d 311 (Mich.App. 1984).

86 *Ibid.*, 46–47, 62.

87 *Ibid.*

88 *Ibid.*, 65.

89 *Ibid.*, 105.

90 429 U.S. 97 (1976).

91 Defendant-Appellant's Brief on Appeal, *supra* note 65, at 76, *People v. Gauntlett*, 352 N.W.2d 311 (Mich.App. 1984).

92 *People v. Gauntlett*, 352 N.W.2d 311, 314 (Mich.App. 1984). *See*: Defendant-Appellant's Appeal Brief, *supra* note 65, at 43–81, for Gauntlett's constitutional arguments and at 82–133 for his statutory arguments on the four points addressed by the Michigan Court of Appeals.

93 *People v. Gauntlett*, 352 N.W.2d 311, 315 (Mich.App. 1984) (citing M.C.L. #77.3[4] and MSA #28.1133[4]).

94 *Ibid.*, 315–16.

95 *Ibid.*, 316.

96 *Ibid.*

97 *Ibid.*, 318.

98 *People v. Gauntlett*, 353 N.W.2d 463 (Mich. 1984).

99 *People v. Gauntlett*, 394 N.W.2d 437, 439–40 (Mich.App. 1986).

100 *Gauntlett v. Kelley*, 658 F.Supp. 1483, 1489 (W.D. Mich. 1987).

101 Habeas corpus (Latin for "you have the body") is "a court order or writ which directs law enforcement officials (prison administrators or police) who have custody of a prisoner to appear in court to determine whether the prisoner is lawfully in prison. . . . The writ is employed procedurally in federal district courts to

challenge the constitutionality of a state court conviction." Black, *supra* note 66, at 638.

102 *Gauntlett v. Kelley*, 658 F.Supp. 1483 (W.D. Mich. 1987).

103 *Gauntlett v. Kelley*, 849 F.2d 213 (6th Cir. 1988).

104 Philip Jenkins, *Moral Panic: Changing Concepts of the Child Molester in the United States* (New Haven, CT: Yale University Press, 1998).

105 Kristen Zagora, "Spin Doctors and Moral Crusaders: The Moral Panic Behind Child Safety Legislation," *Criminal Justice Studies* 17(4): 389–98, at 395 (2004).

106 Sheldon Krantz, *Corrections and Prisoners' Rights*, 2d ed. (St. Paul, MN: West Publishing, 1983), 324.

107 George G. Killinger, Hazel B. Kerper, and Paul F. Cromwell, Jr., *Probation and Parole in the Criminal Justice System* (St. Paul, MN: West Publishing, 1976), 69–72.

108 California Penal Code, §645(a) & (b) (2015). *See*: Audrey Moog, "California Penal Code 645: Legislators Practicing Medicine on Child Molesters," *Journal of Contemporary Health Law and Policy* 15:711–37 (1999).

109 California Penal Code, §645(d) (2015).

110 *Ibid.*

111 Four states follow the California model: Florida, Iowa, Louisiana, and Montana. *See*: Florida Statutes Annotated §794.0235 (2015), Iowa Code §930B.10 (2015), Louisiana Revised Statutes §14:43.6A (2014), and Montana Code Annotated §45-5-512 (2014). The Wisconsin statute is the outlier, because its courts are not involved in Depo-Provera implementation. *See*: Wisconsin Statutes §302.11 (2015).

   Georgia and Oregon enacted statutes that have been repealed. Georgia Code Annotated §16–6-4 was repealed by Georgia Acts 2006, no. 571, Georgia House Bill 1059 (effective July 1, 2006). Oregon Revised Statutes Annotated §144.625 (1) was repealed by Law 2011, C 419 §1 (effective June 17, 2011). In Alabama, Arizona, Colorado, Hawaii, Michigan, Mississippi, Missouri, and Tennessee, legislation was proposed, but not enacted. *See*: Moog, *supra* note 108 at 713, n. 12.

112 Scott and Holmberg, *supra* note 1, at 503–4.

113 *Ibid.*

114 *Ibid.*

115 *Ibid.*

116 *Ibid.*

117 California Penal Code § 645 (2015), Florida Statutes Annotated §794.0235 (2015), Iowa Code §930B.10 (2015), Louisiana Revised Statutes §14:43.6A (2014), Montana Code Annotated §45-5-512 (2014), and Wisconsin Statutes §302.11 (2015).

118 Scott and Holmberg, *supra* note 1, at 505–06.

119 *Ibid.*, 503–04.

120 Wisconsin Statutes §302.11 (2015).

121 John F. Stinneford, "Incapacitation through Maiming: Chemical Castration, the Eighth Amendment, and the Denial of Human Dignity," *University of St. Thomas Law Journal* 3(3): 559–599, 581 (2006).

122 Moog, *supra* note 109, at 731.

123 *Ibid.*, 729 (quoting California Senate. Floor Report, Senate Rules Committee, Assembly Bill 3339 [July 9, 1996]), 8.

124 Fred S. Berlin, "Chemical Castration' for Sex Offenders," *New England Journal of Medicine* 336(154): 1030 (Apr. 3, 1997).

125 Zagora, *supra* 105, at 399.

126 Florida Statutes Annotated §794.0235 (2015).

127 Louisiana Revised Statutes §14:43.6A (2014).

128 Florida Statutes Annotated §794.0235(2)(a) (2015). *See: Jackson v. State*, 907 So.2d 696 (Fla. 4th Dist. App. 2005).

129 California Penal Code §645 (2015), Louisiana Revised Statutes §14:43.6A (2014), and Montana Code Annotated §45-5-512 (2014).

130 California Penal Code §645 (2015), Florida Statutes Annotated §794.0235 (2015), Iowa Code §930B.10 (2015), Louisiana Revised Statutes §14:43.6A (2014), Montana Code Annotated §45-5-512 (2014), and Wisconsin Statutes §302.11 (2015).

131 Louisiana Revised Statutes §14:43.6A (2014).

132 California Penal Code §645 (2015), Florida Statutes Annotated §794.0235 (2015), Iowa Code §930B.10 (2015), Louisiana Revised Statutes §14:43.6A (2014), Montana Code Annotated §45-5-512 (2014).

133 Elizabeth Garfinkle, "Coming of Age in America: The Misapplication of Sex Offender Registration and Community Notification Laws to Juveniles," *California Law Review* 91:163–208, at 173 (2003).

134 Iowa Code §930B.10 (2015), Louisiana Revised Statutes §14:43.6A (2014), Montana Code Annotated §45-5-512 (2014).

135 554 U.S. 407 (2008).

136 Georgia Code Annotated §16-6-4, repealed by Georgia Acts 2006, no. 571, Georgia House Bill 1059 (July 1, 2006).

137 Oregon Revised Statutes Annotated §144.625 (1), repealed by Law 2011, C 419 §1 (June 17, 2011).

138 In his lyrics to "They Can't Take that Away From Me" (1936), Ira Gershwin wrote: "'The song is ended, but as the song writer wrote, the melody lingers on." Music by George Gershwin.

139 Stinneford, *supra* note 121, at 563, n. 17.

140 *People v. Foster*, 101 Cal.App.4th 247 (2007).

141 Memorandum to Lisa Goodner, State Courts Administrator, Florida, from Lee Garringer, Office of State Courts Administrator, 1 (May 27, 2005) (quoted by Tayna Simpson, "'If Your Hand Causes You to Sin . . .': Florida's Chemical Castration Statute Misses the Mark," *Florida State University Law Review* 34[4]: 1239 [2007]).

142 Deidre M. Orazio, Steven Arkowitz, Joy Adams, and Wesley Maram, "The California Sexually Violent Predator Statute: History, Description, and Areas for Improvement," *The California Coalition for Sexual Offending* (2009).

143 Zachary Edmonds Oswald, "Off with His ___: Analyzing the Sex Disparity in Chemical Castration Sentences," *Michigan Journal of Gender and Law* 19(2): 505 (2013).

144 *Houston v. State*, 852 So.2d 425 (Fla. 5th DCA 2003).

145 *Jackson v. State*, 907 So.2d 696, 698–99 (Fla. 4th DCA 2005).

146 *People v. Steele*, 2004 WL 2897955, 2 (2004) (not officially reported).

147 Killinger, Kerper, and Cromwell, *supra* note 107, at 34.

148 Neil P. Cohen and James J. Gobert, *The Law of Probation and Parole* (New York: Shepards/McGraw-Hill, 1983), 379.

149 *Ibid.*, 317–24.

150 Killinger, Kerper, and Cromwell, *supra* note 107, at 72.

151 *Ibid.*

152 *In re Manino*, 14 Cal.App.3d 953, 956 (1971) (quoting *People v. Dominguez*, 256 Cal. App.2d 623, 625–27 1967]).

153 Blumer and Migeon, *supra* note 9, at 135.

154 Barry Maletsky and Gary Fields, "The Biological Treatment of Dangerous Sexual Offenders: A Preliminary Review and Preliminary Report on the Oregon Pilot Program," *Aggression and Violent Behavior* 8:392 (2003).

155 *Ibid.*, 495.

156 Killinger, Kerper, and Cromwell, *supra* note 107, at 72.

157 California Penal Code §645 (2012), Florida Statutes Annotated §794.0235 (2013), Montana Code Annotated §45-5-512 (2014).

158 In the *Gauntlett* case, Judge Borsos did not determine whether medical personnel were available at the Johns Hopkins Clinic. Defendant-Appellant's Brief on Appeal, *supra* note 65, at 97, *People v. Gauntlett*, 352 N.W.2d 311 (Mich.App. 1984).

159 In the *Gauntlett* case, William Fette argued that it was an abuse of discretion for Judge Borsos to impose a Depo-Provera probation condition without a medical examination when he was aware that the drug was controversial, experimental, unlicensed to treat rape offenders, and contraindicated by the defendant's treating physician. The judge, the defendant argued, had become, in effect, a "medical expert. . . . who had sentenced him . . . to participate in a scientific experiment." *Ibid.*, 91, 102–3. The state appellate court agreed. *People v. Gauntlett*, 352 N.W.2d 311, 314–16 (Mich.App. 1984). But the Michigan Supreme Court upheld the appeal on other grounds. *People v. Gauntlett*, 353 N.W.2d 464 (Mich. 1984).

160 American Medical Association, Council on Ethics and Judicial Affairs, "Court Initiated Medical Treatments in Criminal Cases," *Report 4-A-98* (1998). Dr. Berlin stated that it would be unethical for "psychiatrists . . . [to] act as agents of the state" in the use of Depo-Provera. Fred S. Berlin, "Ethical Use of Antiandrogen Medication," *American Journal of Psychiatry* 138(11): 1516 (1981).

161 Scott and Homberg, *supra* note 1, at 505.

162 These statutory probation provisions conform to the Model Penal Code and American Bar Association standards, which suggest a maximum five-year term for felony probation. *See*: American Law Institute, Model Penal Code §301 (1981); and American Bar Association, ABA Standards: Probation, §1,1(d) (1981).

163 Berlin and Meinecke, *supra* note 59, at 607.

164 Scott and Holmberg, *supra* note 1, at 505; Stinneford, *supra* note 121, at 579–80.

165 Killinger, Kerper, and Cromwell, *supra* note 107, at 54.

166 Acceptance or refusal of Depo-Provera raises an issue of voluntary and knowing consent to human experimentation, which has its legal roots in common law and in state and federal statutory and administrative regulations on the use of coercive treatment of and experimentation on incarcerated criminals and mental patients. *See*: Lori Andrews, "Informed Consent Statutes and Decisionmaking," *Journal of Legal Medicine* 5:163–217 (1984). *See also*: George J. Annas, Leonard H. Glantz, and Barbara F. Katz, *Informed Consent to Human Experimentation: The Subject's Dilemma* (Cambridge, MA: Ballinger Publishing, 1977).

167 *Canterbury v. Spence*, 464 F.2d 772, 788 (D.C. Cir. 1972) *See*: Andrews, *supra* note 166, at 176–77.

168 Defendant-Appellant's Brief on Appeal, *supra* note 65, at 112, 124–33, *People v. Gauntlett*, 352 N.W.2d 311 (Mich.App. 1984).

169 Florida, Iowa, and Wisconsin statutes do not provide for informed consent. California, Louisiana, and Montana require their courts to inform the defendant only of the drug's side effects. *See*: Scott and Holmberg, *supra* note 1, at 505–6.

170 Gene G. Abel, Edward B. Blanchard, and Judith V. Becker, "Psychological Treatment of Rapists," 100, in Marcia J. Walker and Stanley L. Broadsky, *Sexual Assault: The Victim and the Rapist* (New York: Lexington Books, 1976).

171 Pierre Gagne concluded that after treatment was terminated, "none of the 40 improved patients returned to his pretreatment behavior."*Supra* note 6, at 646. Berlin and Meinecke found that "the recidivism rate increased dramatically when the patient stopped taking the medicine." Oscar A. Cordoba and James L. Chapel, "Medroxyprogesterone Acetate Antiandrogen Treatment of Hypersexuality in a Pedophiliac Sex Offender," *American Journal of Psychiatry* 140:1037 (1983) (citing Berlin and Meinecke, *supra* note 59, at 607).

172 Cases involving convicted defendants, prisoners, and institutionalized mental patients supporting the right to voluntary consent to Depo-Provera use include *Knecht v. Gillman*, 488 F.2d 1136 (8th Cir. 1973); *Mackey v. Procunier*, 477 F.2d 877 (9th Cir. 1973); *Rogers v. Oakin*, 478 F.Supp. 1342 (D.Mass. 1979); *Rennie v. Klein*, 462 F.Supp. 1131 (D.N.J. 1978); and *Wyatt v. Stickney*, 394 F.Supp. (M.D.Ala. 1972).

173 *Kaimowitz v. Department of Mental Health*, Civil No. 73–19434-Aw (Mich.Cir.Ct. Wayne County, July 10, 1973), summarized at 42 U.S.L.W. 2063 (July 31, 1973) and reprinted in full in Shuman, *supra* note 84, at 200–20.

174 Connecticut Department of Corrections, *supra* note 11, at 6.

175 A probation condition that requires medical or psychiatric treatment may violate a number of a probationer's constitutional rights, including the right to free expression, the prohibition of cruel and unusual punishment, and the invasion of privacy. Cohen and Gobert, *supra* note 148, at 212–17 and 252–56.

176 Defendant-Appellant's Brief on Appeal, *supra* note 65, at 61–81, 112, *People v. Gauntlett*, 352 N.W.2d 311 (Mich.App. 1984).

177 Comment (Stephen Beyer), "Madness and Medicine: The Forcible Administration of Psychotropic Drugs," *Wisconsin Law Review*, 502–3 (1980).

178 *Ibid.*, 502.

179 *See:* Cohen and Gobert, *supra* note 148, at 213 and 252–54; Bruce Greenberg, "Probation Conditions and the First Amendment: When Reasonableness Is Not Enough," *Columbia Journal of Law and Social Problems* 17:45 (1981–1983).

180 381 U.S. 479 (1965). The First Amendment right to mentation is explored by Michael H. Shapiro, *Biological and Behavioral Technologies and the Law* (Westport, CT: Praeger Publishers, 1982).

181 394 U.S. 557, 557 (1969).

182 *See: Kaimowitz v. Department of Mental Health*, Civil No. 73–19434-Aw (Mich.Cir. Ct. Wayne County, July 10, 1973), summarized at 42 U.S.L.W. 2063 (July 31, 1973) and reprinted in full in Shuman, *supra* note 84. *See also: Scott v. Plante*, 532 F.2d 939 (1976); *Mackey v. Procunier*, 477 F.2d 877 (9th Cir. 1973); *Rogers v. Oakin*, 478 F.Supp. 1342 (D.Mass. 1979); and *Rennie v. Klein*, 462 F.Supp. 1131 (D.N.J. 1978); and Note (Craig), "Constitutional Law—Rennie v. Klein: Constitutional Right to Privacy Protects a Mental Patient's Refusal of Psychotropic Medication," *North Carolina Law Review* 57:1481, 1486 (1979).

183 Blumer and Migeon, *supra* note 9, at 128.

184 Money et al., *supra* note 5, at 119.

185 *Rennie v. Klein*, 462 F.Supp. 1131 (D.N.J. 1978).

186 *Ibid.*

187 Abel, Blanchard, and Becker, *supra* note 170, at 108; Gagne, *supra* note 6, at 646.

188 Steven Emanuel, *Constitutional Law* (New York: Wolters Kluwer, 2013), 2–5, 265.

189 *Ibid.*, 2–5, 256–57.

190 Cohen and Gobert, *supra* note 148, at 215.

191 *Knecht v. Gillman*, 488 F.2d 1139 (8th Cir. 1973). *Mackey v. Procunier*, 477 F.2d 877 (9th Cir. 1973), states that characterizing an act as "treatment does not insulate it from Eighth Amendment scrutiny." *See:* Note (S. N. Leinwand). "Aversion Therapy: Punishment as Treatment and Treatment as Cruel and Unusual Punishment," *Southern California Law Review* 49:882 (1976).

192 Defendant-Appellant's Brief on Appeal, *supra* note 65, at 62–63, *People v. Gauntlett*, 352 N.W.2d 311 (Mich.App. 1984)

193 *Rennie v. Klein*, 462 F.Supp. 1131, 1144 (D.N.J. 1978); *Washington v. Harper*, 494 U.S. 210, 215–16 (1990).

194 *People v. Gauntlett*, 352 N.W.2d 310, 316 (Mich.App. 1984).

195 American Medical Association, *supra* note 160.

196 Blumer and Migeon, *supra* note 9, at 622; Tibaut et al., *supra* note 12, at 622; and Meyer, Cole, and Emory, *supra* note 30, at 254.

   Phlebitis is "an "inflammation of a vein and, usually, the formation of a clot in the vein. In the leg, phlebitis causes the leg to swell with fluid and can carry the potential for dislodging blood clots to the lungs." *Mosby's, supra* note 7, at 1849.

   Hypoglycemia, or "low blood sugar, may be associated with anxiety, sweating, tremor, palpitations, nausea, and pallor. Hypoglycemia starves the brain of glucose energy essential for brain function. Lack of glucose energy to the brain can cause headache, mild confusion, abnormal behavior, loss of consciousness, seizure, coma, and death." *Ibid.*, 930.

Dyspnea is "difficult or labored breathing; shortness of breath; and a sign of a serious disease of the airway, lungs, or heart." *Ibid.*, 604.

Hypogonadism is "a condition in which decreased production of gonadal hormones leads to below-normal function of the gonads and to retardation of sexual growth and development in children. The gonads are the ovaries and testes and the hormones they normally produce include estrogen, progesterone, and testosterone." *Ibid.*, 931.

Cerebrovascular disease is "a disease of the blood vessels, especially arteries that supply the brain, usually caused by atherosclerosis and can lead to a stroke." *Ibid.*, 343.

Atherosclerosis is "a progressive thickening and hardening of the walls of medium-sized and large arteries as a result of fat deposits on their inner lining." *Ibid.*, 160.

Chronic renal failure is a chronic kidney disease, which signifies loss of kidney function. People with permanent kidney failure need dialysis or kidney transplant. *Ibid.*, 385.

197 Li et al., *supra* note 61.
198 Raymond A. Lombardo, "Note: California's Unconstitutional Punishment for Heinous Crimes: Chemical Castration of Sex Offenders," *Fordham Law Review* 65:2620 (1997).
199 Stinneford, *supra* note 121, at 577.
200 Defendant-Appellant's Brief on Appeal, *supra* note 65, at 63, *People v. Gauntlett*, 352 N.W.2d 311 (Mich.App. 1984).
201 408 U.S. 238, 272–73 (1972). *See also*: Stinneford, *supra* note 121, at 585–89.
202 356 U.S. 86, 101–02 (1958).
203 Stinneford, *supra* note 121, at 577.
204 *Ibid.*, 568.
205 Defendant Appellant's Brief on Appeal, *supra* note 65, at 111, *People v. Gauntlett*, 352 N.W.2d 311 (Mich.App 1984).
206 *Weems v. United States*, 217 U.S. 349, 380.(1910).
207 408 U.S. 238, 279 (Brennan, J., concurring) and 342 (Marshall, J., concurring) (1972).
208 Thibaut et al., *supra* note 12, at 622; Douglas et al., *supra* note 54, at 395.
209 Maletsky and Fields, *supra* note 154, at 392.
210 Gordon C. Nagayama Hall, "Sexual Offender Recidivism Revisited: A Meta Analysis of Recent Treatment Studies," *Journal of Consulting and Clinical Psychology* 83:807 (1995).
211 Stinneford, *supra* note 121, at 566.
212 Cohen and Gobert, *supra* note 148, at 215, 254–56.
213 *Washington v. Harper*, 494 U.S. 210 (1990).
214 *Rennie v. Klein*, 462 F.Supp. 1131, 1147 (D.N.J. 1978).

215 *Ibid.*

216 Florida Statutes Annotated §794.0235 (2015).

217 Florida Statutes Annotated §794.0235 (2015), Iowa Code §930B.10 (2015).

218 Cases involving involuntarily committed mental patients' right to privacy and to make decisions about psychoactive medication that support a sex offender's right to decide about the use of Depo-Provera include *Mackey v. Procunier*, 477 F.2d 877, 877–78 (9th Cir. 1973); *Rennie v. Klein*, 462 F.Supp. 1131, 1144–45 (D.N.J. 1978); and *Wyatt v. Stickney*, 344 F.Supp. 387 (M.D.Ala. 1972).

219 *Griswold v. Connecticut*, 381 U.S. 479 (1965); *Loving v. Virginia*, 388 U.S. 1 (1967); *Roe v. Wade*, 410 U.S. 113 (1973); *Moore v. East Cleveland*, 431 U.S. 494 (1977); *Zablocki v. Redhail*, 434 U.S. 374 (1978).

220 *Skinner* was, in form, an equal protection case, but the court emphasized in its opinion by Justice Douglas: "We are dealing here with legislation that involves one of the basic rights of man. Marriage and procreation are fundamental to the very existence and survival of the race." *Skinner v. Oklahoma*, 316 U.S. 535, 541 (1942).

221 Gagne, *supra* note 6, at 645; and Cordoba and Chapel, *supra* note 171, at 1038.

222 Connecticut Department of Corrections, *supra* note 11, at 5.

223 *Skinner v. Oklahoma*, 316 U.S. 535, 535 (1942).

224 Emanuel, *supra* note 188.

225 *Ibid.*, 2–5 and 256–57.

226 *Skinner v. Oklahoma*, 316 U.S. 535 (1942). *See*: Emanuel, *supra* note 188, at 379.

227 Emanuel, *supra* note 188, at 334–45.

228 Pharmacia & Upjohn Co., Depo-Provera Contraceptive Injection, Physician Information (2004).

229 Emanuel, *supra* note 188, at 336–39, 262–63. *Craig v. Boren*, 429 U.S. 190 (1976).

230 Emanuel, *supra* note 188, at 256–57.

231 Schizophrenia is a characterized by abnormal social behavior and failure to recognize reality. Schizophrenia may result in hallucinations, delusions, and extremely disordered thinking and behavior. *Mosby's*, *supra* note 7, at 1673–74.

   Substance abuse is the use of a drug, including alcohol, amphetamines, barbiturates, cocaine, cannabis, and morphine, in amounts harmful to the person and others and may result in criminal or antisocial behavior, and long term personality changes. *Ibid.*, 1785.

   An antisocial personality disorder is a chronic mental condition characterized by dysfunctional and destructive thinking and perception of others. A person with this disorder has no regard for right and wrong, has drug and alcohol use problems, behaves violently, and is likely to violate the law. *Ibid.*, 121.

232 "Overinclusive classifications by definition burden some not similarly situated with respect to a rule ... [and] may of course be challenged as denying equal protection," Laurence H. Tribe, *American Constitutional Law*, 2nd ed., (New York: Foundation Press,1988), 1450.

233 Emanuel, *supra* note 188, at 260.

234 470 U.S. 821, 837 (1985).

CONCLUSION

1 U.S. Food and Drug Administration, Public Board of Inquiry on Depo-Provera, *Official Transcript of Proceedings*, 4:32 (Jan. 13, 1983).

2 R. A. Rettig, L. E. Earley, and R. A. Merrill, eds., "Historical Evolution of FDA Advisory Committees," in Food and Drug Administration Advisory Committees. Institute of Medicine Committee to Study the use of Advisory Committees (Washington, DC: National Academies Press, 1992). Available at NCBI Bookshelf: http://ncbi.nlm.nih.gov.

3 U.S. Food and Drug Administration, Fertility and Maternal Health Advisory Committee, *Transcript of Meeting* (June 19, 1992) (Statement by Dr. Solomon Sobel, Director, U.S. Food and Drug Administration, Division of Metabolism and Endocrine Products), 78.

GLOSSARY OF LEGAL AND MEDICAL TERMS

1 Henry Campbell Black, *Black's Law Dictionary* (St. Paul, MN: West Publishing, 1979), 113.

2 *Ibid.*, 171.

3 *Ibid.*, 233.

4 www.archives.gov.

5 Black, *supra* note 1, at 352.

6 *Ibid.*, 250–51.

7 *Ibid.*, 264.

8 *Ibid.*, 931.

9 *Ibid.*, 315.

10 *Ibid.*, 396.

11 *Ibid.*, 413.

12 *Ibid.*, 418–19.

13 *Ibid.*, 484.

14 www.archives.gov.

15 Fed. R. Civil Pro. 60(b).

16 Black, *supra* note 1, at 638.

17 *Ibid.*, 735.

18 Allen Wong, "Products Liability: The Fate of the Learned Intermediary Doctrine," *Journal of Law, Medicine and Ethics* 30(3) 471–72 (2002).

19 Brian Martinotti, "Complex Litigation in the New Jersey and Federal Courts: An Overview of the Current State of Affairs and a Glimpse of What Lies Ahead," *Loyola University of Chicago Law Journal* 44:562, n. 2 (2012).

20 Black, *supra* note 1, at 914.

21 Martinotti, *supra* note 19, at 562, n. 4.

22 Black, *supra* note 1, at 645.

23 Tribe, *American Constitutional Law*, 2nd ed. (New York: Foundation Press, 1988), 1450.

24 Black, *supra* note 1, at 418.
25 *Ibid.*, 1101.
26 *Ibid.*, 362.
27 *Ibid.*, 1335.
28 *Ibid.*, 835.
29 *Ibid.*, 1275.
30 *Ibid.*, 1287.
31 42 U.S.C. 1397.
32 *Ibid.*, 233.
33 Black, *supra* note 1, at 1373.
34 *Ibid.*, 421.
35 *Mosby's Medical Dictionary*, 7th ed. (St. Louis, MO: Mosby, Elsevier, 2006), 44–45.
36 *Ibid.*, 1556.
37 *Ibid.*, 96.
38 *Ibid.*, 121.
39 *Ibid.*, 160.
40 www.fda.gov.
41 *Mosby's*, *supra* note 35, at 343.
42 *Ibid.*, 345–46.
43 *Ibid.*
44 *Ibid.*, 346.
45 William Green, "Chemical Castration," 31–33, in Robert H. Blank and Jenna C. Merrick, eds., *Encyclopedia of U.S. Biomedical Policy* (Westport, CT: Greenwood Press, 1995).
46 *Mosby's*, *supra* note 35, at 385.
47 *Ibid.*, 454.
48 *Ibid.*, 566.
49 *Ibid.*, 586–87.
50 *Ibid.*, 604.
51 *Ibid.*, 235.
52 *Ibid.*, 643–44.
53 *Ibid.*, 644.
54 WHO, at www.who.int.
55 *Mosby's*, *supra* note 35, at 724.
56 *Ibid.*, 733.
57 *Ibid.*, 815–16.
58 *Ibid.*, 842.
59 *Ibid.*, 930.
60 *Ibid.*, 931.
61 *Ibid.*, 937
62 21 C.F.R. 312.3.
63 Harvey Marchvitch, ed., *Black's Medical Dictionary*, 41st ed. (Lanham, MD: Scarecrow Press, 2006), 662–63.
64 *Mosby's*, *supra* note 35, at 1179.

65 *Ibid.*, 1179.
66 *Ibid.*, 1183.
67 *Ibid.*, 1186.
68 *Ibid.*, 1756.
69 *Ibid.*, 1270.
70 WHO Study Group, "WHO Technical Report 843: Assessment of Fracture Risk and Its Application to Screening for Postmenopausal Osteoporosis," *World Health Organization*, 5–6 (1994).
71 *Mosby's, supra* note 35, at 1366.
72 *Ibid.*, 1381.
73 *Ibid.*, 1388.
74 Osborne and Wise, "Paraphilias," 294–95, in Richard Balon and R. Taylor Segraves, *Handbook of Sexual Dysfunctions* (New York: Taylor and Francis, 2005), referencing American Psychological Association, *Diagnostic and Statistical Manual of Disorders*, 4th text revision, 2000.
75 *Ibid.*, 305.
76 *Mosby's, supra* note 35, at 1420.
77 *Ibid.*, 1849.
78 *Ibid.*, 1502.
79 *Ibid.*, 1516.
80 *Black's, supra* note 63, at 583.
81 *Stedman's Medical Dictionary for the Health Professional and Nursing*, 6th ed. (Philadelphia: Lippincott Williams & Wilkins, 2008), 1272.
82 *Mosby's, supra* note 35, at 1540.
83 *Ibid.*, 1556.
84 *Ibid.*, 1575.
85 *Ibid.*, 1589.
86 *Ibid.*, 1629.
87 *Ibid.*, 1654–55.
88 *Ibid.*, 1673–74.
89 *Ibid.*, 1683.
90 *Ibid.*, 1704.
91 *Ibid.*, 1766.
92 *Ibid.*, 1785.
93 *Ibid.*, 1831
94 *Ibid.*, 1831.
95 Philip J. Hilts, *Protecting America's Health: The FDA, Business, and One Hundred Years of Regulation* (Chapel Hill: University of North Carolina Press, 2003), 144–61.
96 *Mosby's, supra* note 35, at 1847.
97 *Ibid.*, 1849.
98 *Ibid.*
99 *Ibid.*, 1846.
100 *Ibid.*, 1903.

INDEX

Adkinson, N. Franklin, 175–76
Administrative Procedure Act, 289n21
Agency for International Development, 64, 71
Alan Guttmacher Institute, 134
Aldana v. Holub (1980), 94
Alexander, Erik, 162
American College of Obstetricians and Gynecologists, 71
American Bar Association, Model Penal Code, 296n162
American Journal of Epidemiology, 132, 138, 182
American Medical Association, 133, 195, 200, 219, 224, 226
animal studies of Depo-Provera, 8, 43, 61,131, 218, 221; results of, 82
Annello, Charles, 38
Anstead, Harry, 122–23
Armistead, J. W., 15, 20–21, 42, 154, 255n51
Askinoise, Barbara, 40
Assenzo, J. Robert, Public Board of Inquiry testimony, 70. *See also* Schwallie and Assenzo Depo-Provera study
Auckland Hospital Department of Medicine, study of osteoporosis, 132
Avery, Byllye, 40

beagle dog studies, 20, 22, 69, 131, 246n42, 252n5; elimination of, 131–32, 140; relevance of, 20, 65, 68, 71–72, 75–76, 131–32; study results of, 20–21, 23, 25, 46, 48, 50, 54, 61–62, 65, 75

Benjamin, David, 102, 104, 108–9, 115, 124–25
Bennett, Ridgely: Depo-Provera marketing approval role of, 142, 145, 147, 166; Fertility and Maternal Health Advisory Committee presentation by, 135, 140, 142; House Select Committee on Population testimony by, 65, 138
Berlin, Fred, 242n5, 288n3, 290–91n51, 296n16; consent forms used by, 176–78; Depo-Provera studies by, 170–71; Depo-Provera use as a probation condition by, 176, 182, 194–95; faults of research studies by, 176–81; *People v. Gauntlett* (1984) and use as a probation condition by, 182–84; practice-of-medicine exception for use of Depo-Provera by, 172–73, 219–220; Public Citizen Health Research Group inquiry of Johns Hopkins Sexual Disorders Clinic headed by, 171–74, 176–79; risk management by, 168–70, 176, 179, 209; Upjohn supply of Depo-Provera to, 174–75. *See also* Johns Hopkins Sexual Disorders Clinic
Berliner, Victor, 20–22, 61, 65
Biometrics and Epidemiology Methodology (BEM) Advisory Committee, 57, 256n89
black box warning, 13, 150–52, 155, 161, 163, 166, 218, 241n29. *See also* bone mineral density; osteoporosis
Black Women's Health Project, 40

(BEM) Advisory Committee: hearing on Depo-Provera, 57–58

Obstetrics and Gynecology and Biometrics and Epidemiology Methodology Advisory (OB/GYN-BEM) Subcommittee: meeting on Depo-Provera, 59

OCs. *See* oral contraceptives

Office of New Drug Evaluation, 33–34

Ohio Products Liability Act (OPLA), 156

Oliver, Adrienne, 129, 154, 160–61, 167, 222

Oliver v. Pharmacia & Upjohn, 153, 155, 160–61, 163–64

oral contraceptives (OCs), 27, 33, 49, 51, 54–55, 60, 73, 87, 92, 136–37, 139

osteoporosis: black box warning for Depo-Provera, 149, 151, 159–63, 165, 167; osteoporosis patient labeling for Depo-Provera (1992), 145; osteoporosis post-approval clinical studies of Depo-Provera, 143–44, 149, 155, 279n110; products liability cases involving Depo-Provera, 156–65, 167–68, 282n166, 282–83n167, 283nn168–69; lessons of osteoporosis products liability litigation, 163–65. *See also* black box warning; Depo-Provera

Ory, Howard, 37–39

Our Bodies Ourselves, 9, 241

ovarian cancer studies, 18, 37, 39, 131, 136, 147

Pap smears, 23, 27, 30, 47, 243n12, 247n74, 253n17

Pardthaisong, Teng, 138, 146

parole conditions: Depo-Provera probation condition, 3, 169, 171, 187, 194, 226; Depo-Provera parole condition, consent to, 195–97; federal constitutional issues raised by use of a Depo-Provera probation condition, 198–208; non-FDA approved use of Depo-Provera as a probation condition, 14; state statutory issues raised by Depo-Provera

parole and probation conditions, 193–97; state parole statutes containing a Depo-Provera condition, 187–89; state court enforcement of a Depo-Provera parole condition, 187–93

Paternetti, Joseph, 106

patients: baseline bone mineral density scans of, 165, 224, 226; baseline bone mineral density scans of, 145, 151, 154, 156, 158, 161, 164, 165; family planning clinics use of Depo-Provera by, 17, 24, 27, 32, 35, 43, 83–84, 92, 103, 105, 107, 118, 174, 218–20; Grady Clinic use of Depo-Provera by, 20, 22, 24–25, 28–35, 220; informed consent forms for, 28, 32, 226; Johns Hopkins Sexual Disorders Clinic and its, 170–71, 173, 175–76, 178, 209, 220; medical malpractice lawsuits by, 4, 82, 90–91, 125–26, 153, 153, 155, 165, 217; National Women's Health Network Registry of, 86; *National Women's Health Network v. Upjohn* (1984) on behalf of, 40–42; osteoporosis patient labeling for Depo-Provera (1992), 145; osteoporosis black box warning (2004) for, 149, 151, 159–163, 165, 167, 241n29; patient package insert, 48–50, 115, 124, 144, 163; package insert for, 85, 108–11, 124–25, 161, 164; patient labeling and brochure (1992) for, 145–46, 148–49, 151, 226–27; physicians as learned intermediaries for, 88, 99, 149; products liability cases by, 156–165, 167–69, 282–83n166 (*see also* class action lawsuits; mass tort cases; multidistrict litigation); risk management by, 5–6, 85, 88, 144; unapproved use by, 19, 22, 41, 83–90, 174

Pearson, Cindy, 148

pedophiles, 180, 184, 194, 207, 223

pedophilia, 180–81, 189, 207

Pelvic Inflammatory Disease (PID), 108

ABOUT THE AUTHOR

William Green is Professor of Government at Morehead State University where he teaches constitutional law and comparative politics. His research and publications explore constitutional and civil liberties issues and the political and legal dimensions of economic development, labor relations, language rights, and pharmaceutical drug policies.